# HIKARU

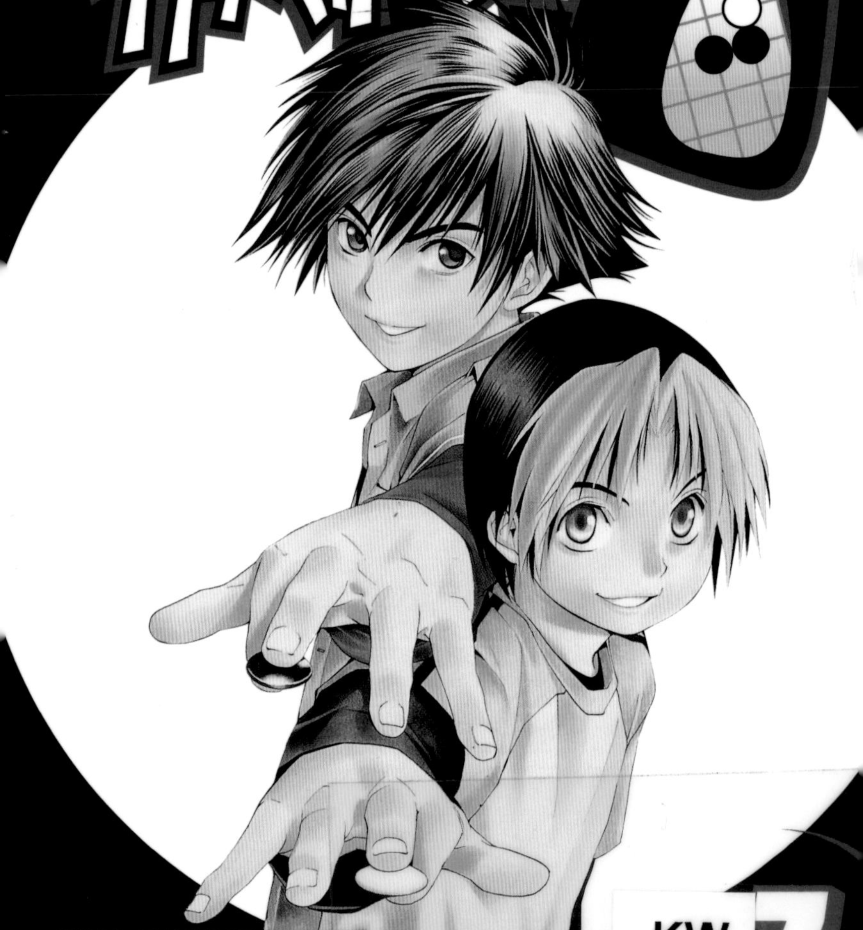

SHONEN**JUMP** MANGA



Story by
**Yumi Hotta**
Art by
**Takeshi Obata**
Supervised by **Yukari Umezawa (5 Dan)**

volume **7**

A PERFECT LOSING STREAK
IN THE BATTLES AGAINST DROWSINESS

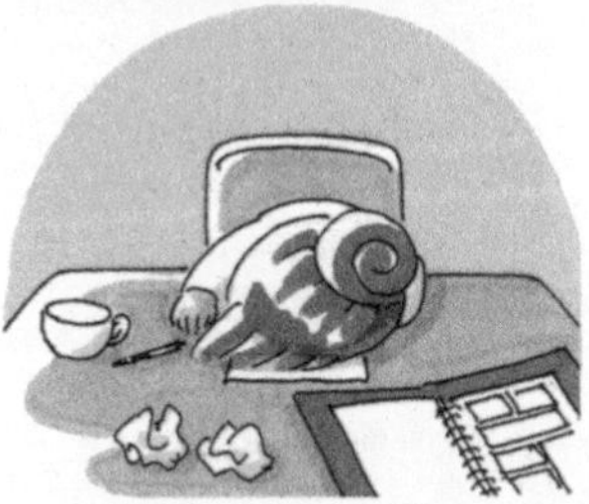

**Yumi Hotta**

I asked professional Go player Yukari Umezawa, who seems very busy, how much sleep she gets on average. I was surprised by her answer—**eight hours!** Yipee! She's just like me!

—Yumi Hotta

It all began when Yumi Hotta played a pick-up game of Go with her father-in-law. As she was learning how to play, Ms. Hotta thought it might be fun to create a story around the traditional board game. More confident in her storytelling abilities than her drawing skills, she submitted the beginnings of **Hikaru no Go** to **Weekly Shonen Jump**'s Story King Award. The Story King Award is an award that picks the best story, manga, character design and youth (under 15) manga submissions every year in Japan. As fate would have it, Ms. Hotta's story (originally named, "***Kokonotsu no Hoshi***"), was a runner-up in the "Story" category of the Story King Award. Many years earlier, Takeshi Obata was a runner-up for the Tezuka Award, another Japanese manga contest sponsored by **Weekly Shonen Jump** and **Monthly Shonen Jump**. An editor assigned to Mr. Obata's artwork came upon Ms. Hotta's story and paired the two for a full-fledged manga about Go. The rest is modern Go history.

## HIKARU NO GO VOL. 7
## SHONEN JUMP Manga Edition

This manga contains material that was originally published in English from
**SHONEN JUMP** #38 to #42.

STORY BY YUMI HOTTA
ART BY TAKESHI OBATA
Supervised by YUKARI UMEZAWA (5 Dan)

Translation & English Adaptation/Andy Nakatani
English Script Consultant/Janice Kim (3 Dan)
Touch-up Art & Lettering/Adam Symons
Design/Courtney Utt
Additional Touch-up/Josh Simpson
Editor/Yuki Takagaki

Printed in the U.S.A.

Published by VIZ Media, LLC
P.O. Box 77010
San Francisco, CA 94107

10 9 8 7 6 5
First printing, July 2006
Fifth printing, May 2016

PARENTAL ADVISORY
HIKARU NO GO is rated A and is
suitable for readers of all ages.
ratings.viz.com

www.viz.com

# HIKARU no GO

## 7

## THE YOUNG LIONS TOURNAMENT

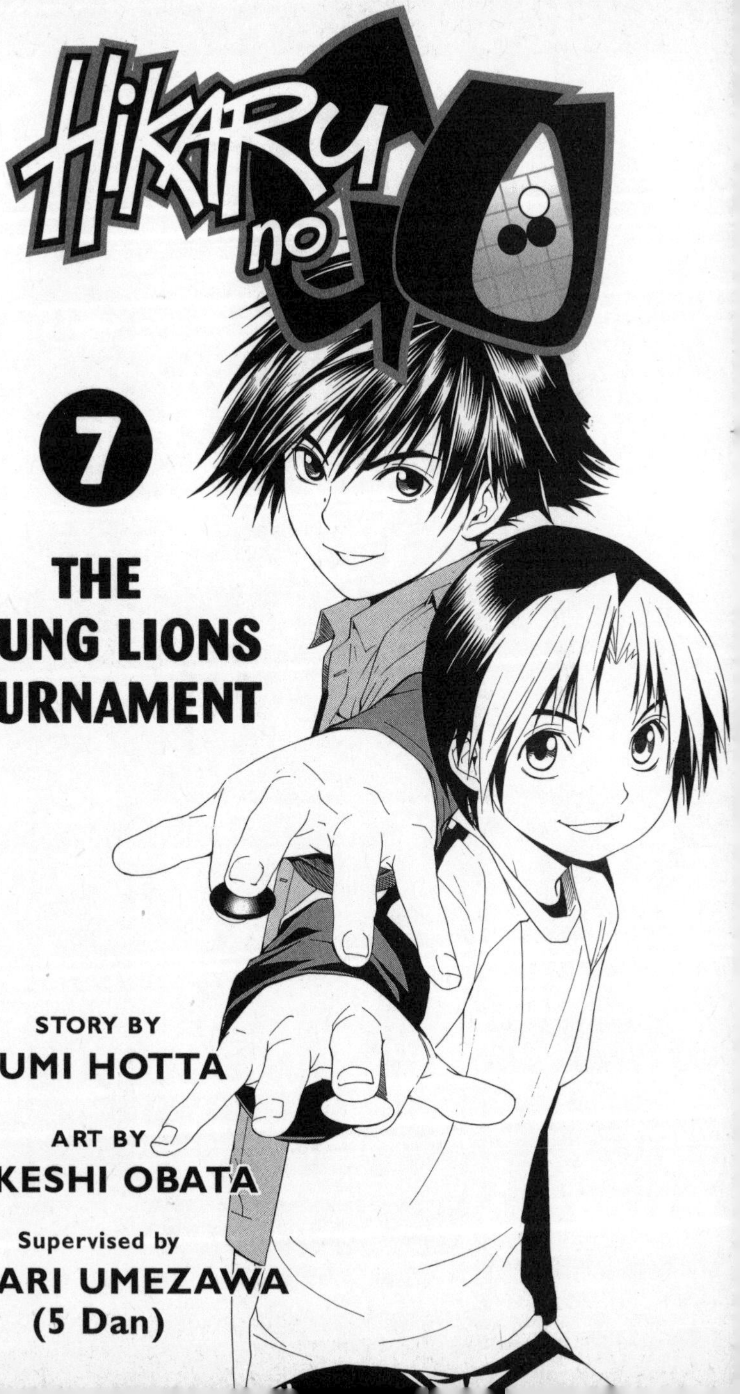


STORY BY
YUMI HOTTA

ART BY
TAKESHI OBATA

Supervised by
YUKARI UMEZAWA
(5 Dan)

# Character Introductions

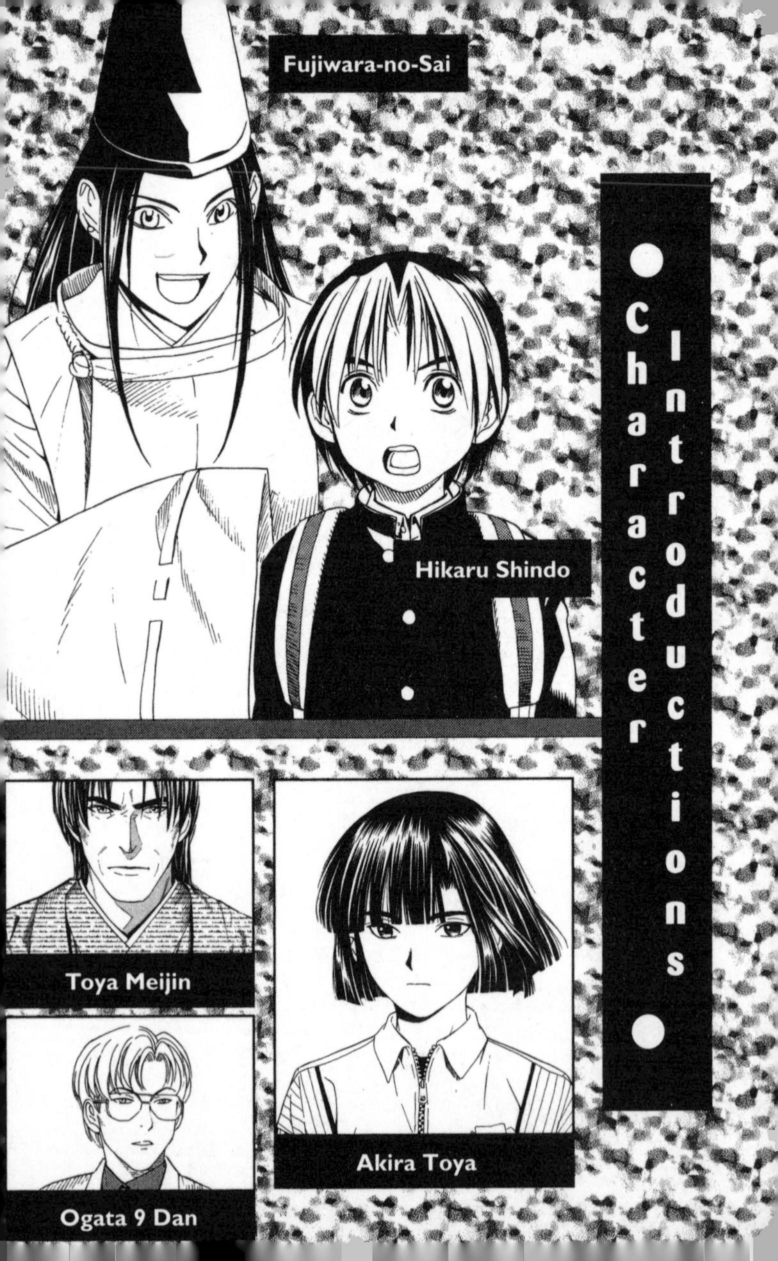
Fujiwara-no-Sai
Hikaru Shindo
Akira Toya
Toya Meijin
Ogata 9 Dan

Akari Fujisaki
Fuku
Yoshitaka Waya
Shirakawa 7 Dan
Yuki Mitani
Ochi
Shinichiro Isumi

## Story Thus Far

One day, Hikaru, a sixth grader, discovers an old Go board in his grandfather's attic. The instant Hikaru touches the board, the spirit of Fujiwara-no-Sai, a genius Go player from Japan's Heian Era, enters Hikaru's consciousness. Inspired by Sai's love of Go, and by his encounter with the prodigy Akira Toya (son of Go master Toya Meijin), Hikaru is slowly drawn to the game.

Hikaru decides to take the insei exam so he can catch up to Akira. On the day of the exam, however, Hikaru is nervous and things don't go well. But the instructor reviews the game records of Hikaru's three simultaneous games, sees the boy's true potential, and lets him join the insei. When Hikaru checks out the insei study room, he blurts out that he is Akira Toya's one and only rival and puts everyone on the defensive. Still, he manages to make friends with two insei — Waya and Isumi. Meanwhile, Akira debuts as a rookie pro in the Shinshodan Series, and his opponent is the holder of the Oza title. Akira goes all out in his game to show Hikaru that they're not in the same league. Back at Haze Middle School, things have quieted down at Hikaru's old Go club while the students wait for Yuki to come back.

# CONTENTS

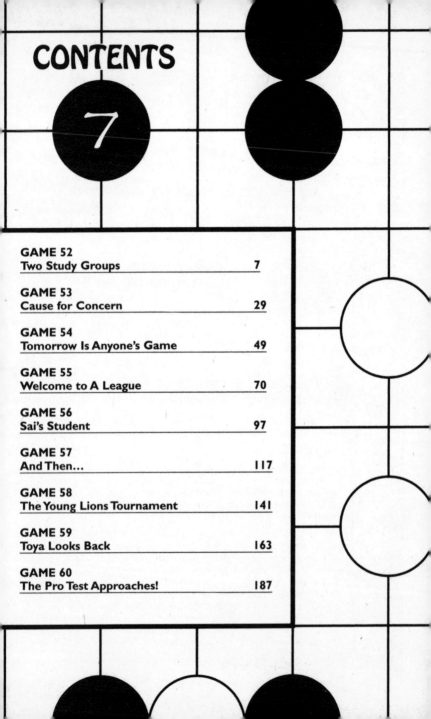

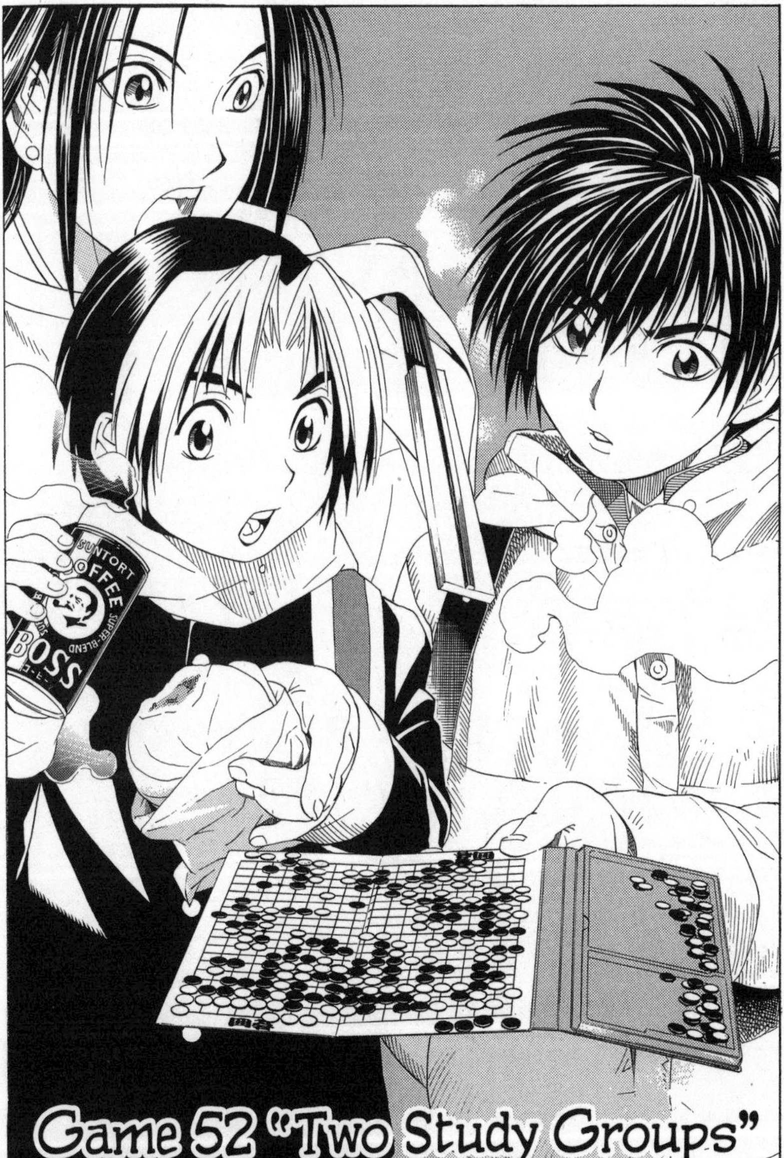
SUNTORY
COFFEE
SUPER-BLEND
BOSS
Game 52 "Two Study Groups"

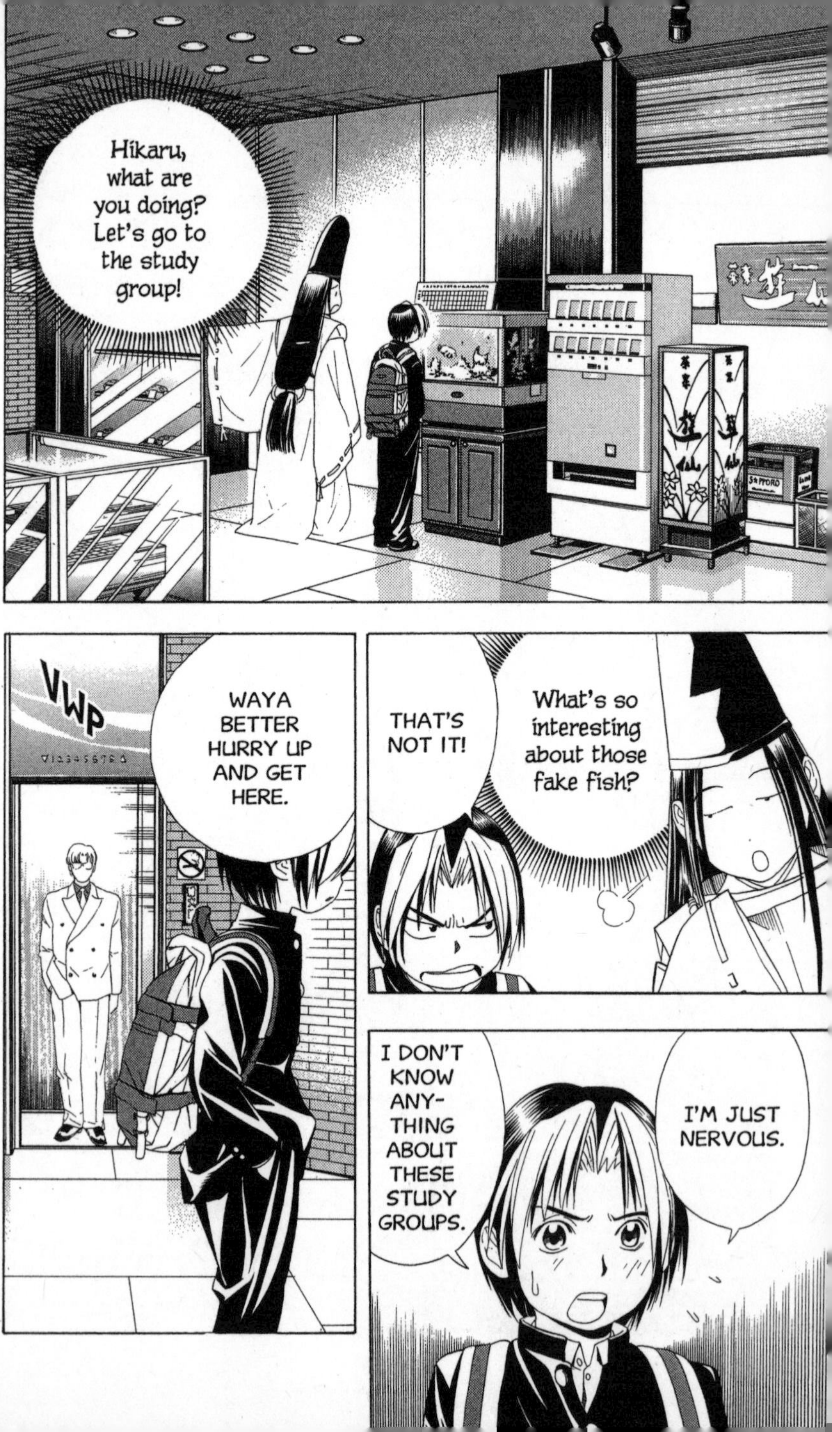

Hikaru, what are you doing? Let's go to the study group!
What's so interesting about those fake fish?
THAT'S NOT IT!
I'M JUST NERVOUS.
I DON'T KNOW ANY-THING ABOUT THESE STUDY GROUPS.
VWP
WAYA BETTER HURRY UP AND GET HERE.

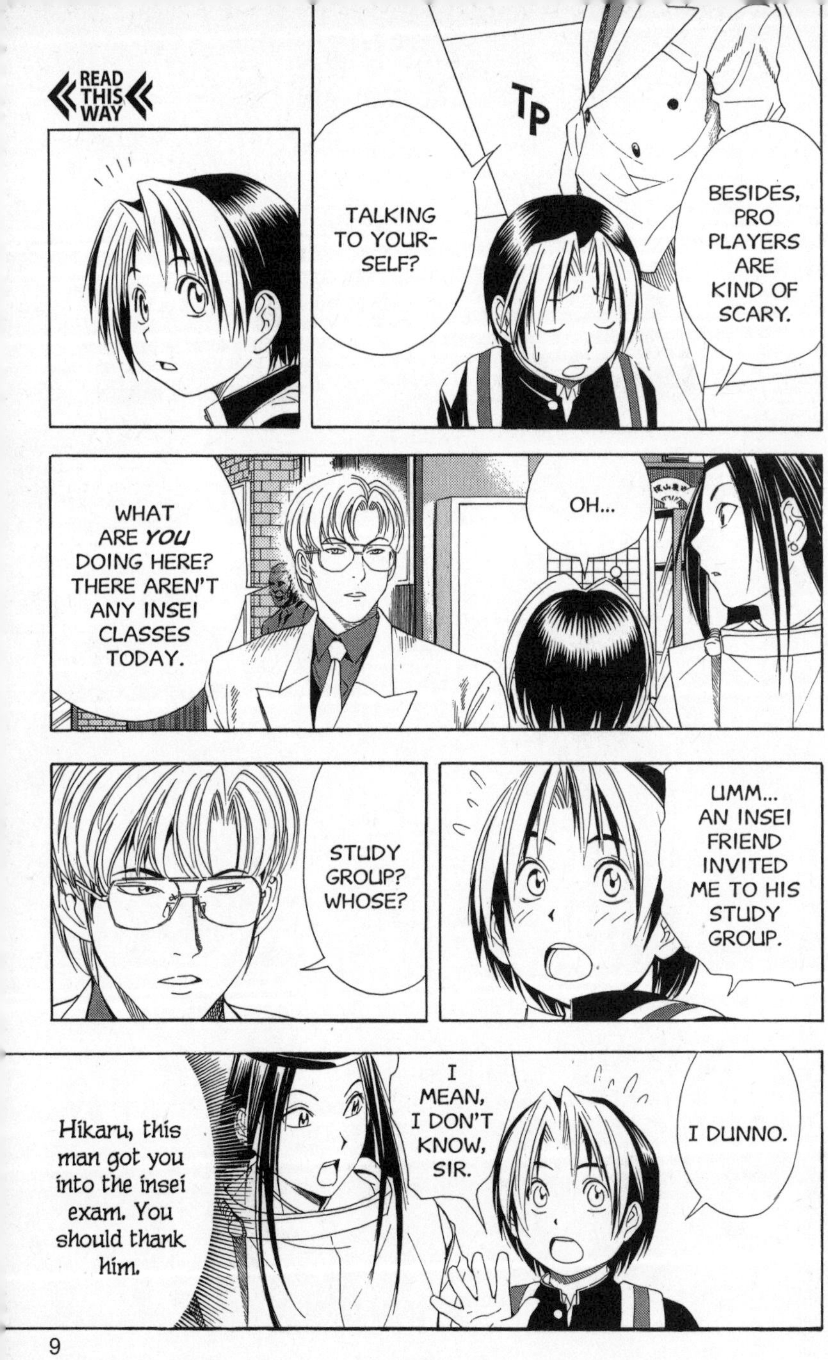
READ THIS WAY
BESIDES, PRO PLAYERS ARE KIND OF SCARY.
TP
TALKING TO YOUR-SELF?
OH...
WHAT ARE *YOU* DOING HERE? THERE AREN'T ANY INSEI CLASSES TODAY.
UMM... AN INSEI FRIEND INVITED ME TO HIS STUDY GROUP.
STUDY GROUP? WHOSE?
I DUNNO.
I MEAN, I DON'T KNOW, SIR.
Hikaru, this man got you into the insei exam. You should thank him.

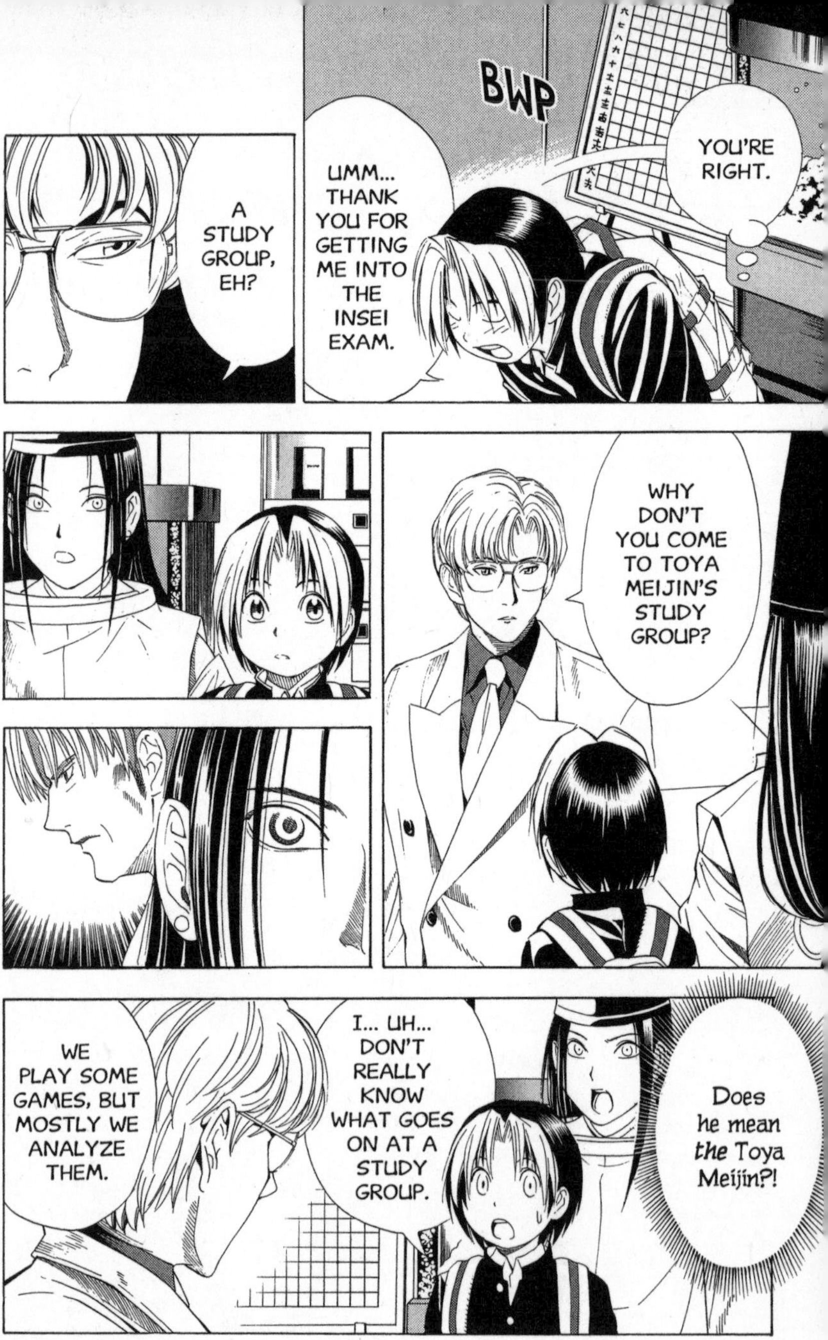
YOU'RE RIGHT.
BWP
UMM... THANK YOU FOR GETTING ME INTO THE INSEI EXAM.
A STUDY GROUP, EH?
WHY DON'T YOU COME TO TOYA MEIJIN'S STUDY GROUP?
Does he mean *the* Toya Meijin?!
I... UH... DON'T REALLY KNOW WHAT GOES ON AT A STUDY GROUP.
WE PLAY SOME GAMES, BUT MOSTLY WE ANALYZE THEM.

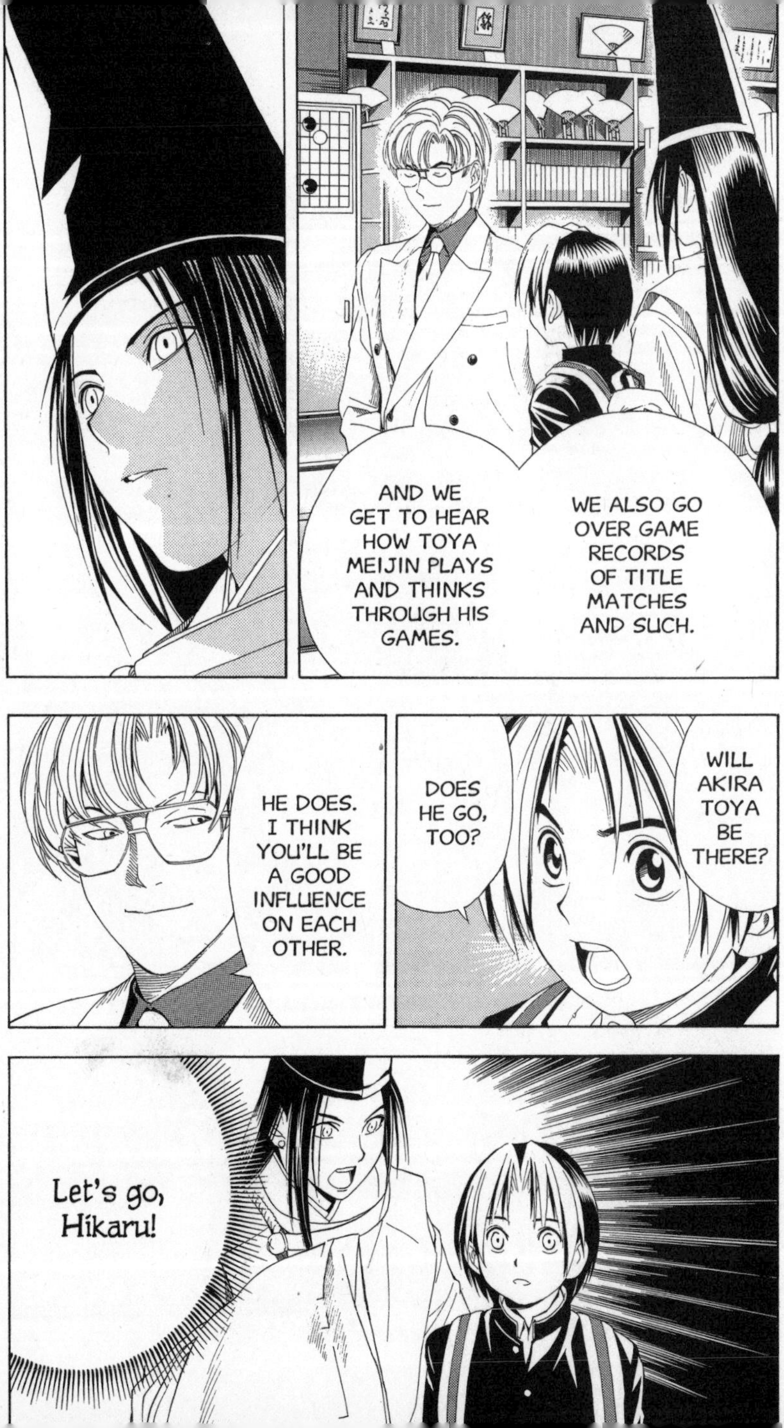
WE ALSO GO OVER GAME RECORDS OF TITLE MATCHES AND SUCH.
AND WE GET TO HEAR HOW TOYA MEIJIN PLAYS AND THINKS THROUGH HIS GAMES.
WILL AKIRA TOYA BE THERE?
DOES HE GO, TOO?
HE DOES. I THINK YOU'LL BE A GOOD INFLUENCE ON EACH OTHER.
Let's go, Hikaru!

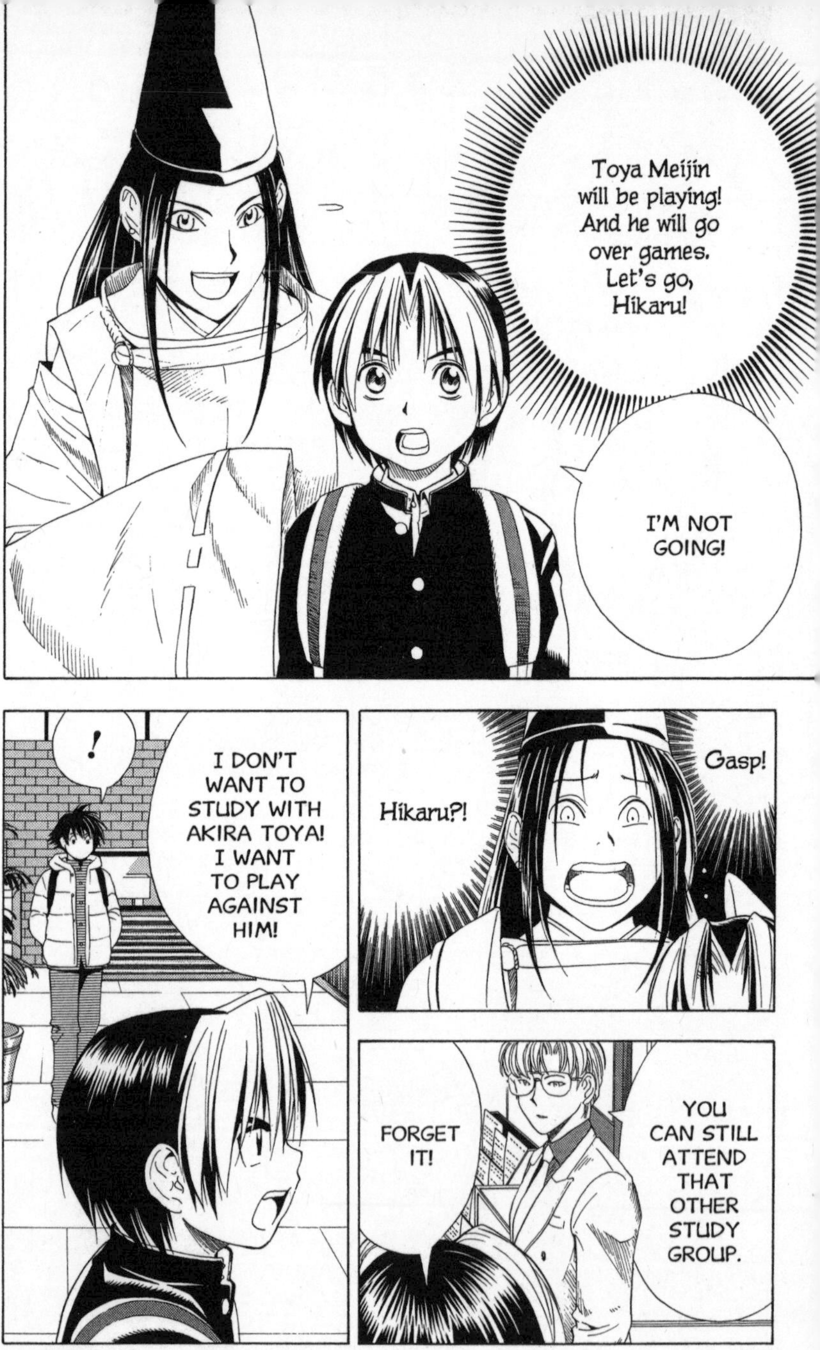
Toya Meijin will be playing! And he will go over games. Let's go, Hikaru!
I'M NOT GOING!
Gasp!
Hikaru?!
YOU CAN STILL ATTEND THAT OTHER STUDY GROUP.
FORGET IT!
!
I DON'T WANT TO STUDY WITH AKIRA TOYA! I WANT TO PLAY AGAINST HIM!

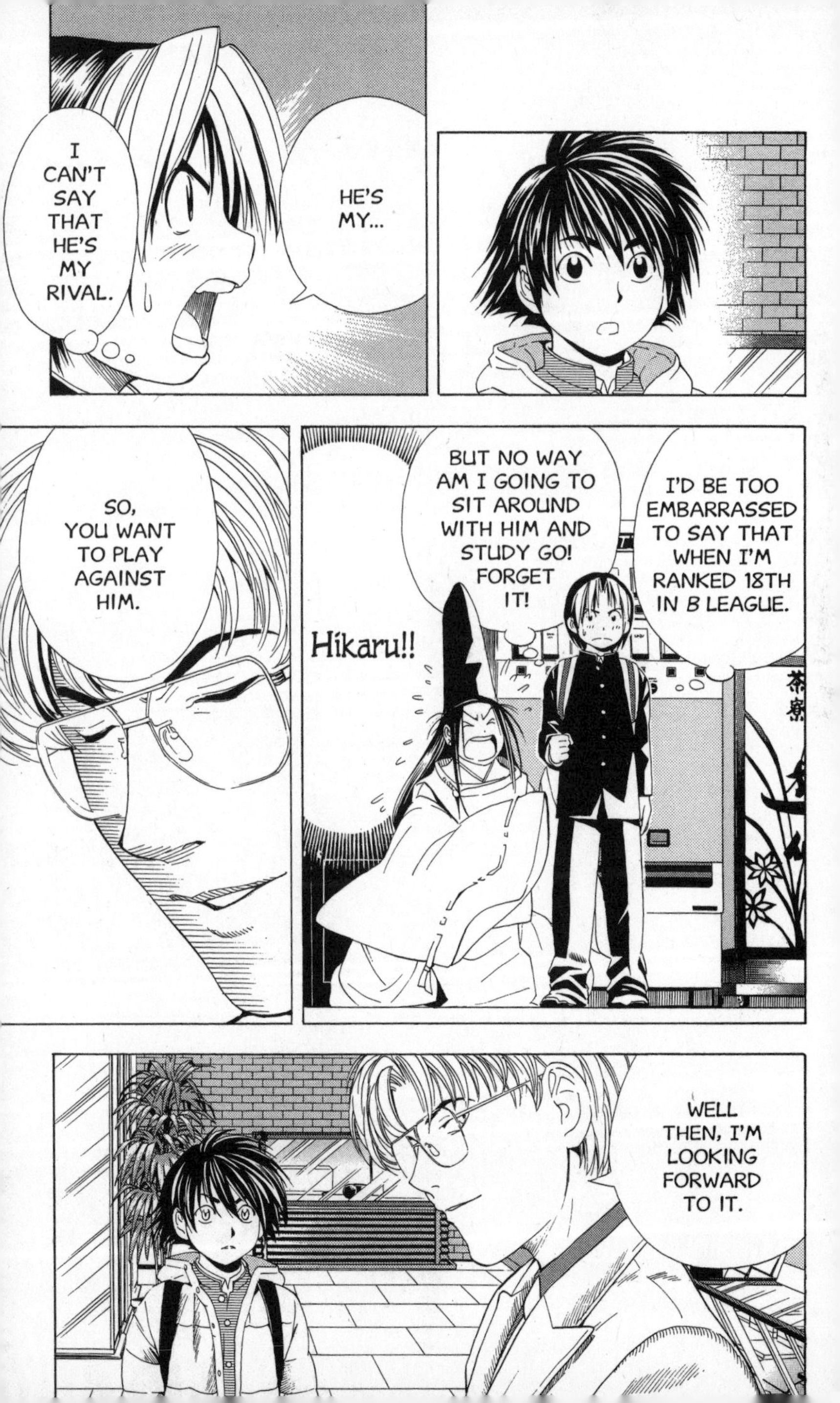
HE'S MY...
I CAN'T SAY THAT HE'S MY RIVAL.
I'D BE TOO EMBARRASSED TO SAY THAT WHEN I'M RANKED 18TH IN *B* LEAGUE.
BUT NO WAY AM I GOING TO SIT AROUND WITH HIM AND STUDY GO! FORGET IT!
Hikaru!!
SO, YOU WANT TO PLAY AGAINST HIM.
WELL THEN, I'M LOOKING FORWARD TO IT.

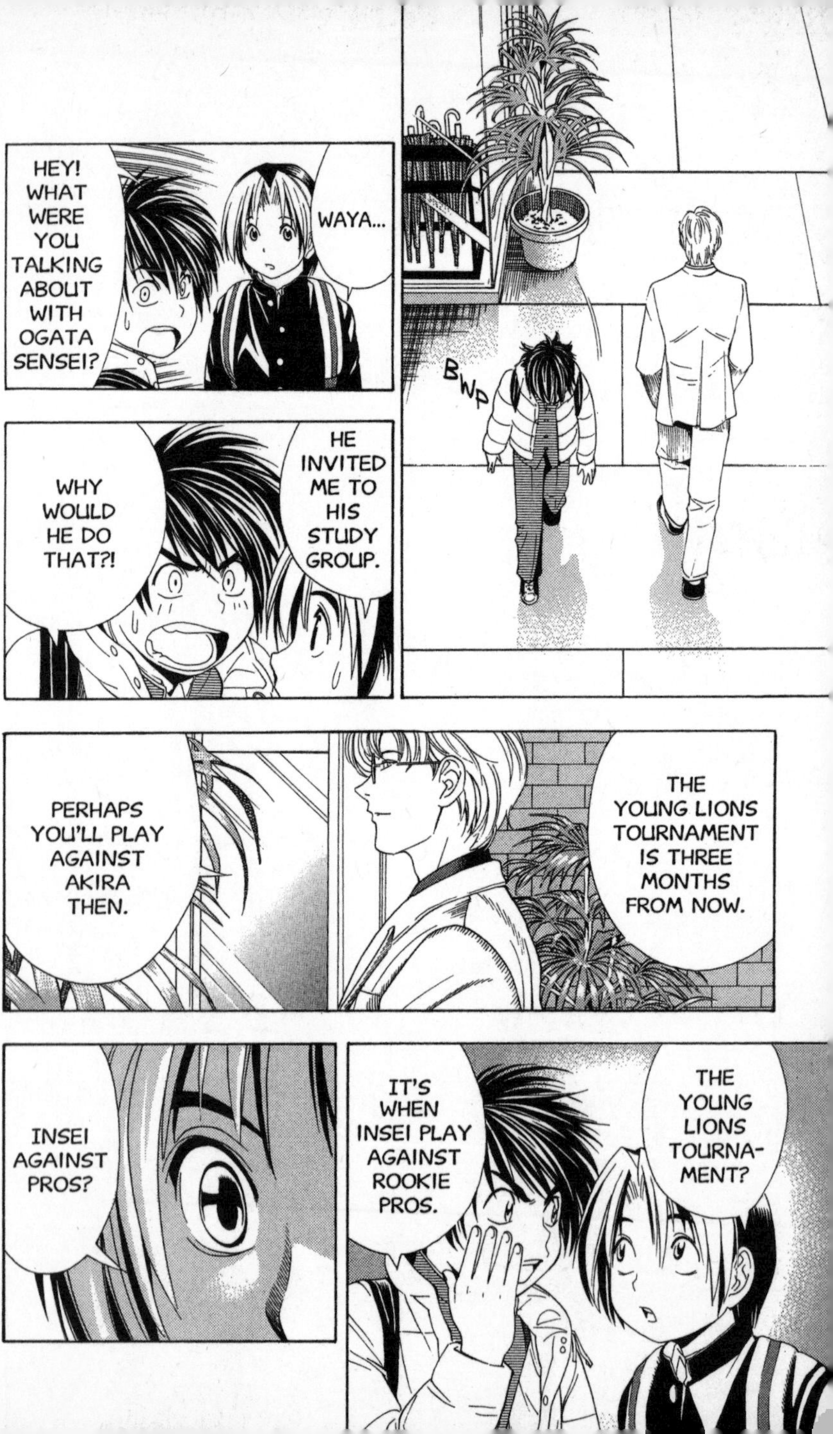
BWP
WAYA...
HEY! WHAT WERE YOU TALKING ABOUT WITH OGATA SENSEI?
HE INVITED ME TO HIS STUDY GROUP.
WHY WOULD HE DO THAT?!
THE YOUNG LIONS TOURNAMENT IS THREE MONTHS FROM NOW.
PERHAPS YOU'LL PLAY AGAINST AKIRA THEN.
THE YOUNG LIONS TOURNA-MENT?
IT'S WHEN INSEI PLAY AGAINST ROOKIE PROS.
INSEI AGAINST PROS?

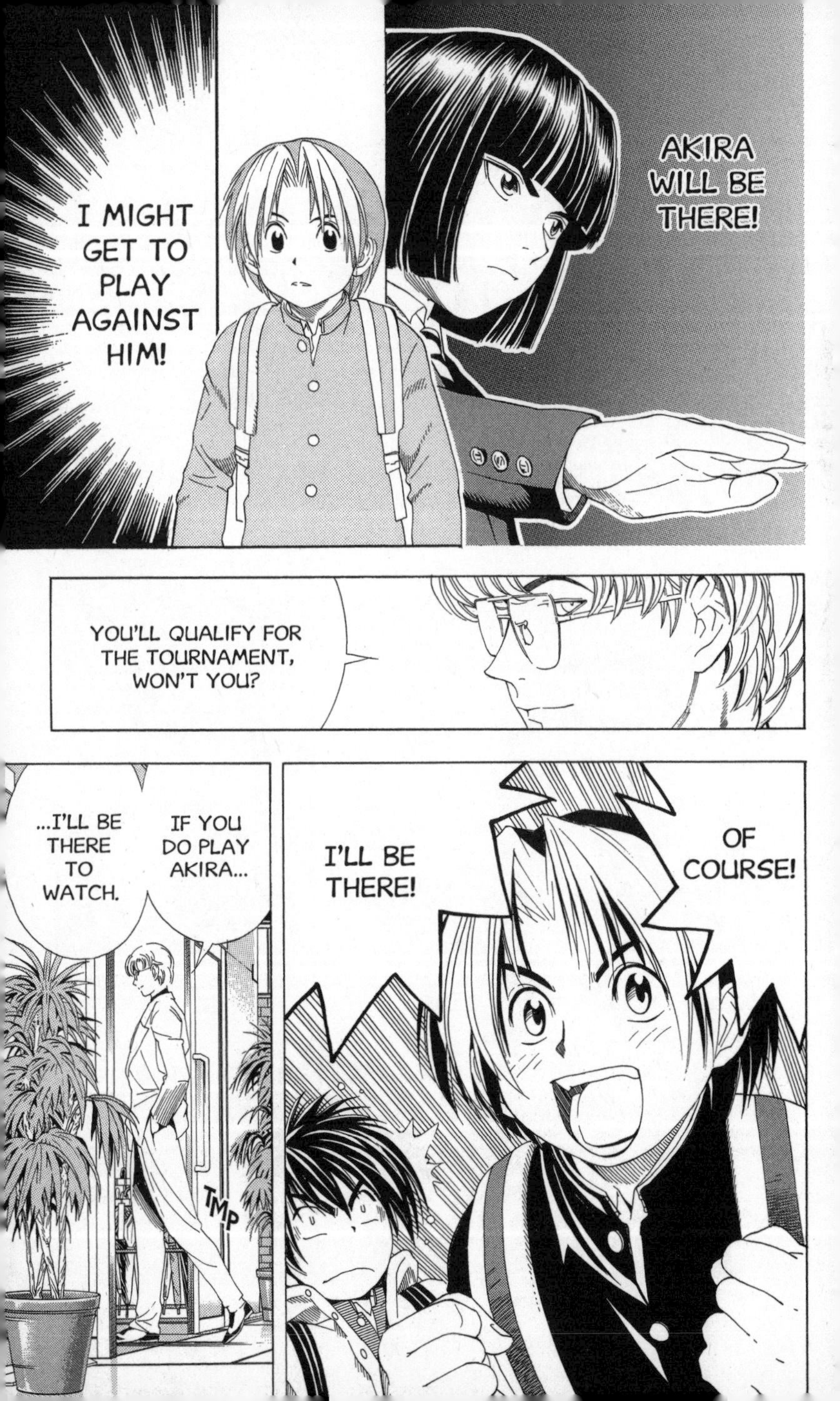
AKIRA WILL BE THERE!
I MIGHT GET TO PLAY AGAINST HIM!
YOU'LL QUALIFY FOR THE TOURNAMENT, WON'T YOU?
OF COURSE!
I'LL BE THERE!
IF YOU DO PLAY AKIRA...
...I'LL BE THERE TO WATCH.
TMP

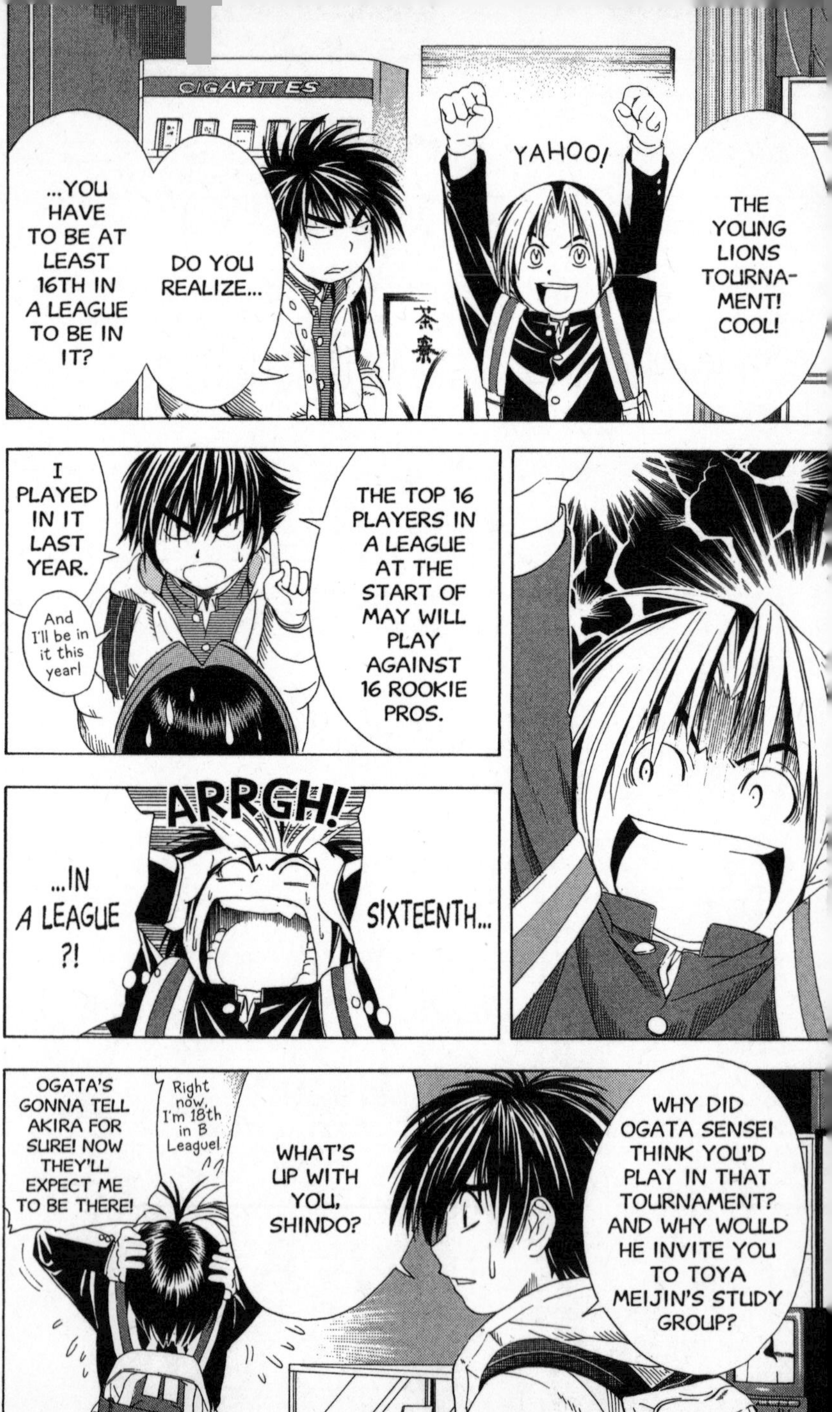
THE YOUNG LIONS TOURNAMENT! COOL!
YAHOO!
CIGARTTES
茶寮
DO YOU REALIZE...
...YOU HAVE TO BE AT LEAST 16TH IN A LEAGUE TO BE IN IT?
THE TOP 16 PLAYERS IN A LEAGUE AT THE START OF MAY WILL PLAY AGAINST 16 ROOKIE PROS.
I PLAYED IN IT LAST YEAR.
And I'll be in it this year!
ARRGH!
SIXTEENTH...
...IN A LEAGUE ?!
WHY DID OGATA SENSEI THINK YOU'D PLAY IN THAT TOURNAMENT? AND WHY WOULD HE INVITE YOU TO TOYA MEIJIN'S STUDY GROUP?
WHAT'S UP WITH YOU, SHINDO?
Right now, I'm 18th in B League!
OGATA'S GONNA TELL AKIRA FOR SURE! NOW THEY'LL EXPECT ME TO BE THERE!

READ THIS WAY

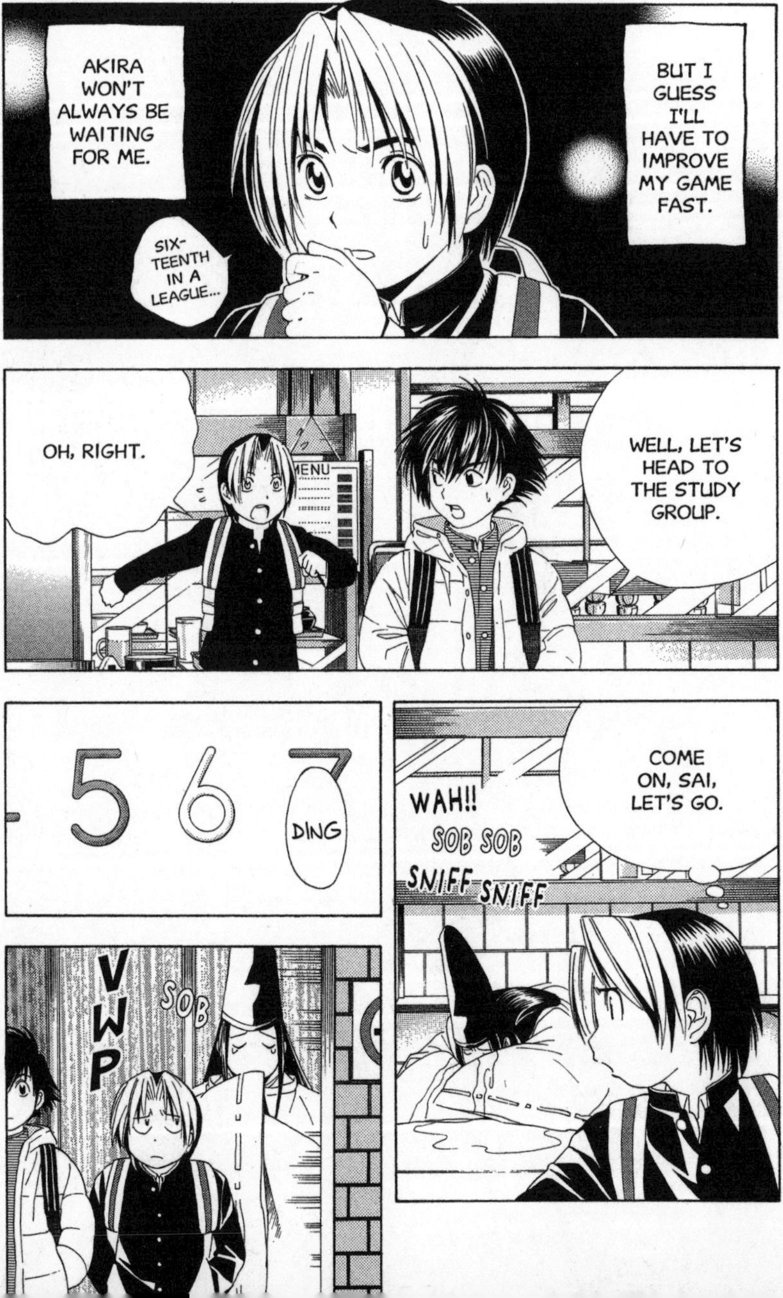
BUT I GUESS I'LL HAVE TO IMPROVE MY GAME FAST.
AKIRA WON'T ALWAYS BE WAITING FOR ME.
SIX-TEENTH IN A LEAGUE...
WELL, LET'S HEAD TO THE STUDY GROUP.
OH, RIGHT.
COME ON, SAI, LET'S GO.
WAH!!
SOB SOB
SNIFF SNIFF
5 6 7
DING
VWP
SOB

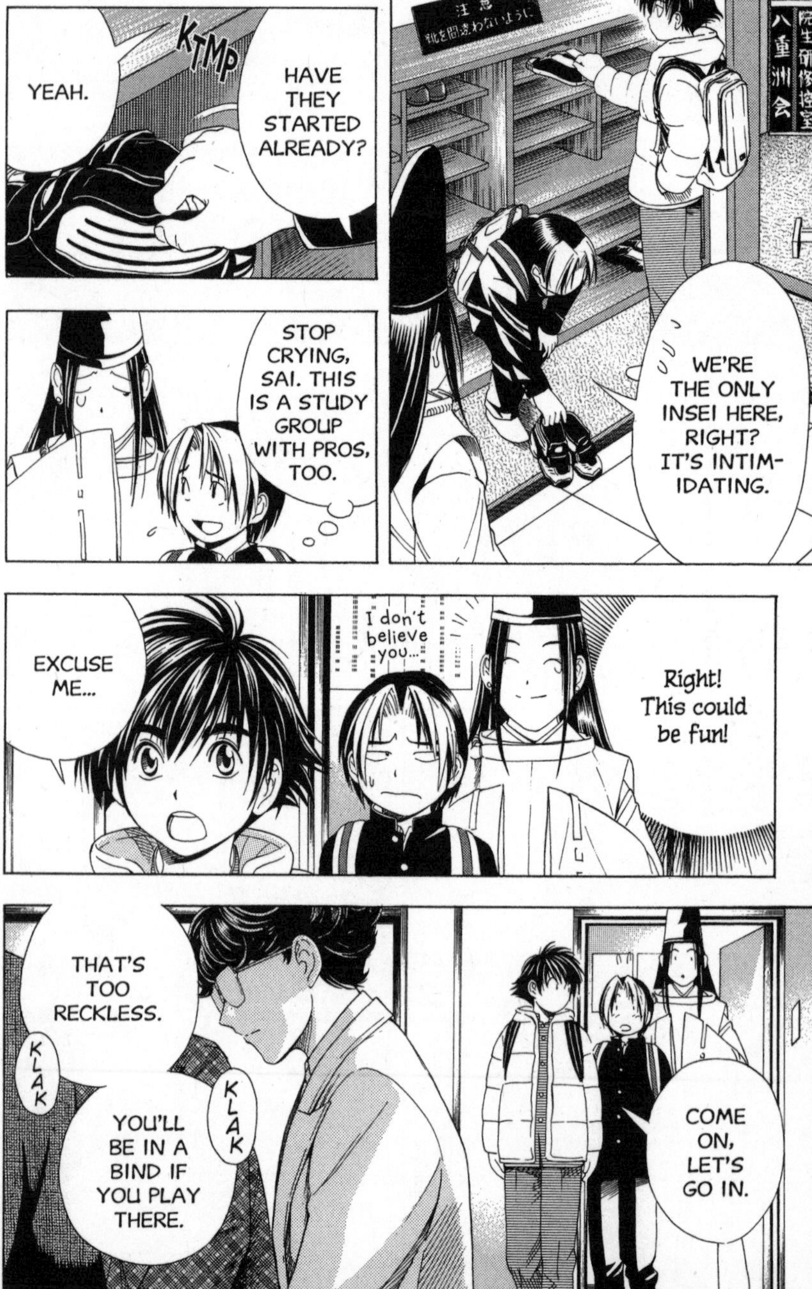
注意
靴を間違わないように
院生研修控室
八重洲会
WE'RE THE ONLY INSEI HERE, RIGHT? IT'S INTIMIDATING.
HAVE THEY STARTED ALREADY?
KTMP
YEAH.
STOP CRYING, SAI. THIS IS A STUDY GROUP WITH PROS, TOO.
Right! This could be fun!
I don't believe you...
EXCUSE ME...
COME ON, LET'S GO IN.
THAT'S TOO RECKLESS.
KLAK
KLAK
YOU'LL BE IN A BIND IF YOU PLAY THERE.

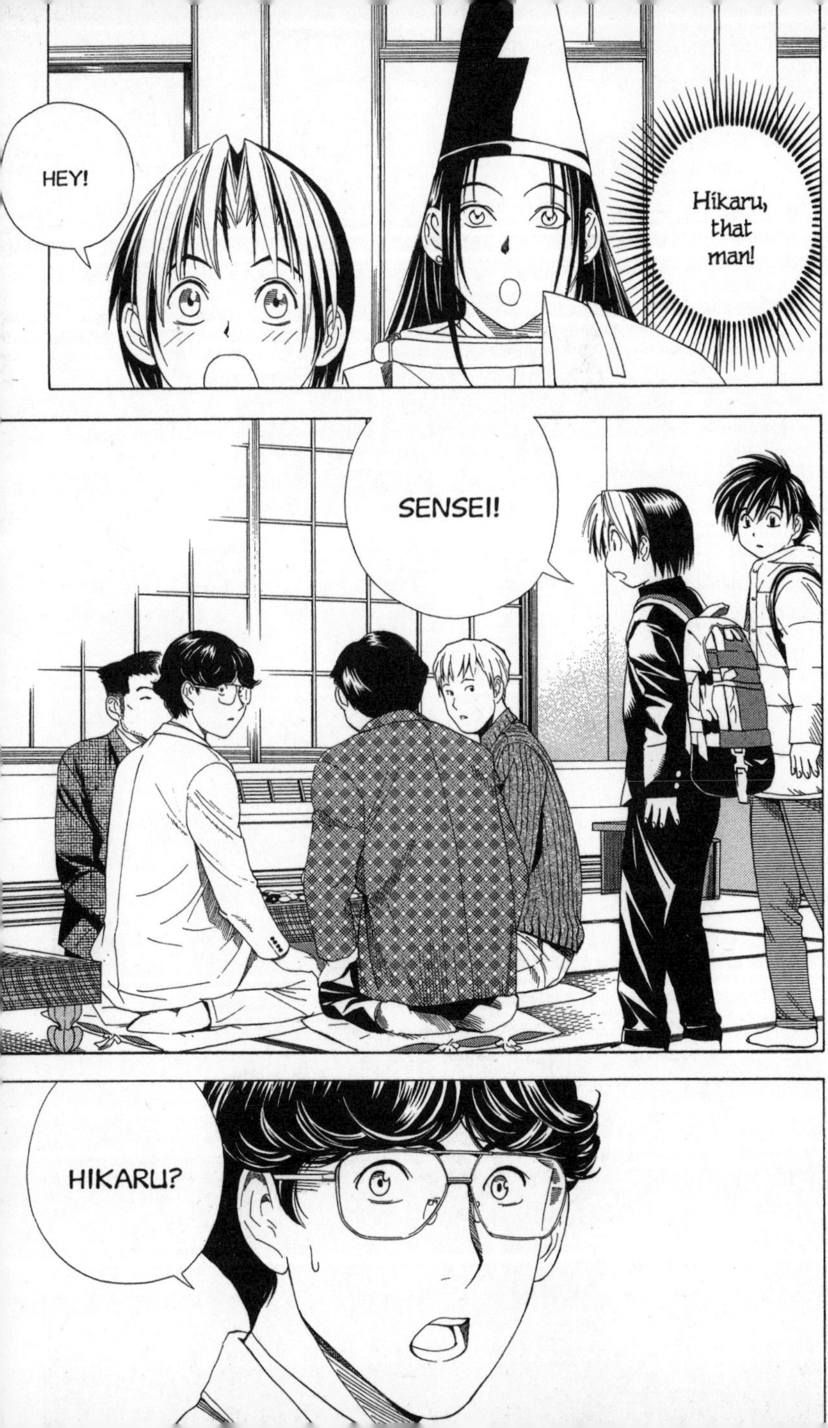
Hikaru, that man!
HEY!
SENSEI!
HIKARU?

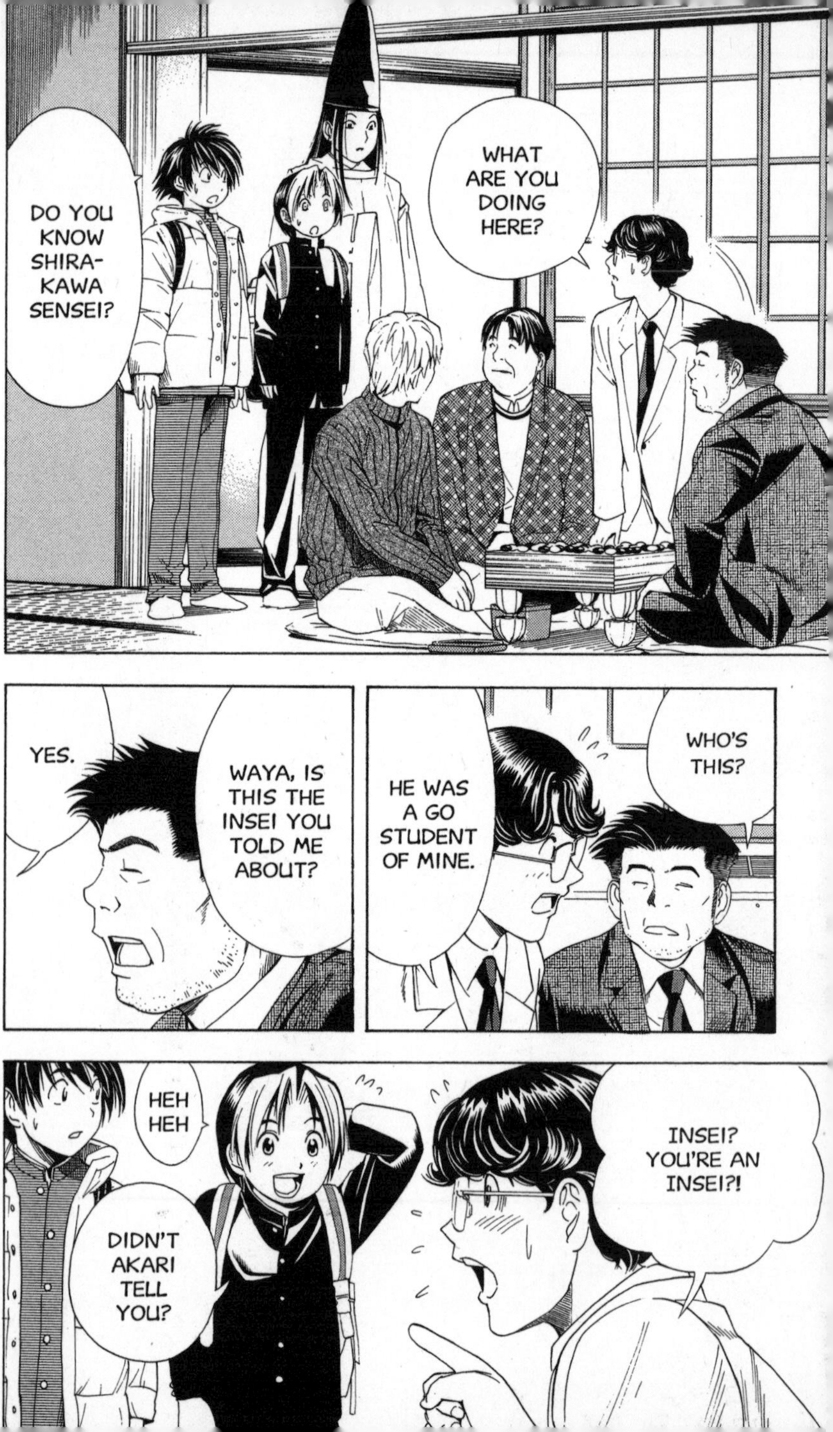
WHAT ARE YOU DOING HERE?
DO YOU KNOW SHIRAKAWA SENSEI?
WHO'S THIS?
HE WAS A GO STUDENT OF MINE.
WAYA, IS THIS THE INSEI YOU TOLD ME ABOUT?
YES.
INSEI? YOU'RE AN INSEI?!
HEH HEH
DIDN'T AKARI TELL YOU?

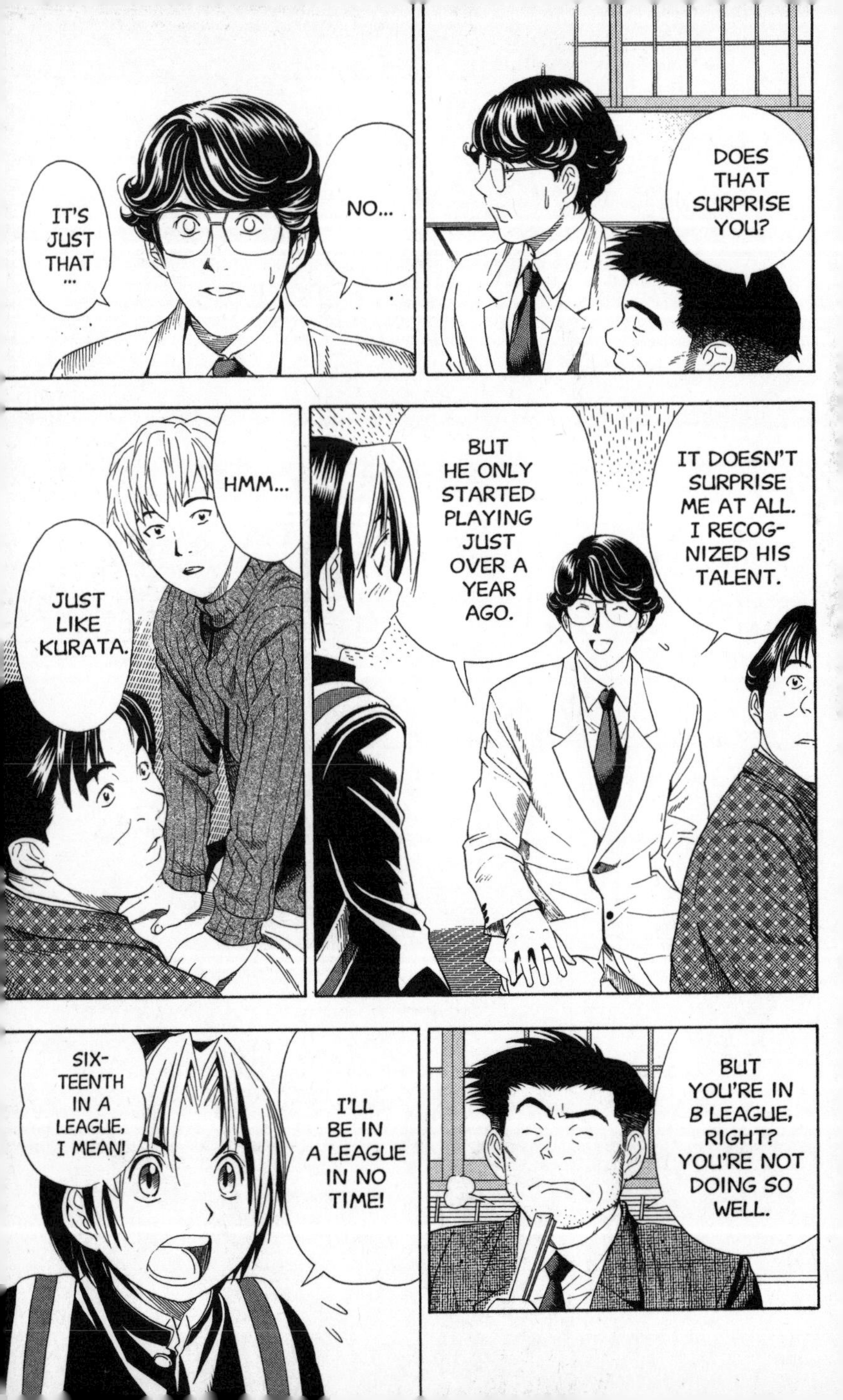
DOES THAT SURPRISE YOU?
NO...
IT'S JUST THAT ...
IT DOESN'T SURPRISE ME AT ALL. I RECOGNIZED HIS TALENT.
BUT HE ONLY STARTED PLAYING JUST OVER A YEAR AGO.
HMM...
JUST LIKE KURATA.
BUT YOU'RE IN *B* LEAGUE, RIGHT? YOU'RE NOT DOING SO WELL.
I'LL BE IN A LEAGUE IN NO TIME!
SIXTEENTH IN A LEAGUE, I MEAN!

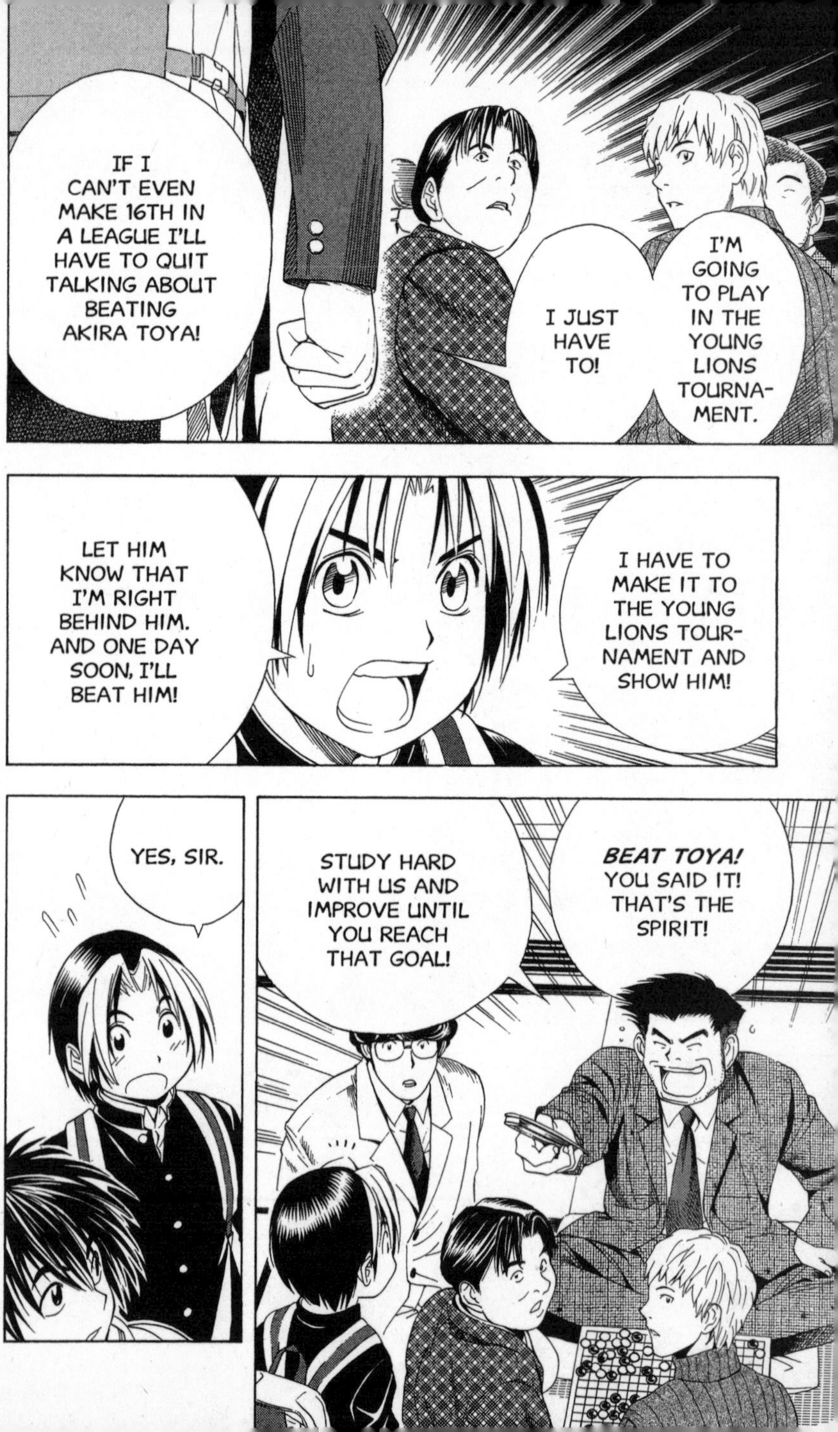
I'M GOING TO PLAY IN THE YOUNG LIONS TOURNAMENT.
I JUST HAVE TO!
IF I CAN'T EVEN MAKE 16TH IN A LEAGUE I'LL HAVE TO QUIT TALKING ABOUT BEATING AKIRA TOYA!
I HAVE TO MAKE IT TO THE YOUNG LIONS TOURNAMENT AND SHOW HIM!
LET HIM KNOW THAT I'M RIGHT BEHIND HIM. AND ONE DAY SOON, I'LL BEAT HIM!
*BEAT TOYA!* YOU SAID IT! THAT'S THE SPIRIT!
STUDY HARD WITH US AND IMPROVE UNTIL YOU REACH THAT GOAL!
YES, SIR.

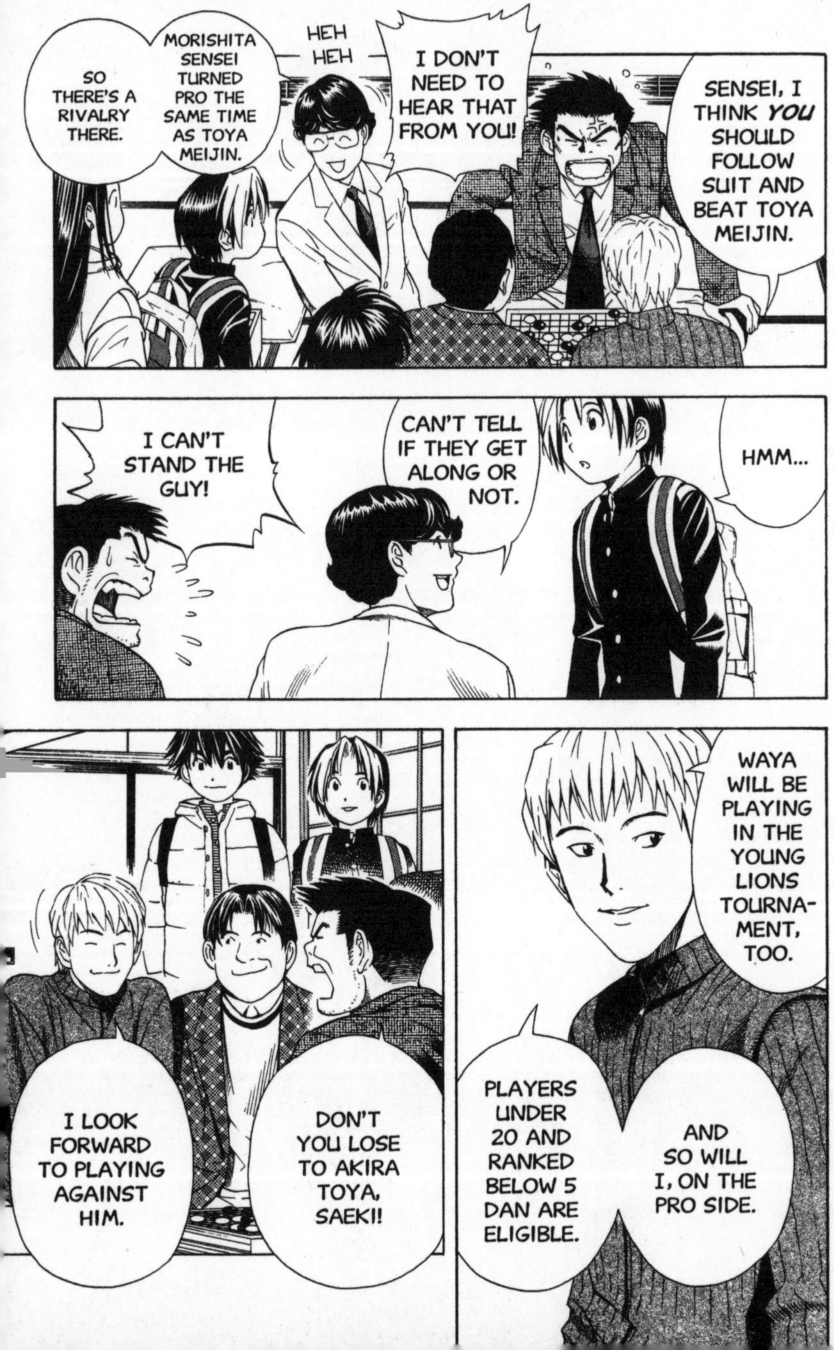
SENSEI, I THINK *YOU* SHOULD FOLLOW SUIT AND BEAT TOYA MEIJIN.
I DON'T NEED TO HEAR THAT FROM YOU!
HEH HEH
MORISHITA SENSEI TURNED PRO THE SAME TIME AS TOYA MEIJIN.
SO THERE'S A RIVALRY THERE.
HMM...
CAN'T TELL IF THEY GET ALONG OR NOT.
I CAN'T STAND THE GUY!
WAYA WILL BE PLAYING IN THE YOUNG LIONS TOURNAMENT, TOO.
AND SO WILL I, ON THE PRO SIDE.
PLAYERS UNDER 20 AND RANKED BELOW 5 DAN ARE ELIGIBLE.
DON'T YOU LOSE TO AKIRA TOYA, SAEKI!
I LOOK FORWARD TO PLAYING AGAINST HIM.

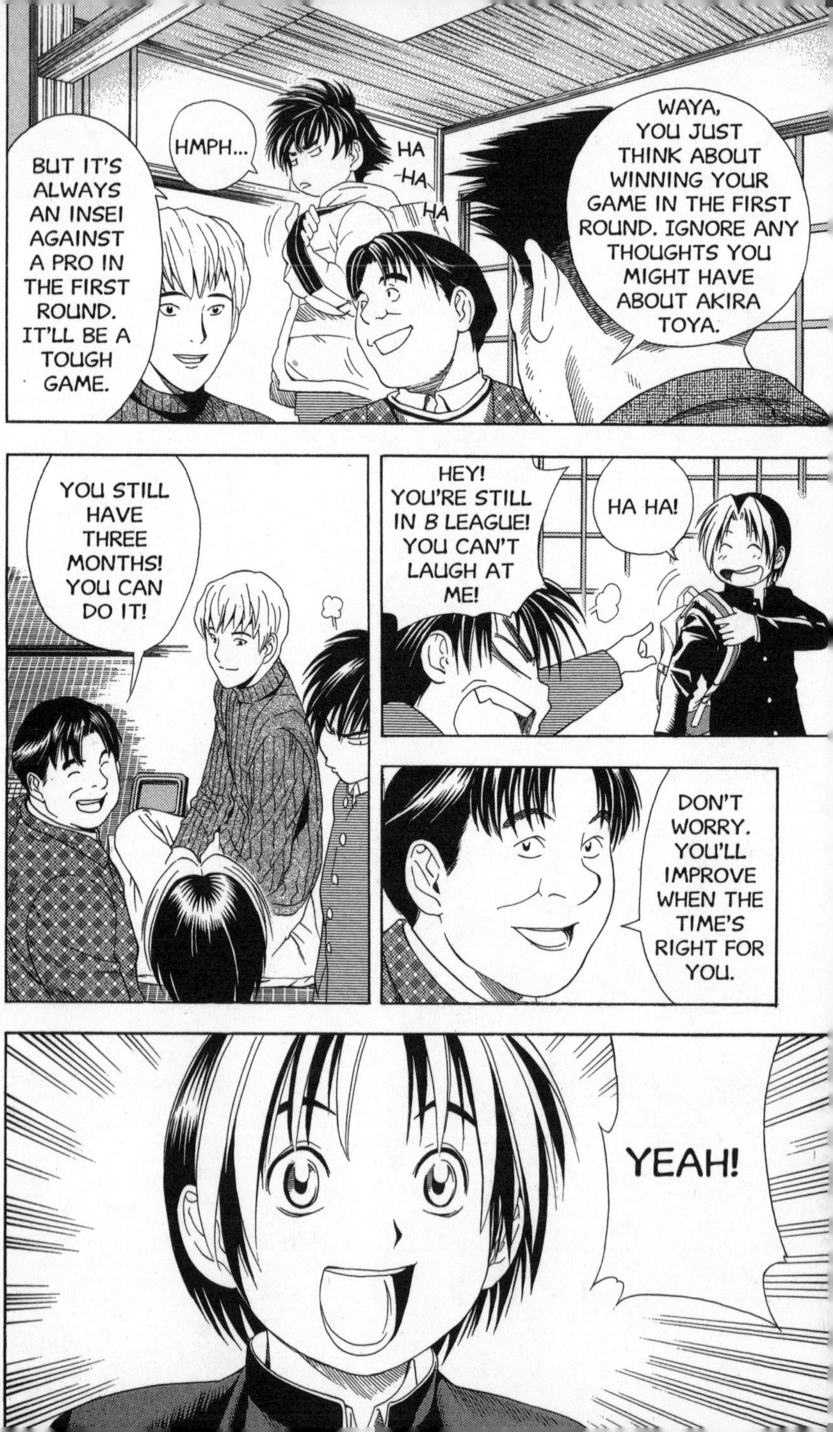
WAYA, YOU JUST THINK ABOUT WINNING YOUR GAME IN THE FIRST ROUND. IGNORE ANY THOUGHTS YOU MIGHT HAVE ABOUT AKIRA TOYA.
HA -HA HA
HMPH...
BUT IT'S ALWAYS AN INSEI AGAINST A PRO IN THE FIRST ROUND. IT'LL BE A TOUGH GAME.
HA HA!
HEY! YOU'RE STILL IN *B* LEAGUE! YOU CAN'T LAUGH AT ME!
DON'T WORRY. YOU'LL IMPROVE WHEN THE TIME'S RIGHT FOR YOU.
YOU STILL HAVE THREE MONTHS! YOU CAN DO IT!
YEAH!

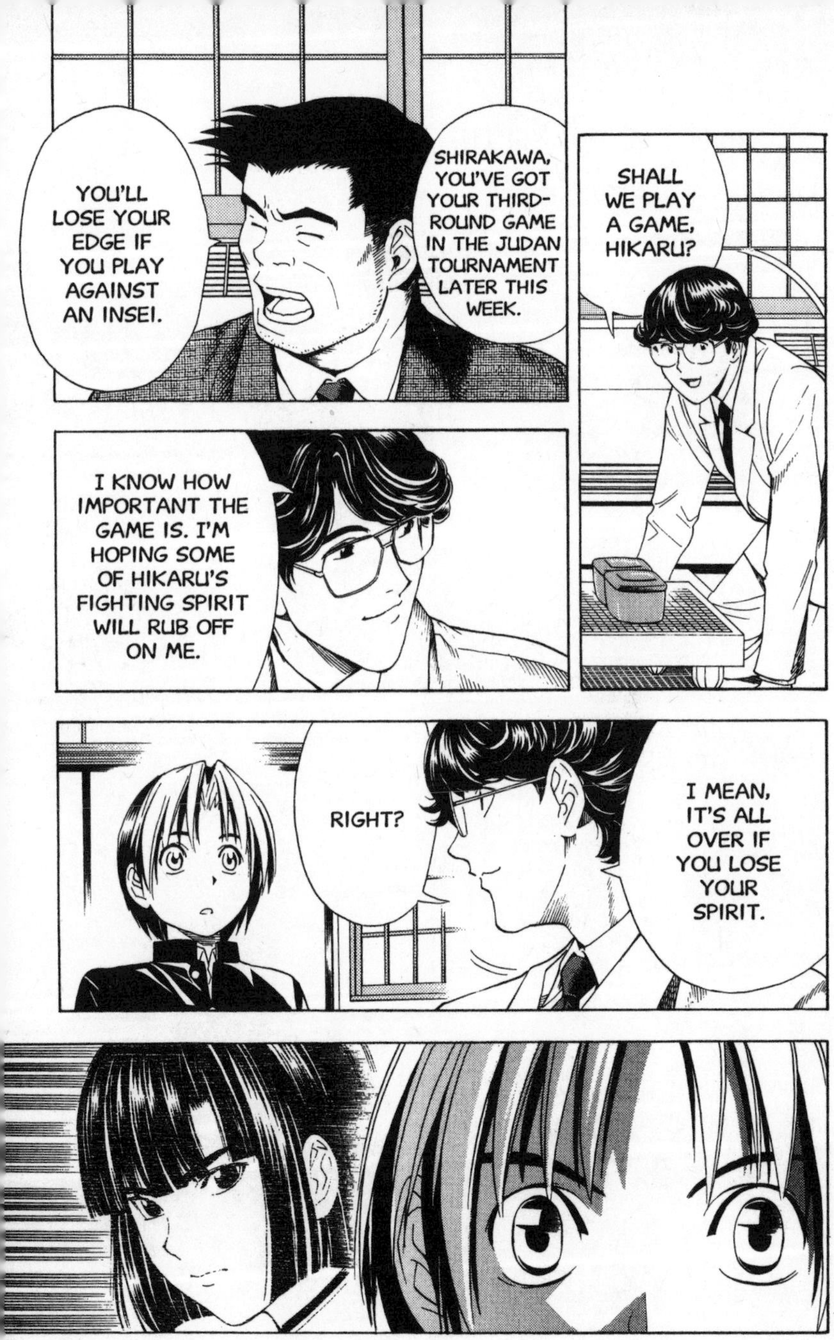
SHALL WE PLAY A GAME, HIKARU?
SHIRAKAWA, YOU'VE GOT YOUR THIRD-ROUND GAME IN THE JUDAN TOURNAMENT LATER THIS WEEK.
YOU'LL LOSE YOUR EDGE IF YOU PLAY AGAINST AN INSEI.
I KNOW HOW IMPORTANT THE GAME IS. I'M HOPING SOME OF HIKARU'S FIGHTING SPIRIT WILL RUB OFF ON ME.
I MEAN, IT'S ALL OVER IF YOU LOSE YOUR SPIRIT.
RIGHT?

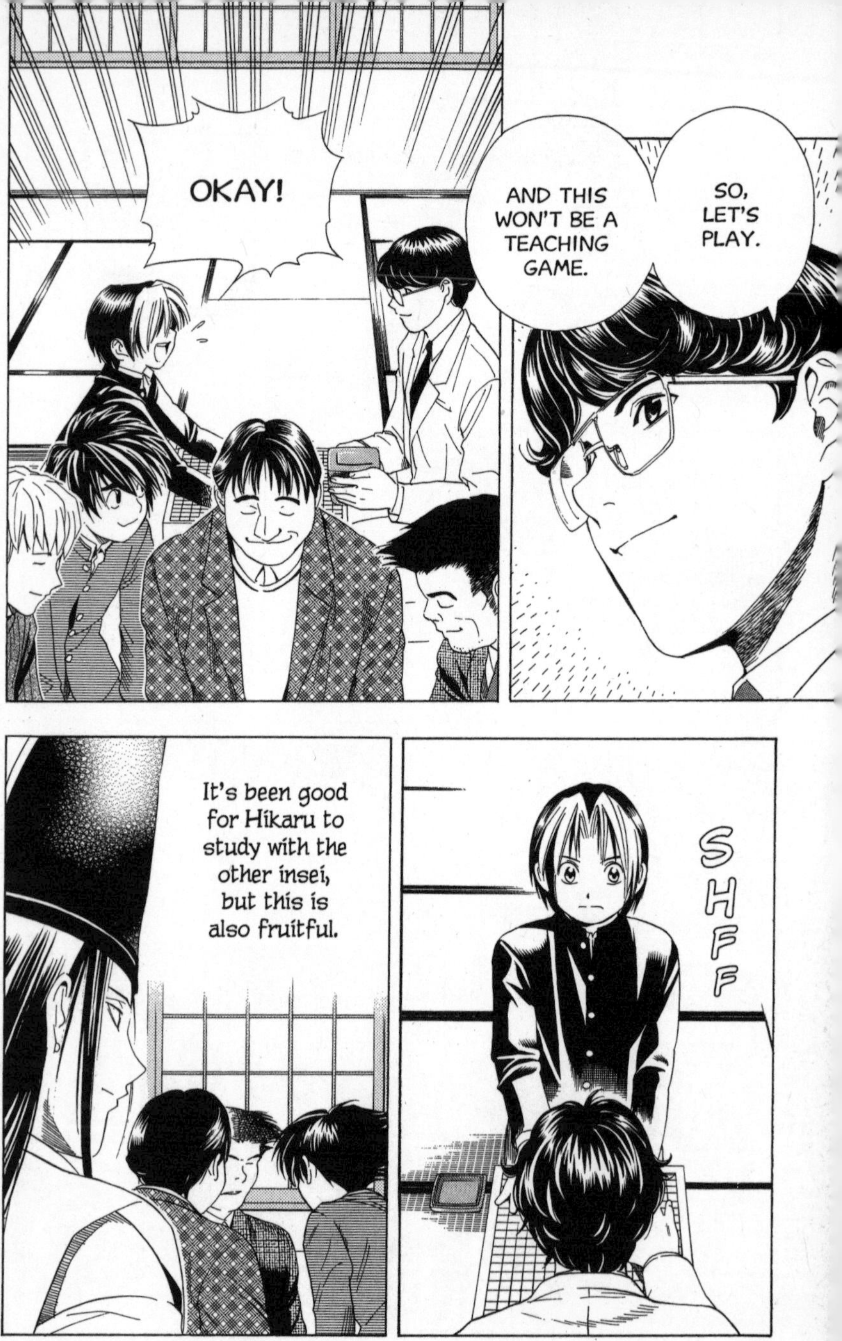
SO, LET'S PLAY.
AND THIS WON'T BE A TEACHING GAME.
OKAY!
SHFF
It's been good for Hikaru to study with the other insei, but this is also fruitful.

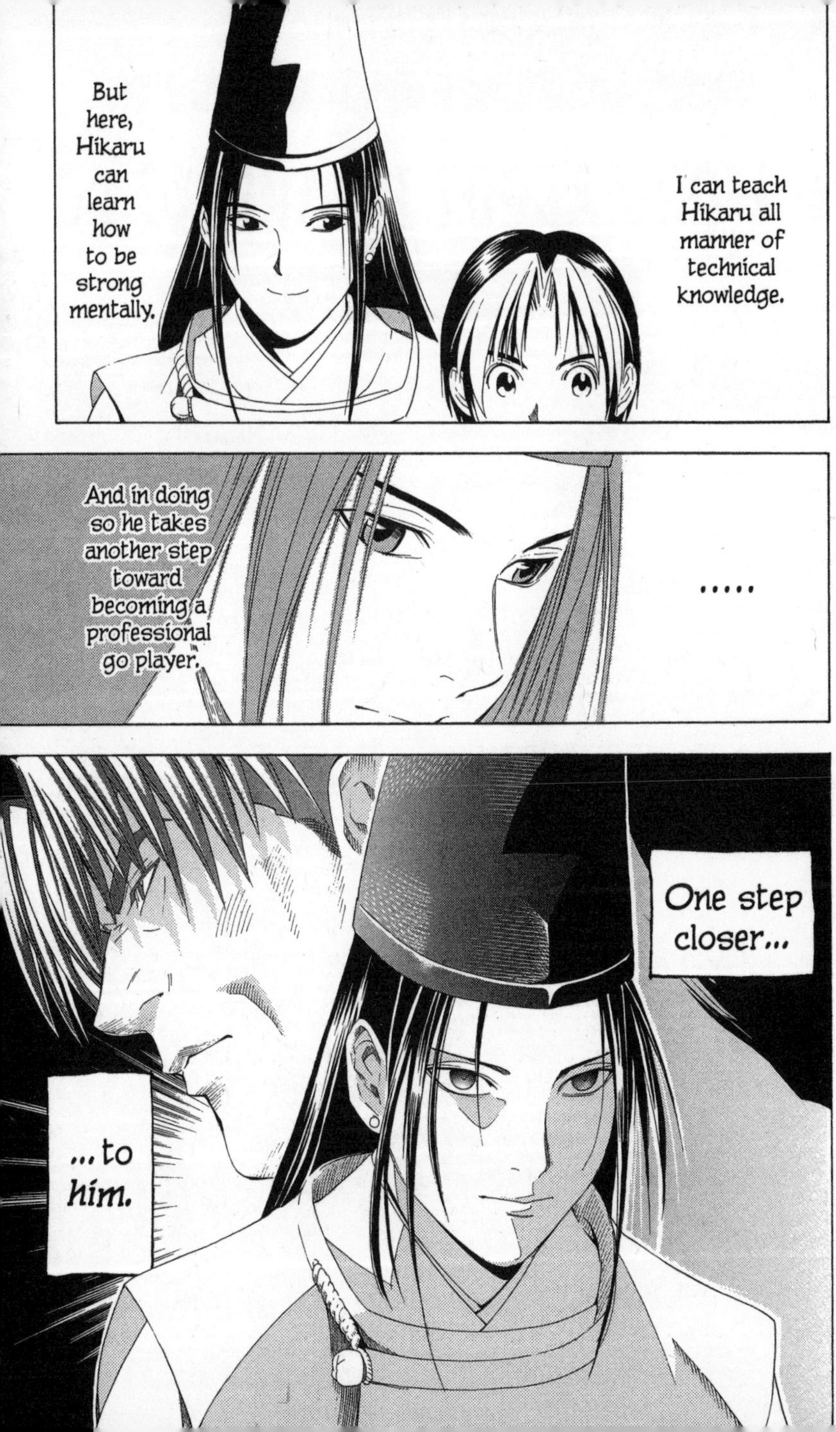
I can teach Hikaru all manner of technical knowledge.
But here, Hikaru can learn how to be strong mentally.
.....
And in doing so he takes another step toward becoming a professional go player.
One step closer...
...to *him.*

# A WORD ABOUT HIKARU NO GO

## BECOMING A PRO

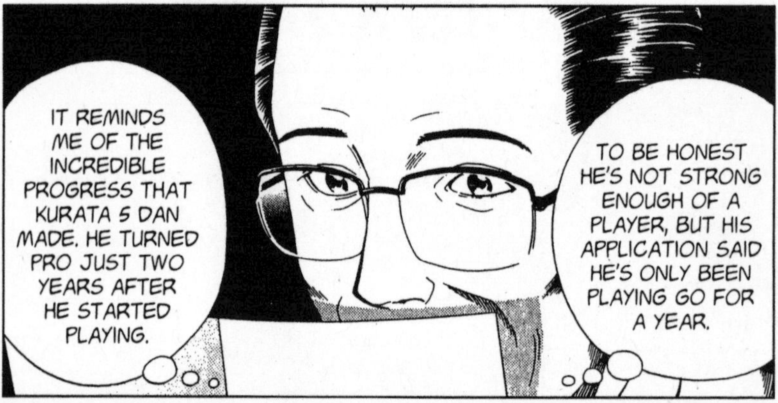
TO BE HONEST HE'S NOT STRONG ENOUGH OF A PLAYER, BUT HIS APPLICATION SAID HE'S ONLY BEEN PLAYING GO FOR A YEAR.
IT REMINDS ME OF THE INCREDIBLE PROGRESS THAT KURATA 5 DAN MADE. HE TURNED PRO JUST TWO YEARS AFTER HE STARTED PLAYING.

THERE ACTUALLY ARE PEOPLE WHO WENT ON TO BECOME PROFESSIONAL GO PLAYERS ONLY TWO YEARS AFTER THEY BEGAN PLAYING. SOME HAVE DONE IT IN THREE YEARS. THE AGE LIMIT FOR TURNING PRO IS 30 YEARS OF AGE.

THAT'S RIGHT! YOU STILL HAVE A CHANCE TO GO PRO!

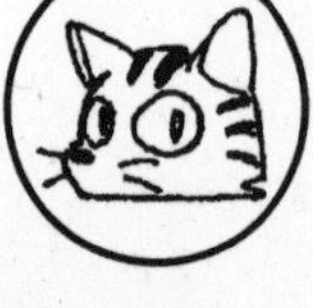

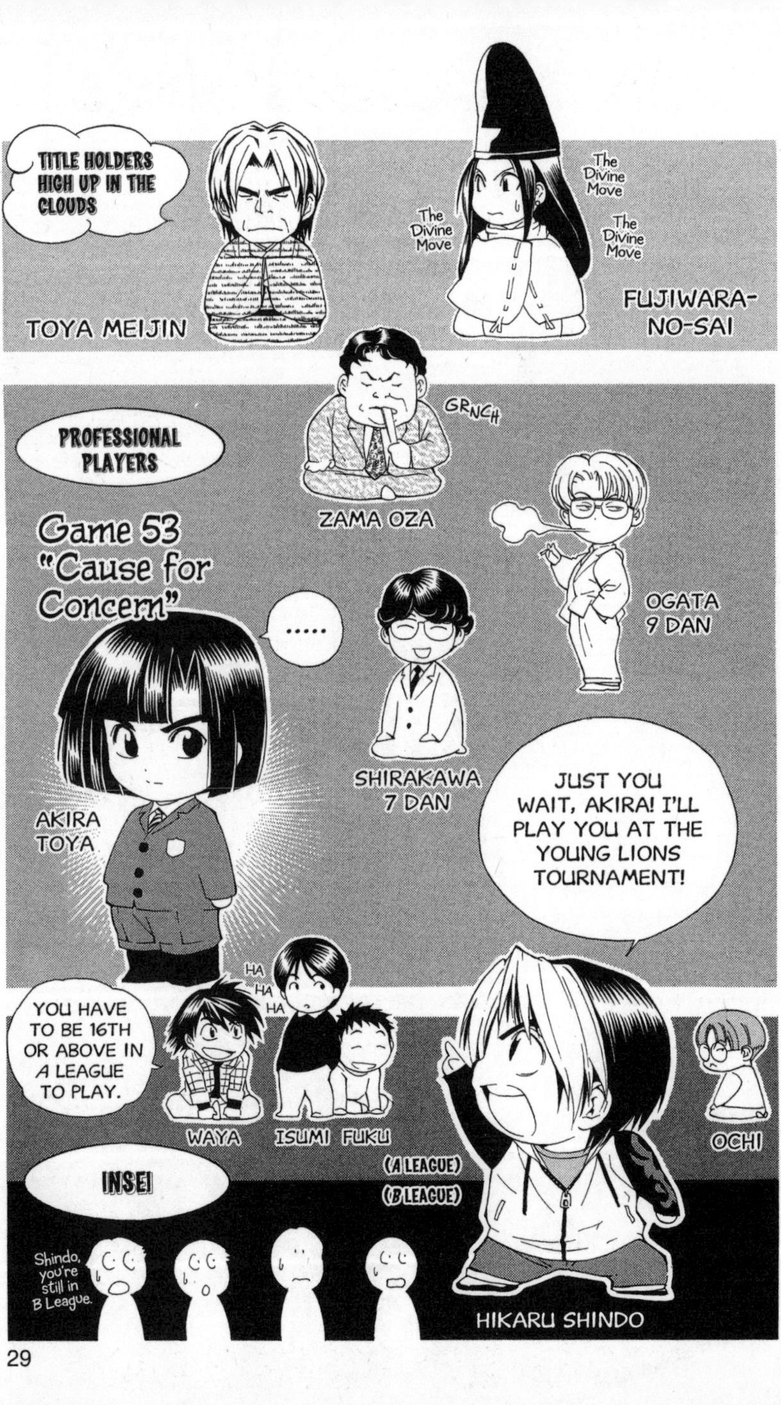
TITLE HOLDERS HIGH UP IN THE CLOUDS
The Divine Move
The Divine Move
The Divine Move
FUJIWARA-NO-SAI
TOYA MEIJIN
PROFESSIONAL PLAYERS
GRNCH
ZAMA OZA
OGATA 9 DAN
Game 53 "Cause for Concern"
SHIRAKAWA 7 DAN
.....
AKIRA TOYA
JUST YOU WAIT, AKIRA! I'LL PLAY YOU AT THE YOUNG LIONS TOURNAMENT!
HA HA HA
YOU HAVE TO BE 16TH OR ABOVE IN A LEAGUE TO PLAY.
OCHI
FUKU
ISUMI
WAYA
(A LEAGUE)
(B LEAGUE)
INSEI
HIKARU SHINDO
Shindo, you're still in B League.

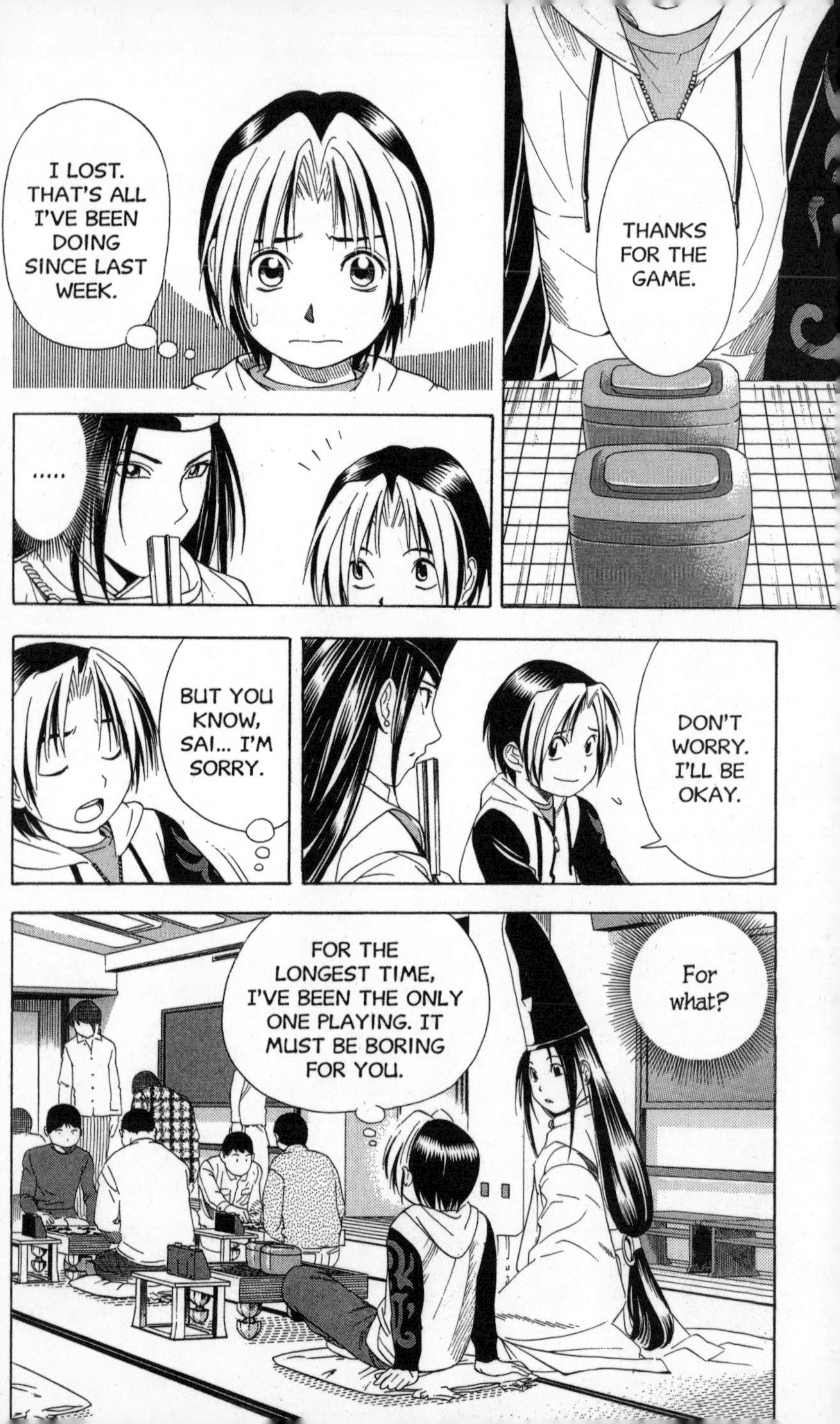
THANKS FOR THE GAME.
I LOST. THAT'S ALL I'VE BEEN DOING SINCE LAST WEEK.
.....
DON'T WORRY. I'LL BE OKAY.
BUT YOU KNOW, SAI... I'M SORRY.
For what?
FOR THE LONGEST TIME, I'VE BEEN THE ONLY ONE PLAYING. IT MUST BE BORING FOR YOU.

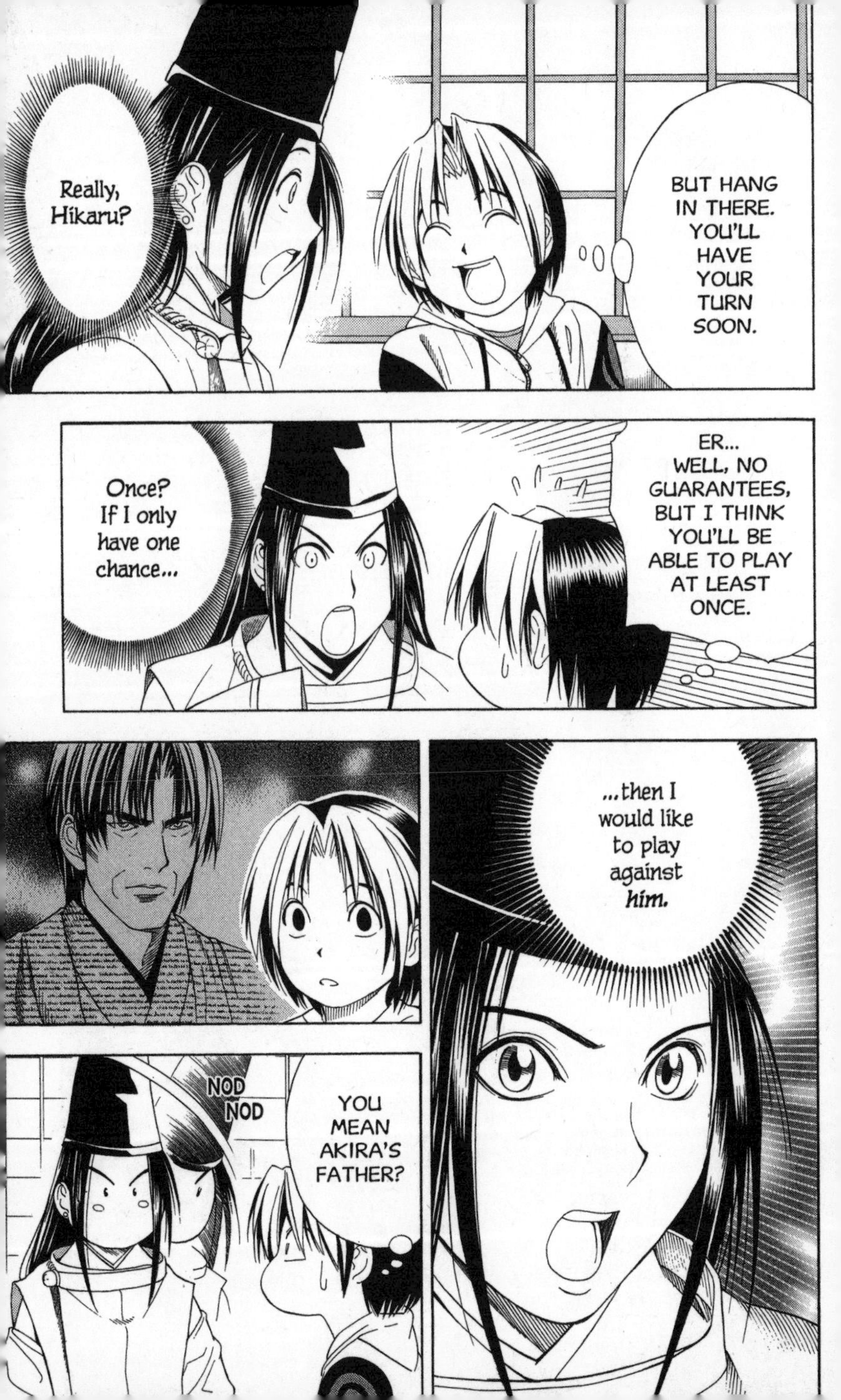
BUT HANG IN THERE. YOU'LL HAVE YOUR TURN SOON.
Really, Hikaru?
ER... WELL, NO GUARANTEES, BUT I THINK YOU'LL BE ABLE TO PLAY AT LEAST ONCE.
Once? If I only have one chance...
...then I would like to play against *him.*
YOU MEAN AKIRA'S FATHER?
NOD NOD

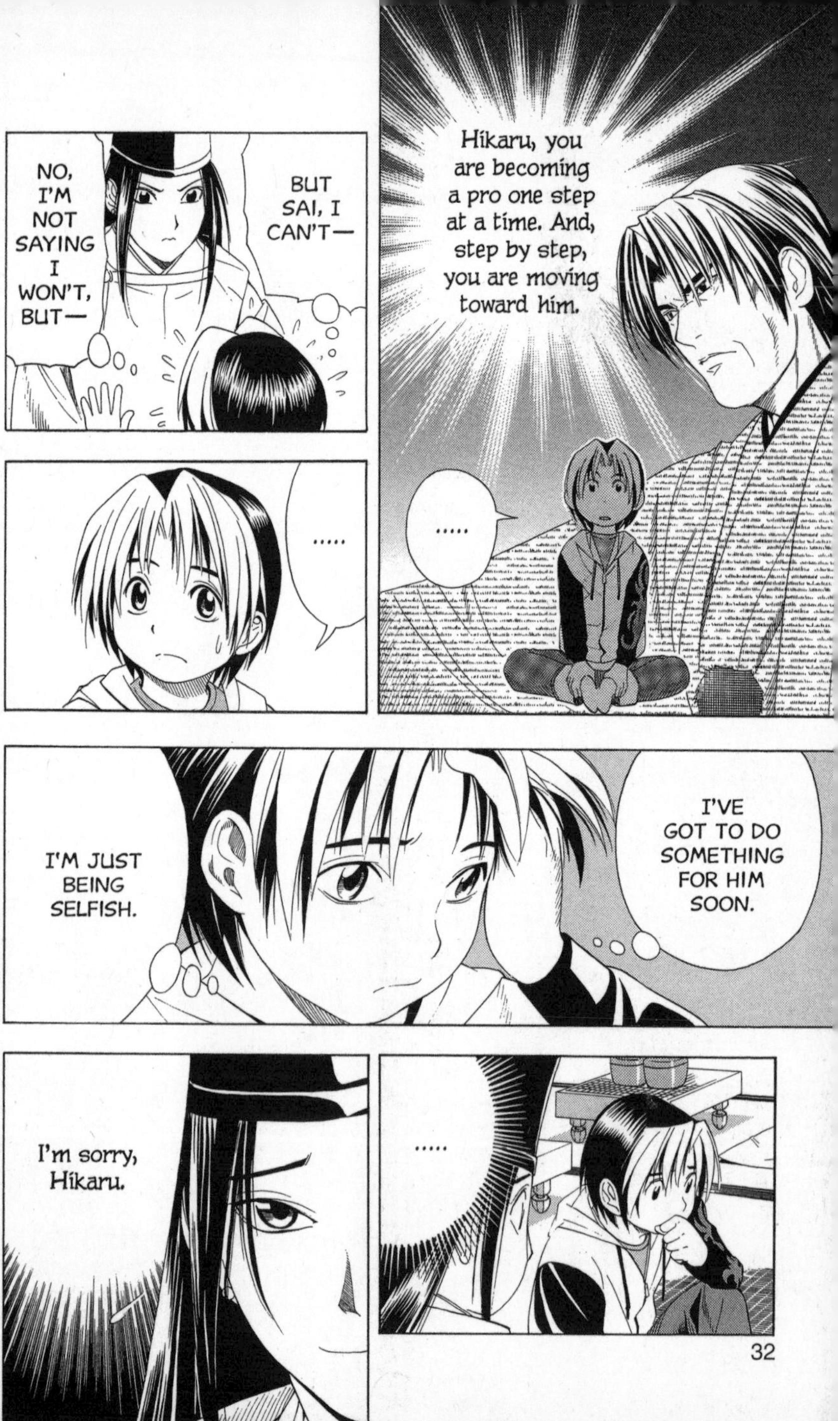

Hikaru, you are becoming a pro one step at a time. And, step by step, you are moving toward him.
.....
BUT SAI, I CAN'T—
NO, I'M NOT SAYING I WON'T, BUT—
.....
I'VE GOT TO DO SOMETHING FOR HIM SOON.
I'M JUST BEING SELFISH.
.....
I'm sorry, Hikaru.

READ THIS WAY

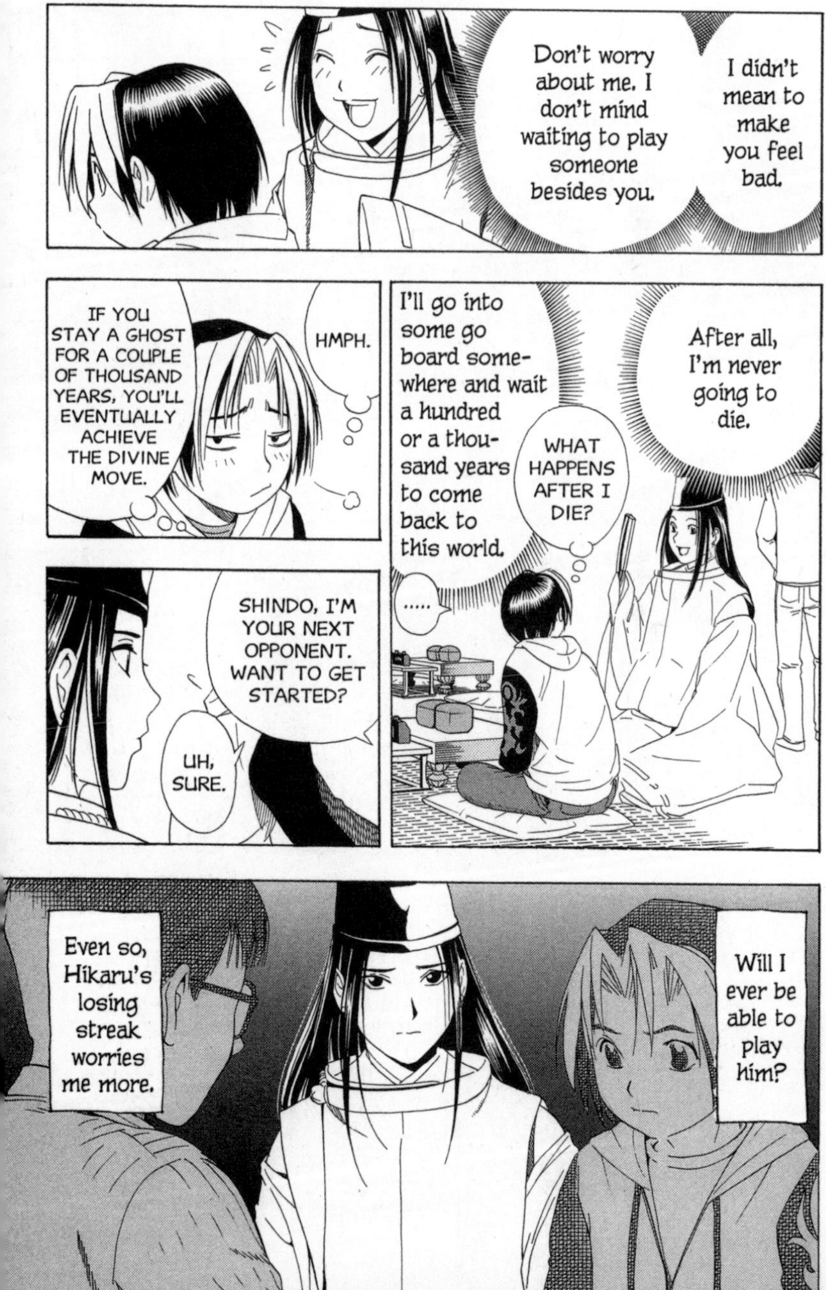

I didn't mean to make you feel bad.
Don't worry about me. I don't mind waiting to play someone besides you.
After all, I'm never going to die.
I'll go into some go board somewhere and wait a hundred or a thousand years to come back to this world.
WHAT HAPPENS AFTER I DIE?
.....
HMPH.
IF YOU STAY A GHOST FOR A COUPLE OF THOUSAND YEARS, YOU'LL EVENTUALLY ACHIEVE THE DIVINE MOVE.
SHINDO, I'M YOUR NEXT OPPONENT. WANT TO GET STARTED?
UH, SURE.
Will I ever be able to play him?
Even so, Hikaru's losing streak worries me more.

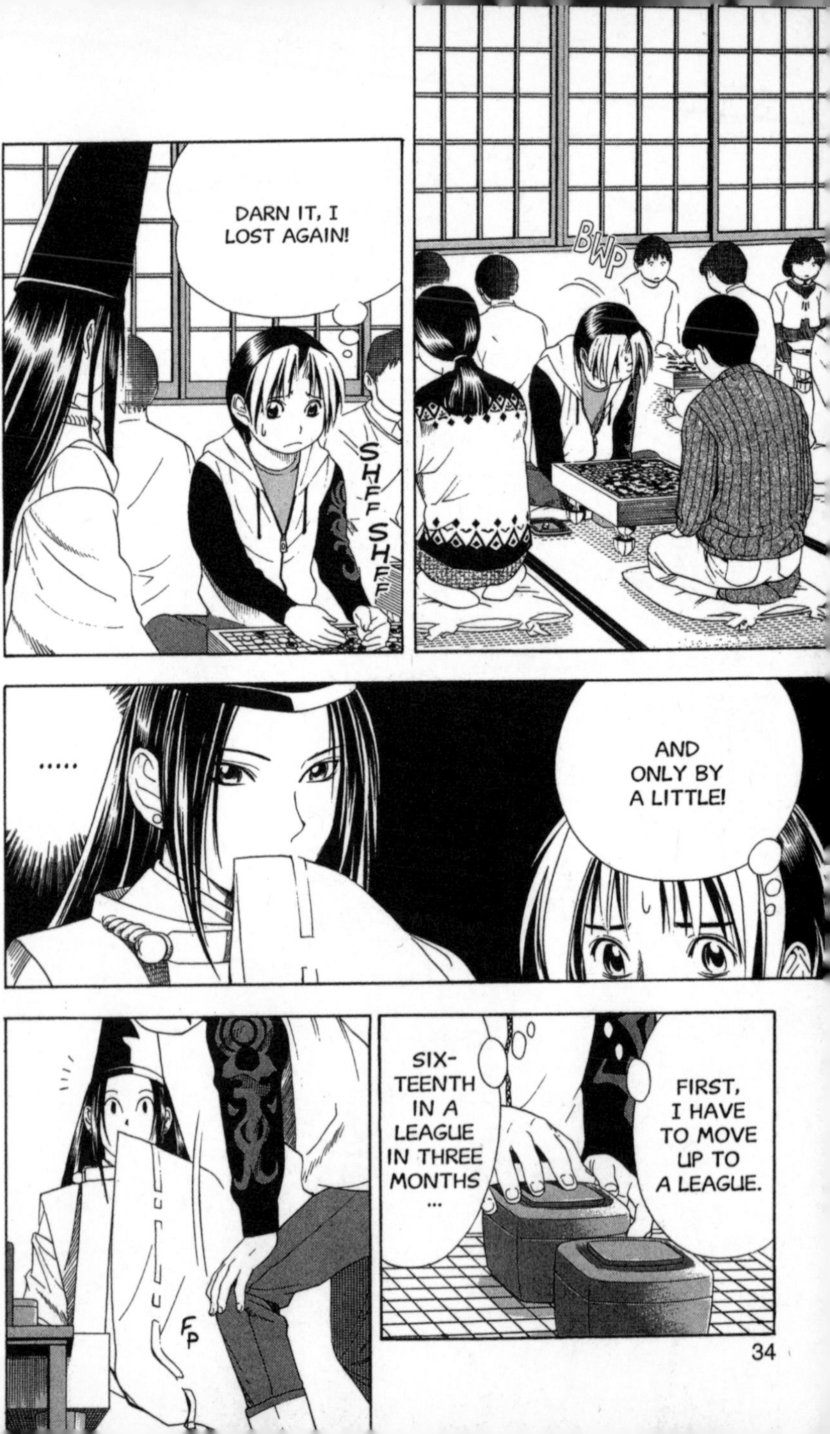
BWP
DARN IT, I LOST AGAIN!
SHFF SHFF
AND ONLY BY A LITTLE!
.....
FIRST, I HAVE TO MOVE UP TO A LEAGUE.
SIX-TEENTH IN A LEAGUE IN THREE MONTHS ...
FP

READ THIS WAY

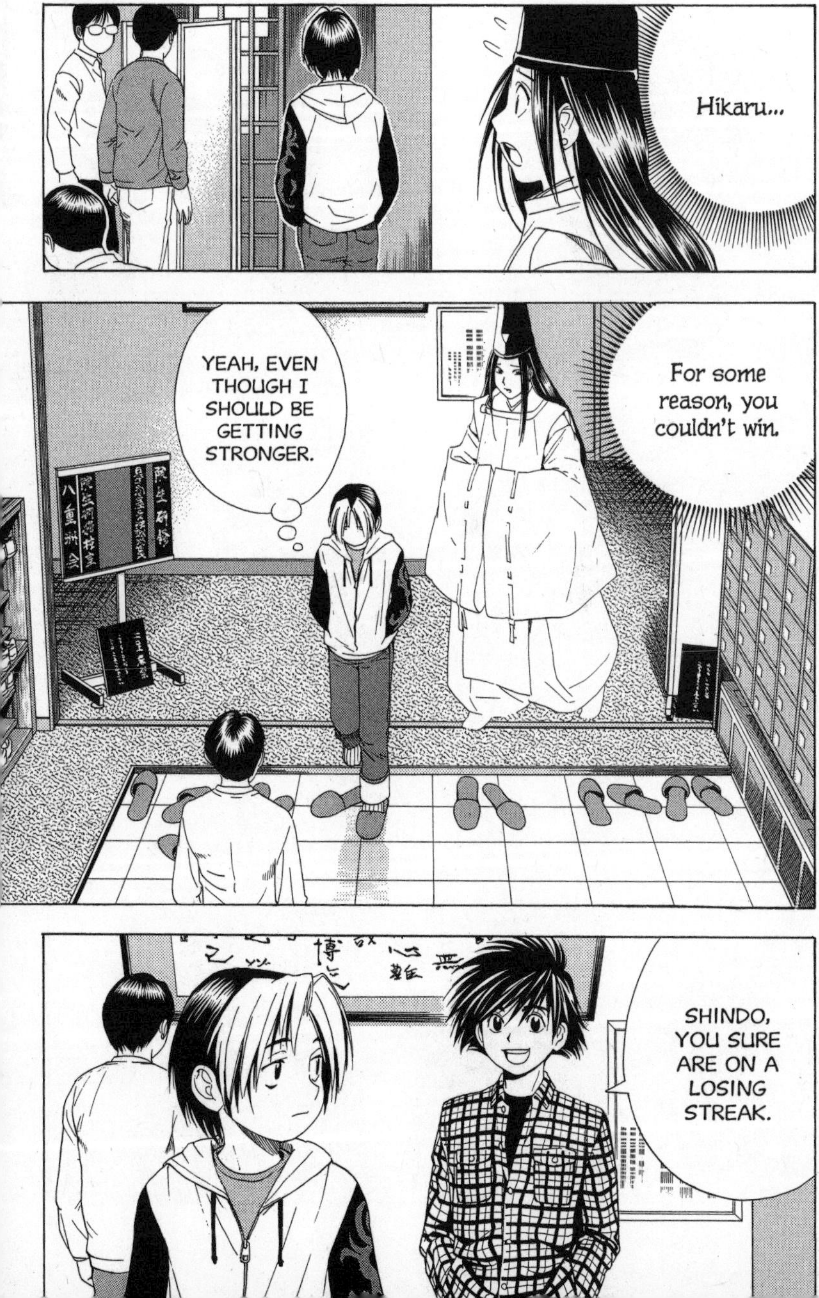
Hikaru...
For some reason, you couldn't win.
YEAH, EVEN THOUGH I SHOULD BE GETTING STRONGER.
SHINDO, YOU SURE ARE ON A LOSING STREAK.

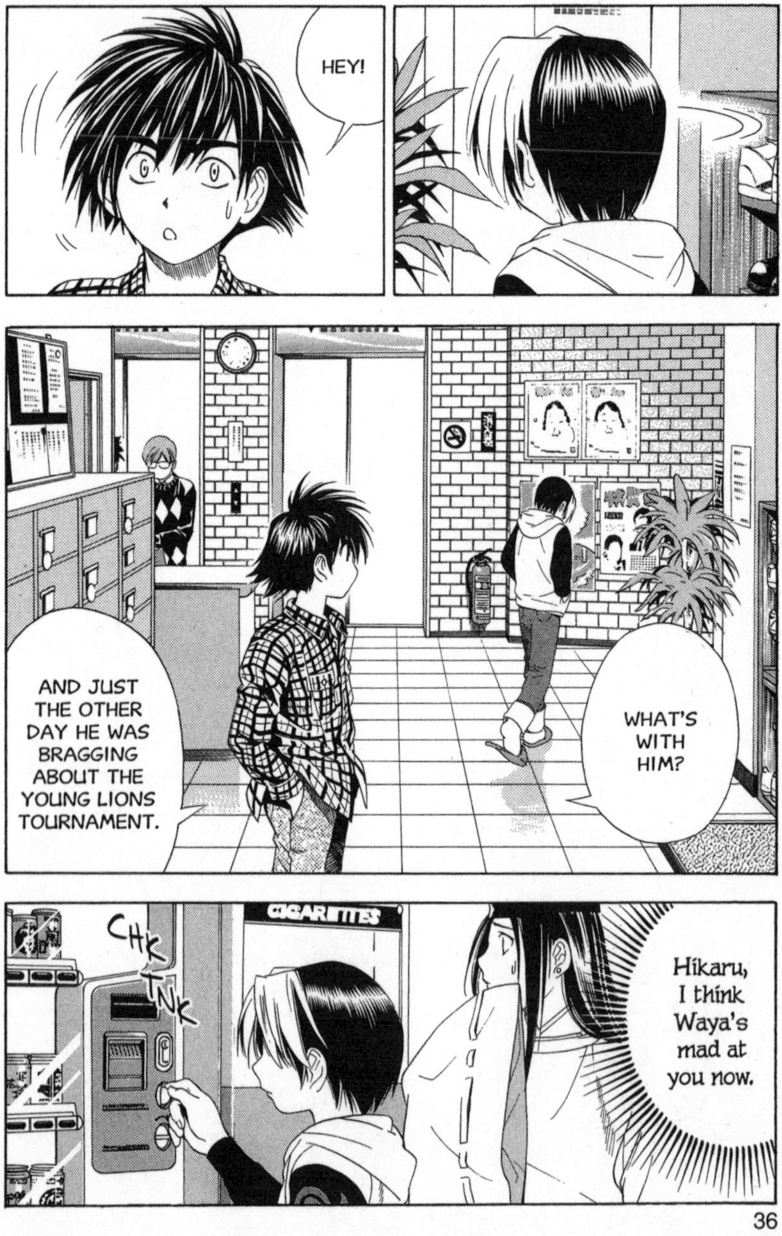
HEY!
WHAT'S WITH HIM?
AND JUST THE OTHER DAY HE WAS BRAGGING ABOUT THE YOUNG LIONS TOURNAMENT.
Hikaru, I think Waya's mad at you now.
CIGARETTES
CHK TNK

READ THIS WAY

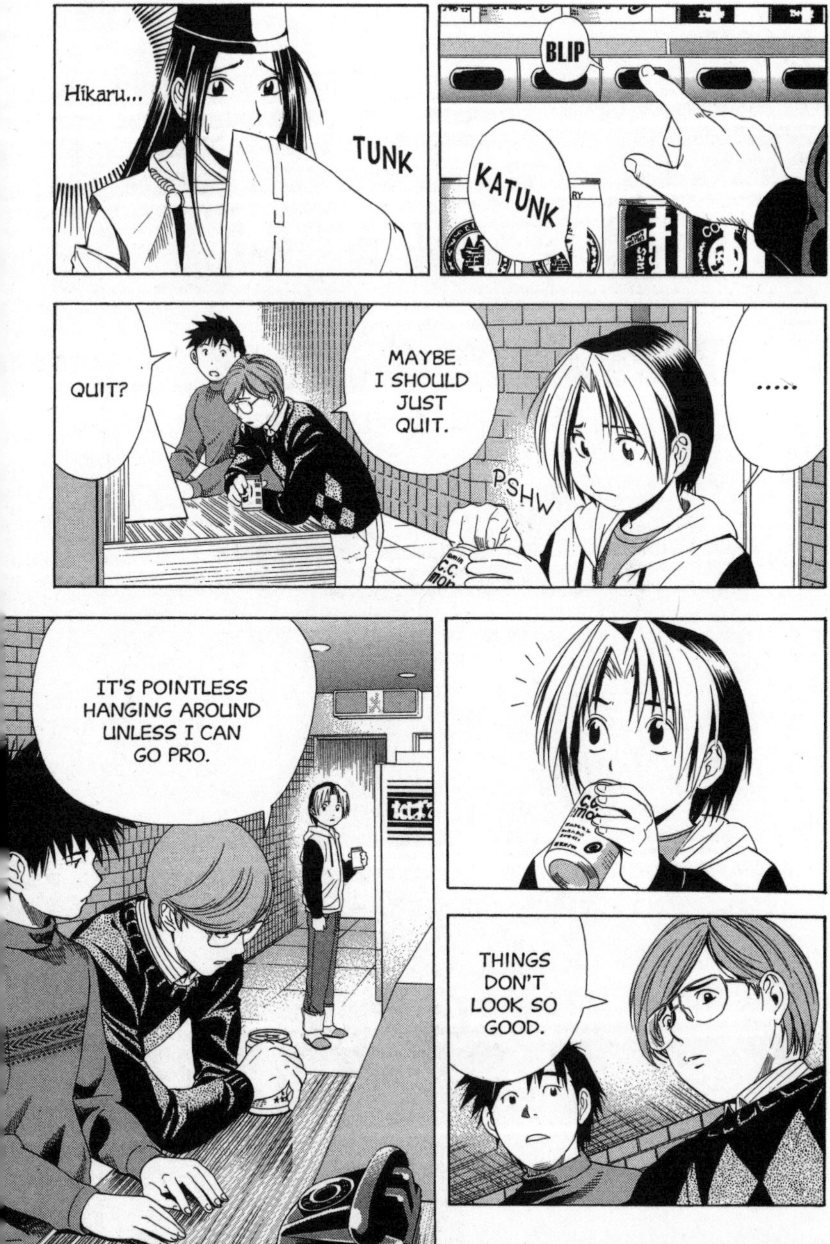
BLIP
KATUNK
Hikaru...
TUNK
.....
PSHW
MAYBE I SHOULD JUST QUIT.
QUIT?
THINGS DON'T LOOK SO GOOD.
IT'S POINTLESS HANGING AROUND UNLESS I CAN GO PRO.

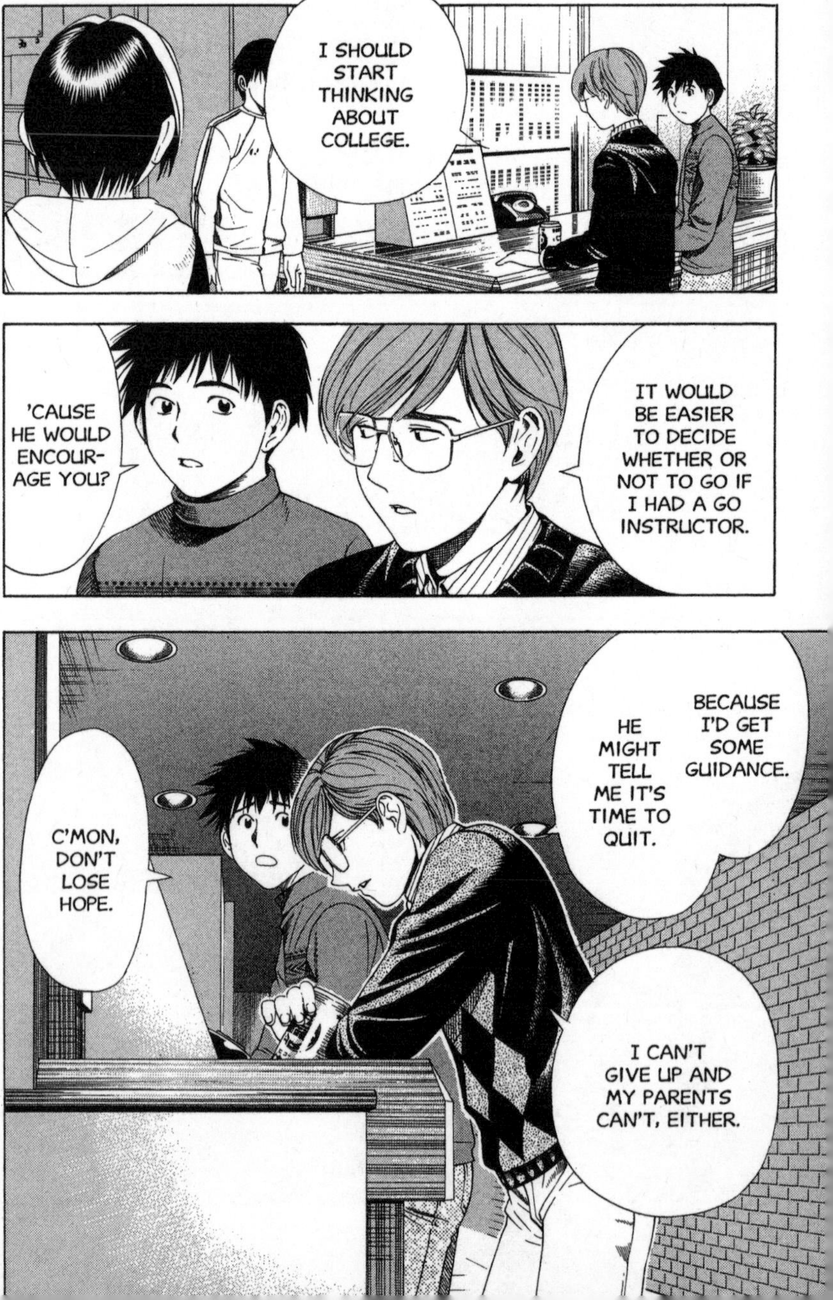
I SHOULD START THINKING ABOUT COLLEGE.
IT WOULD BE EASIER TO DECIDE WHETHER OR NOT TO GO IF I HAD A GO INSTRUCTOR.
'CAUSE HE WOULD ENCOUR-AGE YOU?
BECAUSE I'D GET SOME GUIDANCE.
HE MIGHT TELL ME IT'S TIME TO QUIT.
C'MON, DON'T LOSE HOPE.
I CAN'T GIVE UP AND MY PARENTS CAN'T, EITHER.

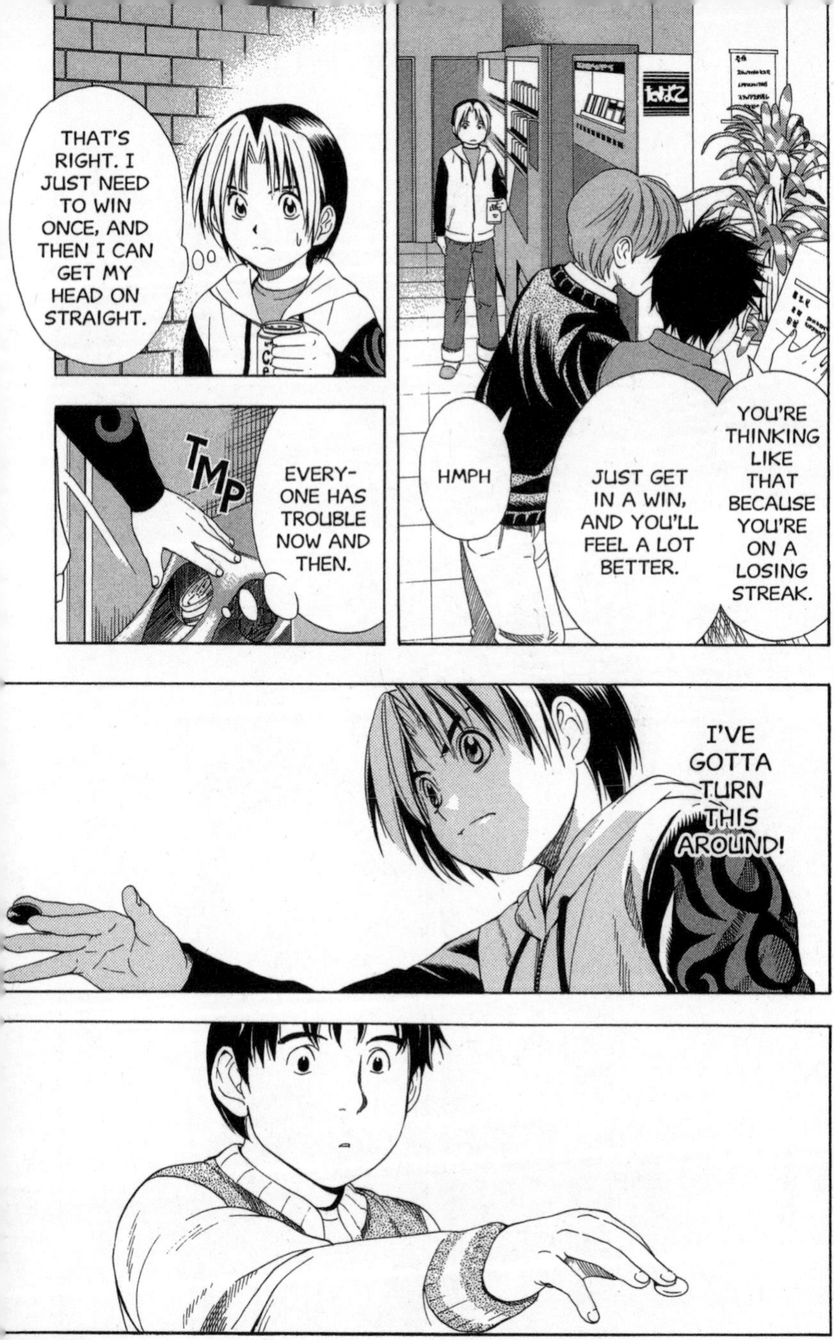
YOU'RE THINKING LIKE THAT BECAUSE YOU'RE ON A LOSING STREAK.
JUST GET IN A WIN, AND YOU'LL FEEL A LOT BETTER.
HMPH
THAT'S RIGHT. I JUST NEED TO WIN ONCE, AND THEN I CAN GET MY HEAD ON STRAIGHT.
EVERY-ONE HAS TROUBLE NOW AND THEN.
TMP
I'VE GOTTA TURN THIS AROUND!

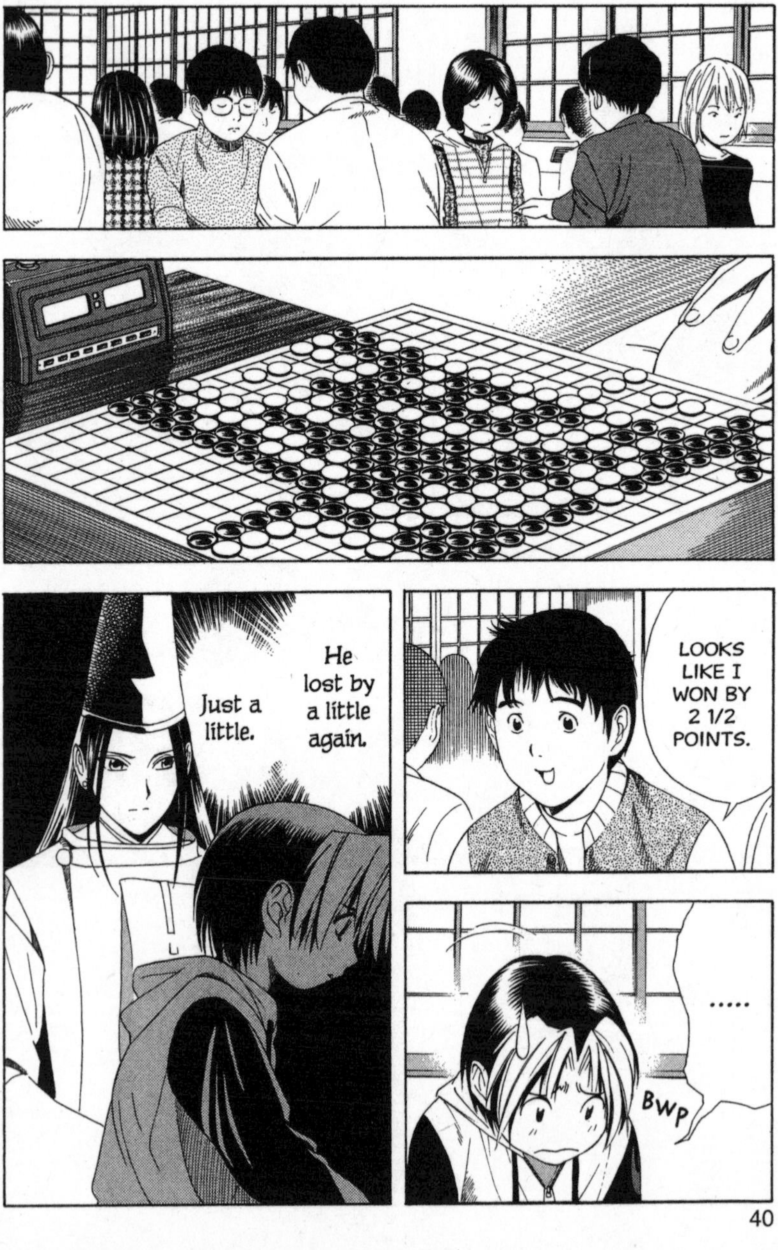

LOOKS LIKE I WON BY 2 1/2 POINTS.
.....
BWP
He lost by a little again.
Just a little.

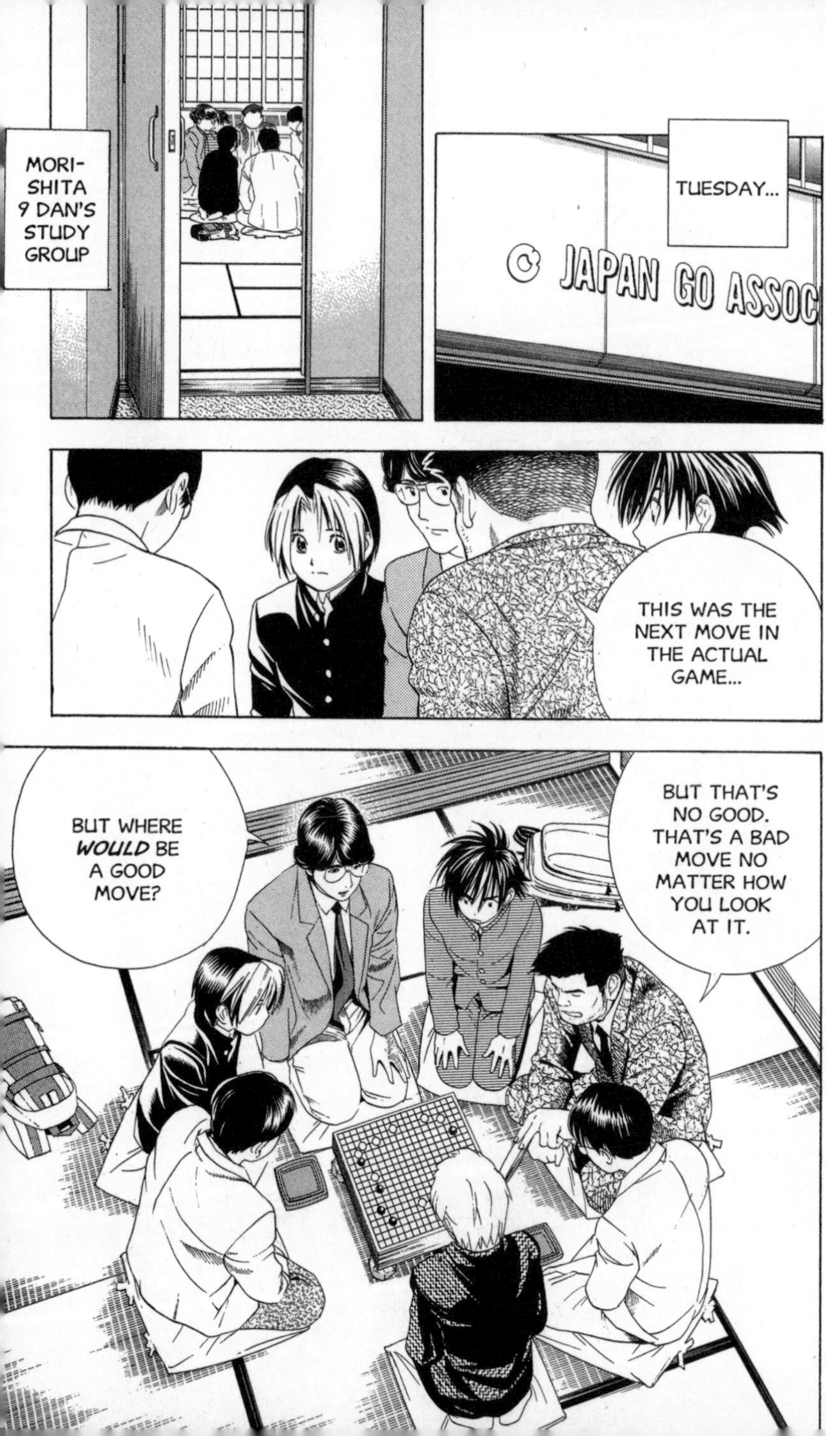
TUESDAY...
JAPAN GO ASSOC
MORI-SHITA 9 DAN'S STUDY GROUP
THIS WAS THE NEXT MOVE IN THE ACTUAL GAME...
BUT THAT'S NO GOOD. THAT'S A BAD MOVE NO MATTER HOW YOU LOOK AT IT.
BUT WHERE *WOULD* BE A GOOD MOVE?

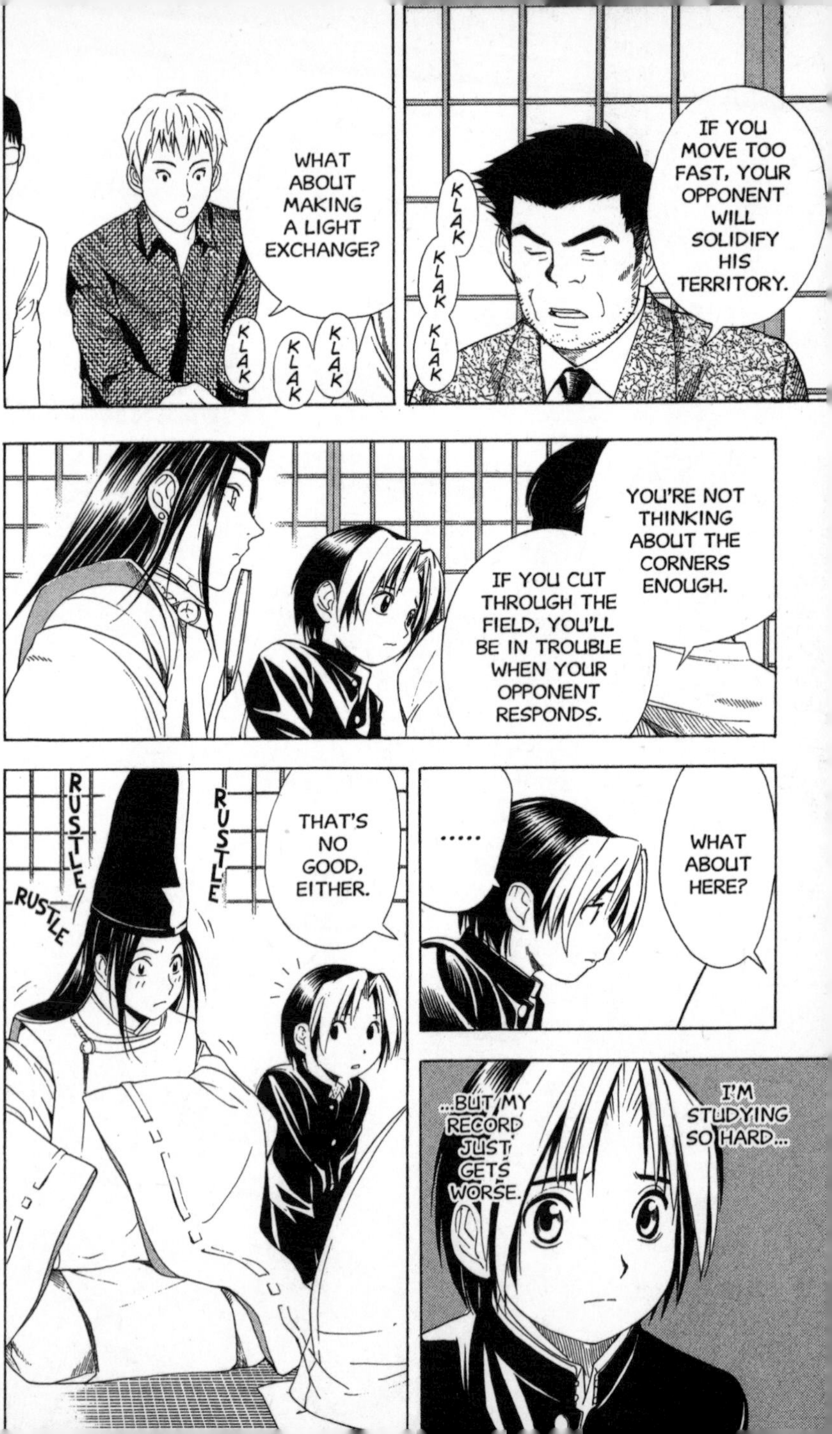
IF YOU MOVE TOO FAST, YOUR OPPONENT WILL SOLIDIFY HIS TERRITORY.
KLAK KLAK KLAK
WHAT ABOUT MAKING A LIGHT EXCHANGE?
KLAK KLAK KLAK
YOU'RE NOT THINKING ABOUT THE CORNERS ENOUGH.
IF YOU CUT THROUGH THE FIELD, YOU'LL BE IN TROUBLE WHEN YOUR OPPONENT RESPONDS.
WHAT ABOUT HERE?
.....
I'M STUDYING SO HARD...
...BUT MY RECORD JUST GETS WORSE.
RUSTLE
THAT'S NO GOOD, EITHER.
RUSTLE
RUSTLE

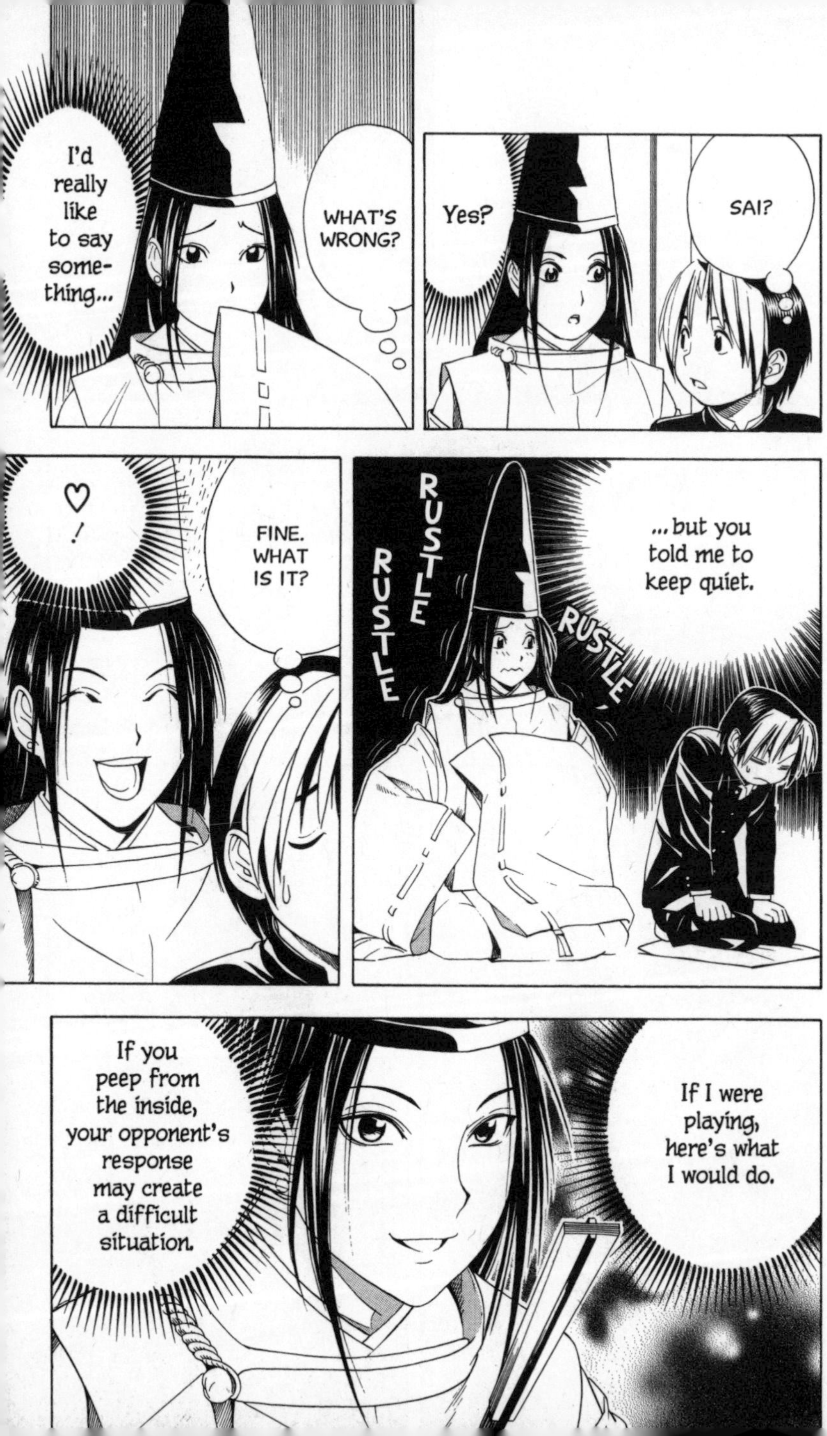
SAI?
Yes?
WHAT'S WRONG?
I'd really like to say something...
...but you told me to keep quiet.
RUSTLE
RUSTLE
RUSTLE
FINE. WHAT IS IT?
♡ !
If I were playing, here's what I would do.
If you peep from the inside, your opponent's response may create a difficult situation.

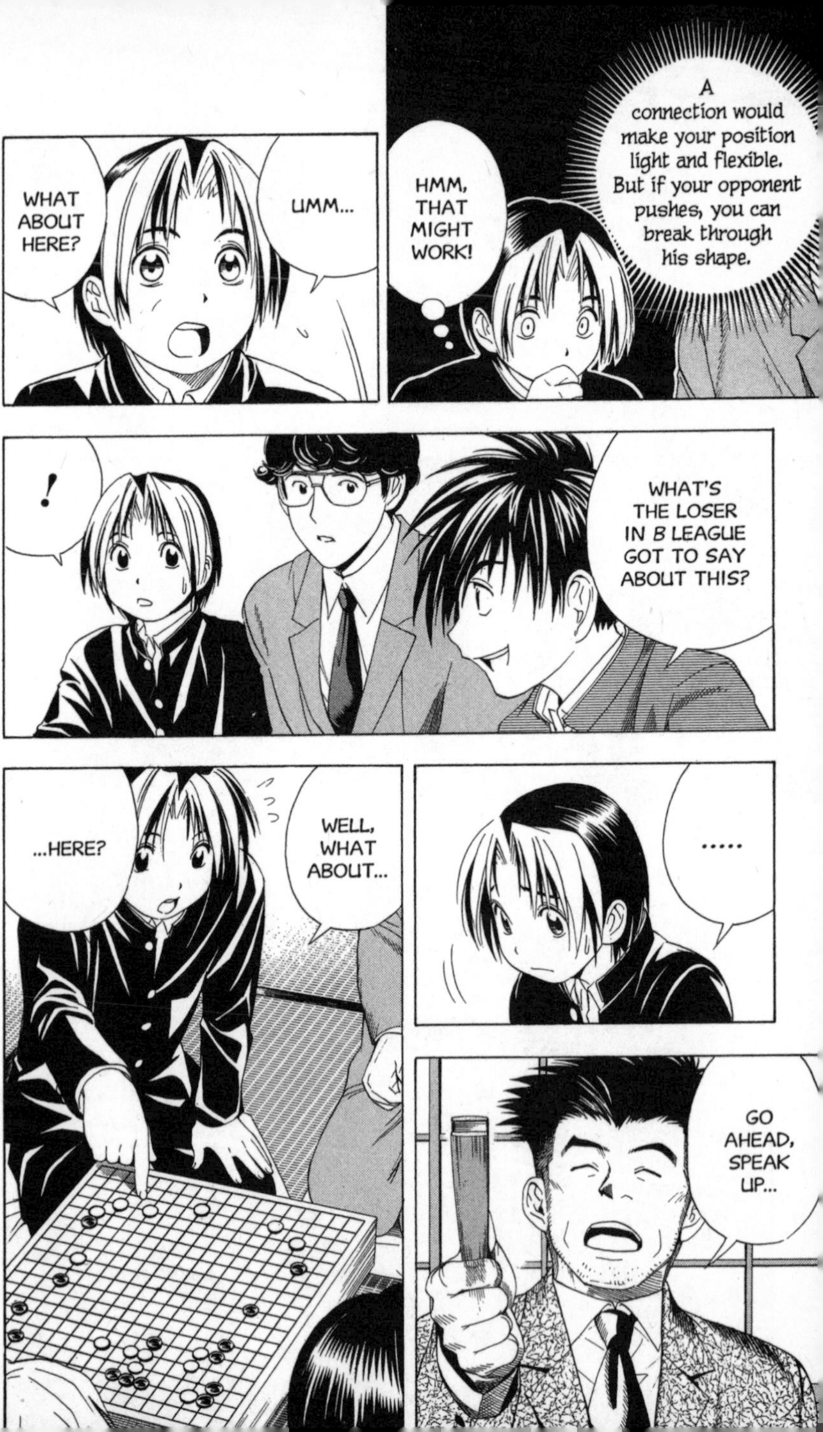
A connection would make your position light and flexible. But if your opponent pushes, you can break through his shape.
HMM, THAT MIGHT WORK!
UMM...
WHAT ABOUT HERE?
WHAT'S THE LOSER IN *B* LEAGUE GOT TO SAY ABOUT THIS?
!
.....
WELL, WHAT ABOUT...
...HERE?
GO AHEAD, SPEAK UP...

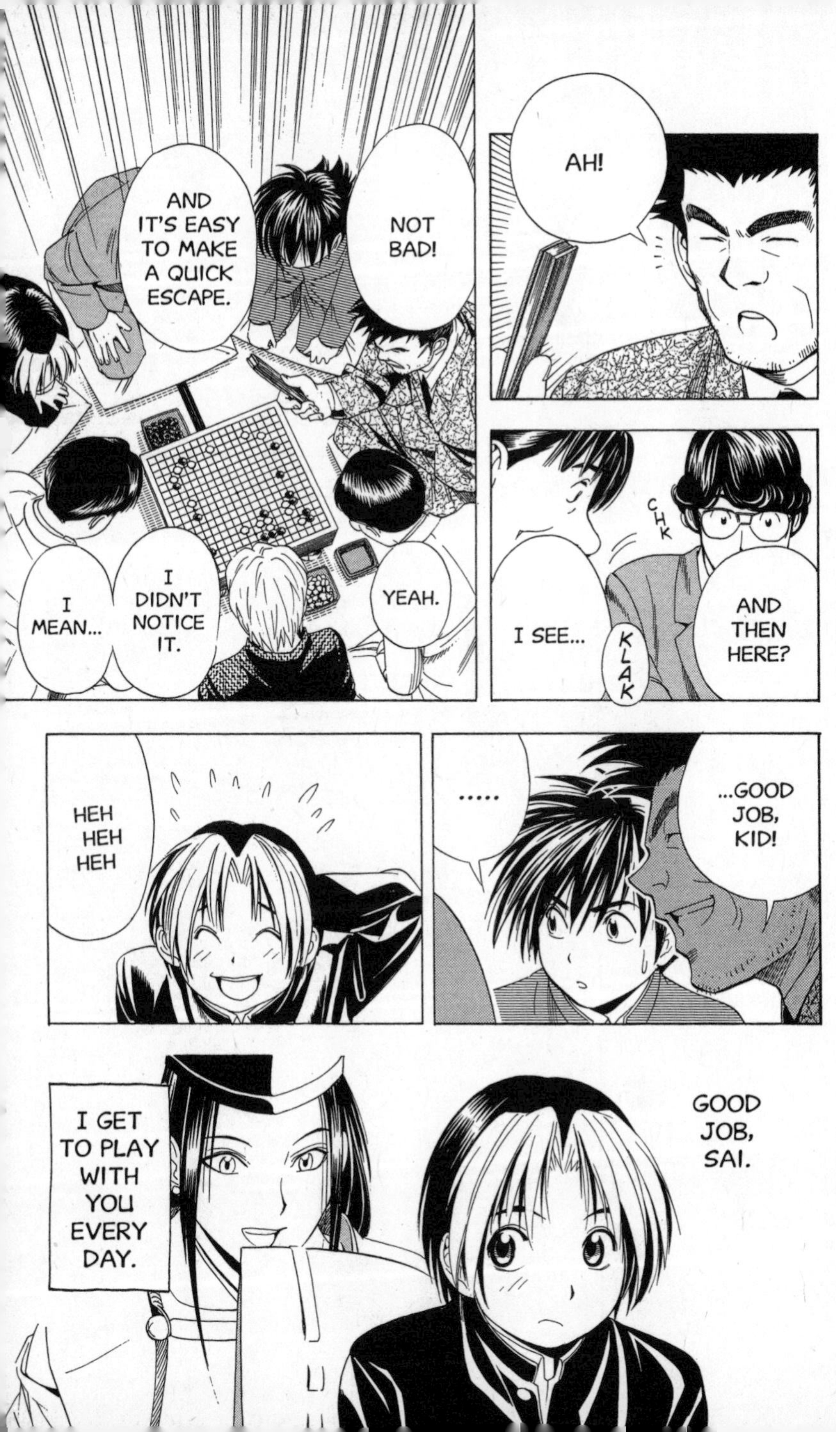
AH!
AND THEN HERE?
CHK
KLAK
I SEE...
NOT BAD!
AND IT'S EASY TO MAKE A QUICK ESCAPE.
YEAH.
I DIDN'T NOTICE IT.
I MEAN...
...GOOD JOB, KID!
.....
HEH HEH HEH
GOOD JOB, SAI.
I GET TO PLAY WITH YOU EVERY DAY.

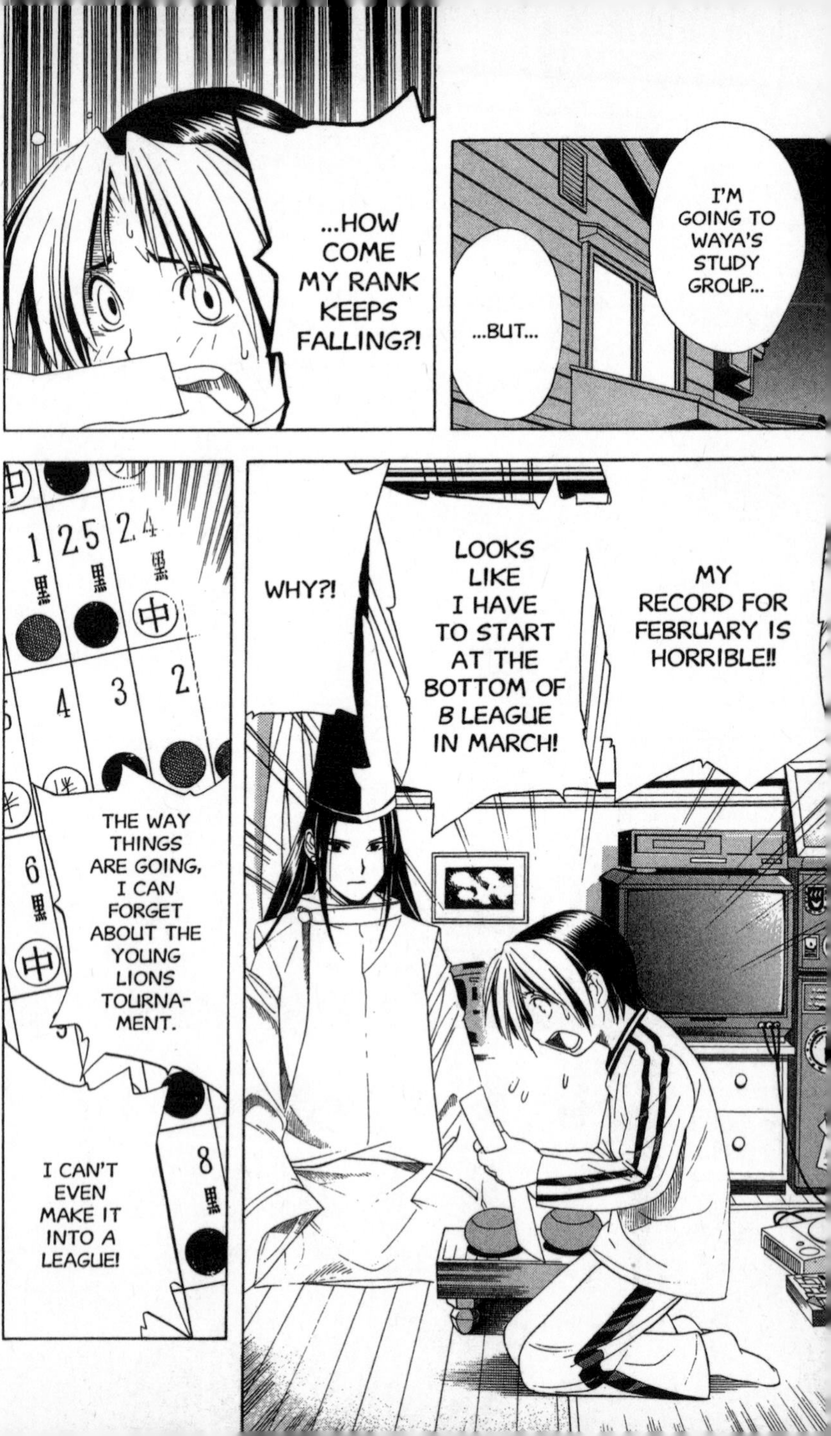
I'M GOING TO WAYA'S STUDY GROUP...
...BUT...
...HOW COME MY RANK KEEPS FALLING?!
MY RECORD FOR FEBRUARY IS HORRIBLE!!
LOOKS LIKE I HAVE TO START AT THE BOTTOM OF B LEAGUE IN MARCH!
WHY?!
THE WAY THINGS ARE GOING, I CAN FORGET ABOUT THE YOUNG LIONS TOURNAMENT.
I CAN'T EVEN MAKE IT INTO A LEAGUE!

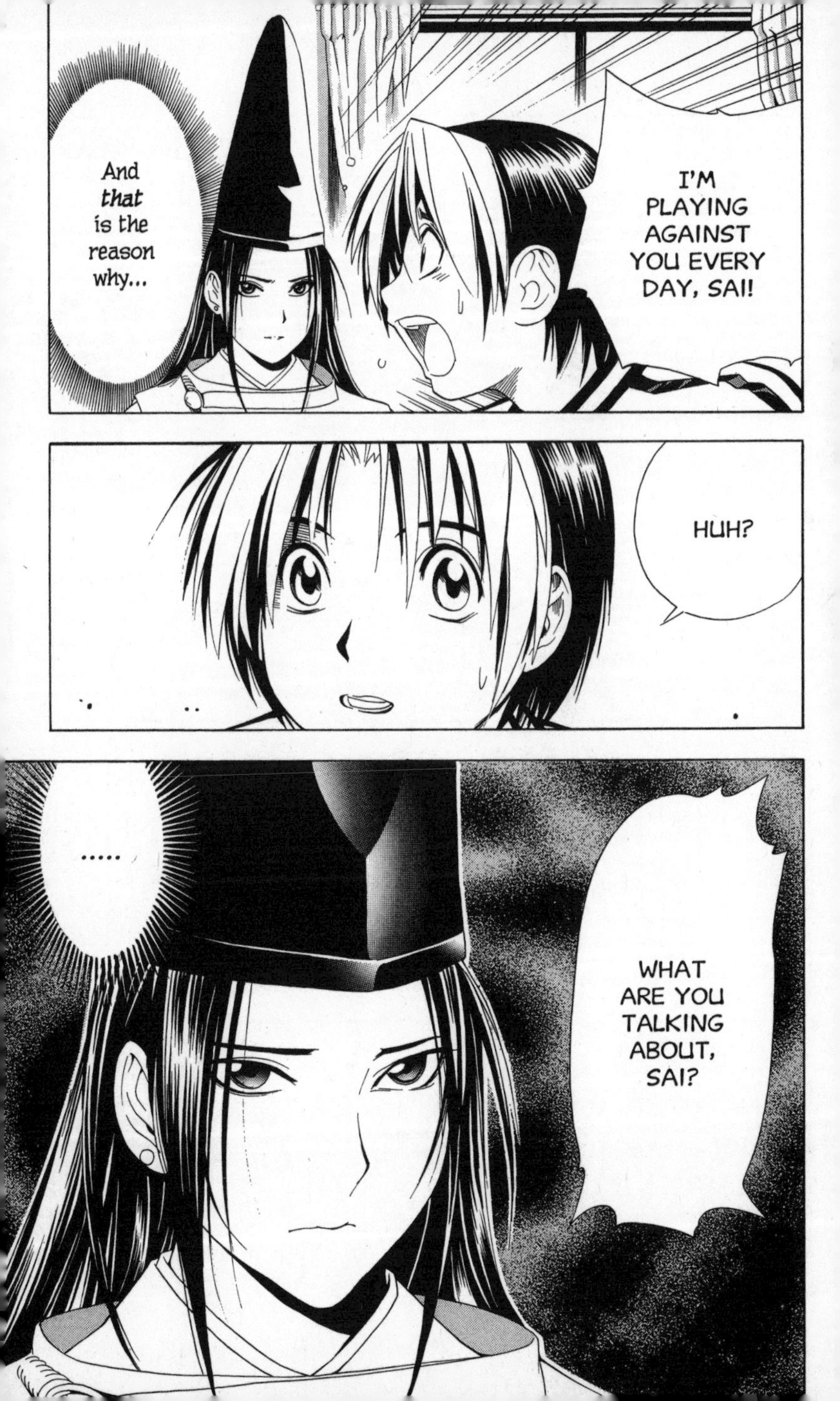
I'M PLAYING AGAINST YOU EVERY DAY, SAI!
And *that* is the reason why...
HUH?
WHAT ARE YOU TALKING ABOUT, SAI?
.....

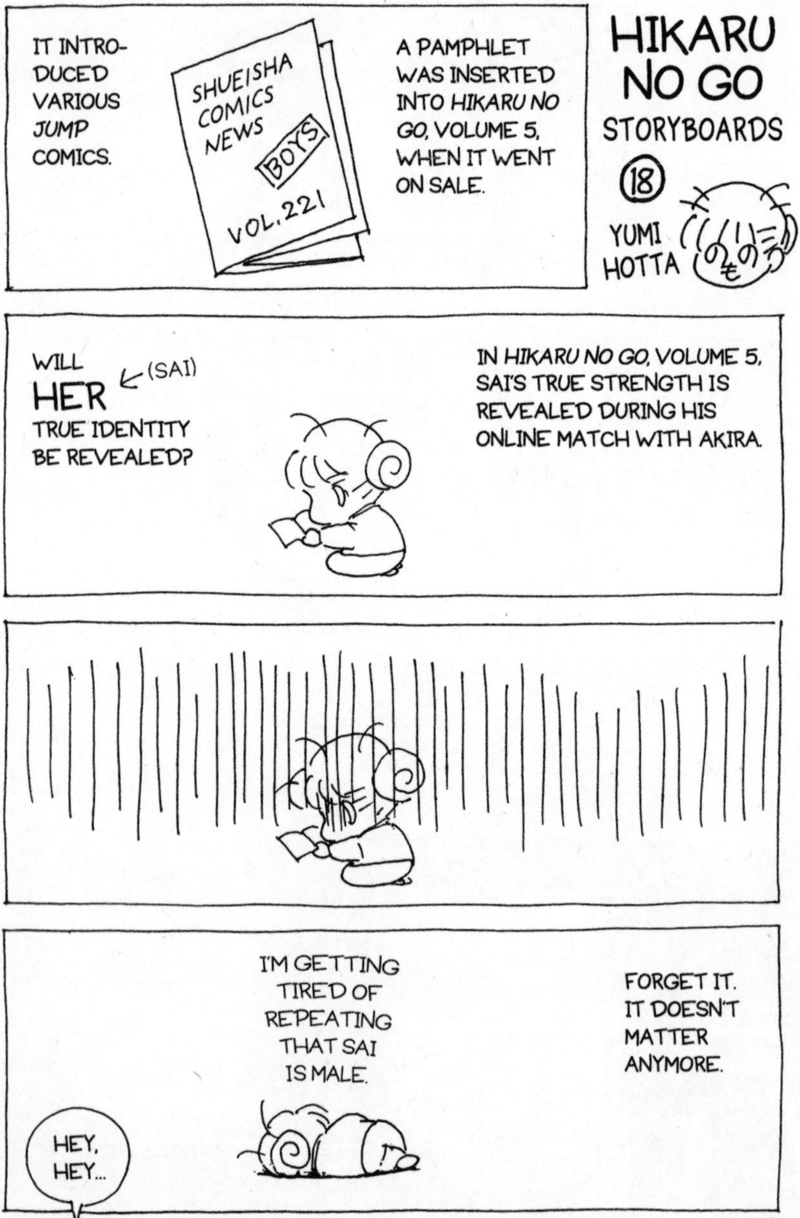

HIKARU NO GO STORYBOARDS
18
YUMI HOTTA
A PAMPHLET WAS INSERTED INTO HIKARU NO GO, VOLUME 5, WHEN IT WENT ON SALE.
SHUEISHA COMICS NEWS
BOYS
VOL.221
IT INTRODUCED VARIOUS JUMP COMICS.
IN HIKARU NO GO, VOLUME 5, SAI'S TRUE STRENGTH IS REVEALED DURING HIS ONLINE MATCH WITH AKIRA.
WILL HER TRUE IDENTITY BE REVEALED?
(SAI)
FORGET IT. IT DOESN'T MATTER ANYMORE.
I'M GETTING TIRED OF REPEATING THAT SAI IS MALE.
HEY, HEY...

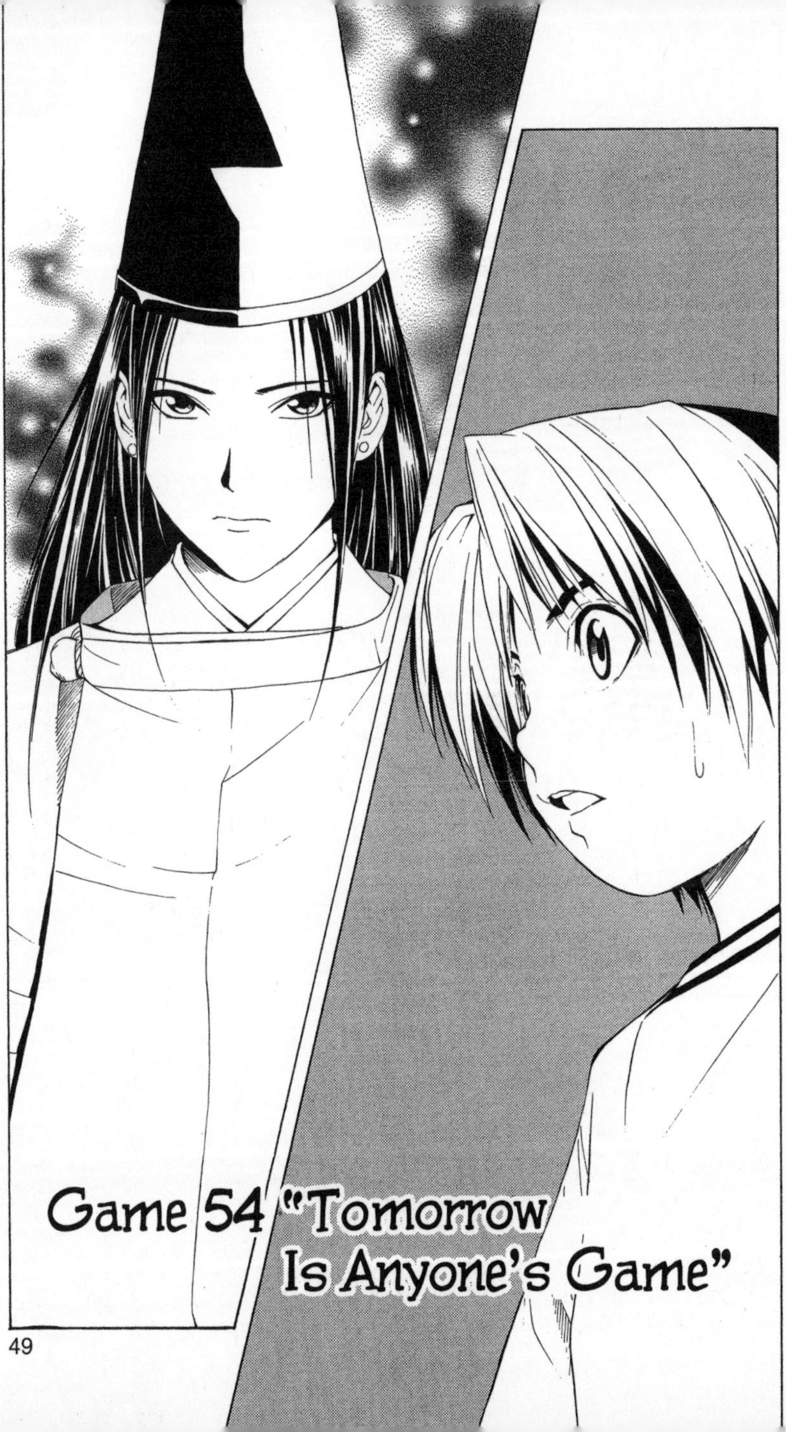
Game 54 "Tomorrow Is Anyone's Game"

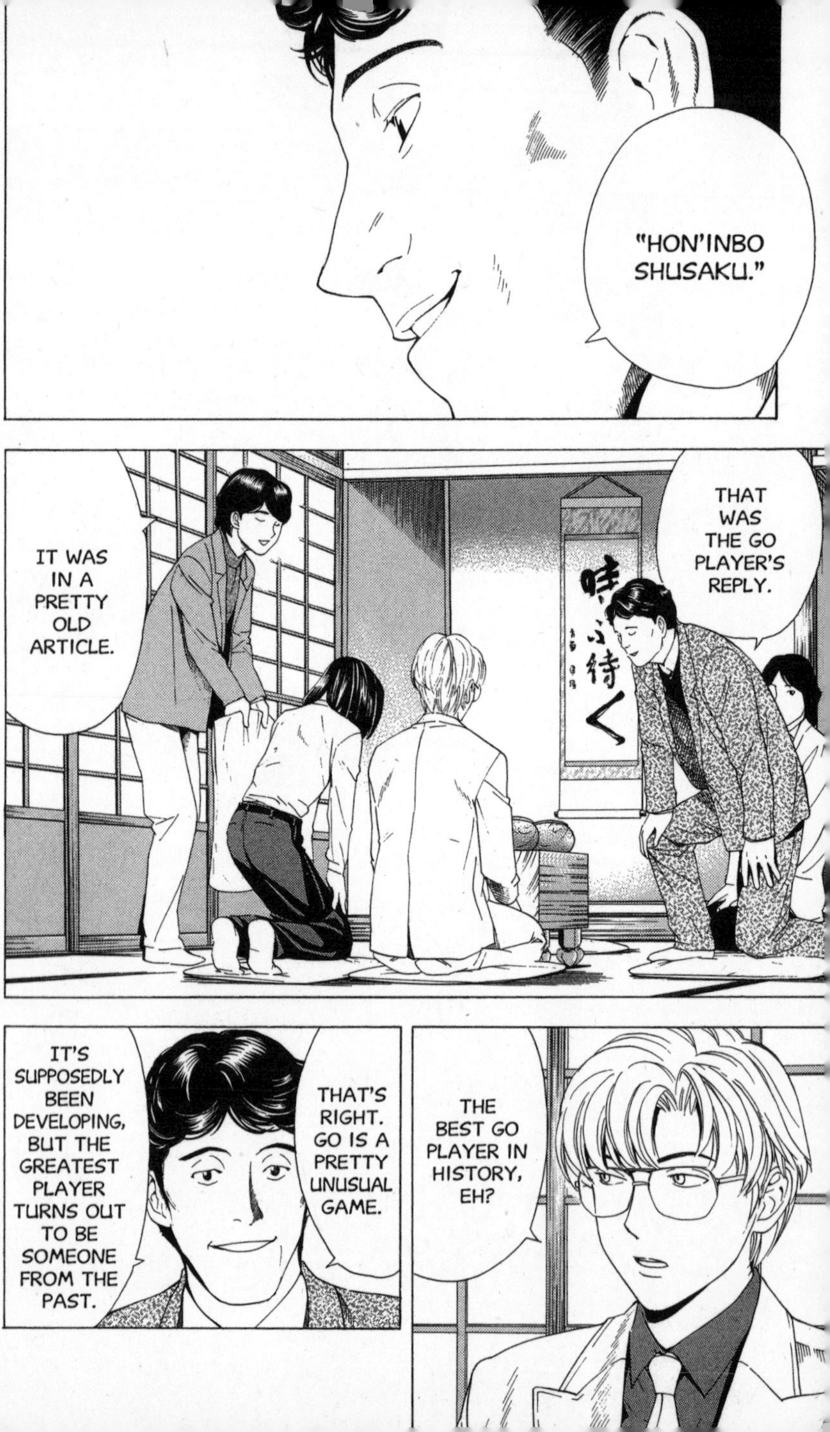
"HON'INBO SHUSAKU."
THAT WAS THE GO PLAYER'S REPLY.
IT WAS IN A PRETTY OLD ARTICLE.
THE BEST GO PLAYER IN HISTORY, EH?
THAT'S RIGHT. GO IS A PRETTY UNUSUAL GAME.
IT'S SUPPOSEDLY BEEN DEVELOPING, BUT THE GREATEST PLAYER TURNS OUT TO BE SOMEONE FROM THE PAST.

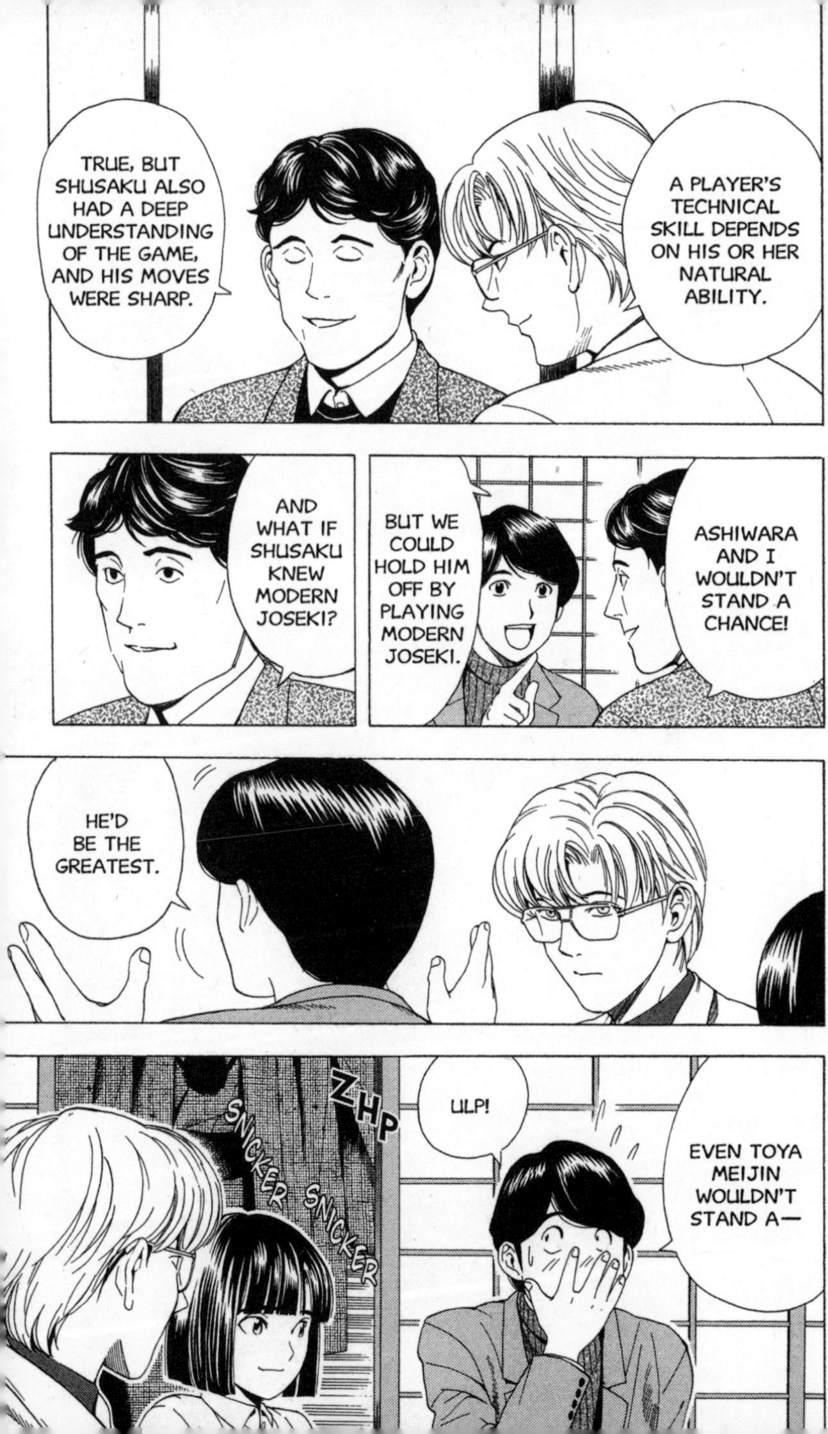

A PLAYER'S TECHNICAL SKILL DEPENDS ON HIS OR HER NATURAL ABILITY.
TRUE, BUT SHUSAKU ALSO HAD A DEEP UNDERSTANDING OF THE GAME, AND HIS MOVES WERE SHARP.
ASHIWARA AND I WOULDN'T STAND A CHANCE!
BUT WE COULD HOLD HIM OFF BY PLAYING MODERN JOSEKI.
AND WHAT IF SHUSAKU KNEW MODERN JOSEKI?
HE'D BE THE GREATEST.
EVEN TOYA MEIJIN WOULDN'T STAND A—
ULP!
ZHP
SNICKER
SNICKER

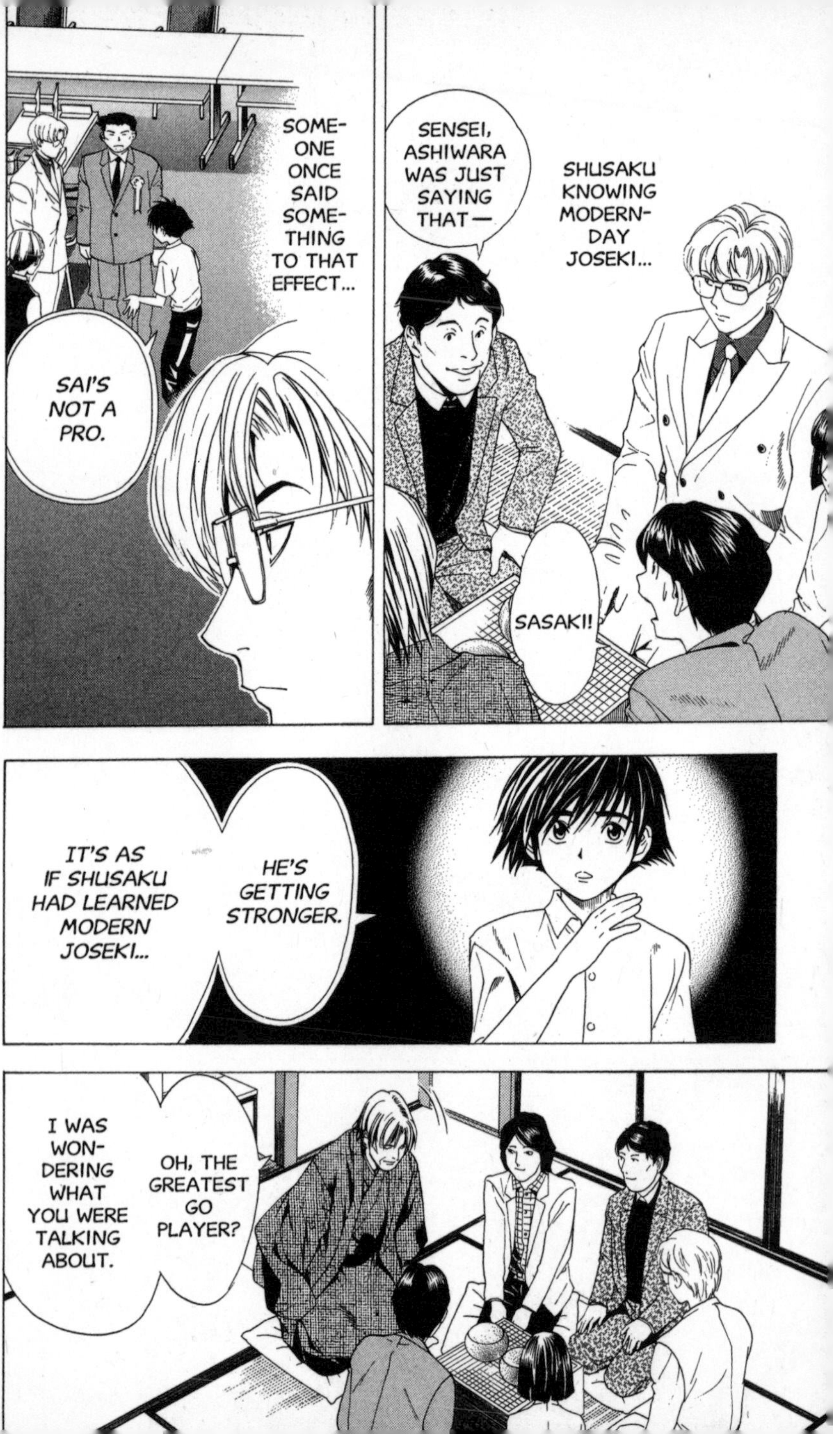
SHUSAKU KNOWING MODERN-DAY JOSEKI...
SENSEI, ASHIWARA WAS JUST SAYING THAT—
SASAKI!
SOME-ONE ONCE SAID SOME-THING TO THAT EFFECT...
SAI'S NOT A PRO.
HE'S GETTING STRONGER.
IT'S AS IF SHUSAKU HAD LEARNED MODERN JOSEKI...
OH, THE GREATEST GO PLAYER?
I WAS WON-DERING WHAT YOU WERE TALKING ABOUT.

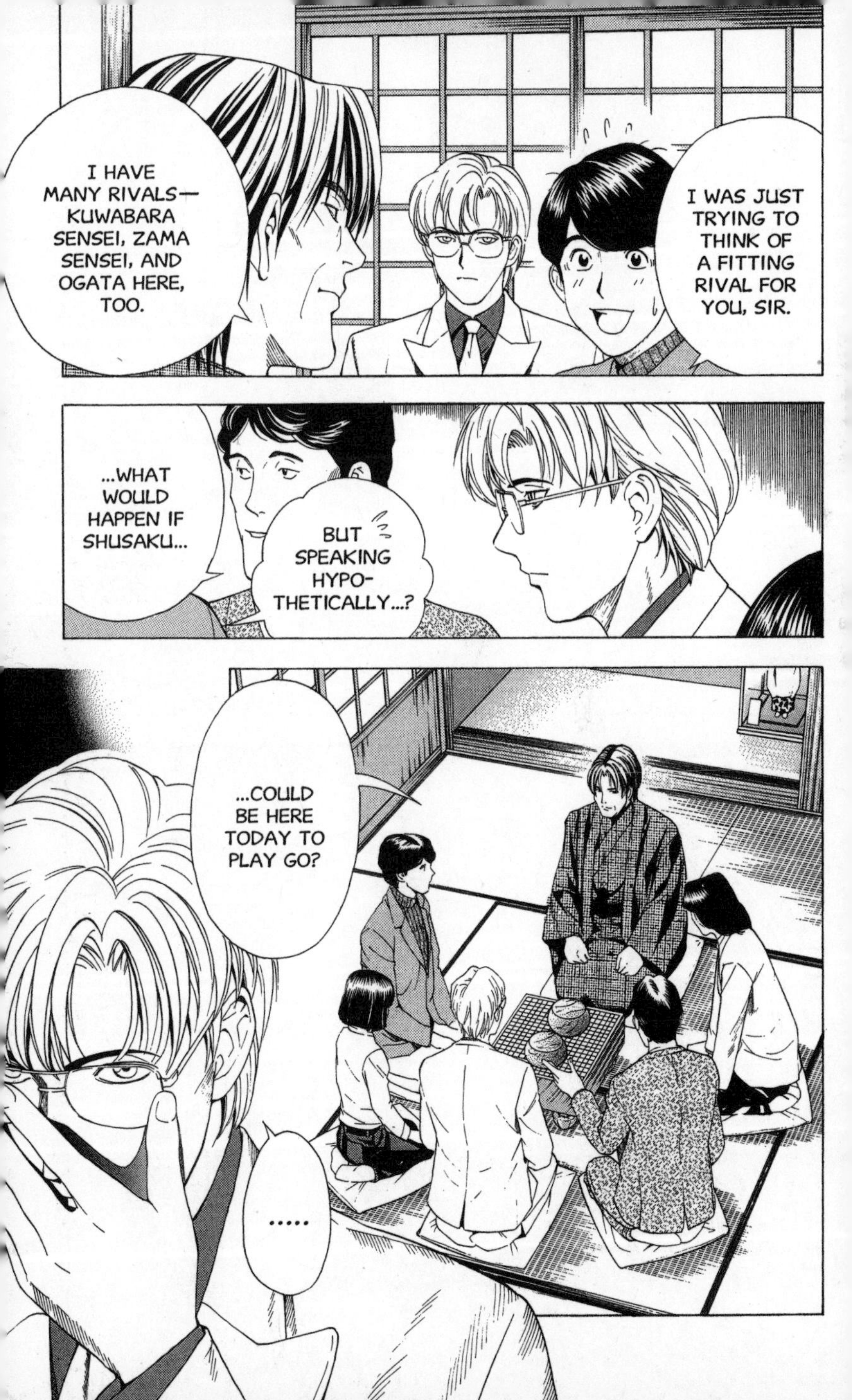
I WAS JUST TRYING TO THINK OF A FITTING RIVAL FOR YOU, SIR.
I HAVE MANY RIVALS—KUWABARA SENSEI, ZAMA SENSEI, AND OGATA HERE, TOO.
BUT SPEAKING HYPOTHETICALLY...?
...WHAT WOULD HAPPEN IF SHUSAKU...
...COULD BE HERE TODAY TO PLAY GO?
.....

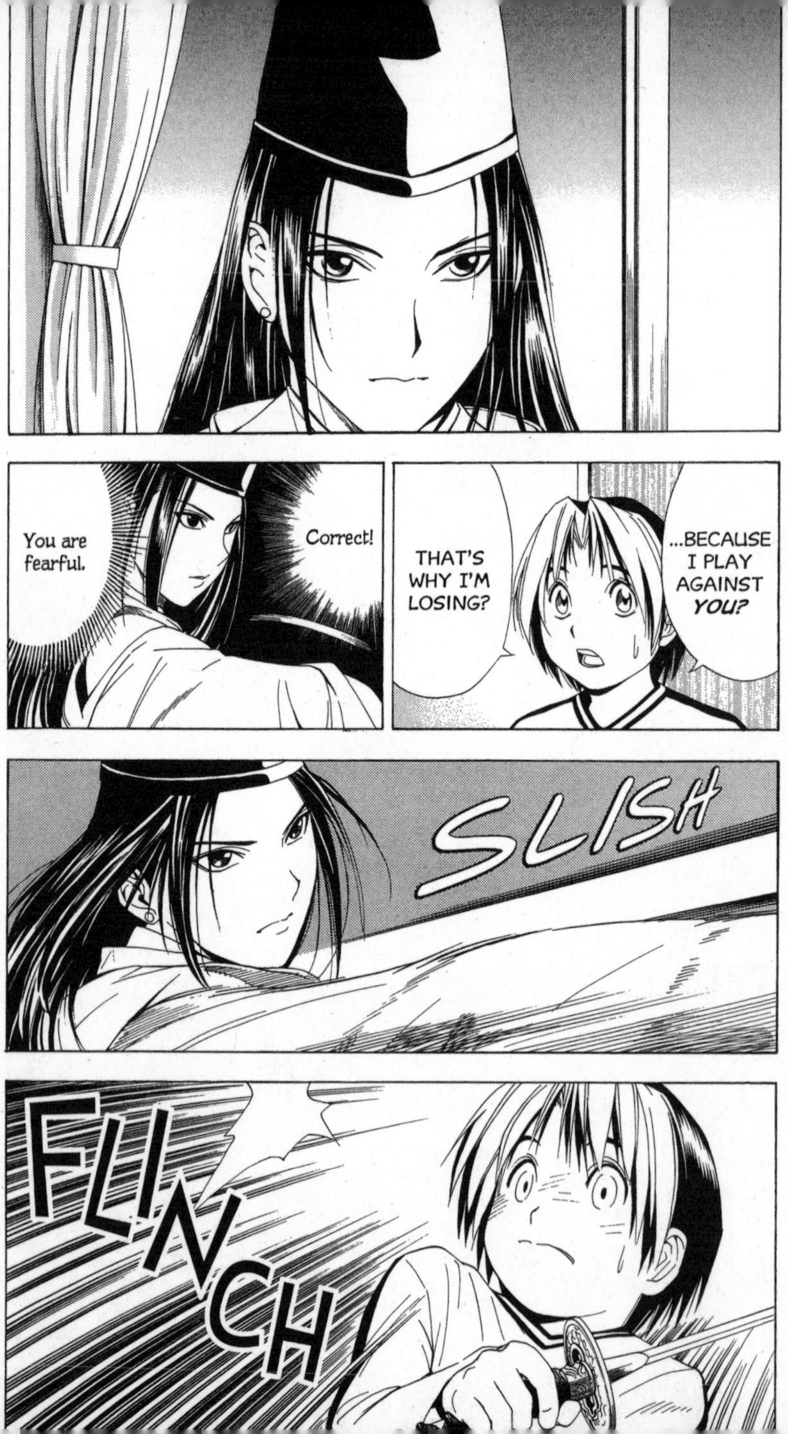
...BECAUSE I PLAY AGAINST *YOU?*
THAT'S WHY I'M LOSING?
Correct!
You are fearful.
SLISH
FLINCH

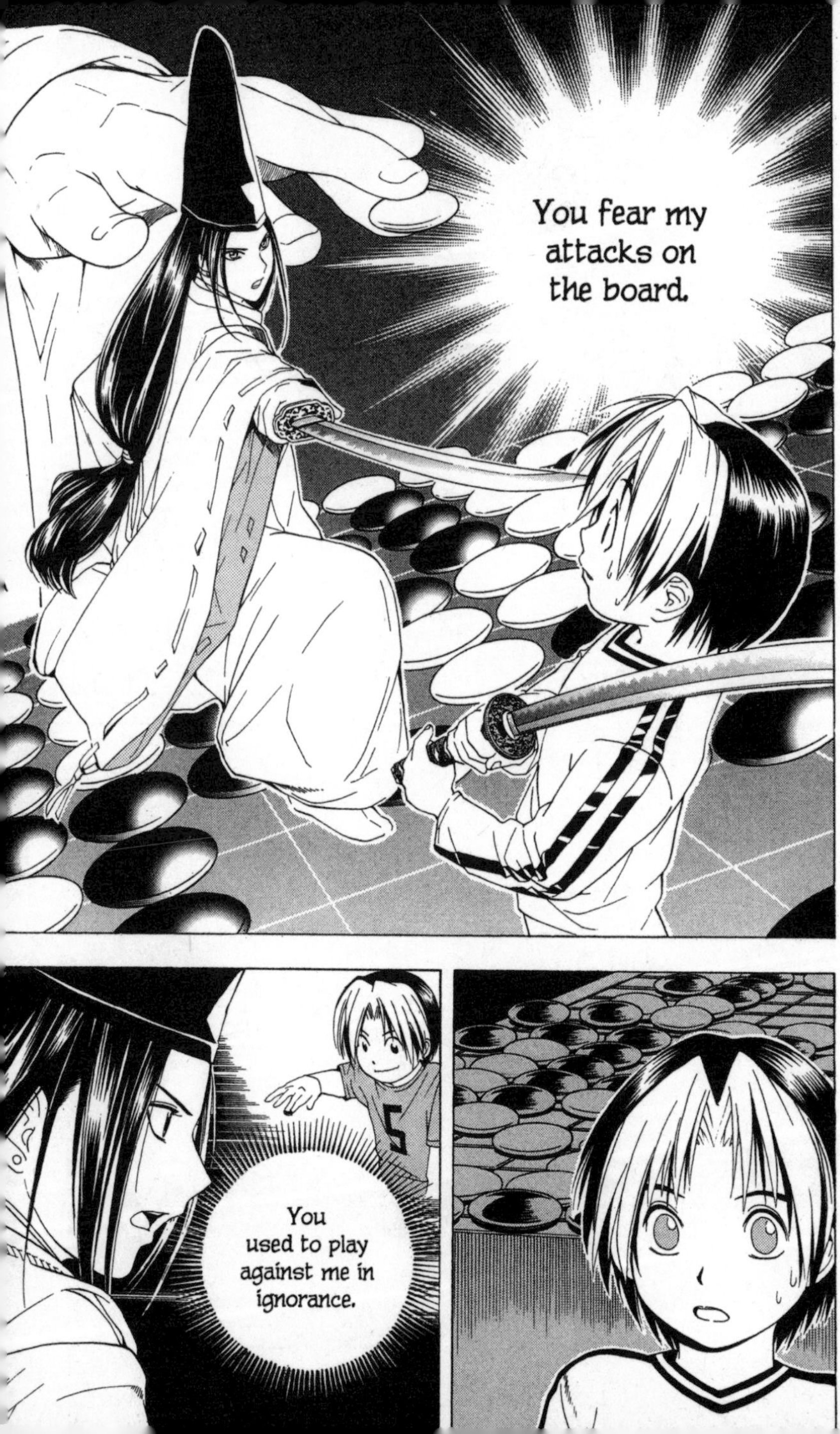
You fear my attacks on the board.
You used to play against me in ignorance.

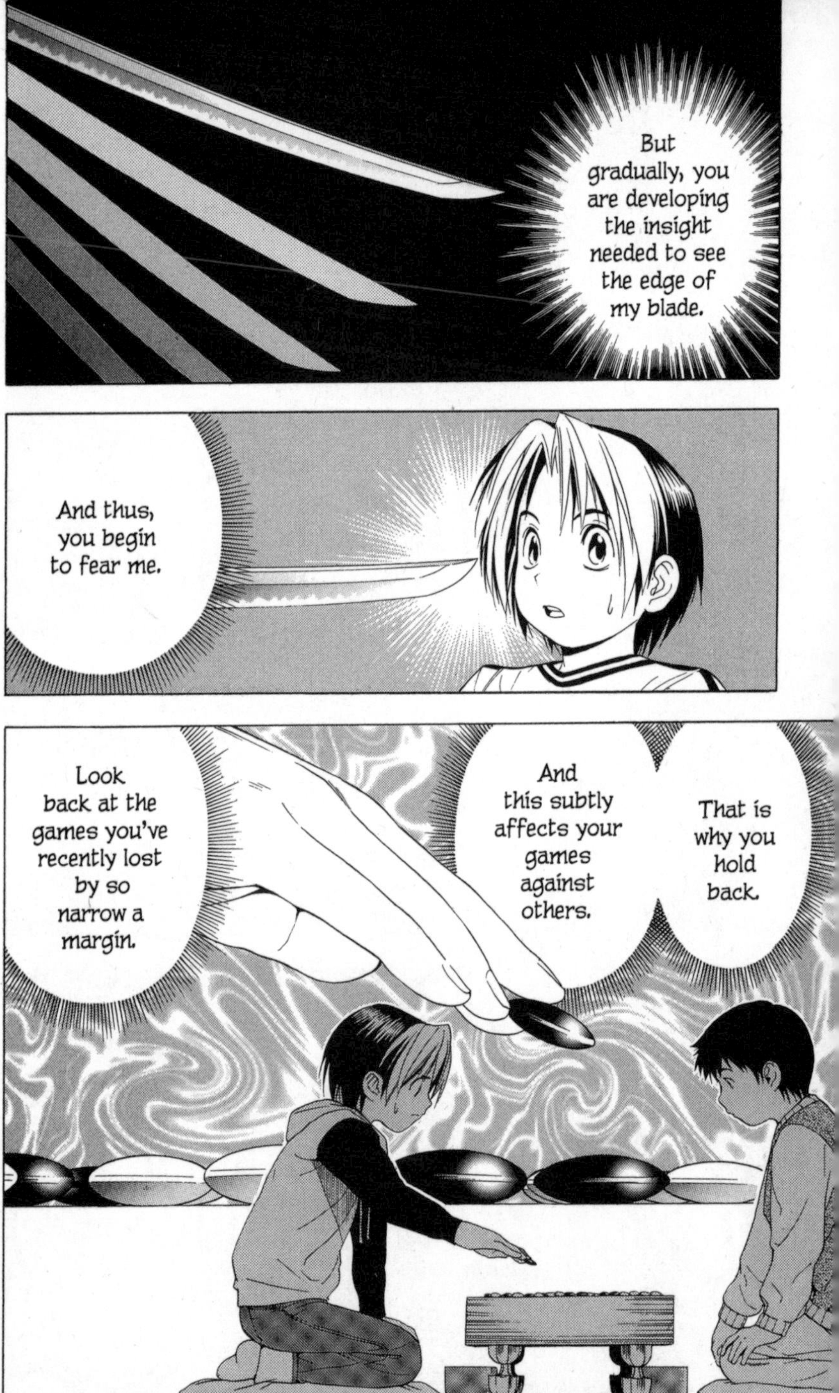
But gradually, you are developing the insight needed to see the edge of my blade.
And thus, you begin to fear me.
That is why you hold back.
And this subtly affects your games against others.
Look back at the games you've recently lost by so narrow a margin.

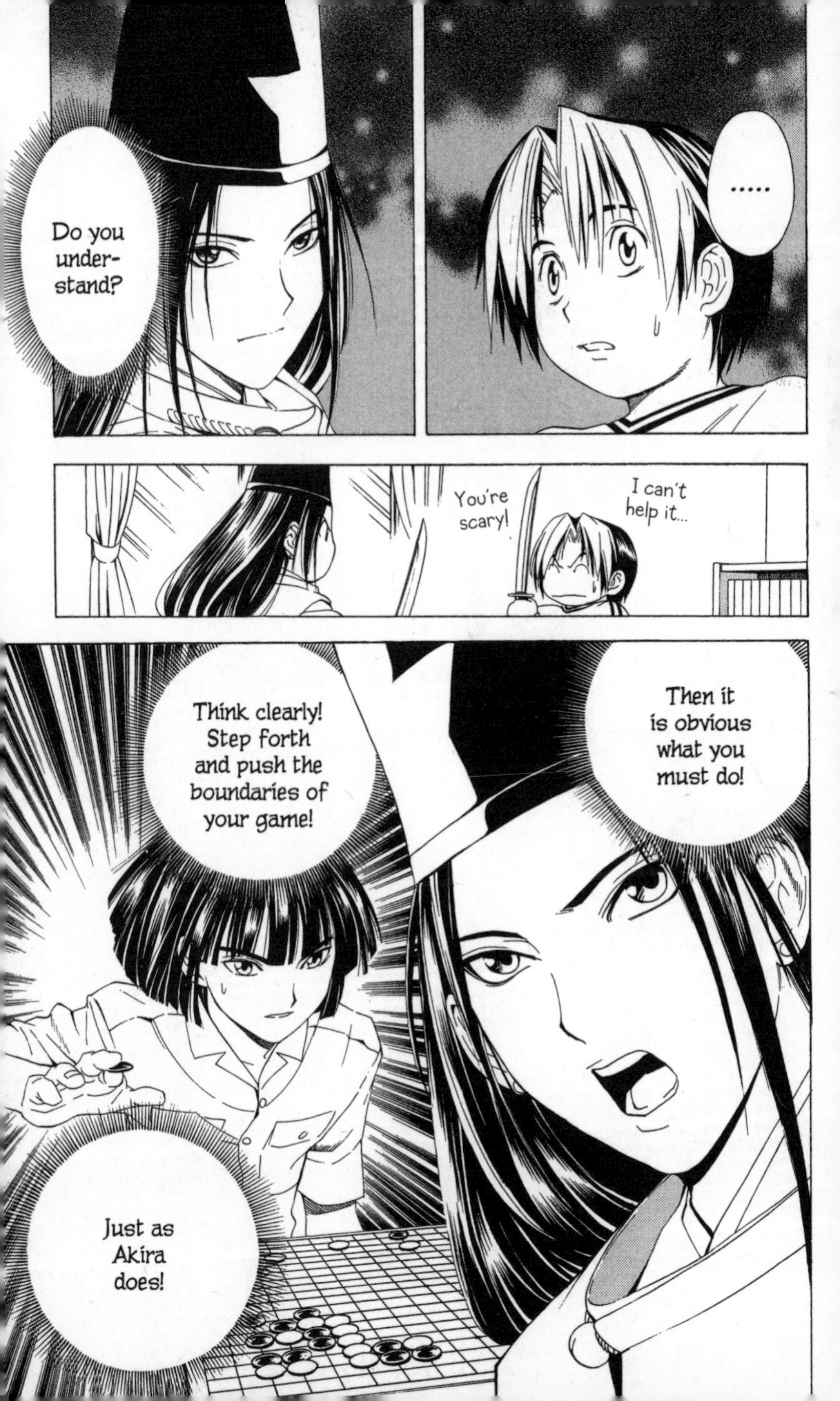
.....
Do you under-stand?
I can't help it...
You're scary!
Then it is obvious what you must do!
Think clearly! Step forth and push the boundaries of your game!
Just as Akira does!

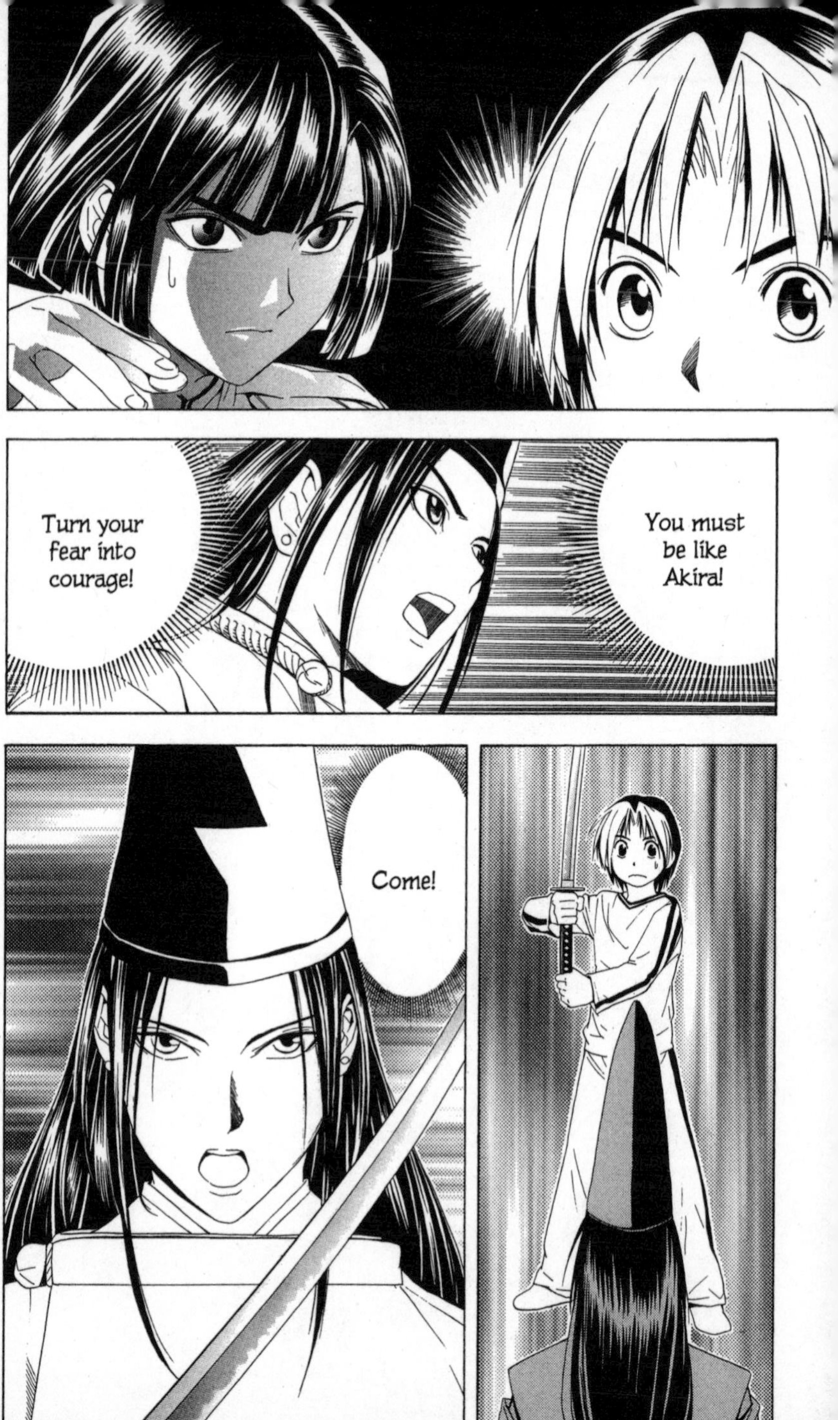
You must be like Akira!
Turn your fear into courage!
Come!

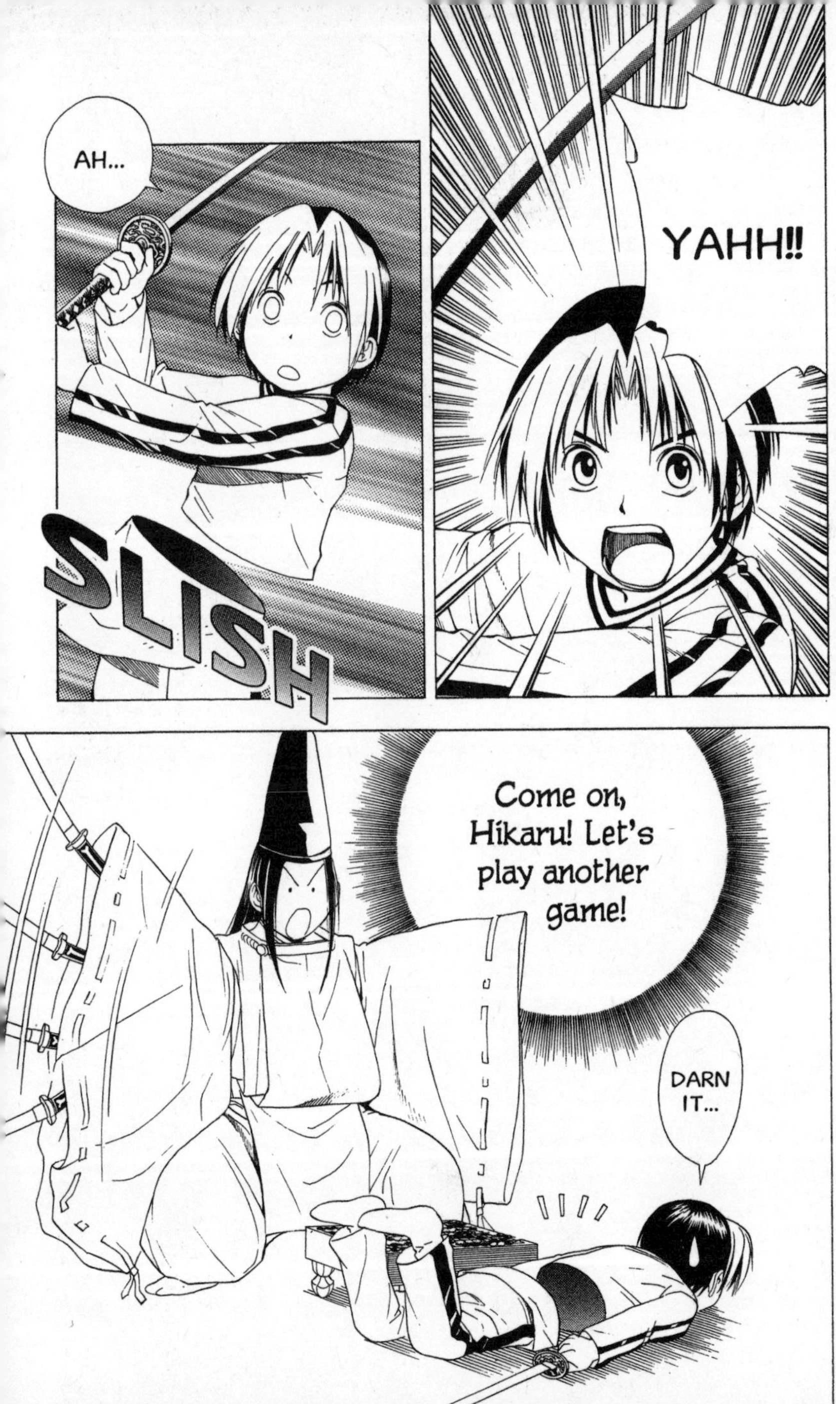
YAHH!!
AH...
SLISH
Come on, Hikaru! Let's play another game!
DARN IT...

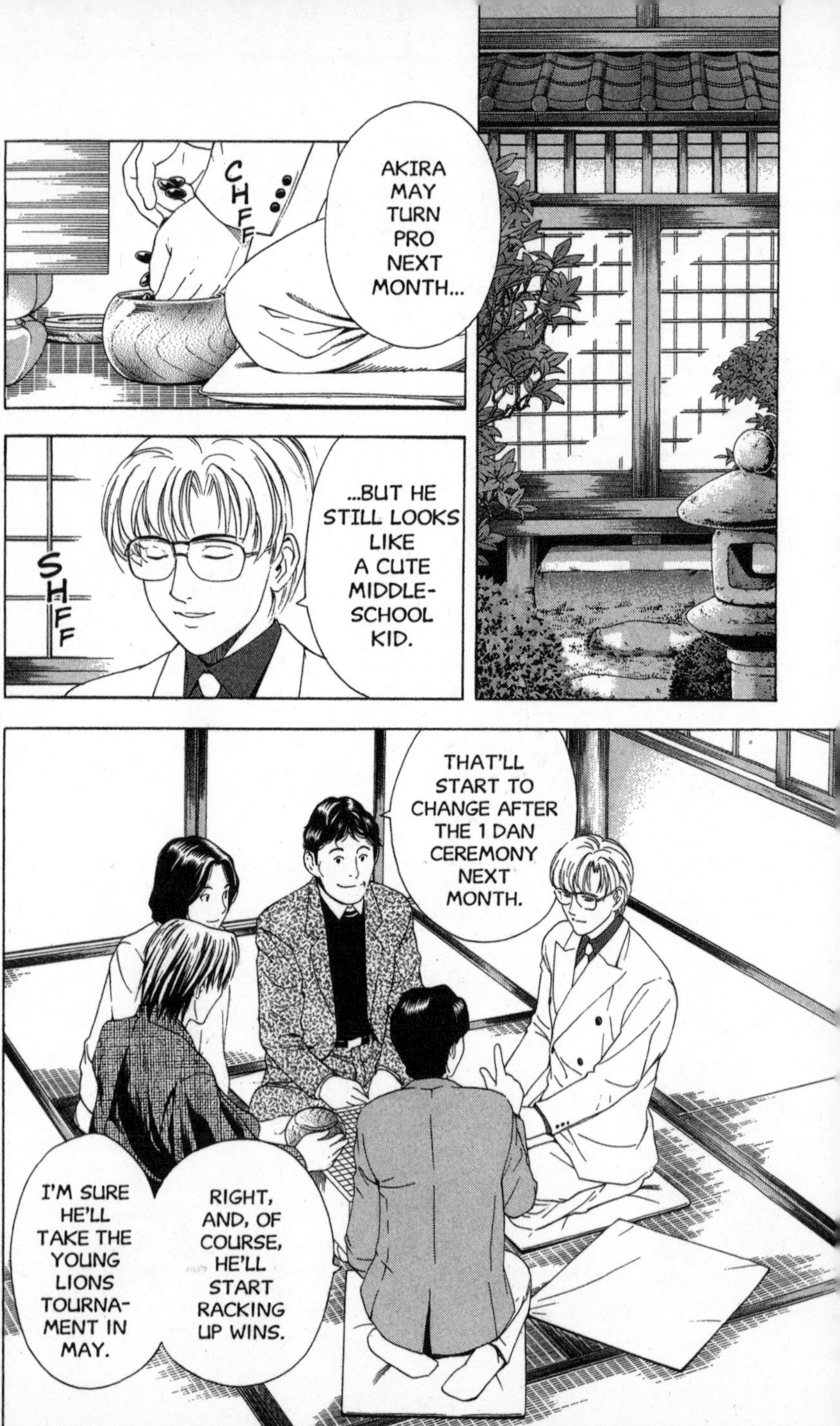
AKIRA MAY TURN PRO NEXT MONTH...
CHFF
...BUT HE STILL LOOKS LIKE A CUTE MIDDLE-SCHOOL KID.
SHFF
THAT'LL START TO CHANGE AFTER THE 1 DAN CEREMONY NEXT MONTH.
RIGHT, AND, OF COURSE, HE'LL START RACKING UP WINS.
I'M SURE HE'LL TAKE THE YOUNG LIONS TOURNA-MENT IN MAY.

READ THIS WAY

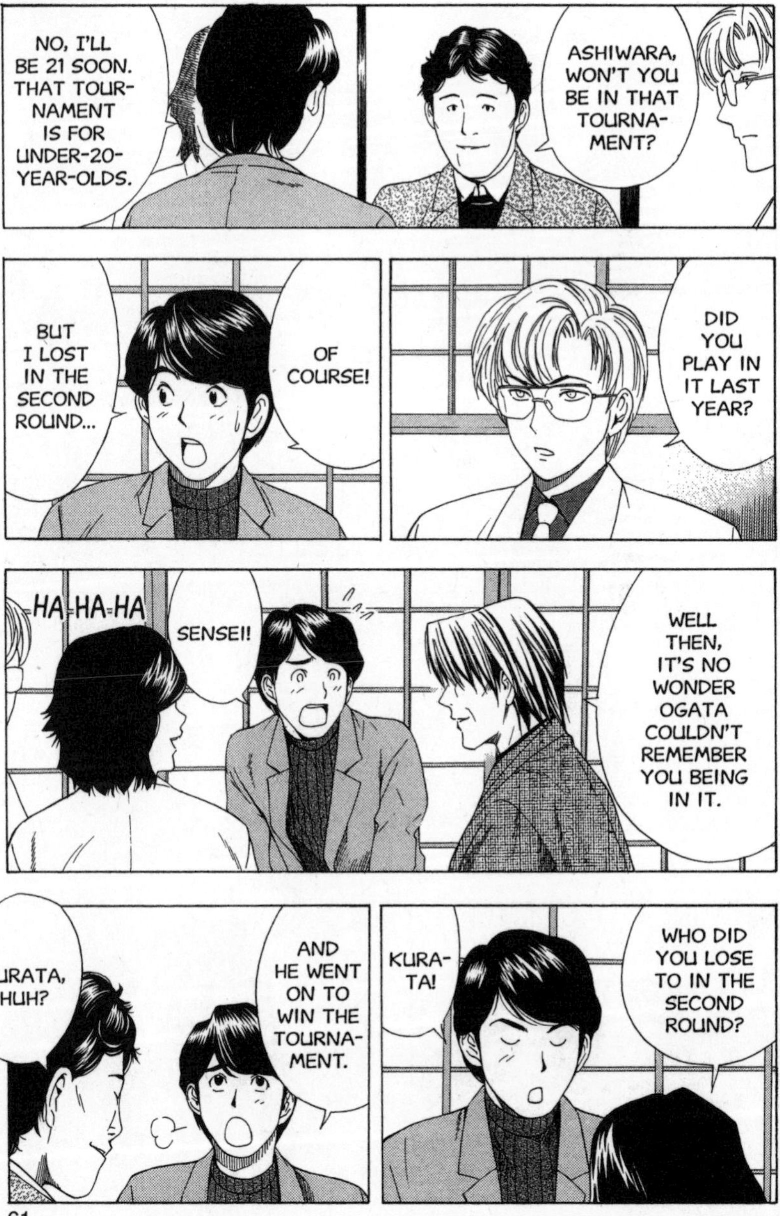
ASHIWARA, WON'T YOU BE IN THAT TOURNAMENT?
NO, I'LL BE 21 SOON. THAT TOURNAMENT IS FOR UNDER-20-YEAR-OLDS.
DID YOU PLAY IN IT LAST YEAR?
OF COURSE!
BUT I LOST IN THE SECOND ROUND...
WELL THEN, IT'S NO WONDER OGATA COULDN'T REMEMBER YOU BEING IN IT.
SENSEI!
HA HA HA
WHO DID YOU LOSE TO IN THE SECOND ROUND?
KURATA!
AND HE WENT ON TO WIN THE TOURNAMENT.
KURATA, HUH?

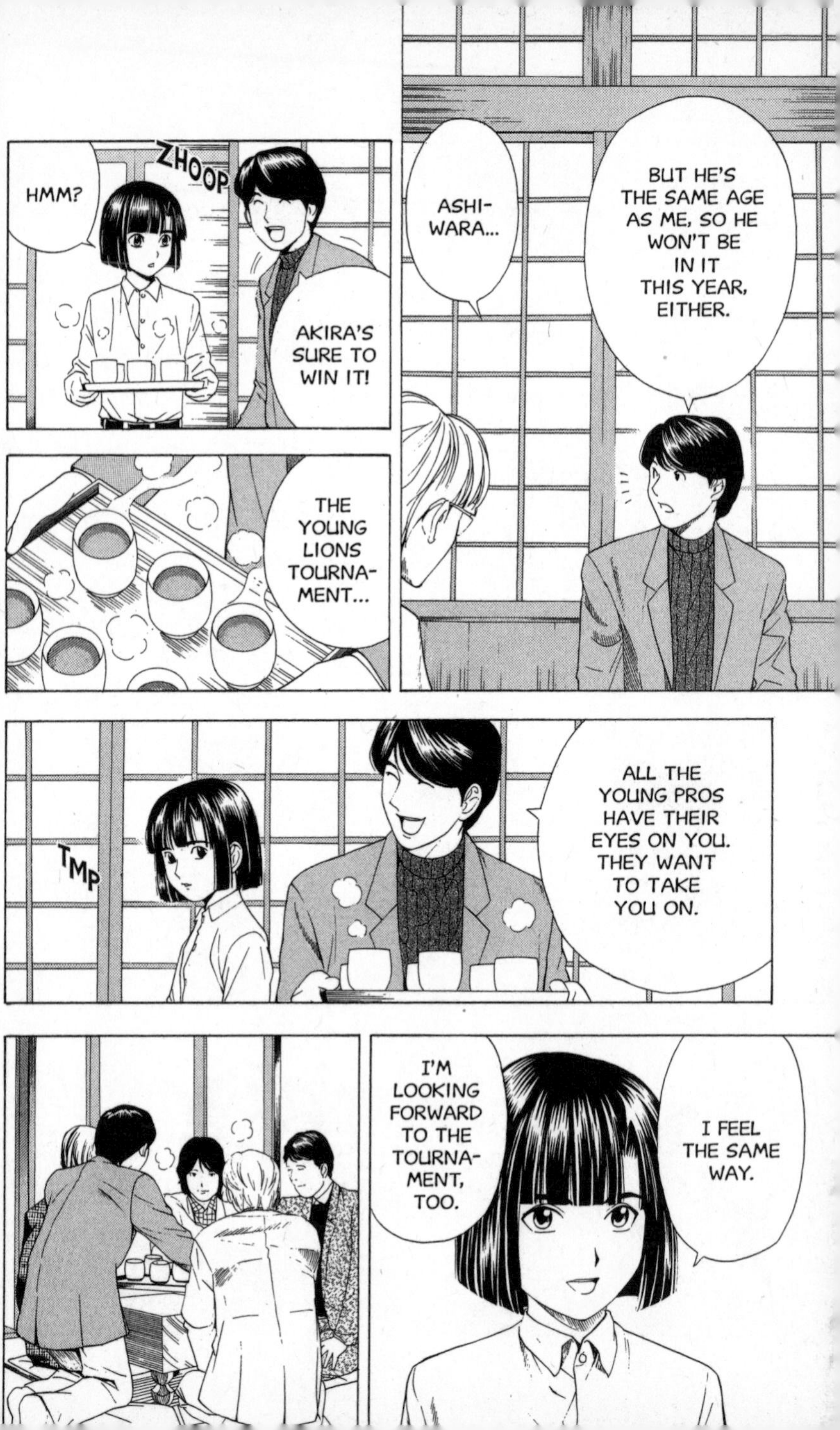
BUT HE'S THE SAME AGE AS ME, SO HE WON'T BE IN IT THIS YEAR, EITHER.
ASHI-WARA...
AKIRA'S SURE TO WIN IT!
ZHOOP
HMM?
THE YOUNG LIONS TOURNA-MENT...
ALL THE YOUNG PROS HAVE THEIR EYES ON YOU. THEY WANT TO TAKE YOU ON.
TMP
I FEEL THE SAME WAY.
I'M LOOKING FORWARD TO THE TOURNA-MENT, TOO.

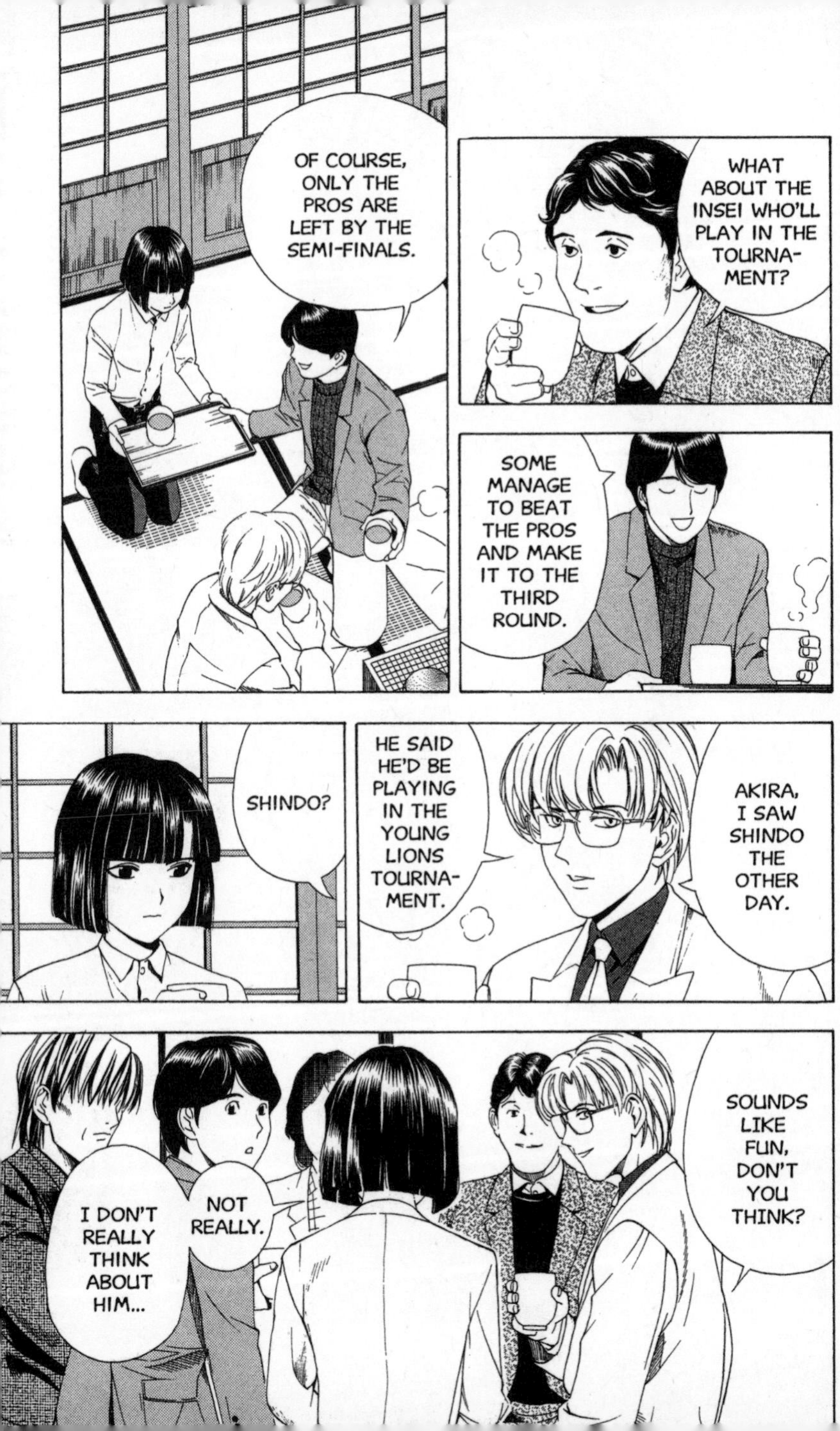
WHAT ABOUT THE INSEI WHO'LL PLAY IN THE TOURNAMENT?
SOME MANAGE TO BEAT THE PROS AND MAKE IT TO THE THIRD ROUND.
OF COURSE, ONLY THE PROS ARE LEFT BY THE SEMI-FINALS.
AKIRA, I SAW SHINDO THE OTHER DAY.
HE SAID HE'D BE PLAYING IN THE YOUNG LIONS TOURNAMENT.
SHINDO?
SOUNDS LIKE FUN, DON'T YOU THINK?
NOT REALLY.
I DON'T REALLY THINK ABOUT HIM...

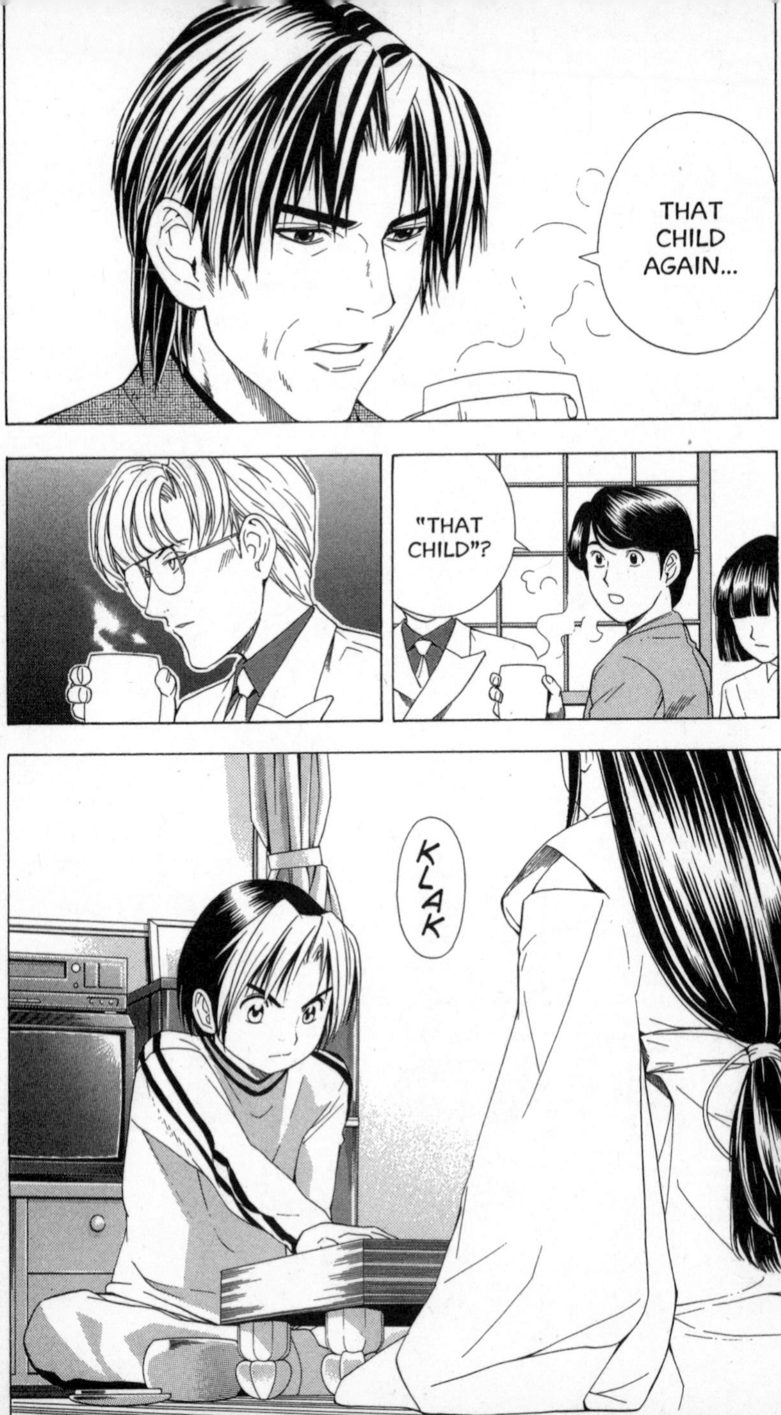
THAT CHILD AGAIN...
"THAT CHILD"?
KLAK

READ THIS WAY

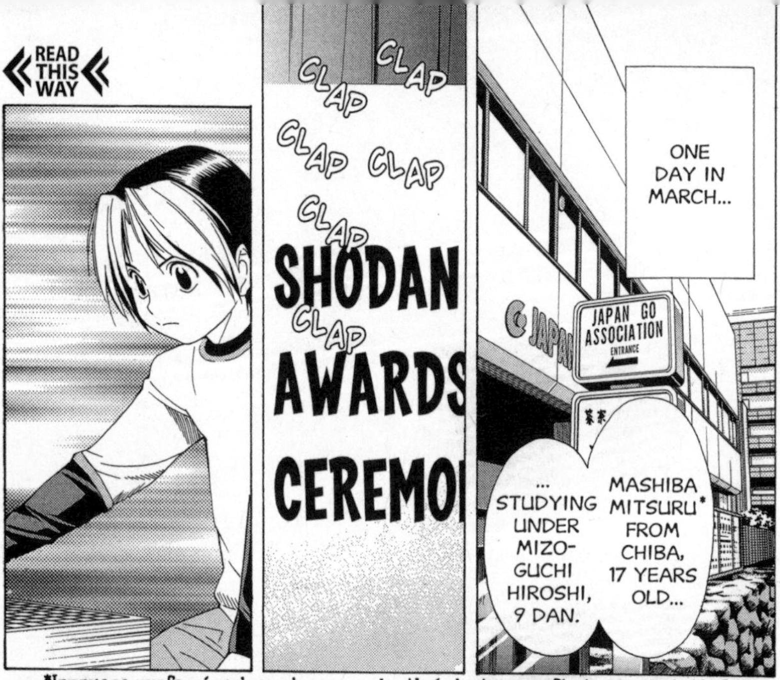
ONE DAY IN MARCH...
JAPAN GO ASSOCIATION ENTRANCE
MASHIBA MITSURU* FROM CHIBA, 17 YEARS OLD...
... STUDYING UNDER MIZO-GUCHI HIROSHI, 9 DAN.
CLAP CLAP CLAP CLAP CLAP CLAP
SHODAN AWARDS CEREMO

*Japanese professional go players go by their last name first, even outside Japan.

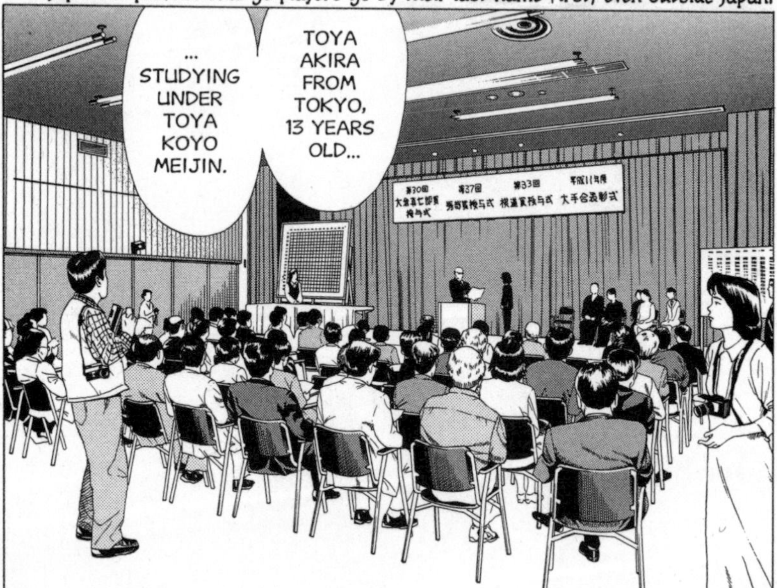
TOYA AKIRA FROM TOKYO, 13 YEARS OLD...
... STUDYING UNDER TOYA KOYO MEIJIN.

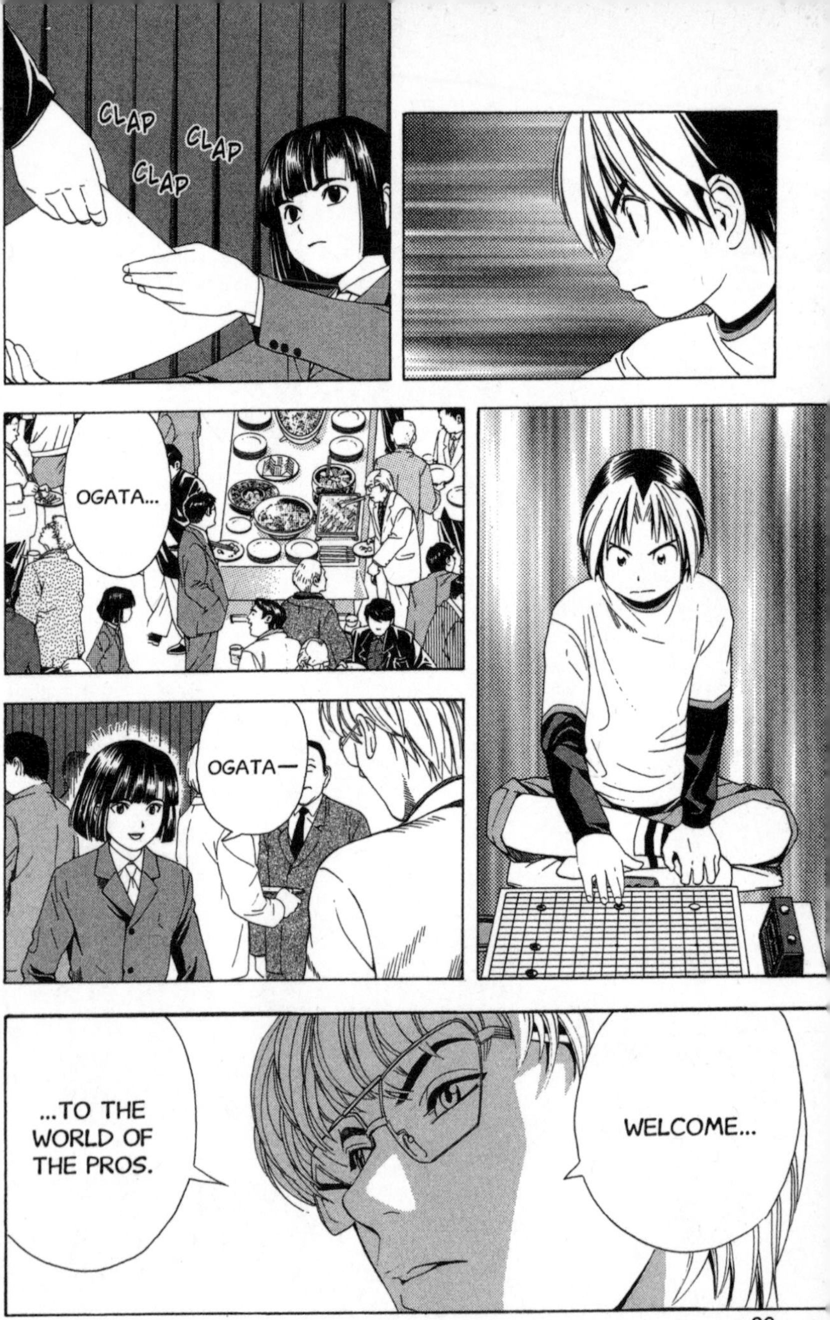
CLAP
CLAP
CLAP
OGATA...
OGATA—
WELCOME...
...TO THE WORLD OF THE PROS.

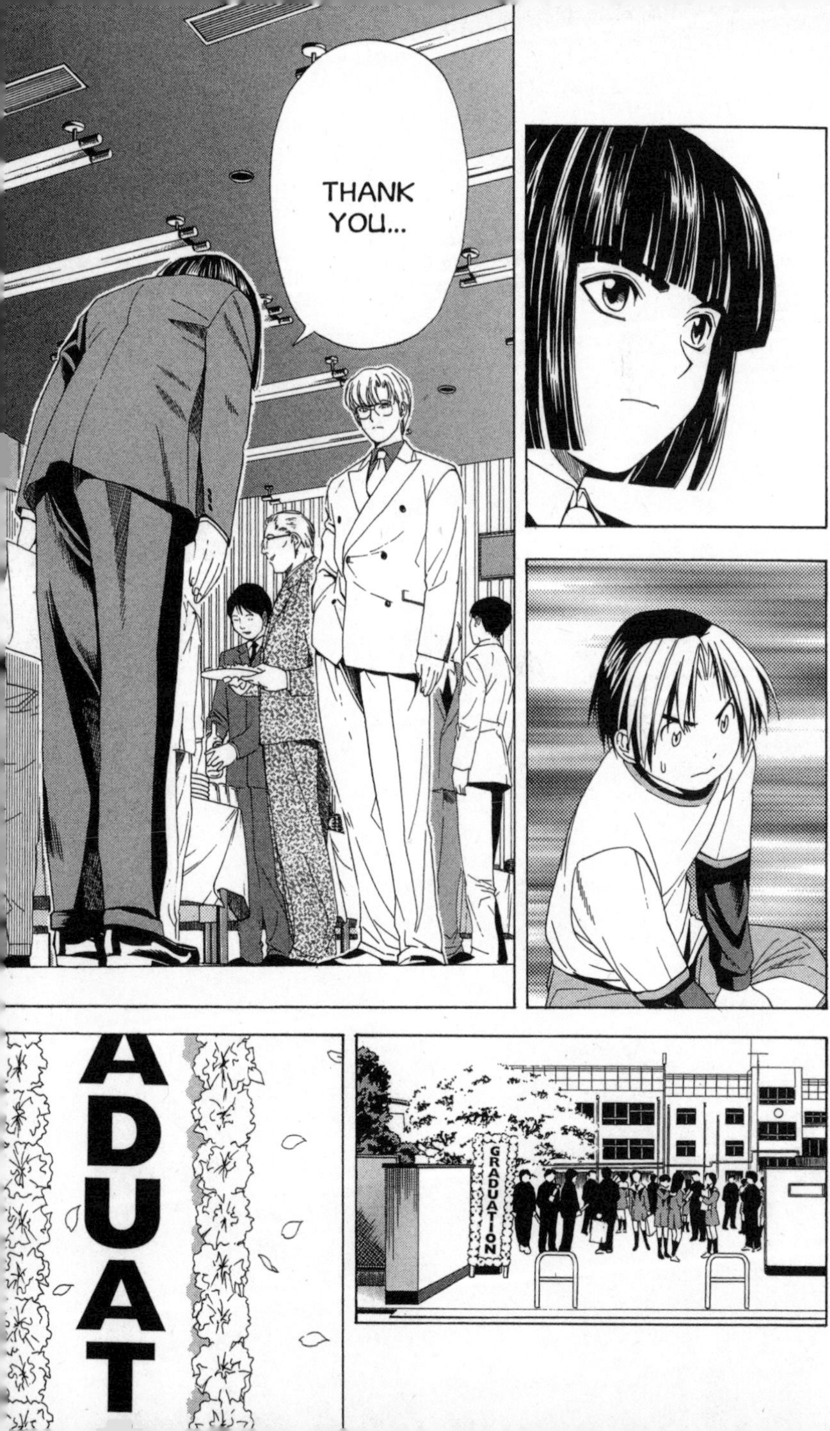
THANK YOU...
GRADUATION
ADUAT

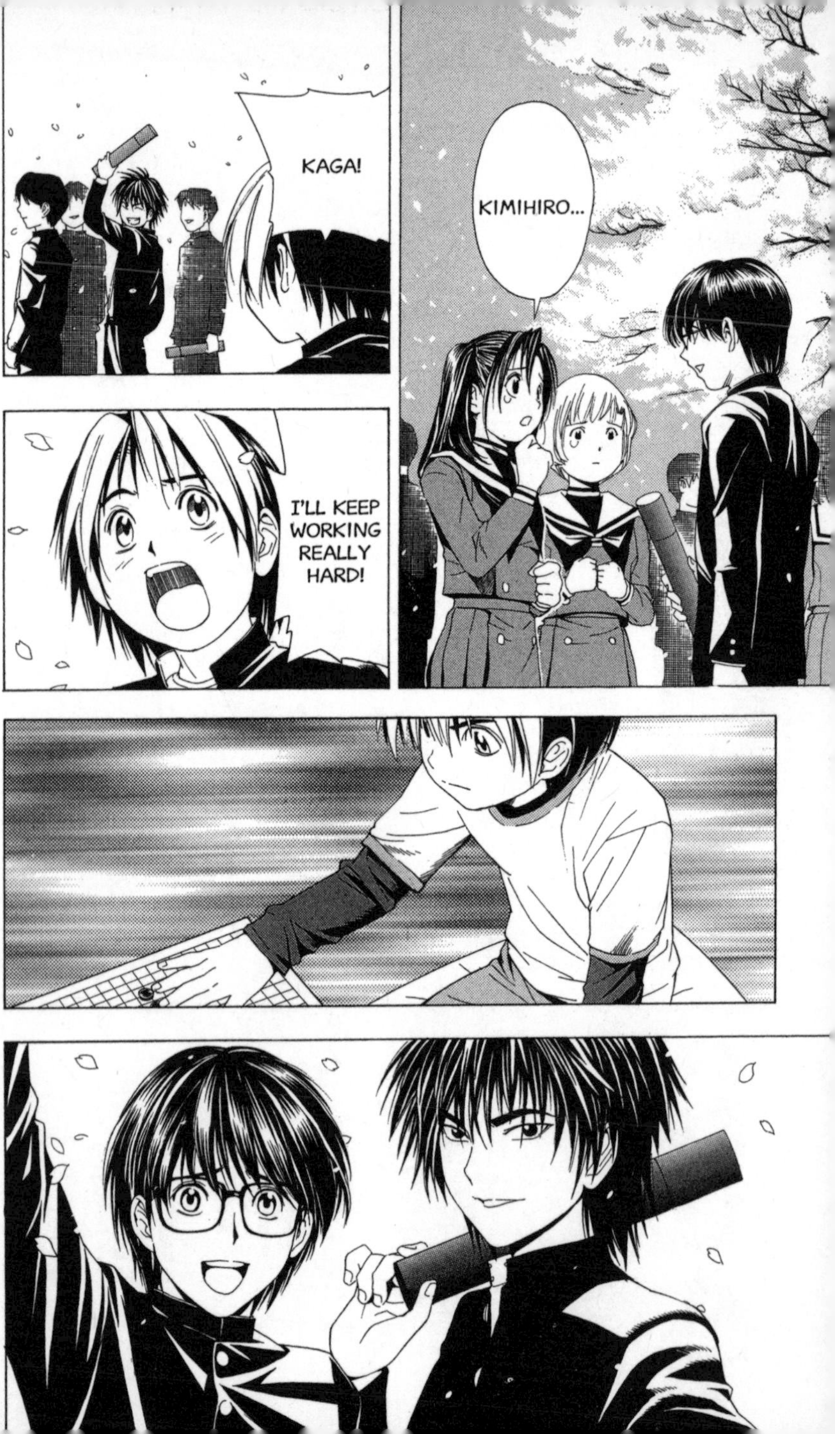
KIMIHIRO...
KAGA!
I'LL KEEP WORKING REALLY HARD!

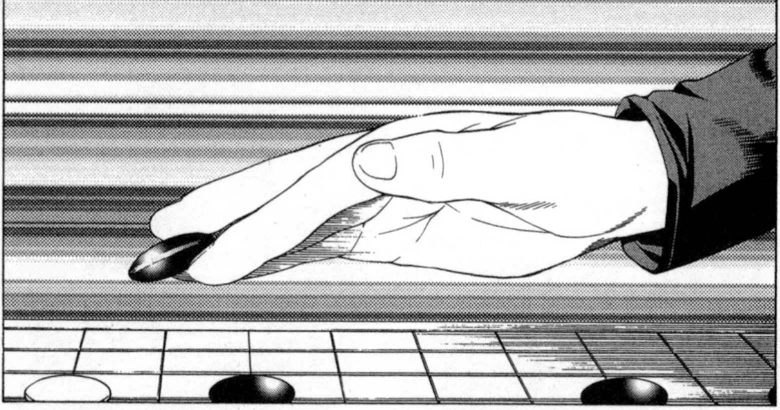

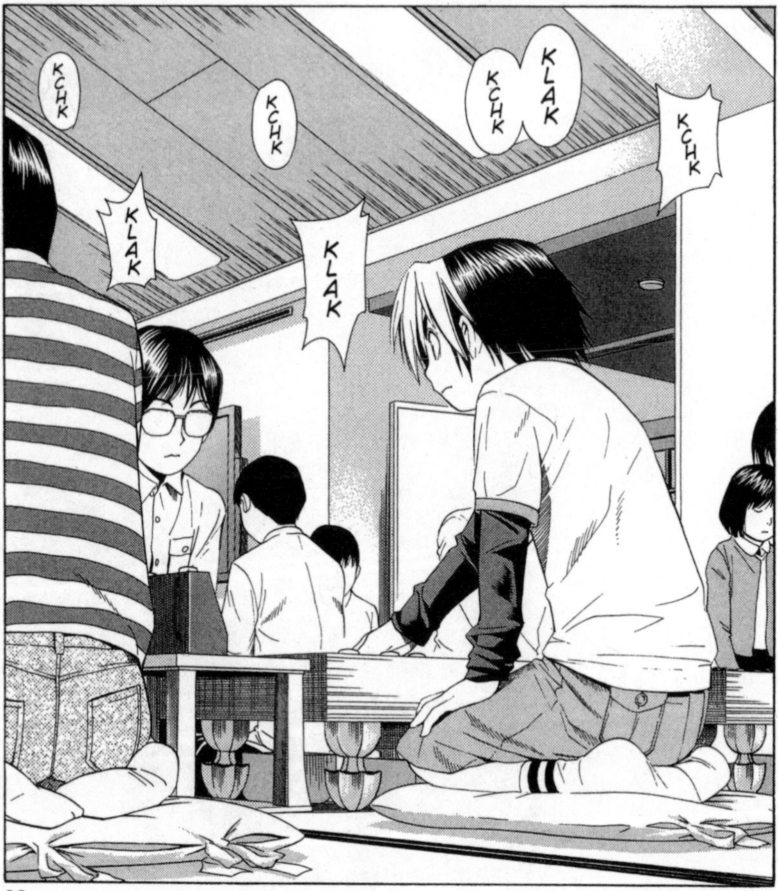
KCHK
KLAK
KCHK
KCHK
KLAK
KCHK
KLAK

# Game 55
# "Welcome to A League"

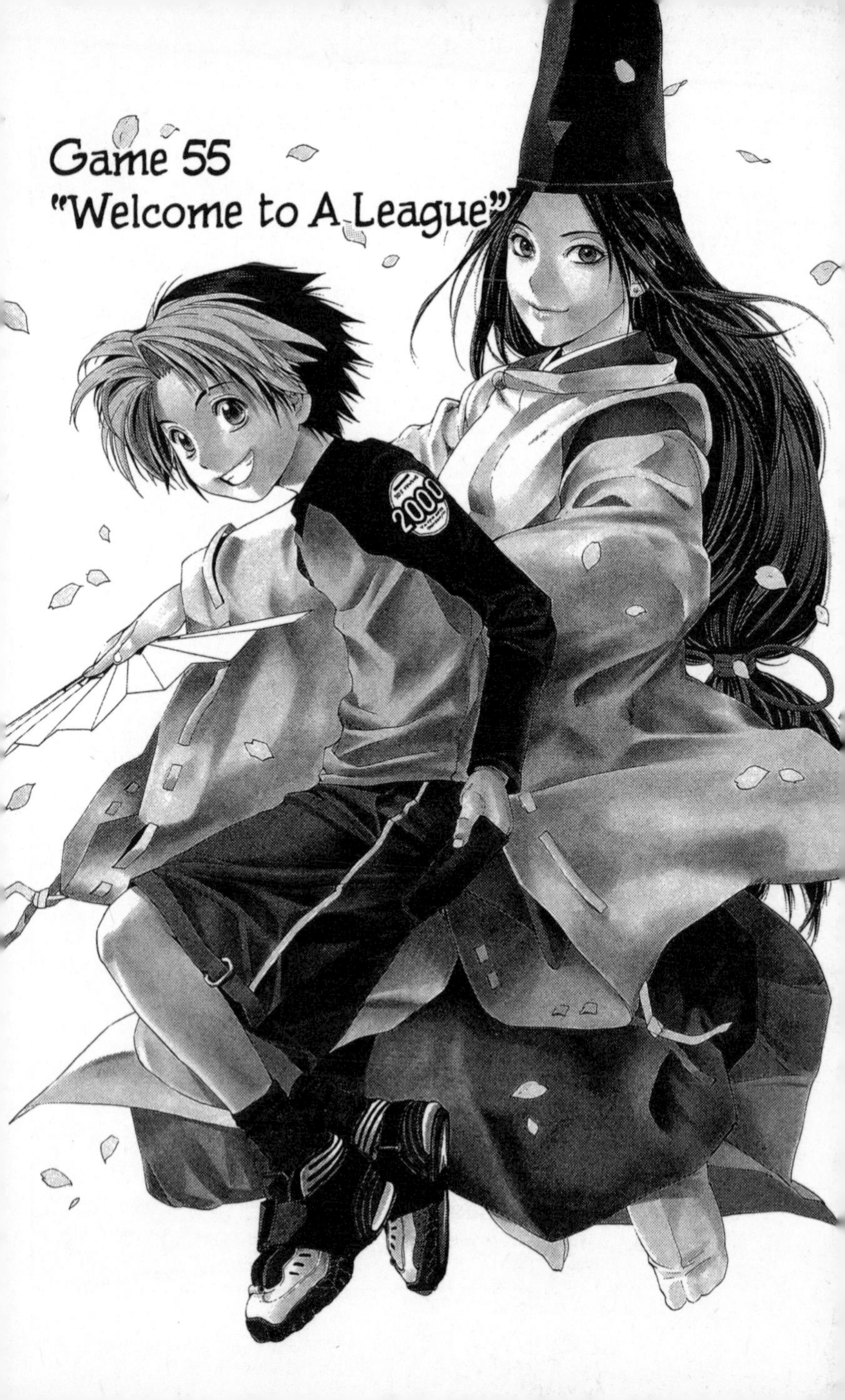

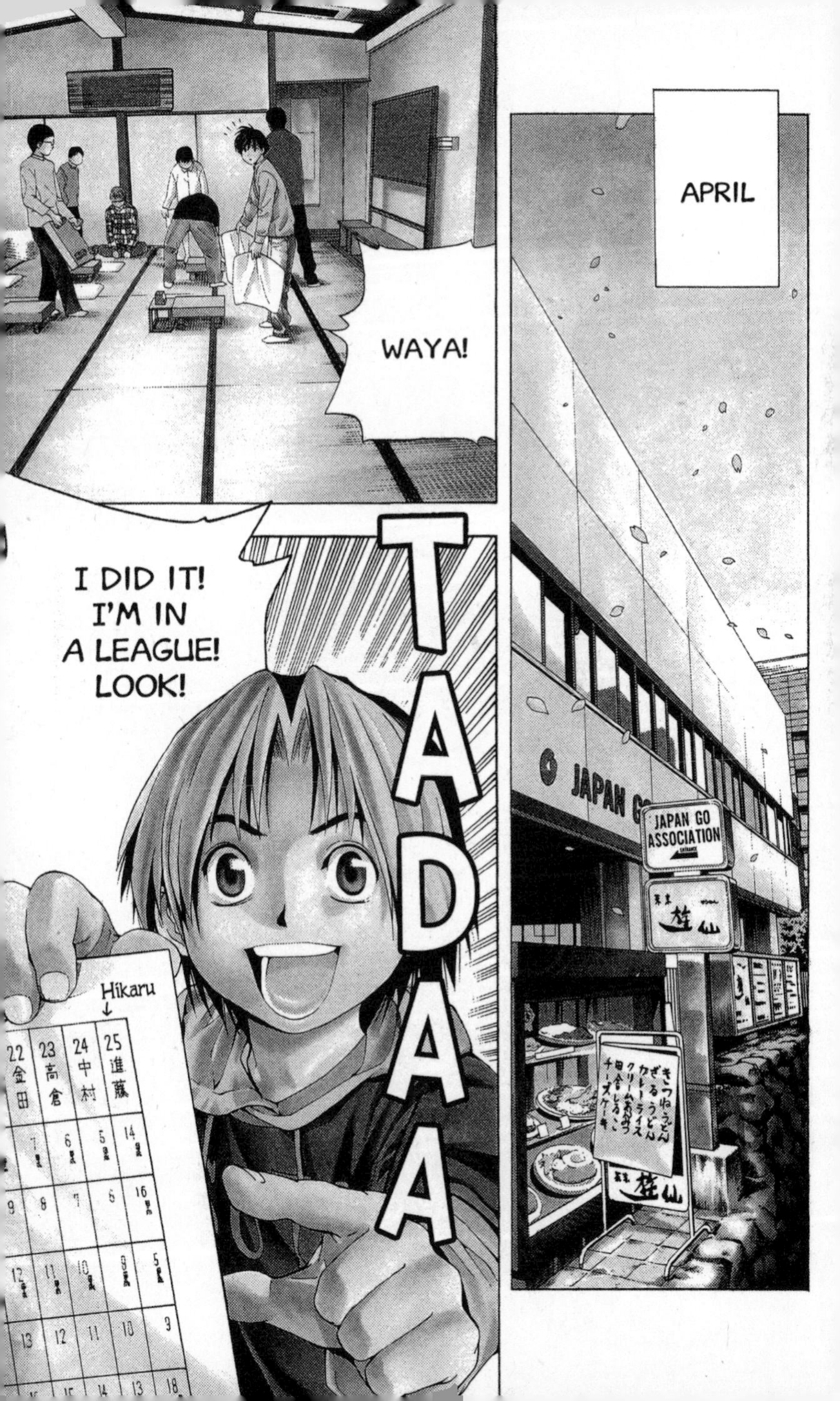
APRIL
JAPAN GO
JAPAN GO ASSOCIATION
きつねうどん
ざるうどん
カレーライス
クリームあんみつ
田舎しるこ
チーズケーキ
WAYA!
I DID IT! I'M IN A LEAGUE! LOOK!
TADAA
Hikaru
22 金田
23 高倉
24 中村
25 進藤

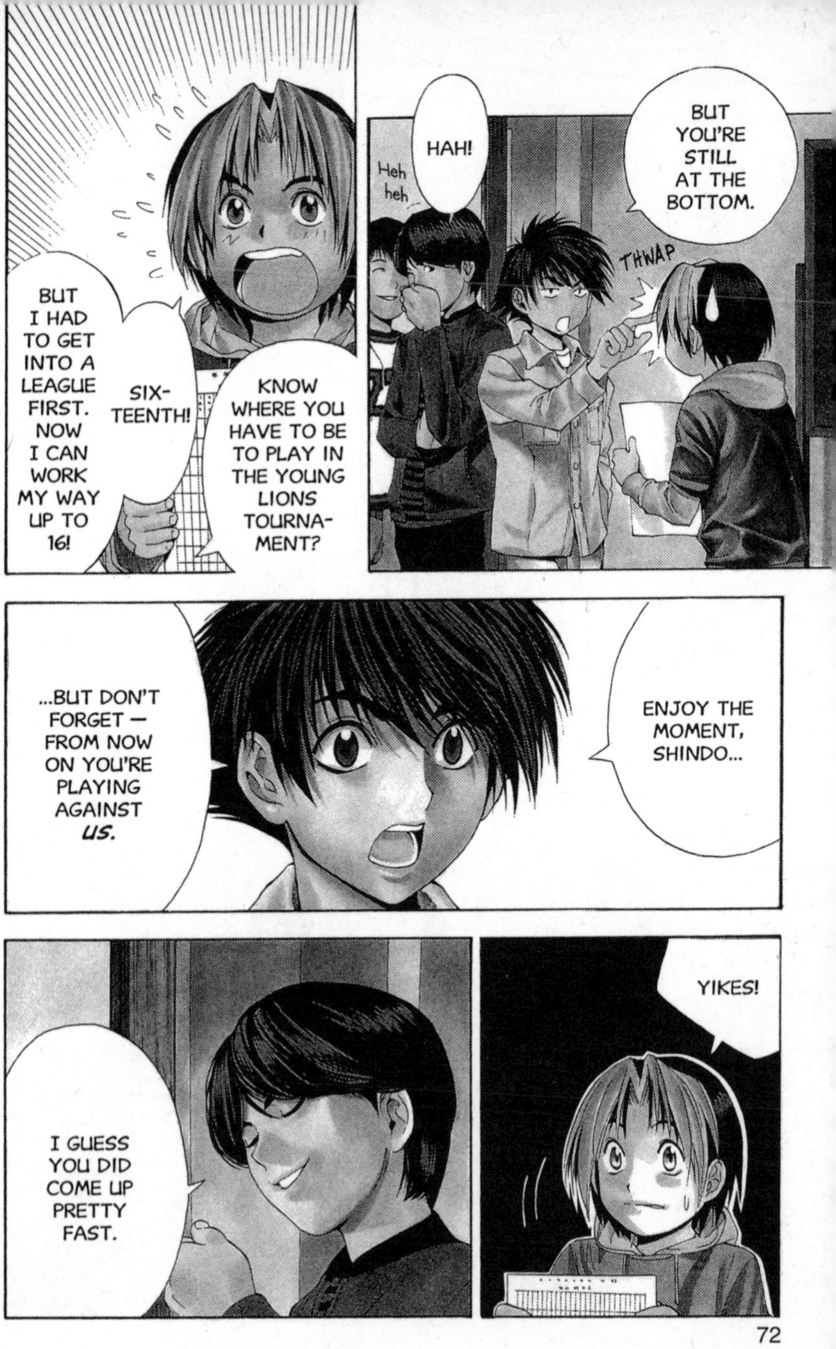
BUT YOU'RE STILL AT THE BOTTOM.
THWAP
HAH!
Heh heh
KNOW WHERE YOU HAVE TO BE TO PLAY IN THE YOUNG LIONS TOURNA-MENT?
SIX-TEENTH!
BUT I HAD TO GET INTO A LEAGUE FIRST. NOW I CAN WORK MY WAY UP TO 16!
ENJOY THE MOMENT, SHINDO...
...BUT DON'T FORGET — FROM NOW ON YOU'RE PLAYING AGAINST *US*.
YIKES!
I GUESS YOU DID COME UP PRETTY FAST.

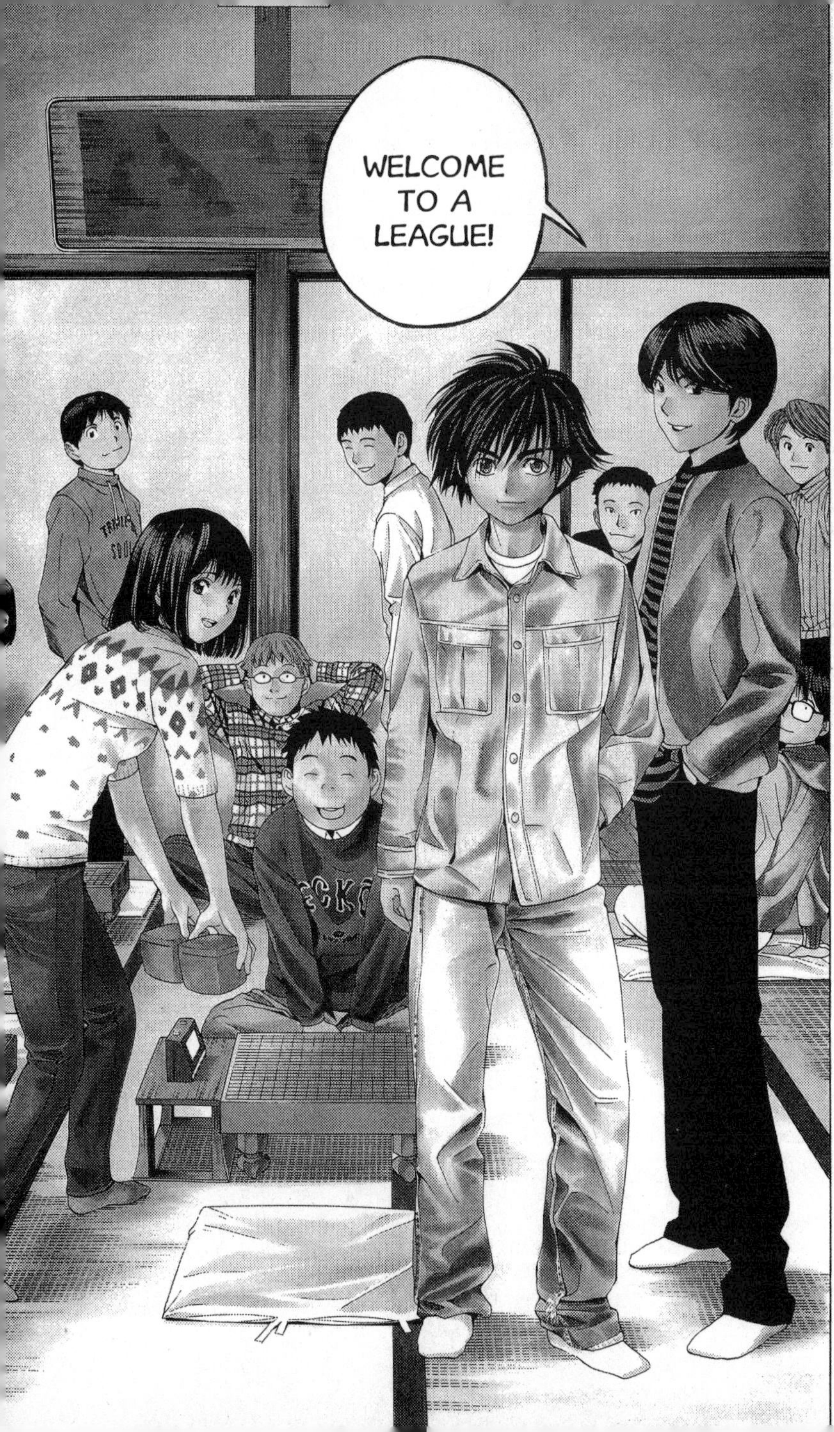
WELCOME TO A LEAGUE!

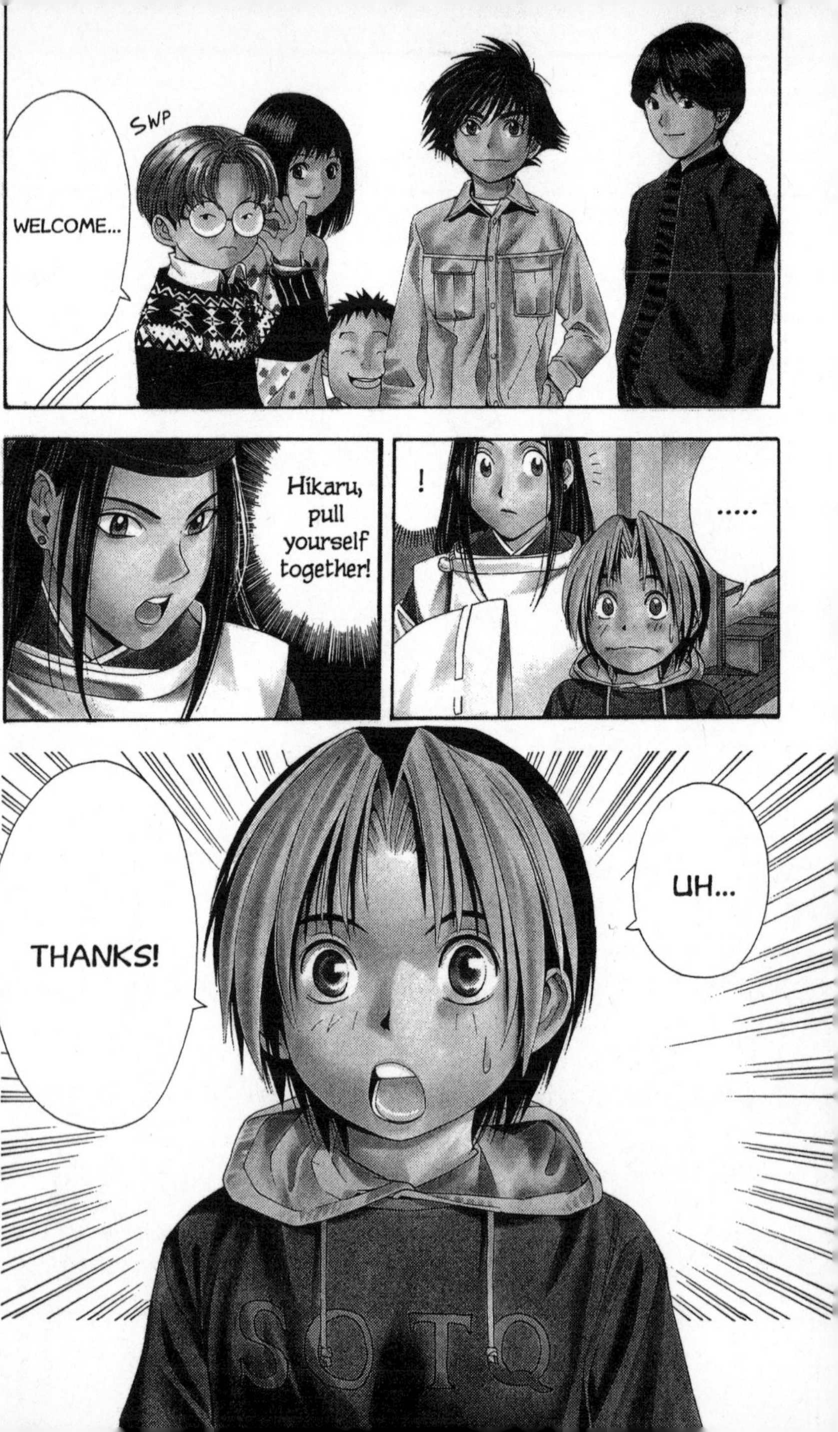
SWP
WELCOME...
!
.....
Hikaru, pull yourself together!
UH...
THANKS!

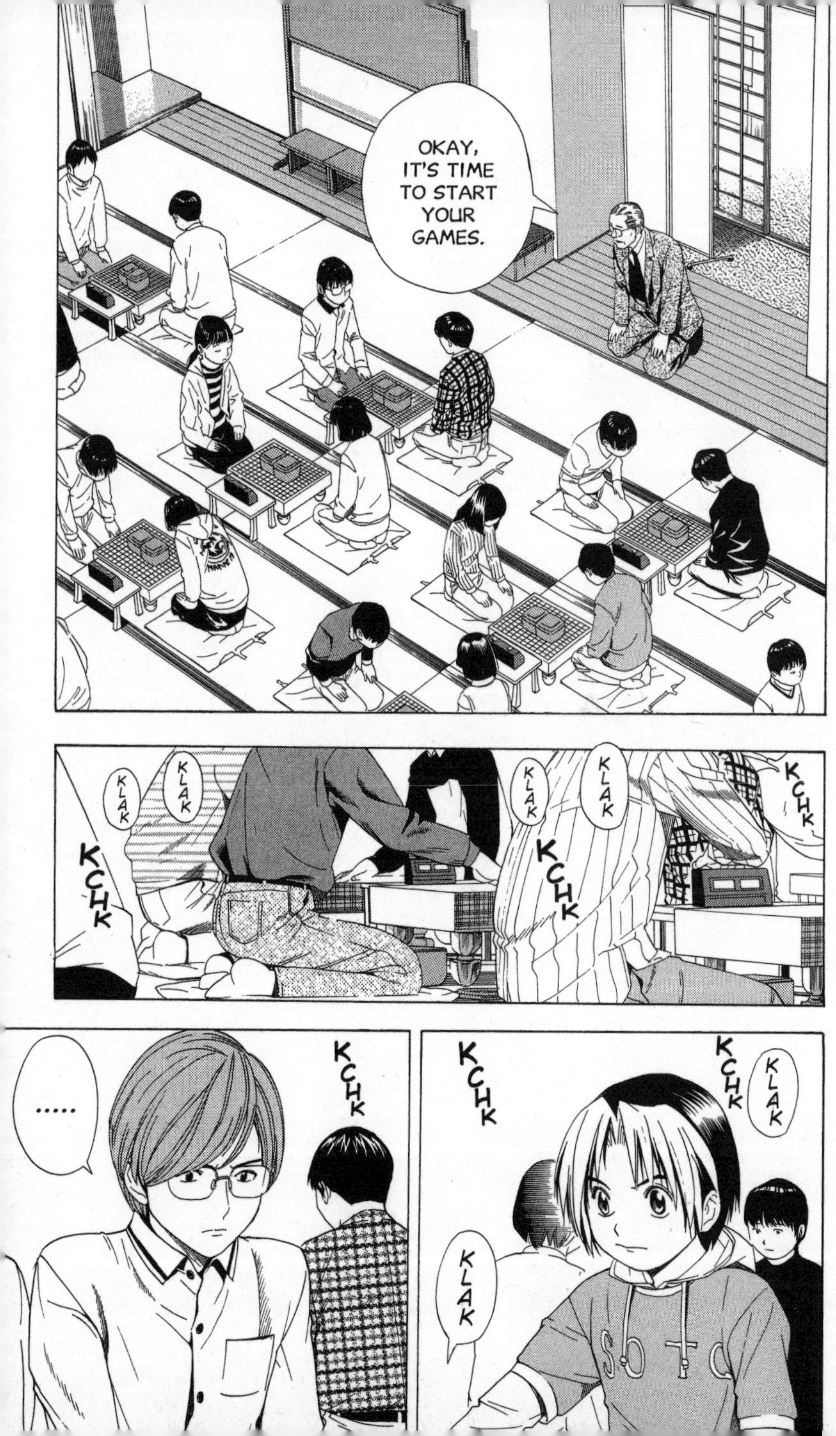
OKAY, IT'S TIME TO START YOUR GAMES.
KCHK
KLAK
KCHK
KLAK
KLAK
KLAK
KCHK
KCHK
KLAK
KCHK
KLAK
KCHK
.....

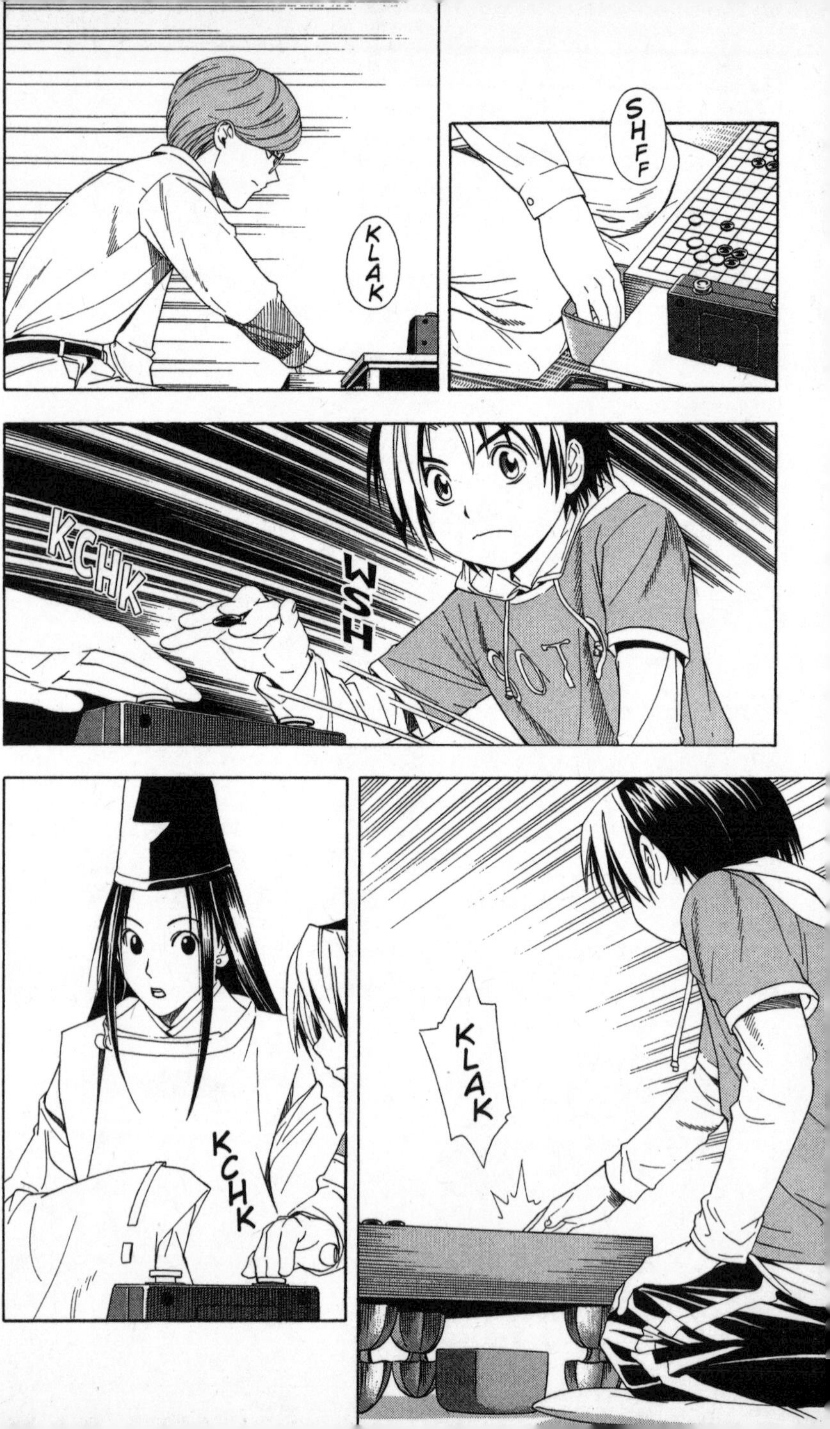
SHFF
KLAK
WSH
KCHK
KLAK
KCHK

READ THIS WAY

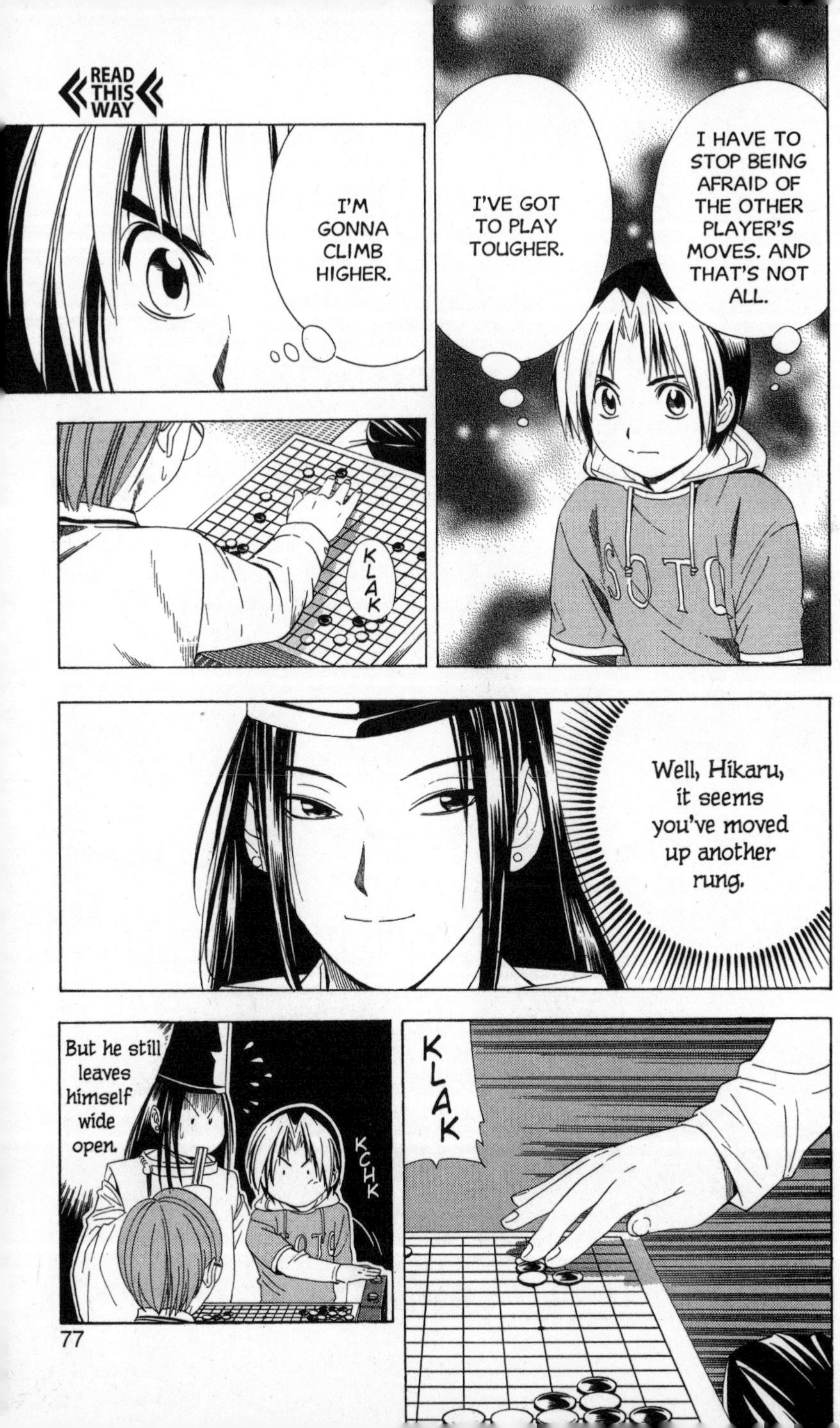

I HAVE TO STOP BEING AFRAID OF THE OTHER PLAYER'S MOVES. AND THAT'S NOT ALL.
I'VE GOT TO PLAY TOUGHER.
I'M GONNA CLIMB HIGHER.
KLAK
Well, Hikaru, it seems you've moved up another rung.
KLAK
But he still leaves himself wide open.
KCHK

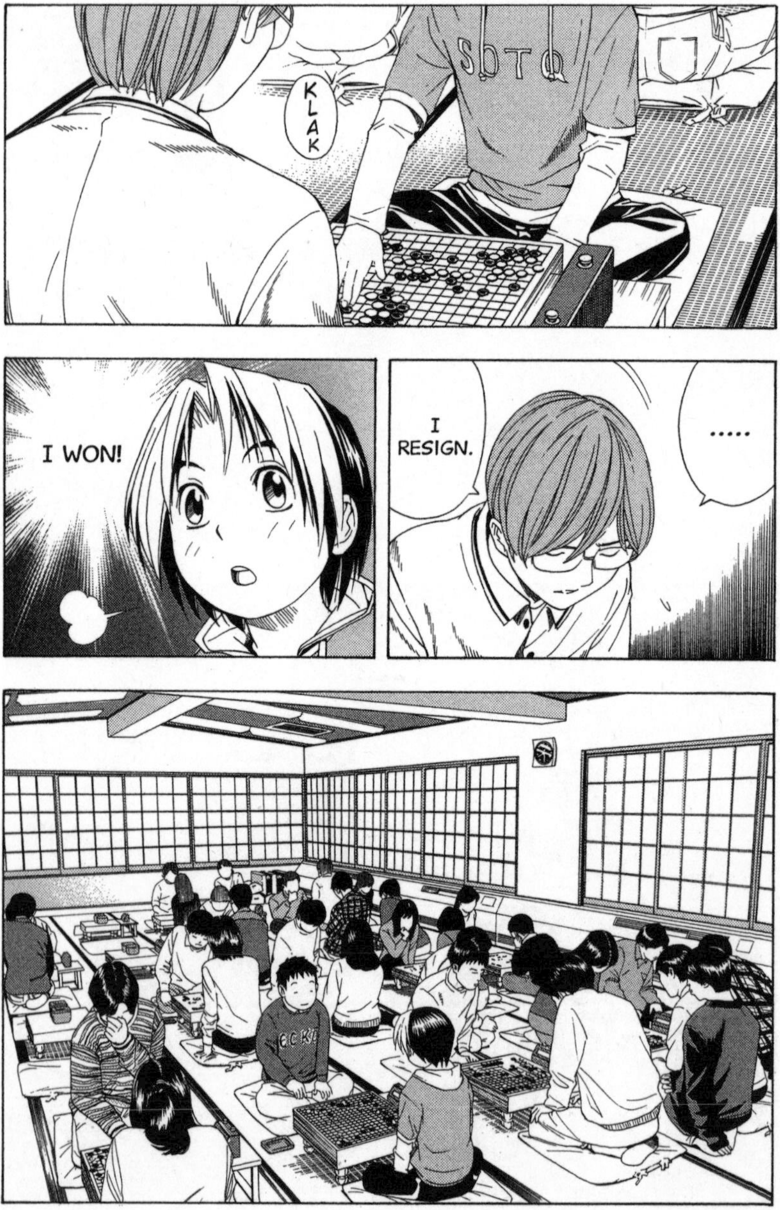
KLAK
.....
I RESIGN.
I WON!

READ THIS WAY

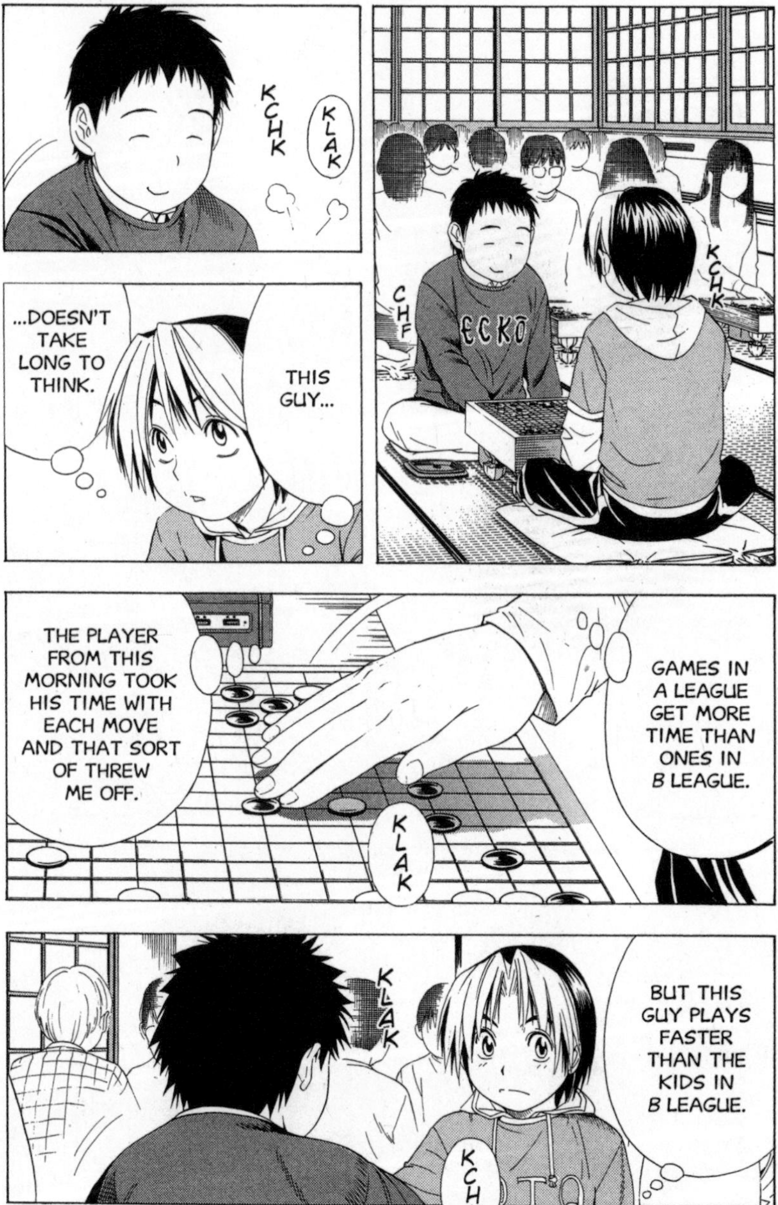

KCHK
CHF
KLAK
KCHK
THIS GUY...
...DOESN'T TAKE LONG TO THINK.
GAMES IN A LEAGUE GET MORE TIME THAN ONES IN B LEAGUE.
KLAK
THE PLAYER FROM THIS MORNING TOOK HIS TIME WITH EACH MOVE AND THAT SORT OF THREW ME OFF.
BUT THIS GUY PLAYS FASTER THAN THE KIDS IN B LEAGUE.
KLAK
KCHK

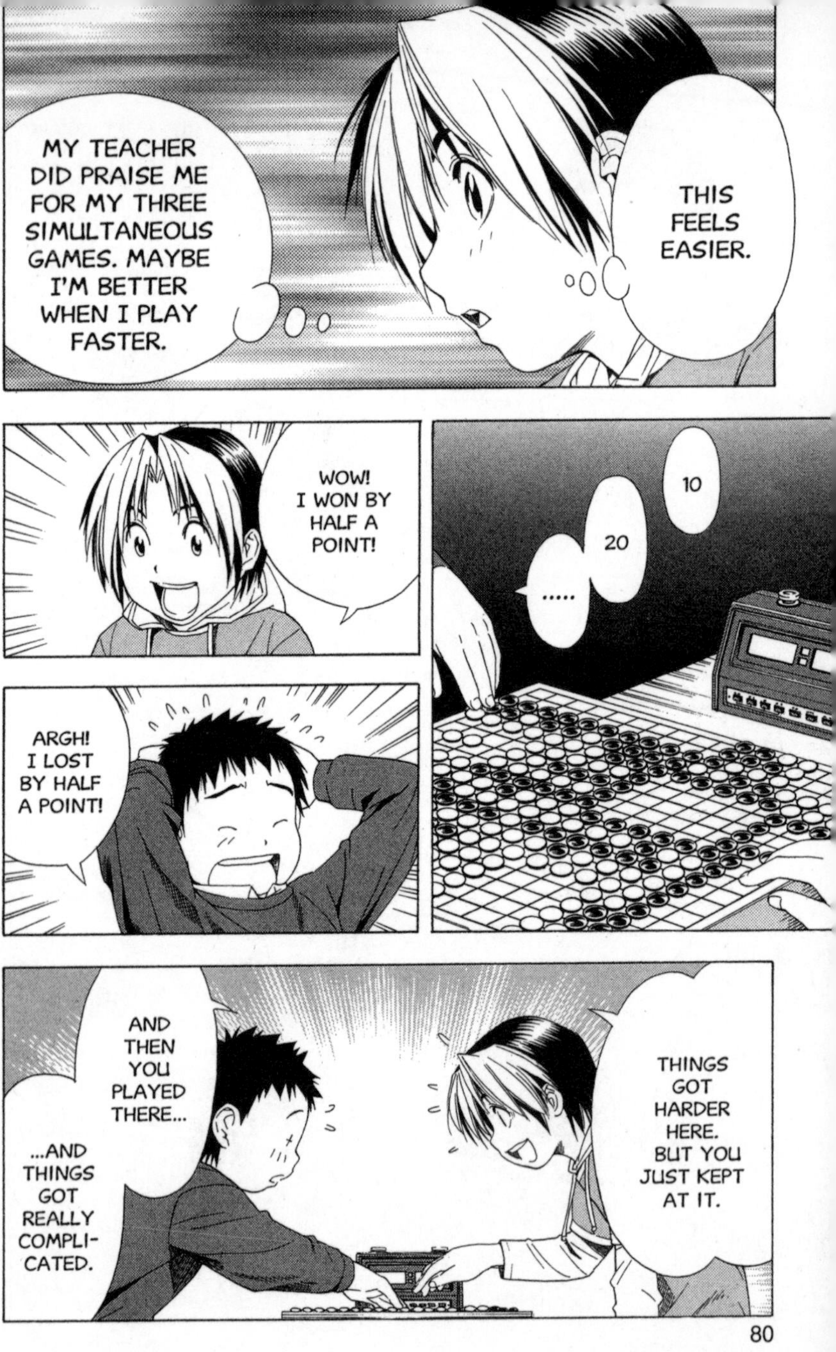
THIS FEELS EASIER.
MY TEACHER DID PRAISE ME FOR MY THREE SIMULTANEOUS GAMES. MAYBE I'M BETTER WHEN I PLAY FASTER.
10
20
.....
WOW! I WON BY HALF A POINT!
ARGH! I LOST BY HALF A POINT!
THINGS GOT HARDER HERE. BUT YOU JUST KEPT AT IT.
AND THEN YOU PLAYED THERE...
...AND THINGS GOT REALLY COMPLICATED.

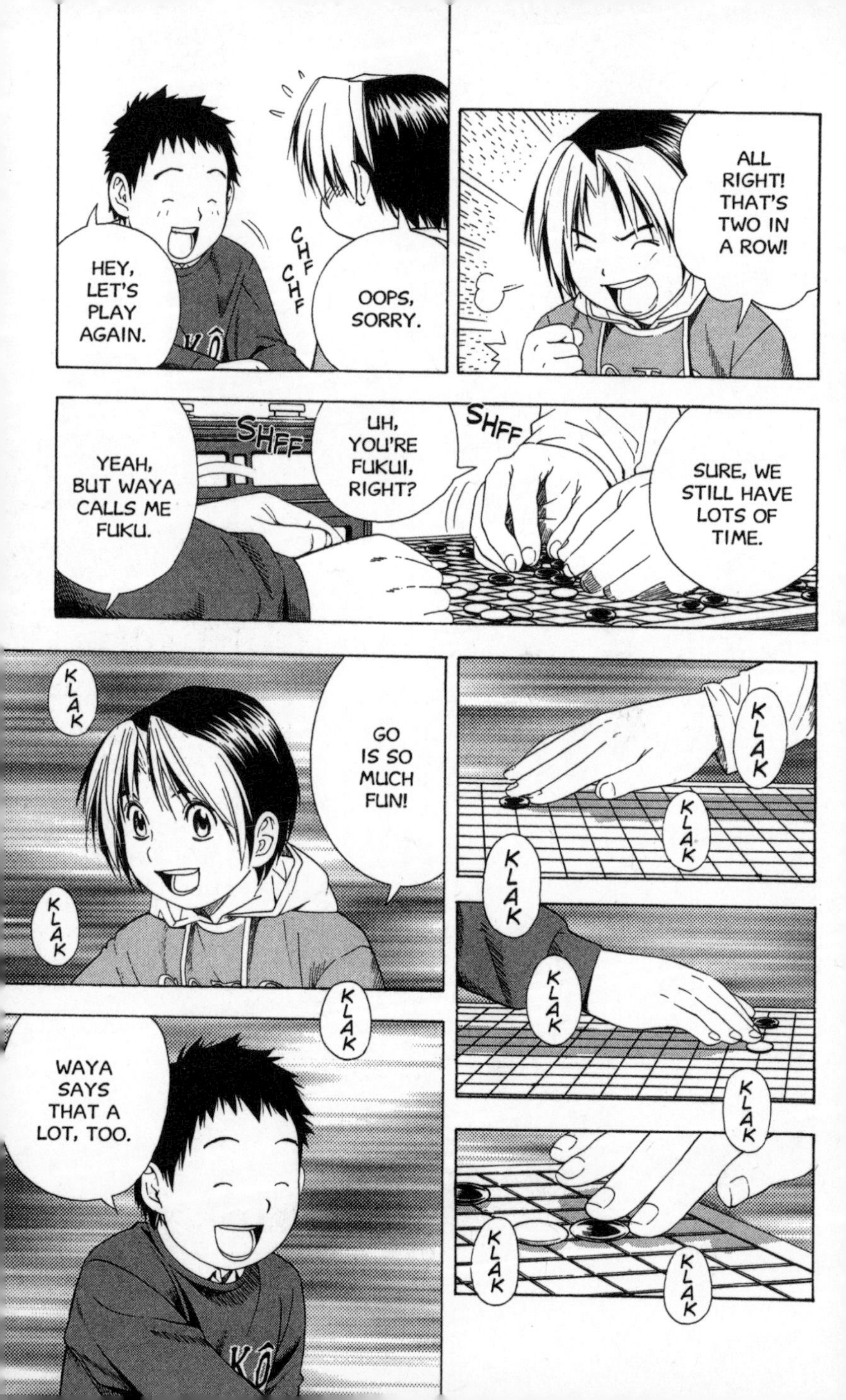
ALL RIGHT! THAT'S TWO IN A ROW!
OOPS, SORRY.
CHF CHF
HEY, LET'S PLAY AGAIN.
SURE, WE STILL HAVE LOTS OF TIME.
SHFF
UH, YOU'RE FUKUI, RIGHT?
SHFF
YEAH, BUT WAYA CALLS ME FUKU.
KLAK
KLAK
KLAK
KLAK
KLAK
KLAK
KLAK
GO IS SO MUCH FUN!
KLAK
KLAK
KLAK
WAYA SAYS THAT A LOT, TOO.

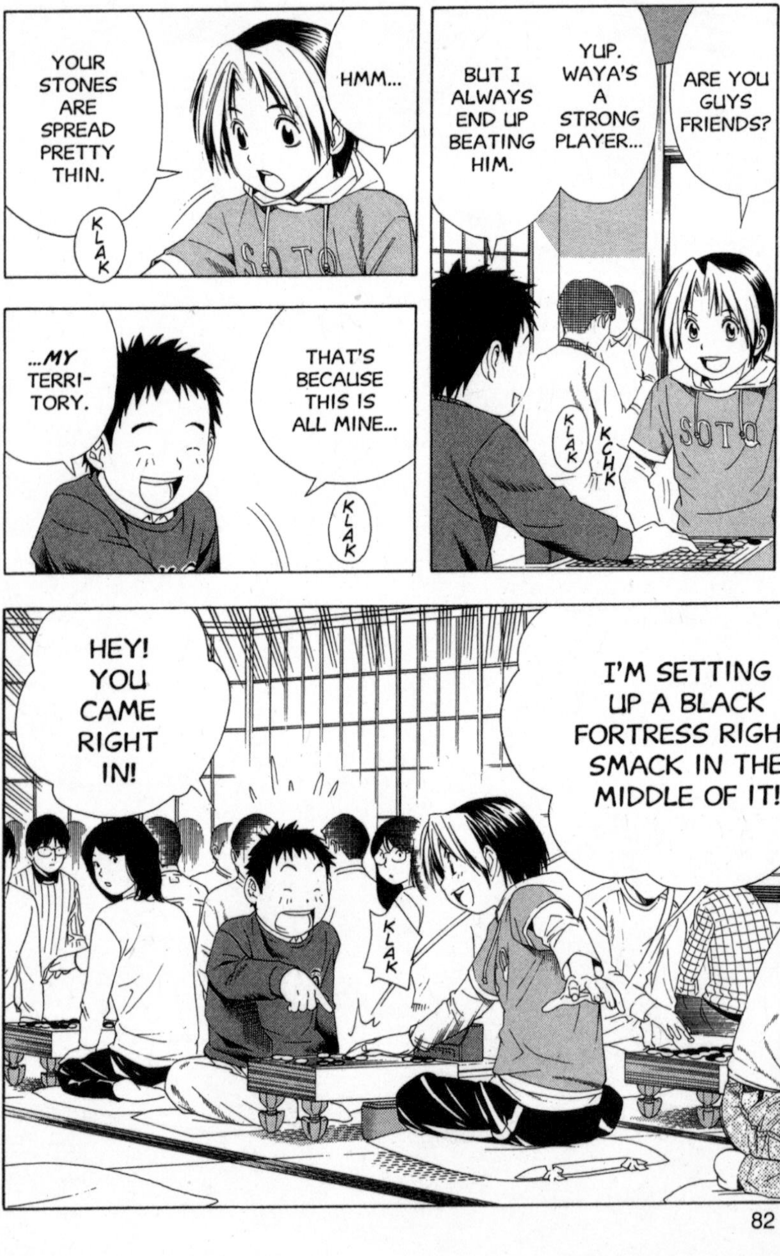
ARE YOU GUYS FRIENDS?
YUP. WAYA'S A STRONG PLAYER...
BUT I ALWAYS END UP BEATING HIM.
KLAK
KCHK
HMM...
YOUR STONES ARE SPREAD PRETTY THIN.
KLAK
THAT'S BECAUSE THIS IS ALL MINE...
...*MY* TERRITORY.
KLAK
I'M SETTING UP A BLACK FORTRESS RIGHT SMACK IN THE MIDDLE OF IT!
HEY! YOU CAME RIGHT IN!
KLAK

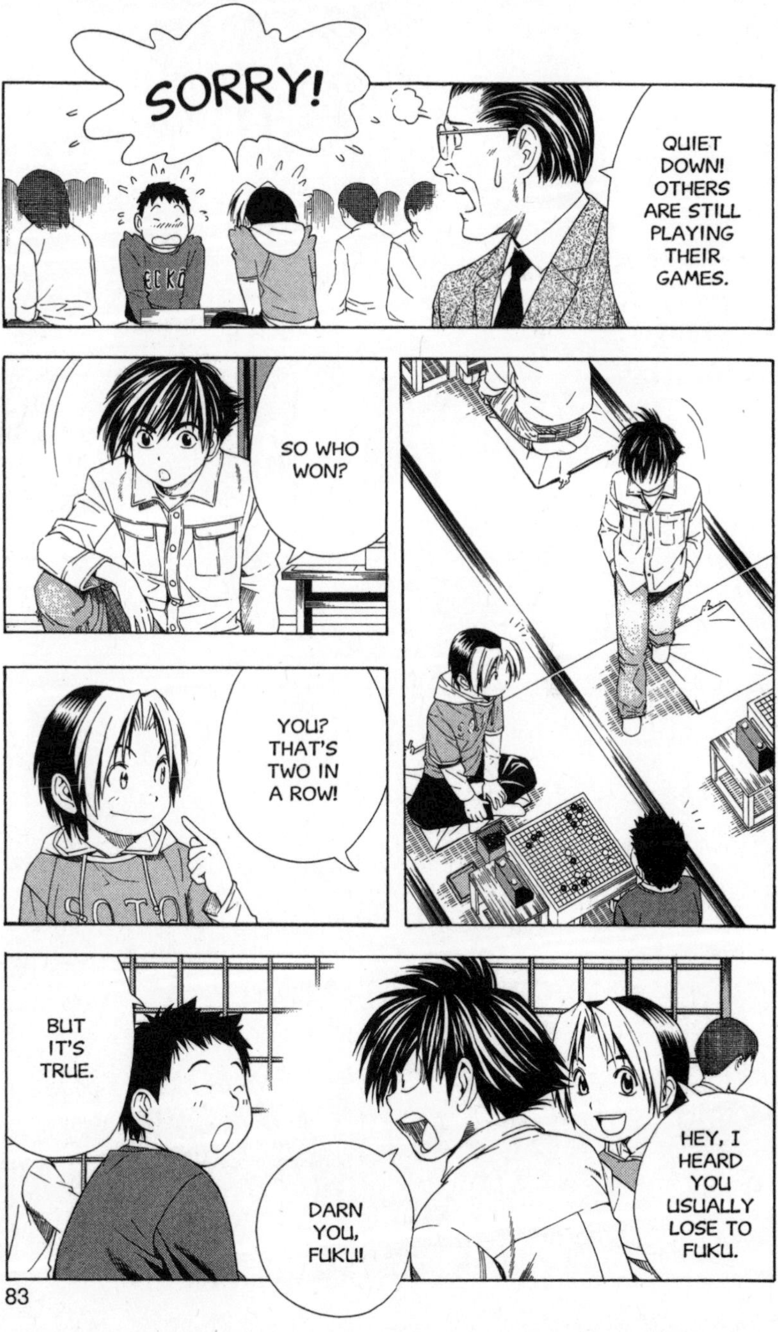
SORRY!
QUIET DOWN! OTHERS ARE STILL PLAYING THEIR GAMES.
SO WHO WON?
YOU? THAT'S TWO IN A ROW!
HEY, I HEARD YOU USUALLY LOSE TO FUKU.
DARN YOU, FUKU!
BUT IT'S TRUE.

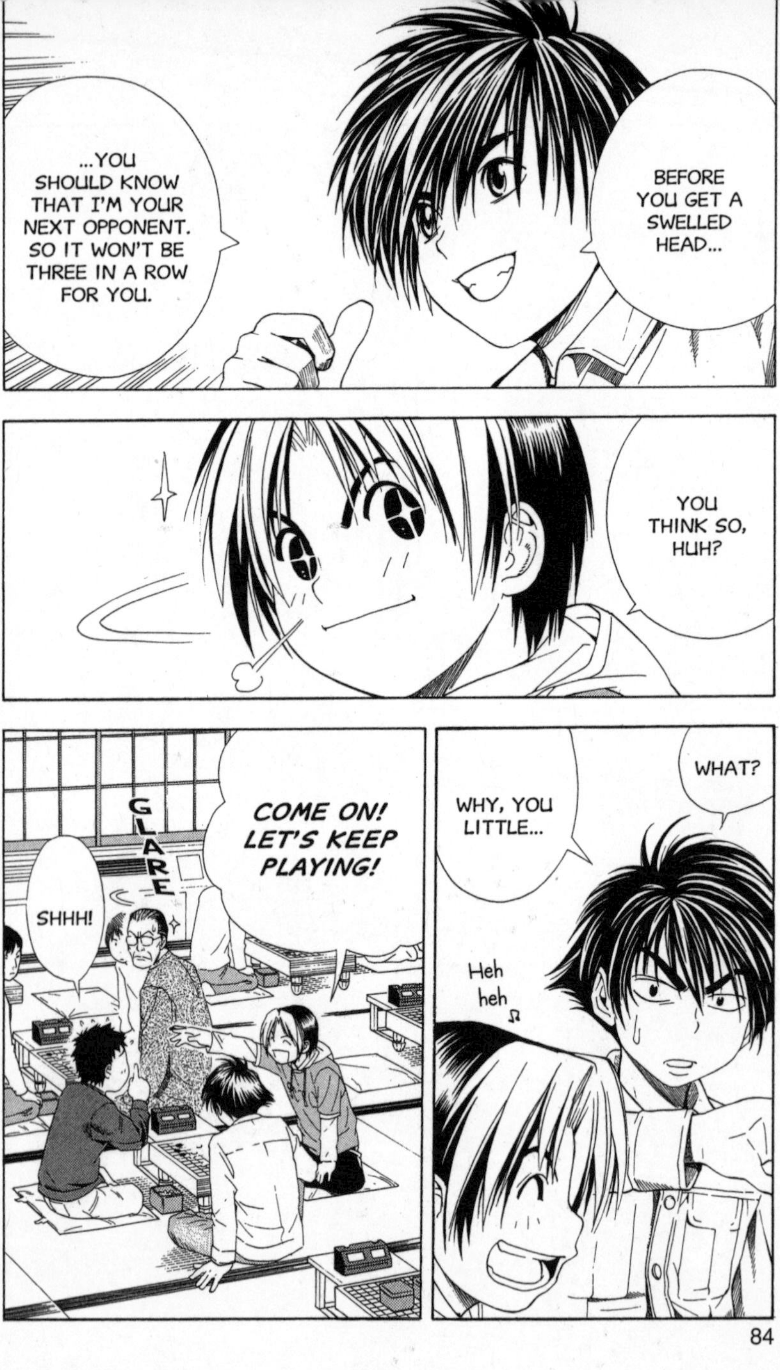
BEFORE YOU GET A SWELLED HEAD...
...YOU SHOULD KNOW THAT I'M YOUR NEXT OPPONENT. SO IT WON'T BE THREE IN A ROW FOR YOU.
YOU THINK SO, HUH?
WHAT?
WHY, YOU LITTLE...
Heh heh
COME ON! LET'S KEEP PLAYING!
GLARE
SHHH!

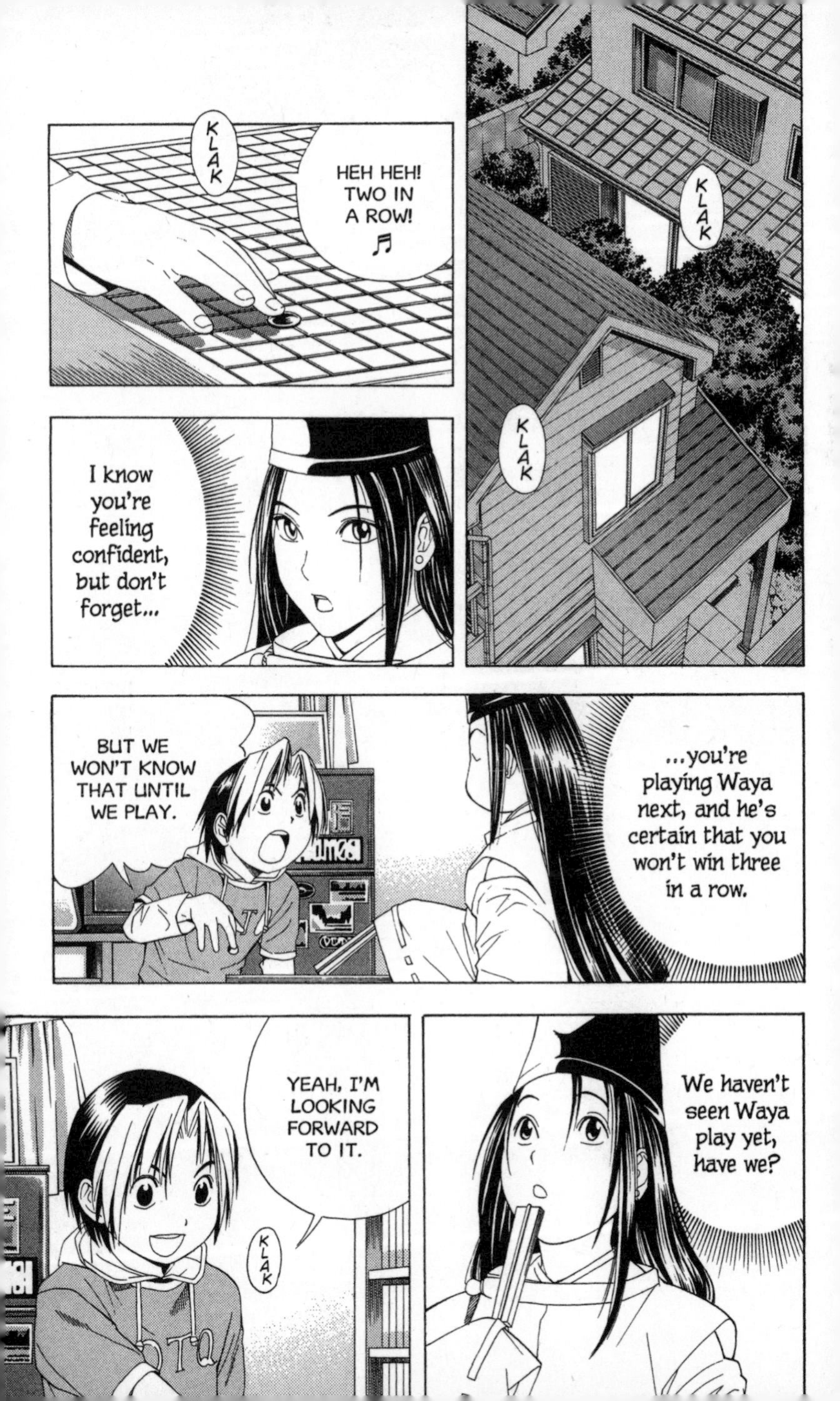
KLAK
KLAK
KLAK
HEH HEH! TWO IN A ROW! ♬
I know you're feeling confident, but don't forget...
...you're playing Waya next, and he's certain that you won't win three in a row.
BUT WE WON'T KNOW THAT UNTIL WE PLAY.
We haven't seen Waya play yet, have we?
YEAH, I'M LOOKING FORWARD TO IT.
KLAK

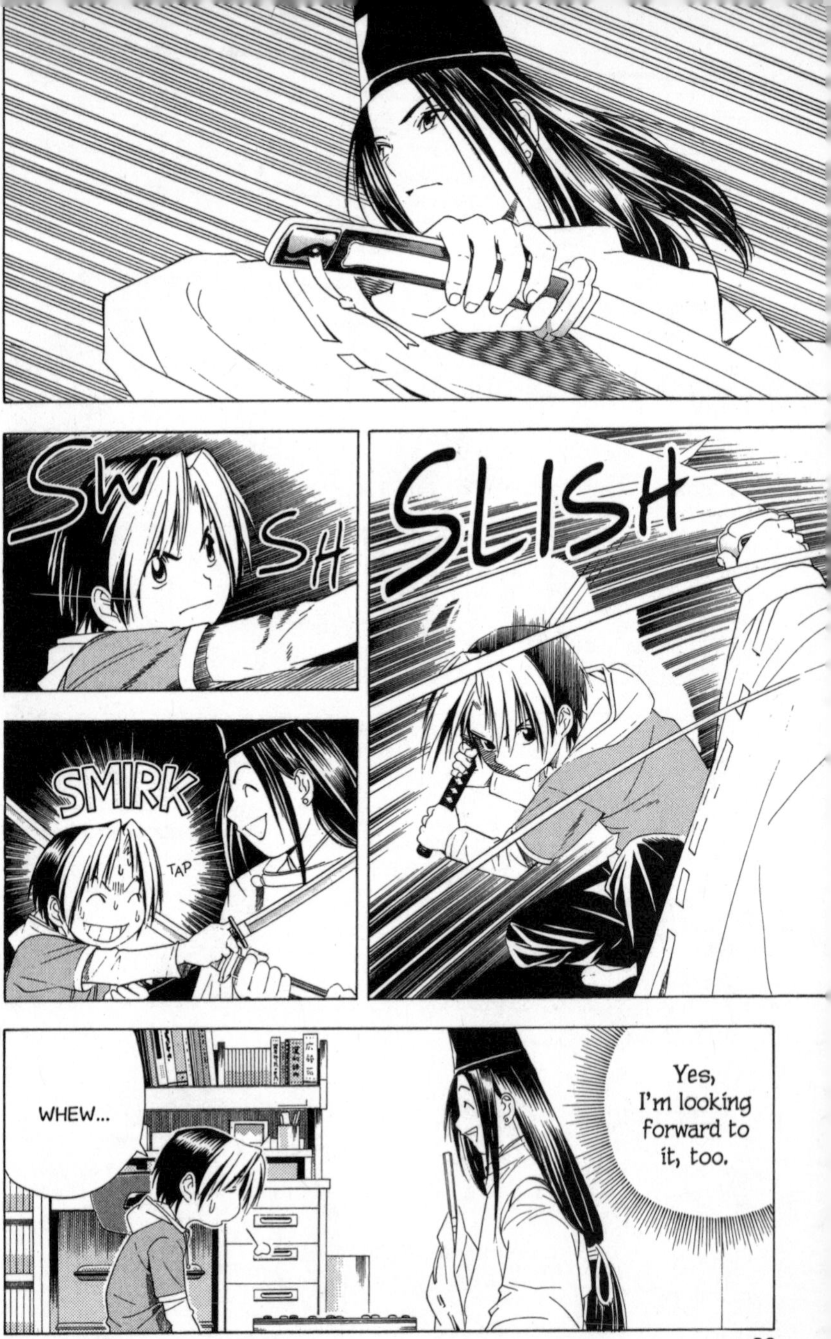
SLISH
SWSH
SMIRK
TAP
Yes, I'm looking forward to it, too.
WHEW...

READ THIS WAY

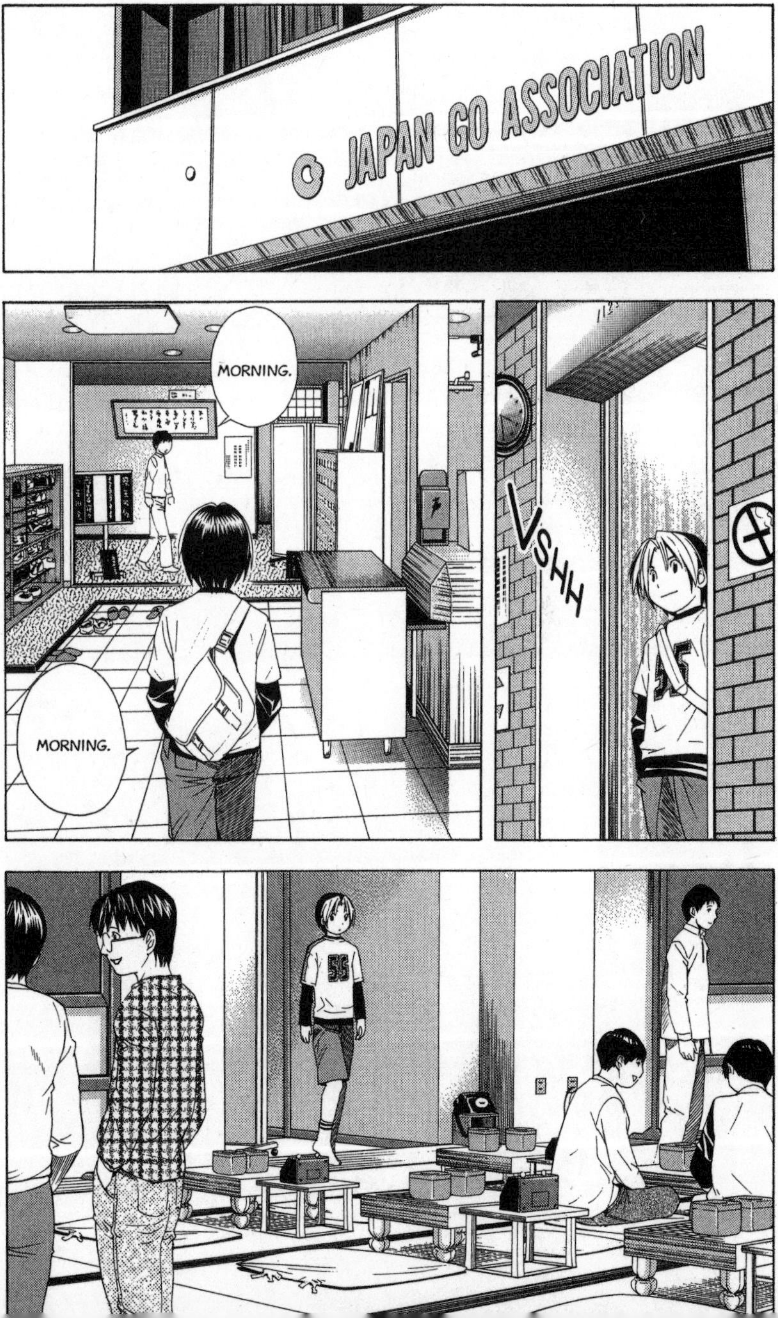
JAPAN GO ASSOCIATION
VSHH
MORNING.
MORNING.

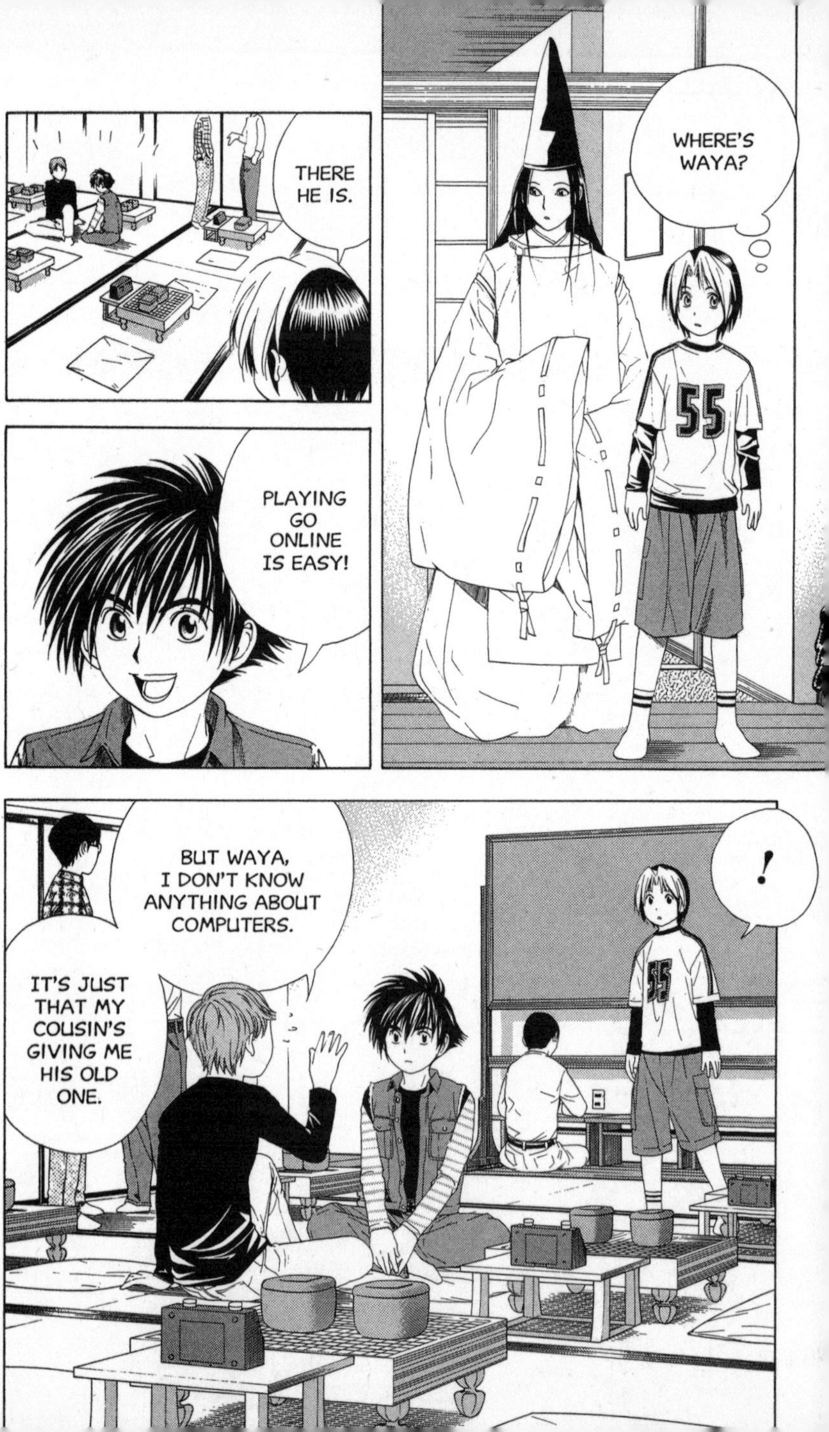
WHERE'S WAYA?
THERE HE IS.
PLAYING GO ONLINE IS EASY!
!
BUT WAYA, I DON'T KNOW ANYTHING ABOUT COMPUTERS.
IT'S JUST THAT MY COUSIN'S GIVING ME HIS OLD ONE.

READ THIS WAY

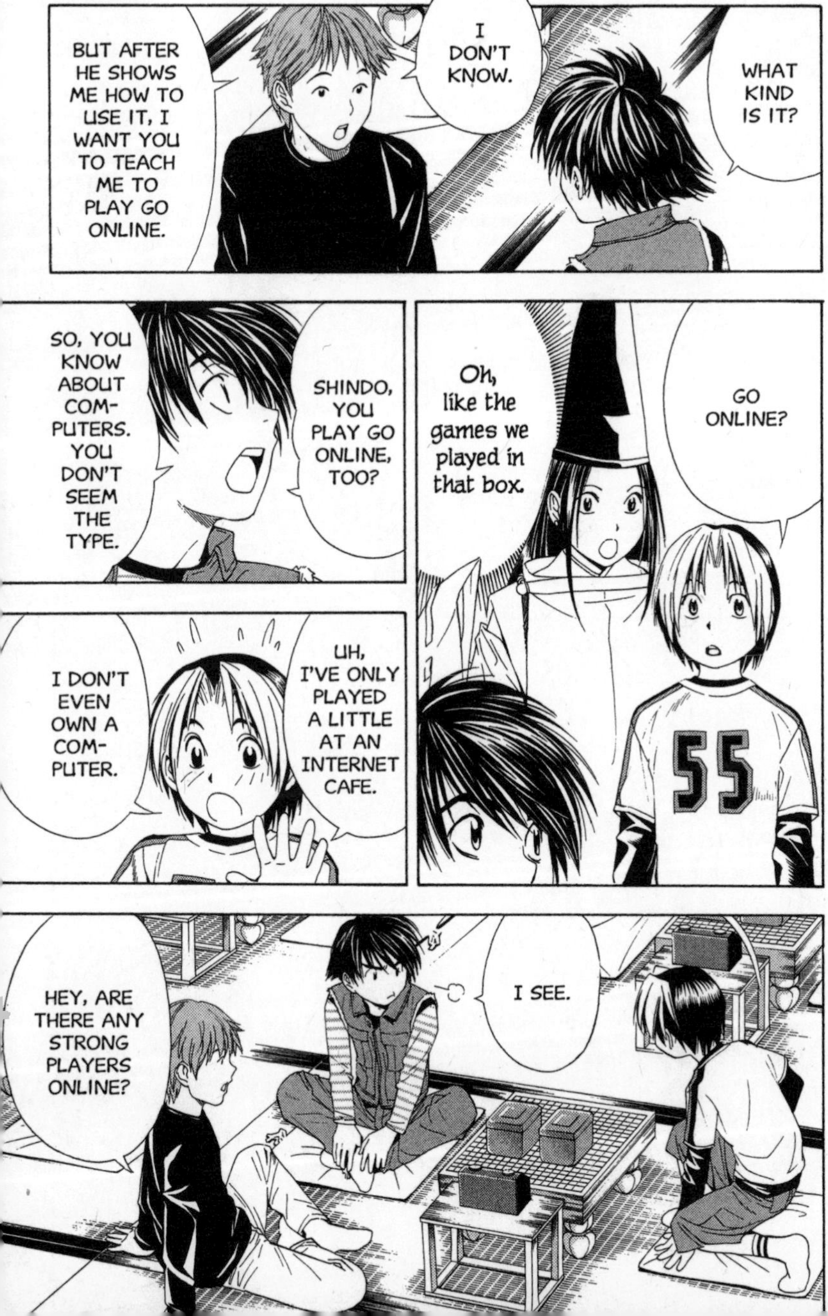
WHAT KIND IS IT?
I DON'T KNOW.
BUT AFTER HE SHOWS ME HOW TO USE IT, I WANT YOU TO TEACH ME TO PLAY GO ONLINE.
GO ONLINE?
Oh, like the games we played in that box.
SHINDO, YOU PLAY GO ONLINE, TOO?
SO, YOU KNOW ABOUT COM-PUTERS. YOU DON'T SEEM THE TYPE.
UH, I'VE ONLY PLAYED A LITTLE AT AN INTERNET CAFE.
I DON'T EVEN OWN A COM-PUTER.
I SEE.
HEY, ARE THERE ANY STRONG PLAYERS ONLINE?

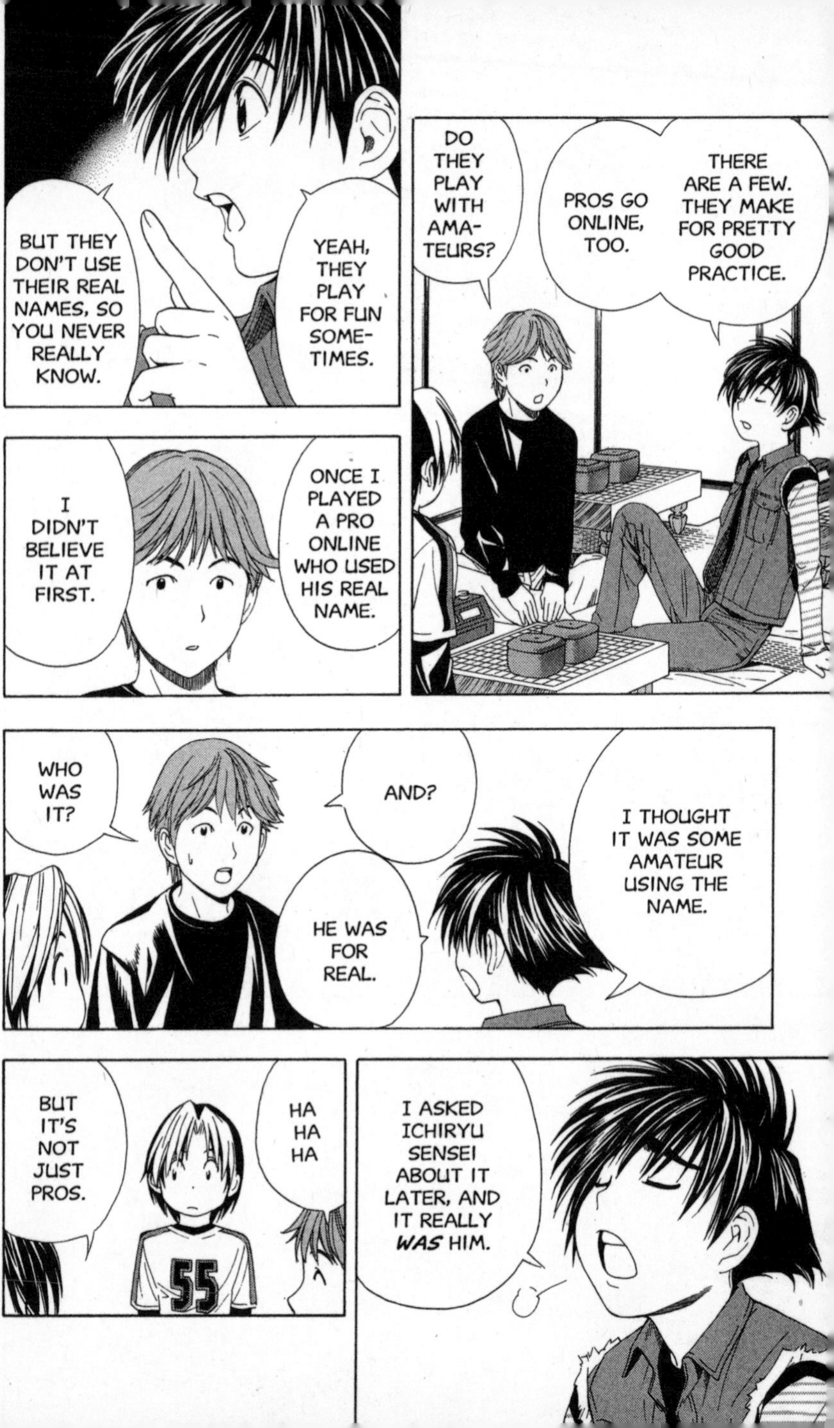
THERE ARE A FEW. THEY MAKE FOR PRETTY GOOD PRACTICE.
PROS GO ONLINE, TOO.
DO THEY PLAY WITH AMA-TEURS?
YEAH, THEY PLAY FOR FUN SOME-TIMES.
BUT THEY DON'T USE THEIR REAL NAMES, SO YOU NEVER REALLY KNOW.
ONCE I PLAYED A PRO ONLINE WHO USED HIS REAL NAME.
I DIDN'T BELIEVE IT AT FIRST.
I THOUGHT IT WAS SOME AMATEUR USING THE NAME.
AND?
HE WAS FOR REAL.
WHO WAS IT?
I ASKED ICHIRYU SENSEI ABOUT IT LATER, AND IT REALLY *WAS* HIM.
HA HA HA
BUT IT'S NOT JUST PROS.

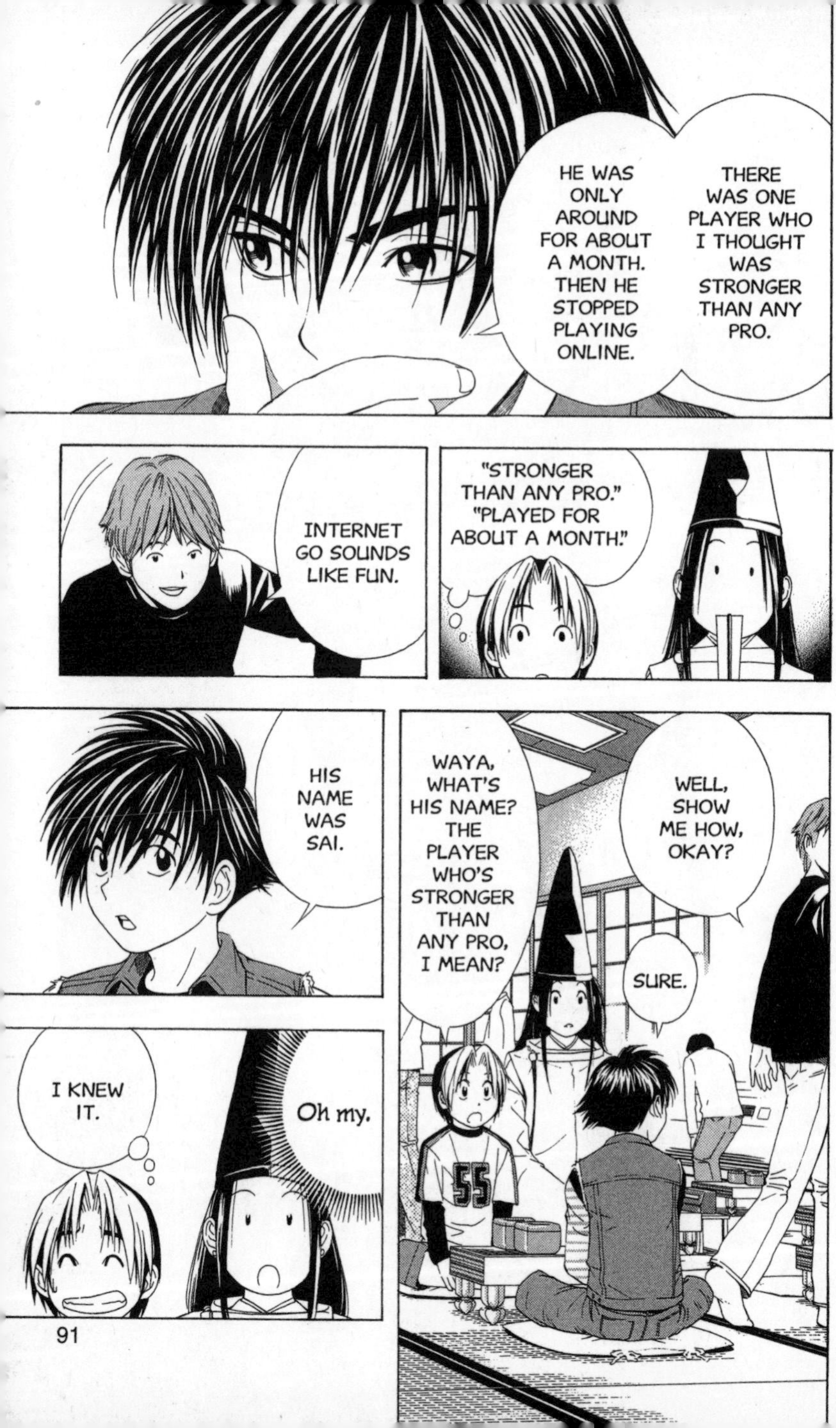
THERE WAS ONE PLAYER WHO I THOUGHT WAS STRONGER THAN ANY PRO.
HE WAS ONLY AROUND FOR ABOUT A MONTH. THEN HE STOPPED PLAYING ONLINE.
"STRONGER THAN ANY PRO." "PLAYED FOR ABOUT A MONTH."
INTERNET GO SOUNDS LIKE FUN.
WELL, SHOW ME HOW, OKAY?
WAYA, WHAT'S HIS NAME? THE PLAYER WHO'S STRONGER THAN ANY PRO, I MEAN?
SURE.
HIS NAME WAS SAI.
Oh my.
I KNEW IT.

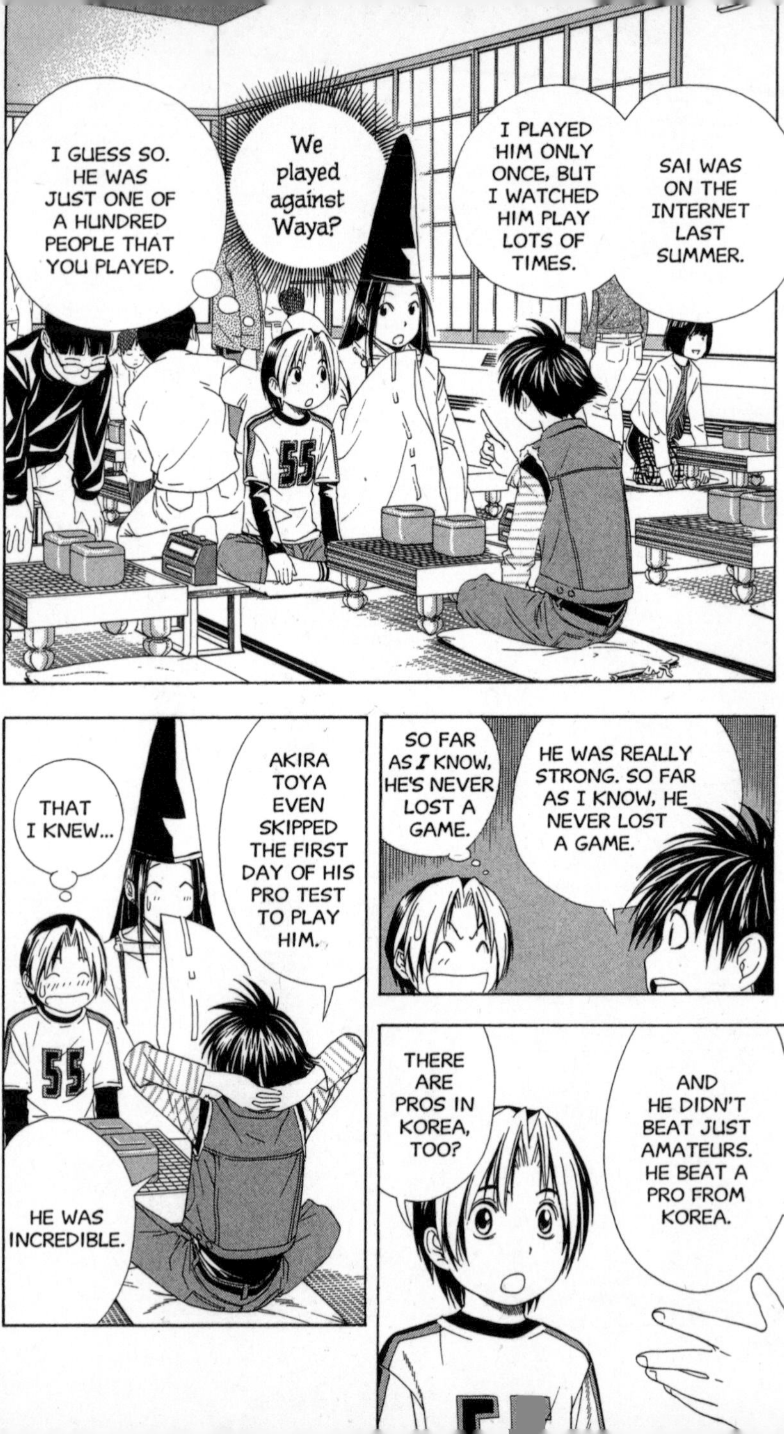
SAI WAS ON THE INTERNET LAST SUMMER.
I PLAYED HIM ONLY ONCE, BUT I WATCHED HIM PLAY LOTS OF TIMES.
We played against Waya?
I GUESS SO. HE WAS JUST ONE OF A HUNDRED PEOPLE THAT YOU PLAYED.
HE WAS REALLY STRONG. SO FAR AS I KNOW, HE NEVER LOST A GAME.
SO FAR AS *I* KNOW, HE'S NEVER LOST A GAME.
AND HE DIDN'T BEAT JUST AMATEURS. HE BEAT A PRO FROM KOREA.
THERE ARE PROS IN KOREA, TOO?
AKIRA TOYA EVEN SKIPPED THE FIRST DAY OF HIS PRO TEST TO PLAY HIM.
THAT I KNEW...
HE WAS INCREDIBLE.

READ THIS WAY

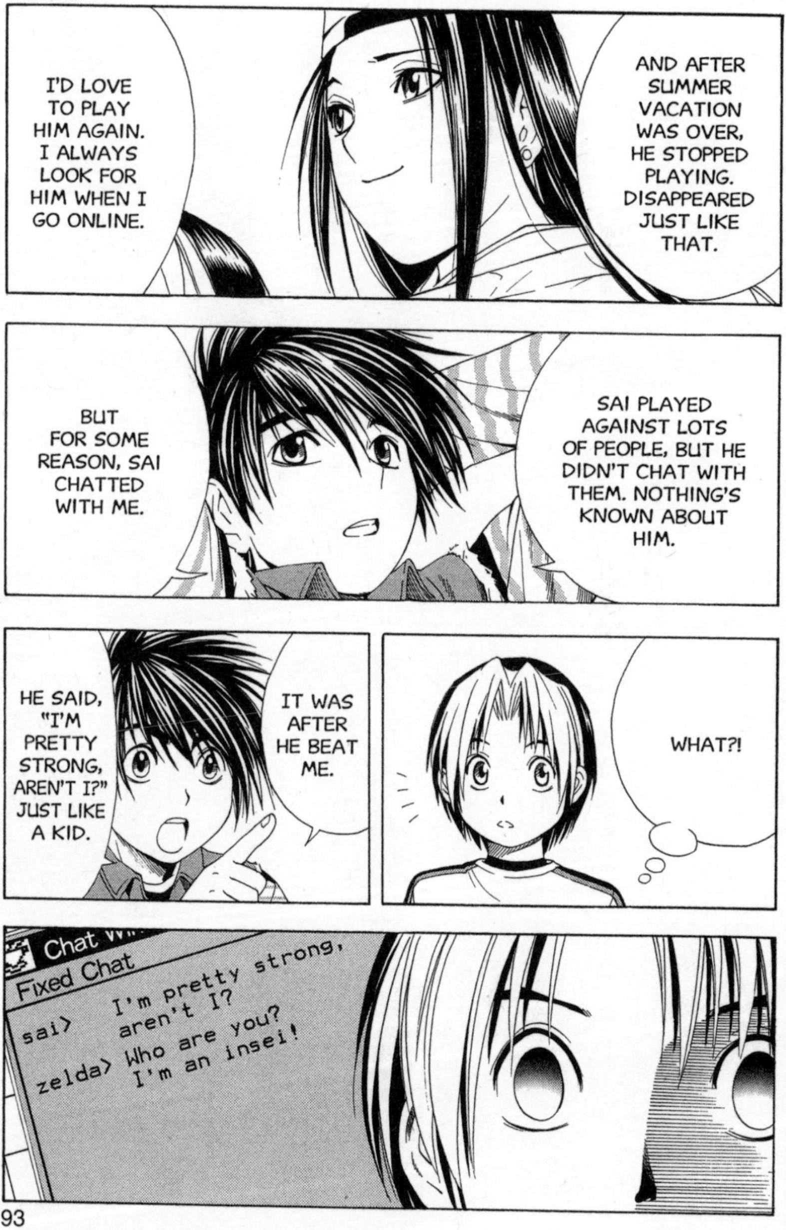
AND AFTER SUMMER VACATION WAS OVER, HE STOPPED PLAYING. DISAPPEARED JUST LIKE THAT.
I'D LOVE TO PLAY HIM AGAIN. I ALWAYS LOOK FOR HIM WHEN I GO ONLINE.
SAI PLAYED AGAINST LOTS OF PEOPLE, BUT HE DIDN'T CHAT WITH THEM. NOTHING'S KNOWN ABOUT HIM.
BUT FOR SOME REASON, SAI CHATTED WITH ME.
WHAT?!
IT WAS AFTER HE BEAT ME.
HE SAID, "I'M PRETTY STRONG, AREN'T I?" JUST LIKE A KID.
Fixed Chat
sai> I'm pretty strong, aren't I?
zelda> Who are you? I'm an insei!

WAYA! *YOU'RE* ZELDA?!

THEN YOU SAID, "I'M AN INSEI"!!

Hikaru!

OOPS!

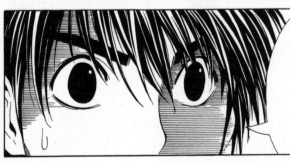

HOW DO YOU KNOW WHAT SAI AND I SAID TO EACH OTHER?

READ THIS WAY

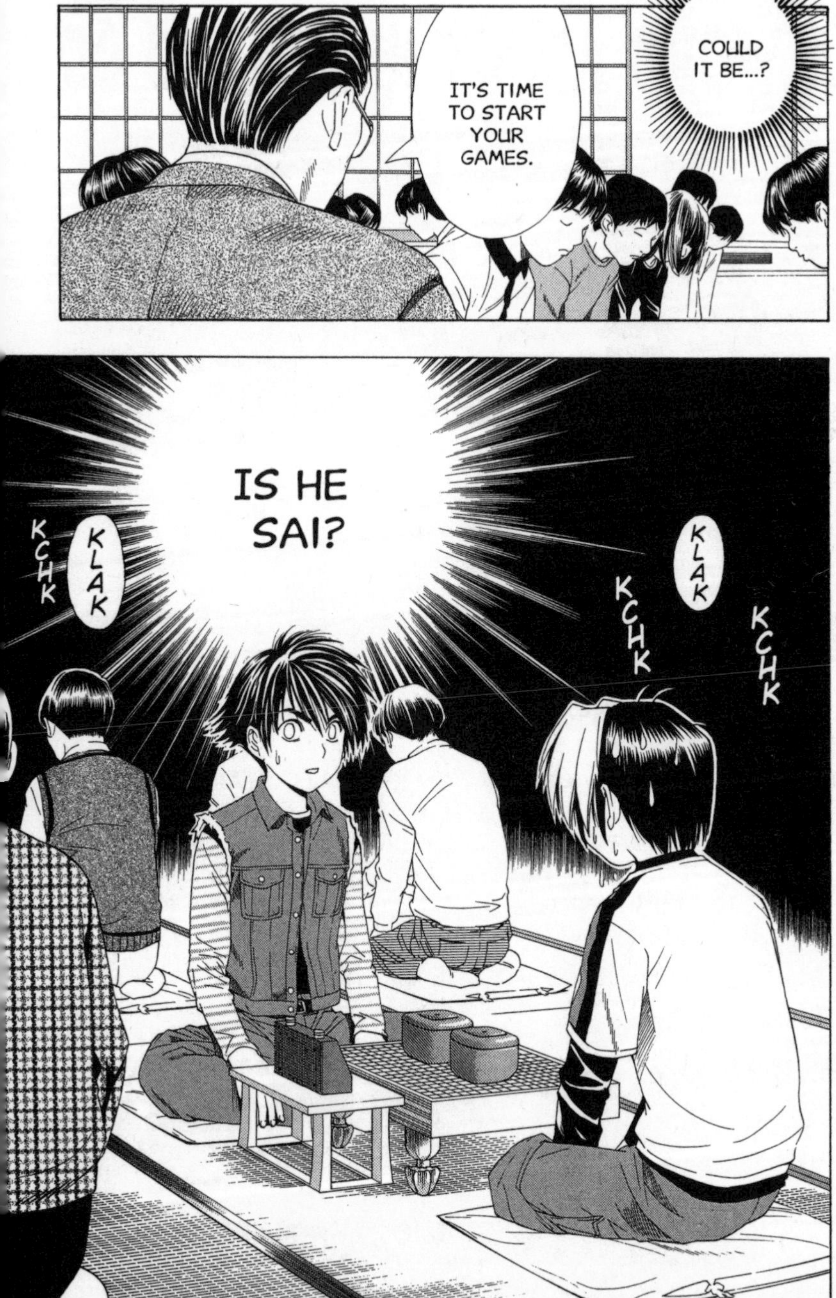
COULD IT BE...?
IT'S TIME TO START YOUR GAMES.
IS HE SAI?
KCHK
KLAK
KCHK
KLAK
KCHK

# A WORD ABOUT HIKARU NO GO

## FOREIGN TRANSLATIONS OF THE MANGA

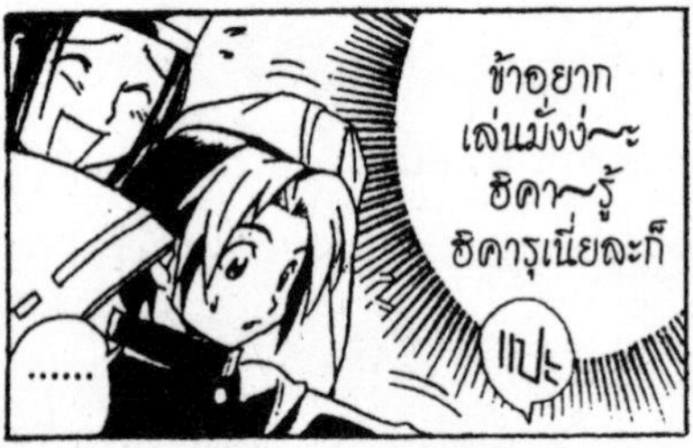
ข้าอยาก
เล่นมั่งง่~ะ
ฮิคา~รู้
ฮิคารุเนี่ยละก็
แปะ
......

THAI VERSION

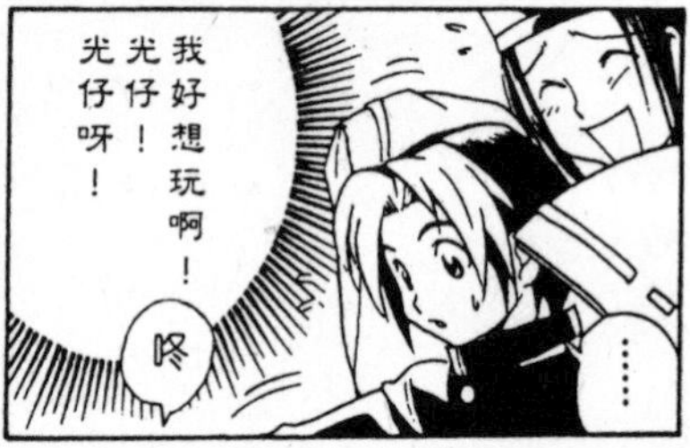
我好想玩啊！
光仔！
光仔呀！
咚
......

HONG KONG VERSION

TAIWAN, THAILAND, HONG KONG, SINGAPORE, KOREA...

IN TAIWAN, *HIKARU NO GO* IS CALLED *GO PLAYER SPIRIT KING*, WHILE IN HONG KONG IT'S *GO PLAYER SPIRIT*. THE THAI VERSION READS FROM RIGHT TO LEFT, AND THE HONG KONG VERSION INCLUDES ARTICLES ABOUT THE HONG KONG GO ASSOCIATION.

IT'S FUN SEEING ALL THE DIFFERENT TRANSLATIONS.

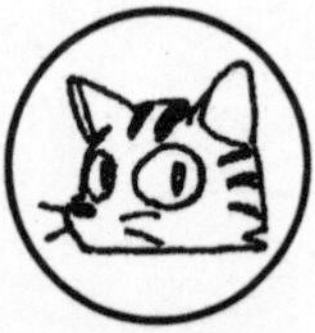

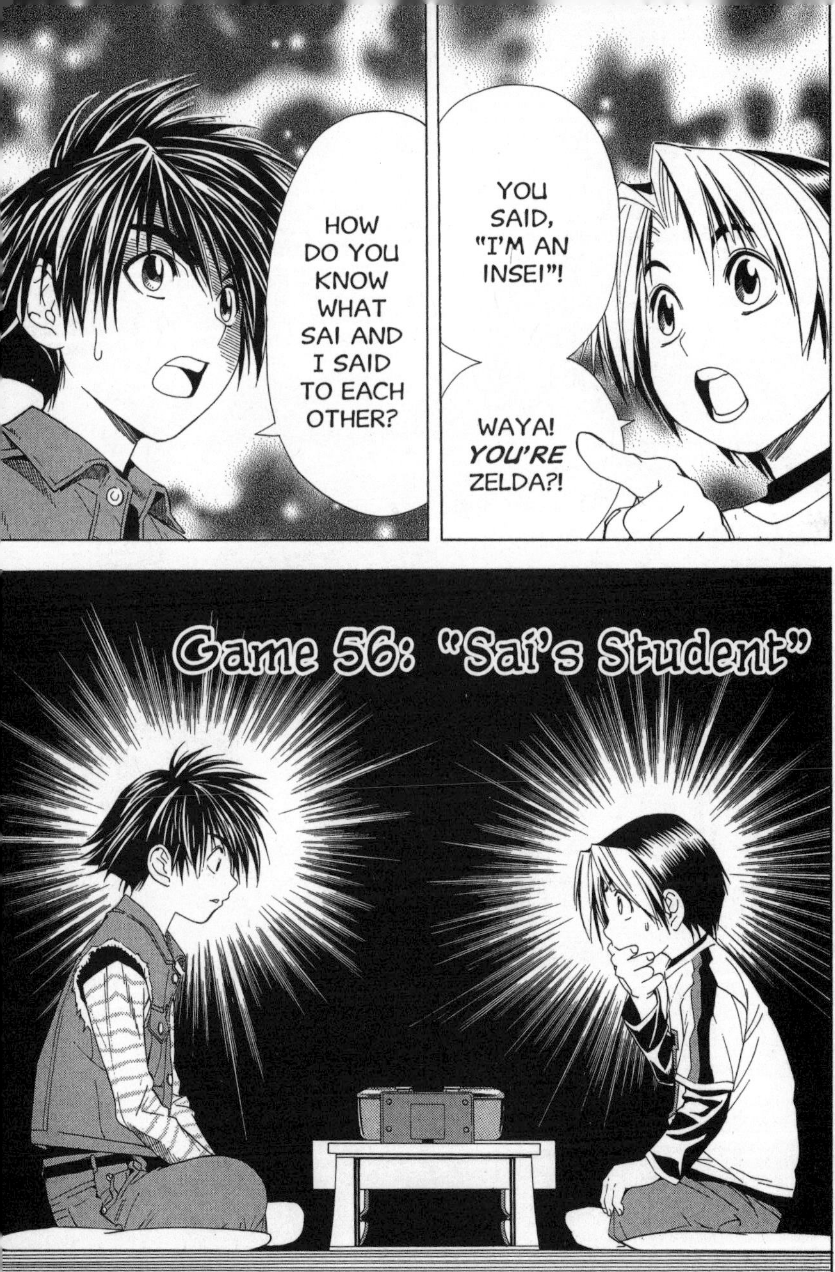
YOU SAID, "I'M AN INSEI"!
WAYA! *YOU'RE* ZELDA?!
HOW DO YOU KNOW WHAT SAI AND I SAID TO EACH OTHER?
Game 56: "Sai's Student"

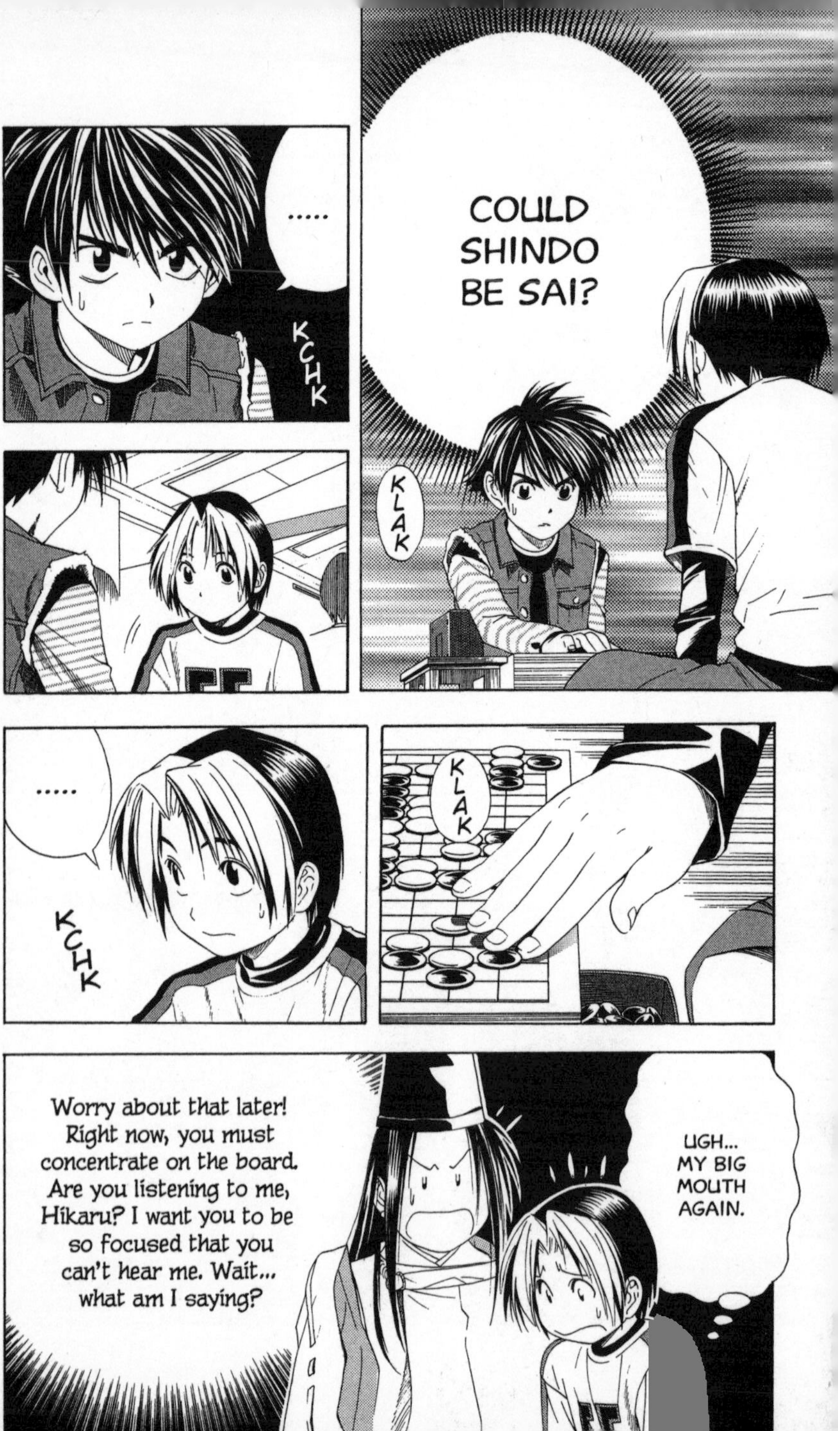
COULD SHINDO BE SAI?
KLAK
.....
KCHK
KLAK
.....
KCHK
UGH... MY BIG MOUTH AGAIN.
Worry about that later! Right now, you must concentrate on the board. Are you listening to me, Hikaru? I want you to be so focused that you can't hear me. Wait... what am I saying?

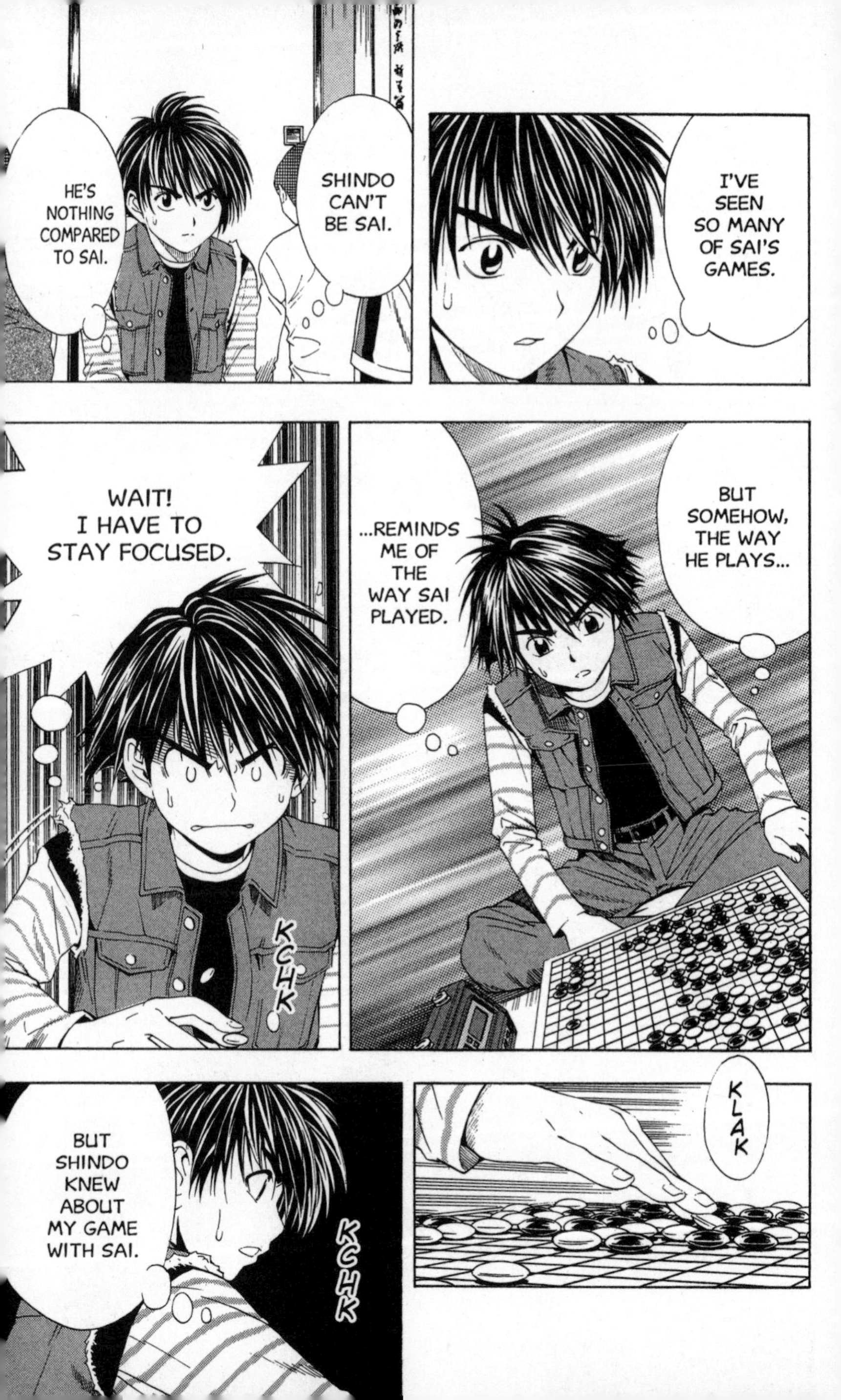
I'VE SEEN SO MANY OF SAI'S GAMES.
SHINDO CAN'T BE SAI.
HE'S NOTHING COMPARED TO SAI.
BUT SOMEHOW, THE WAY HE PLAYS...
...REMINDS ME OF THE WAY SAI PLAYED.
WAIT! I HAVE TO STAY FOCUSED.
KCHK
KLAK
BUT SHINDO KNEW ABOUT MY GAME WITH SAI.
KCHK

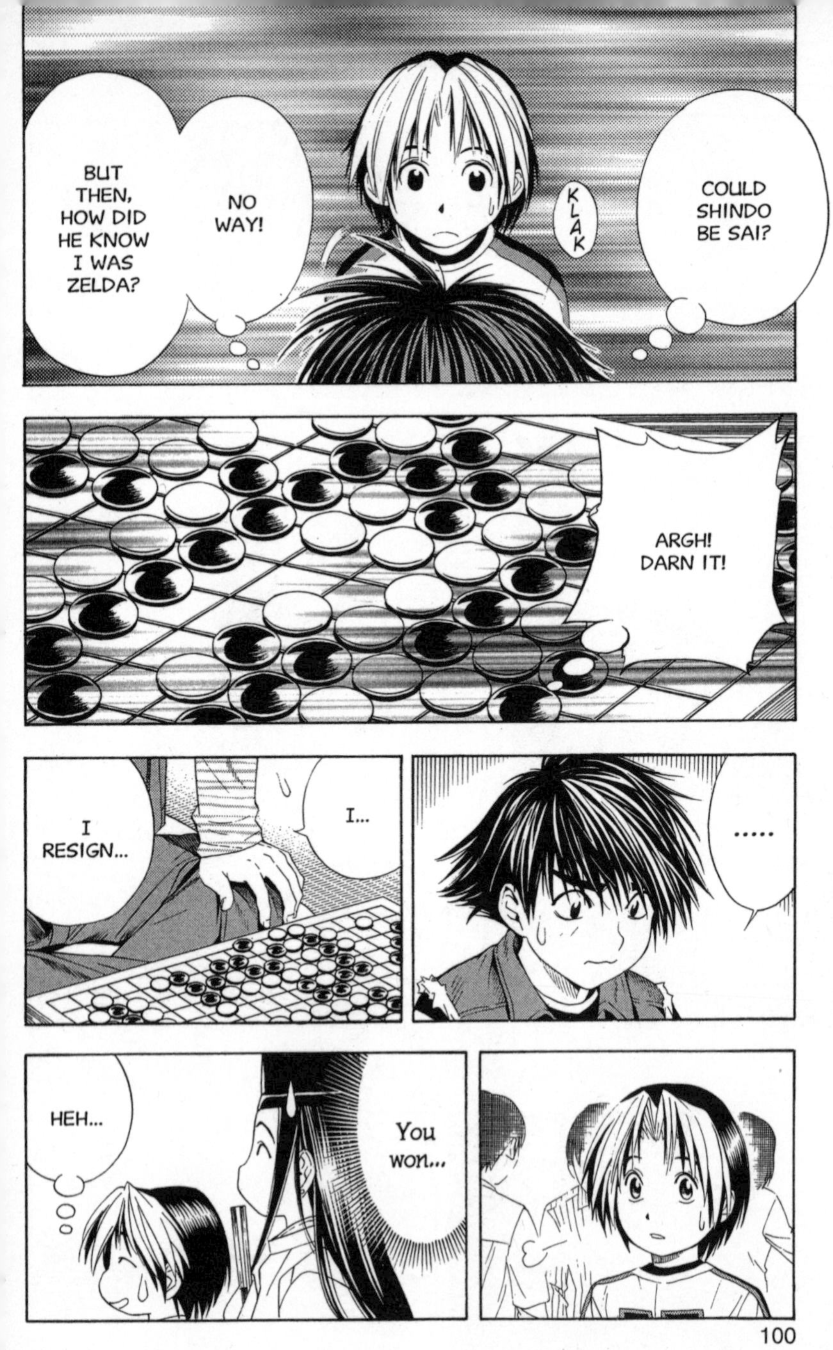
COULD SHINDO BE SAI?
KLAK
NO WAY!
BUT THEN, HOW DID HE KNOW I WAS ZELDA?
ARGH! DARN IT!
.....
I...
I RESIGN...
You won...
HEH...

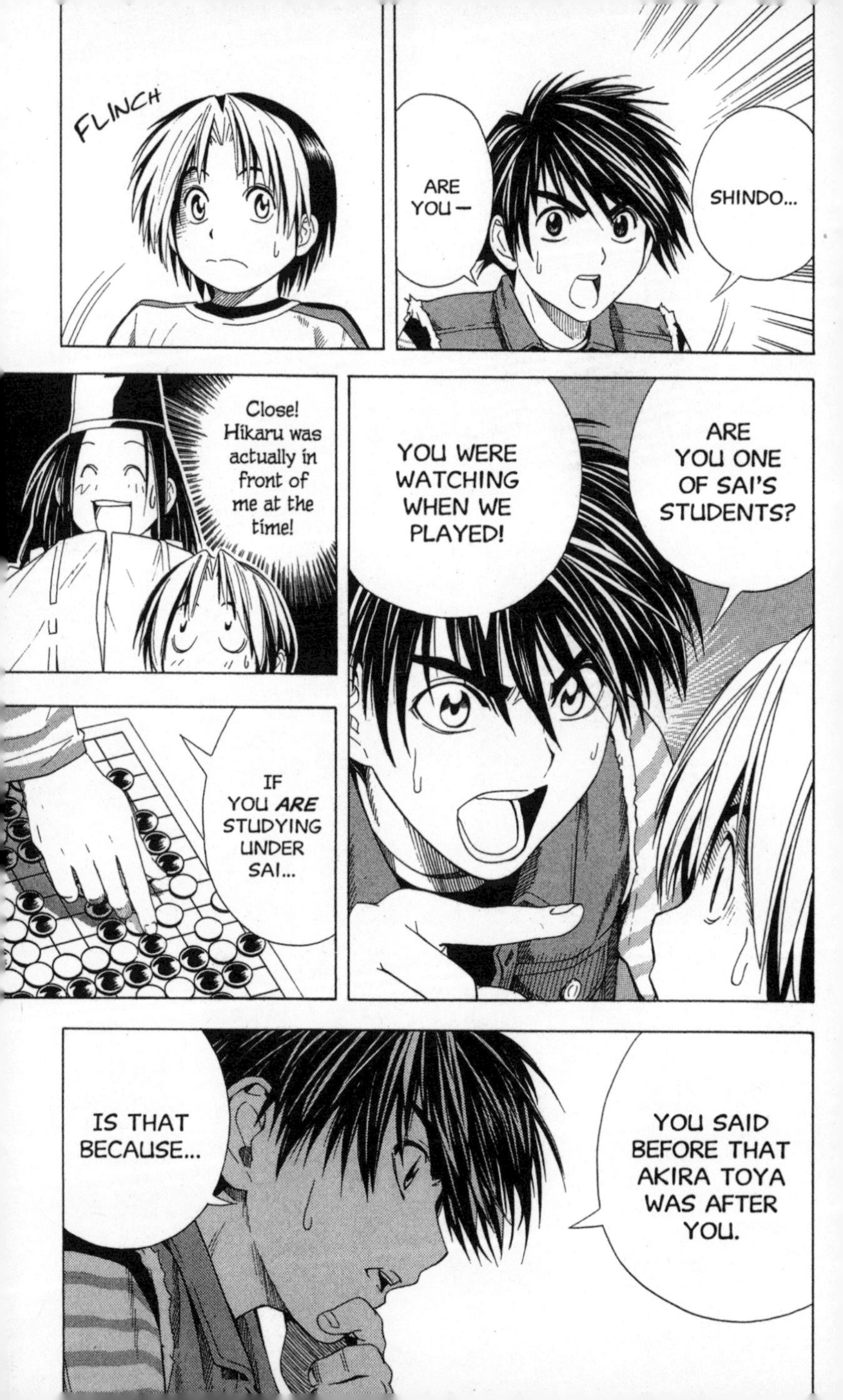
SHINDO...
ARE YOU—
FLINCH
ARE YOU ONE OF SAI'S STUDENTS?
YOU WERE WATCHING WHEN WE PLAYED!
Close! Hikaru was actually in front of me at the time!
IF YOU *ARE* STUDYING UNDER SAI...
YOU SAID BEFORE THAT AKIRA TOYA WAS AFTER YOU.
IS THAT BECAUSE...

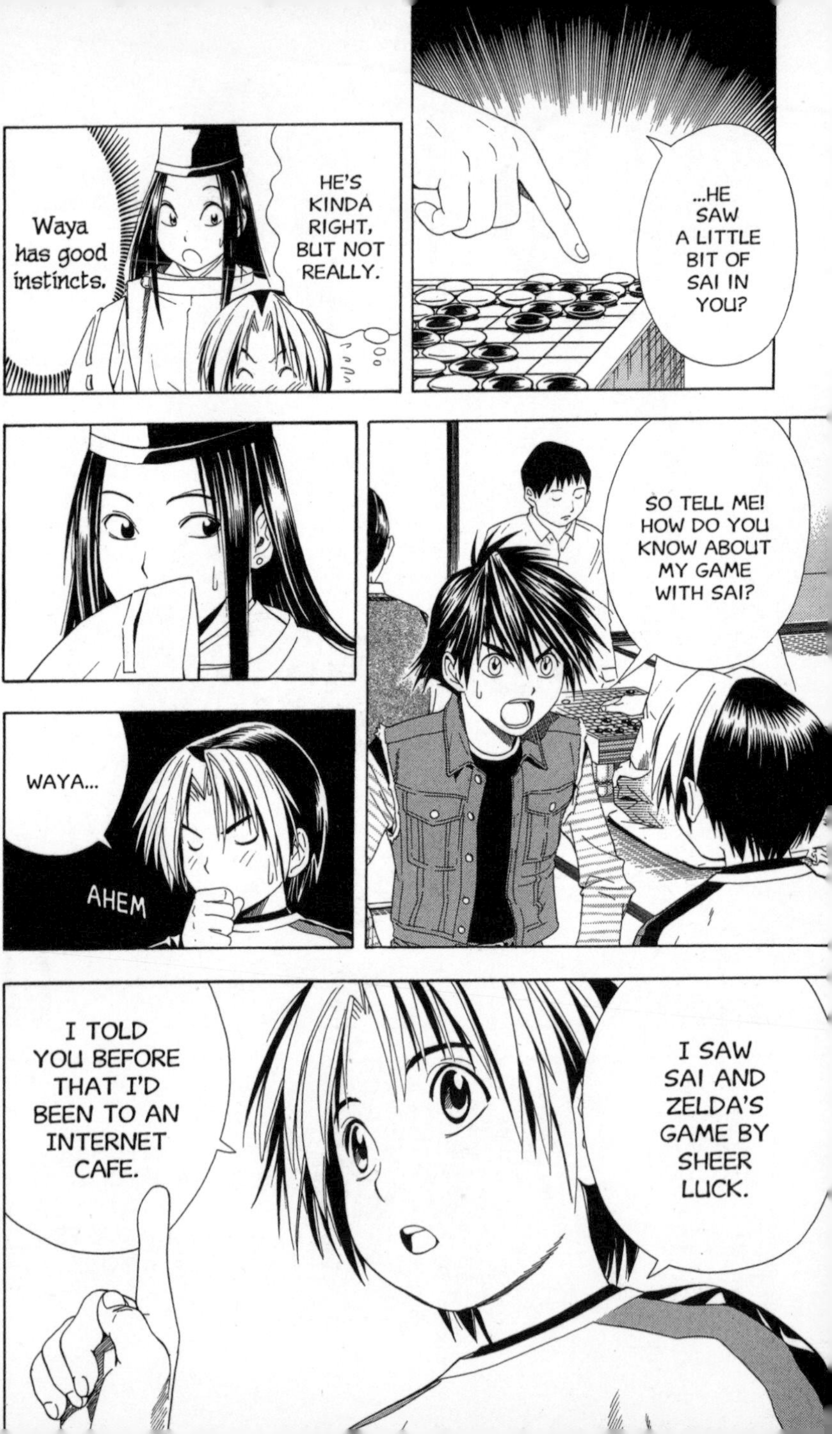
...HE SAW A LITTLE BIT OF SAI IN YOU?
HE'S KINDA RIGHT, BUT NOT REALLY.
Waya has good instincts.
SO TELL ME! HOW DO YOU KNOW ABOUT MY GAME WITH SAI?
WAYA...
AHEM
I SAW SAI AND ZELDA'S GAME BY SHEER LUCK.
I TOLD YOU BEFORE THAT I'D BEEN TO AN INTERNET CAFE.

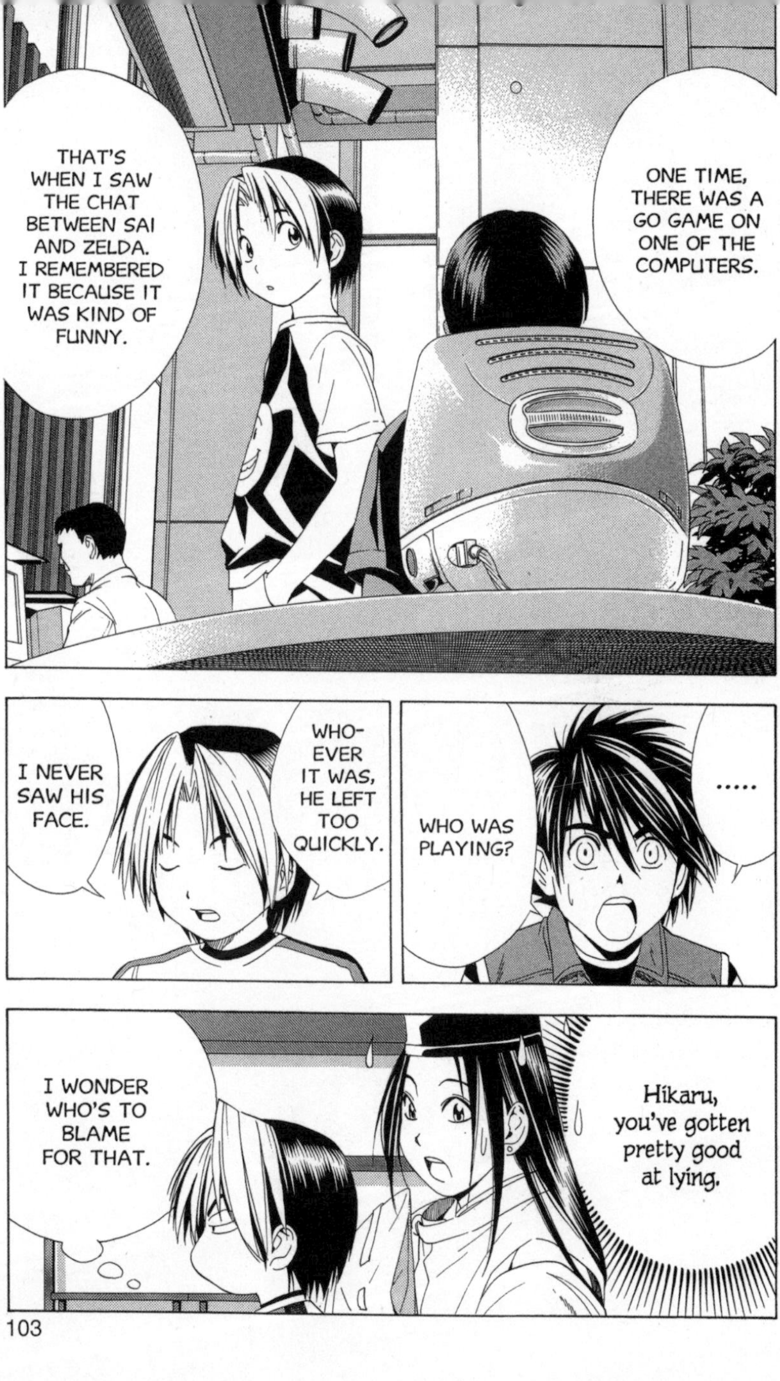
ONE TIME, THERE WAS A GO GAME ON ONE OF THE COMPUTERS.
THAT'S WHEN I SAW THE CHAT BETWEEN SAI AND ZELDA. I REMEMBERED IT BECAUSE IT WAS KIND OF FUNNY.
.....
WHO WAS PLAYING?
WHO-EVER IT WAS, HE LEFT TOO QUICKLY.
I NEVER SAW HIS FACE.
Hikaru, you've gotten pretty good at lying.
I WONDER WHO'S TO BLAME FOR THAT.

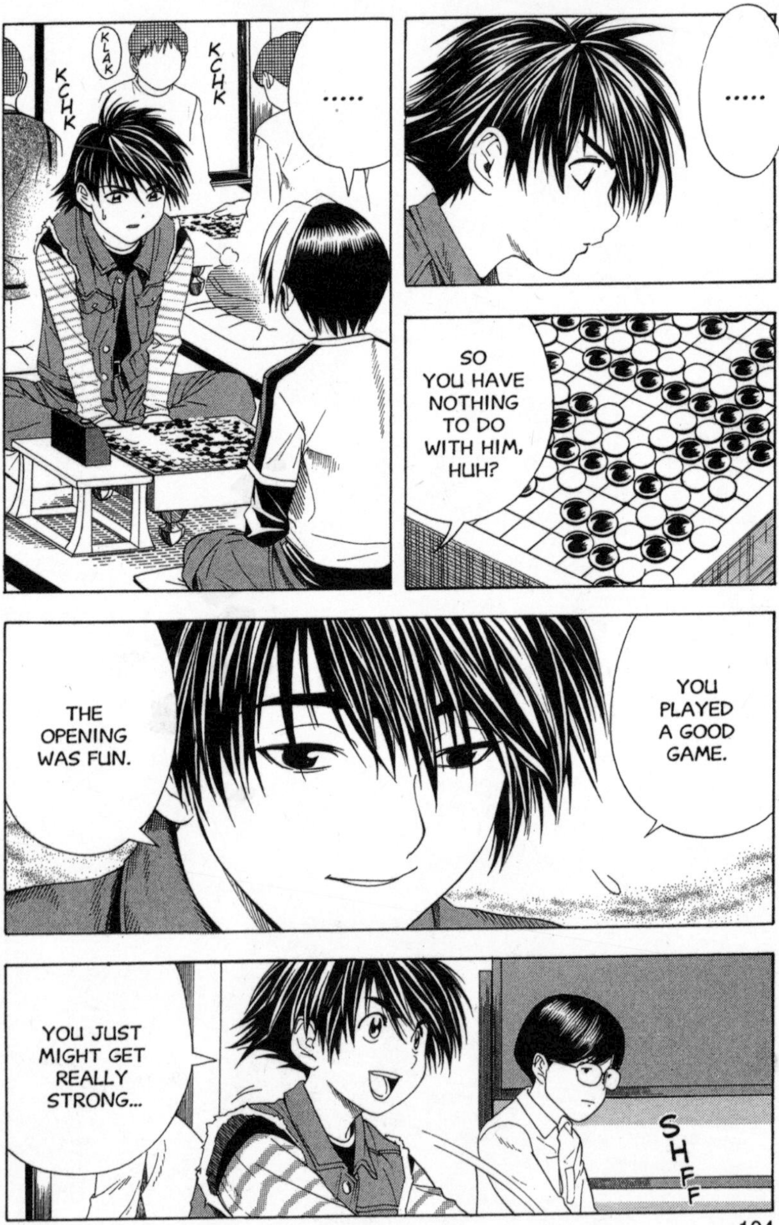
.....
SO YOU HAVE NOTHING TO DO WITH HIM, HUH?
.....
KCHK
KLAK
KCHK
YOU PLAYED A GOOD GAME.
THE OPENING WAS FUN.
SHFF
YOU JUST MIGHT GET REALLY STRONG...

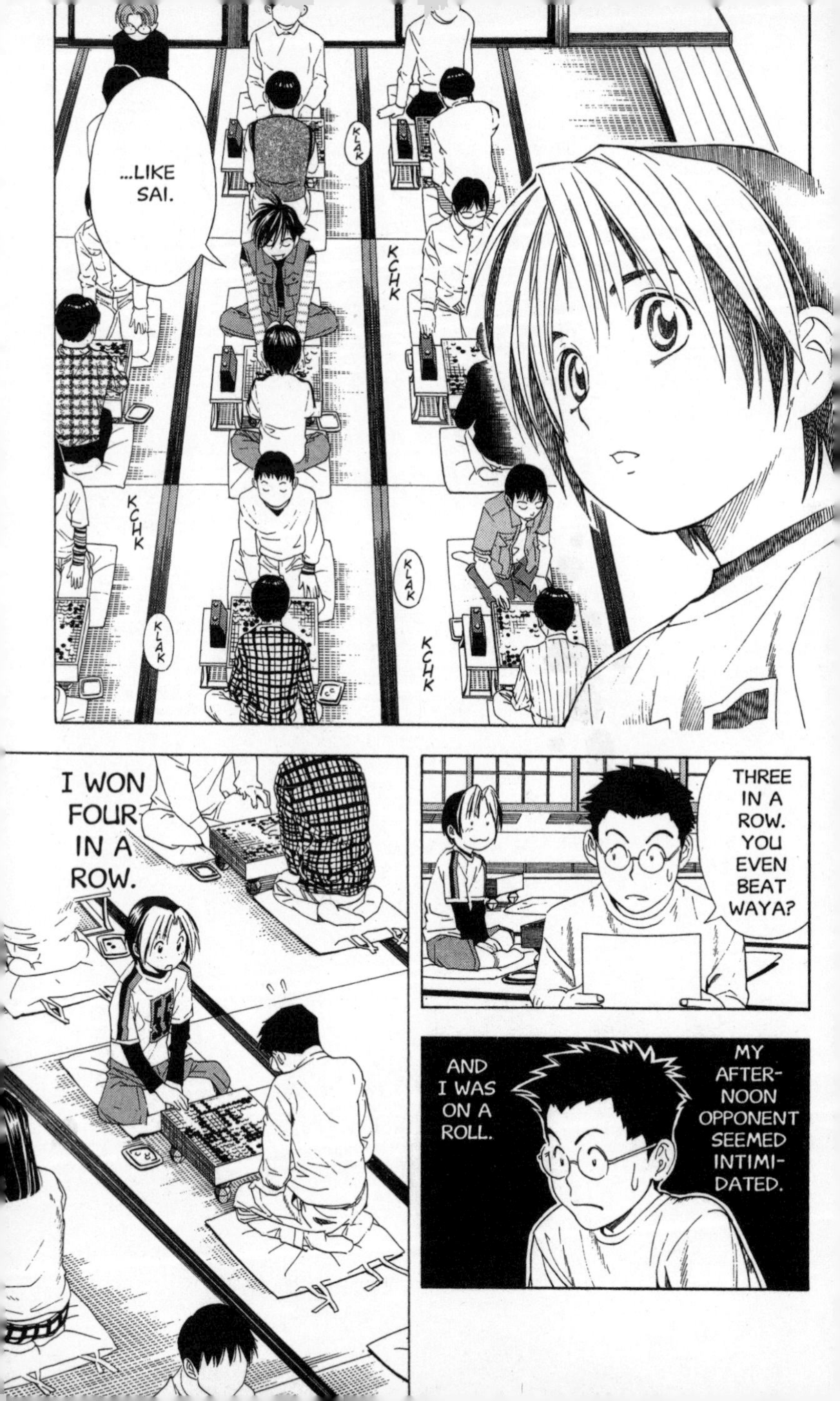
KLAK
...LIKE SAI.
KCHK
KLAK
KCHK
KCHK
KLAK
THREE IN A ROW. YOU EVEN BEAT WAYA?
MY AFTER-NOON OPPONENT SEEMED INTIMI-DATED.
AND I WAS ON A ROLL.
I WON FOUR IN A ROW.

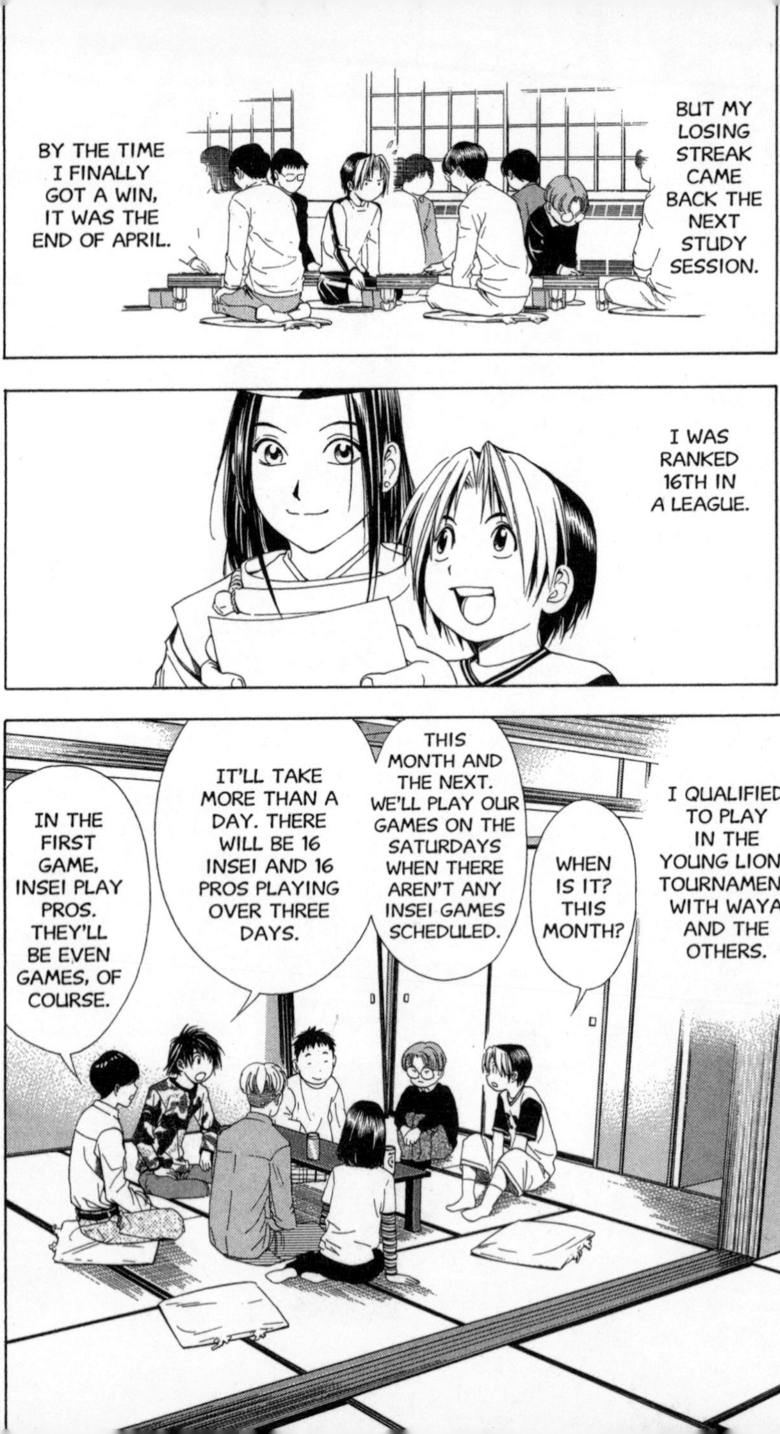
BY THE TIME I FINALLY GOT A WIN, IT WAS THE END OF APRIL.
BUT MY LOSING STREAK CAME BACK THE NEXT STUDY SESSION.
I WAS RANKED 16TH IN A LEAGUE.
I QUALIFIED TO PLAY IN THE YOUNG LIONS TOURNAMENT WITH WAYA AND THE OTHERS.
WHEN IS IT? THIS MONTH?
THIS MONTH AND THE NEXT. WE'LL PLAY OUR GAMES ON THE SATURDAYS WHEN THERE AREN'T ANY INSEI GAMES SCHEDULED.
IT'LL TAKE MORE THAN A DAY. THERE WILL BE 16 INSEI AND 16 PROS PLAYING OVER THREE DAYS.
IN THE FIRST GAME, INSEI PLAY PROS. THEY'LL BE EVEN GAMES, OF COURSE.

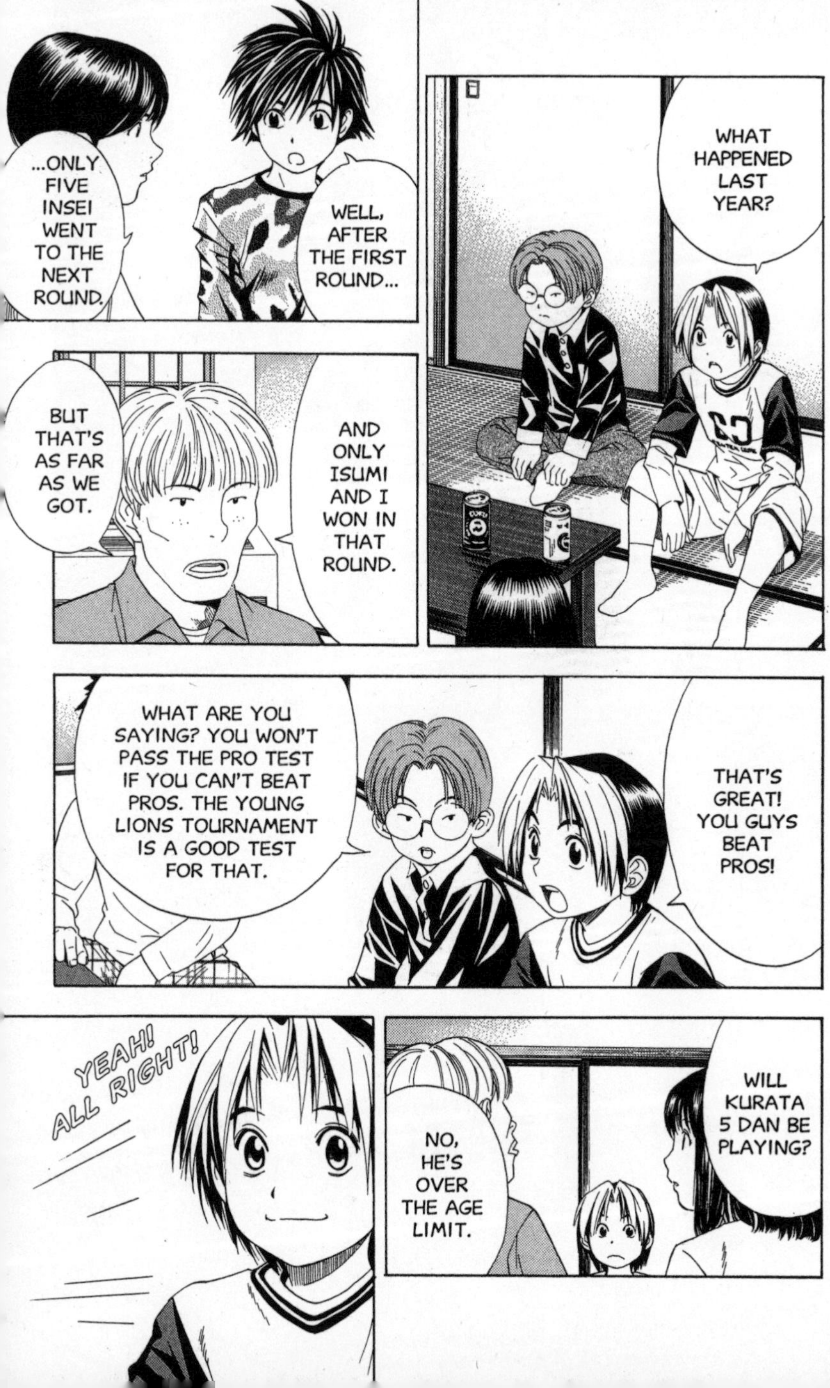
WHAT HAPPENED LAST YEAR?
WELL, AFTER THE FIRST ROUND...
...ONLY FIVE INSEI WENT TO THE NEXT ROUND.
AND ONLY ISUMI AND I WON IN THAT ROUND.
BUT THAT'S AS FAR AS WE GOT.
THAT'S GREAT! YOU GUYS BEAT PROS!
WHAT ARE YOU SAYING? YOU WON'T PASS THE PRO TEST IF YOU CAN'T BEAT PROS. THE YOUNG LIONS TOURNAMENT IS A GOOD TEST FOR THAT.
WILL KURATA 5 DAN BE PLAYING?
NO, HE'S OVER THE AGE LIMIT.
YEAH! ALL RIGHT!

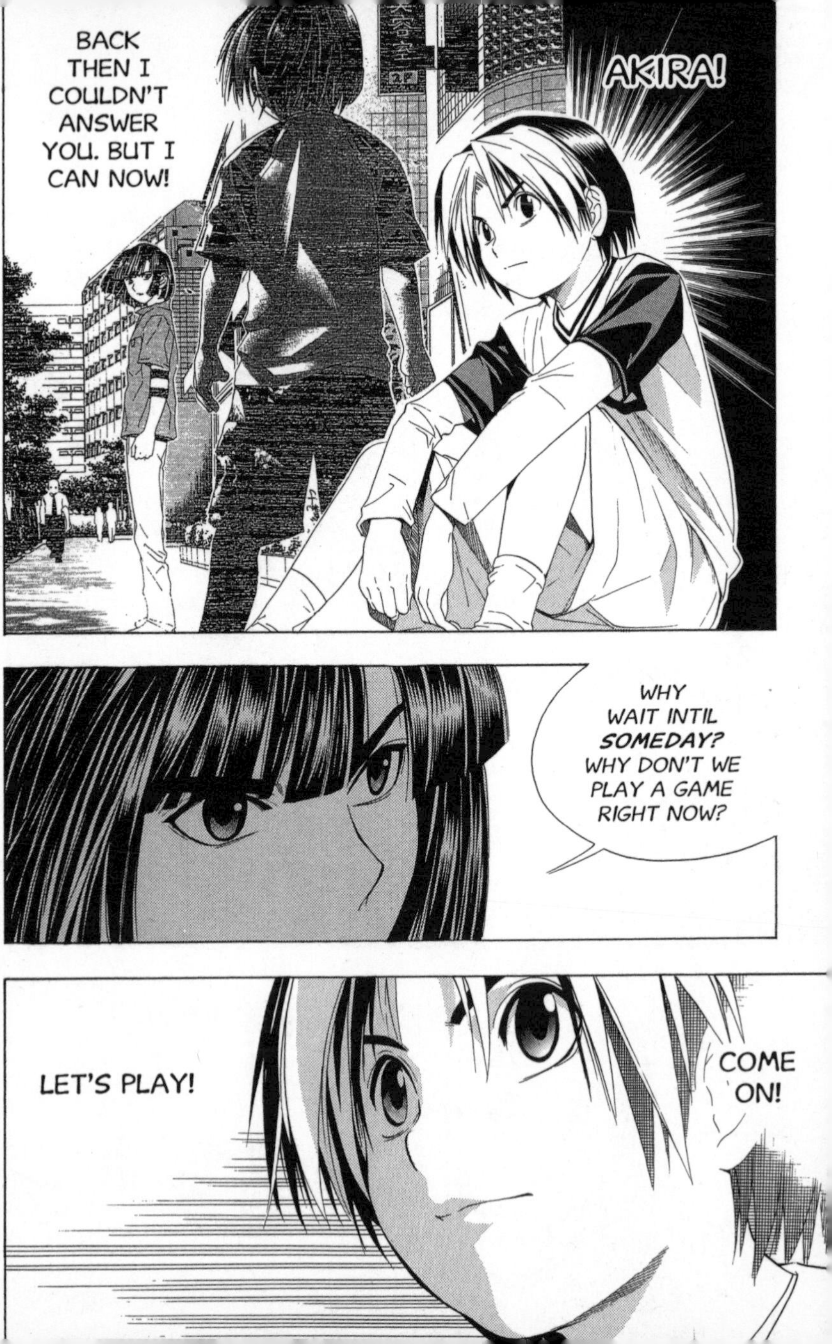
AKIRA!
BACK THEN I COULDN'T ANSWER YOU. BUT I CAN NOW!
WHY WAIT INTIL SOMEDAY? WHY DON'T WE PLAY A GAME RIGHT NOW?
COME ON!
LET'S PLAY!

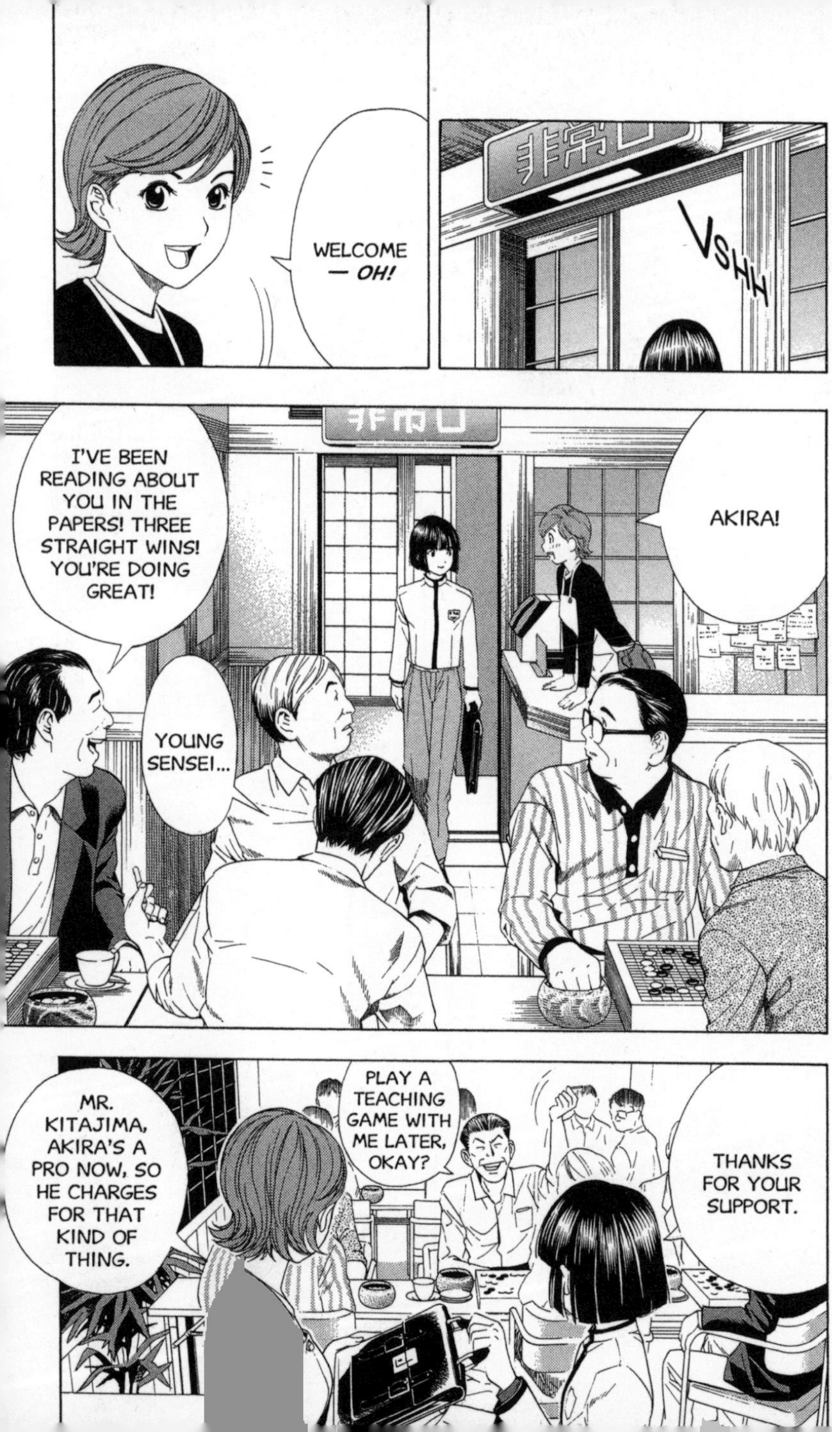
非常口
VSHH
WELCOME — OH!
AKIRA!
I'VE BEEN READING ABOUT YOU IN THE PAPERS! THREE STRAIGHT WINS! YOU'RE DOING GREAT!
YOUNG SENSEI...
THANKS FOR YOUR SUPPORT.
PLAY A TEACHING GAME WITH ME LATER, OKAY?
MR. KITAJIMA, AKIRA'S A PRO NOW, SO HE CHARGES FOR THAT KIND OF THING.

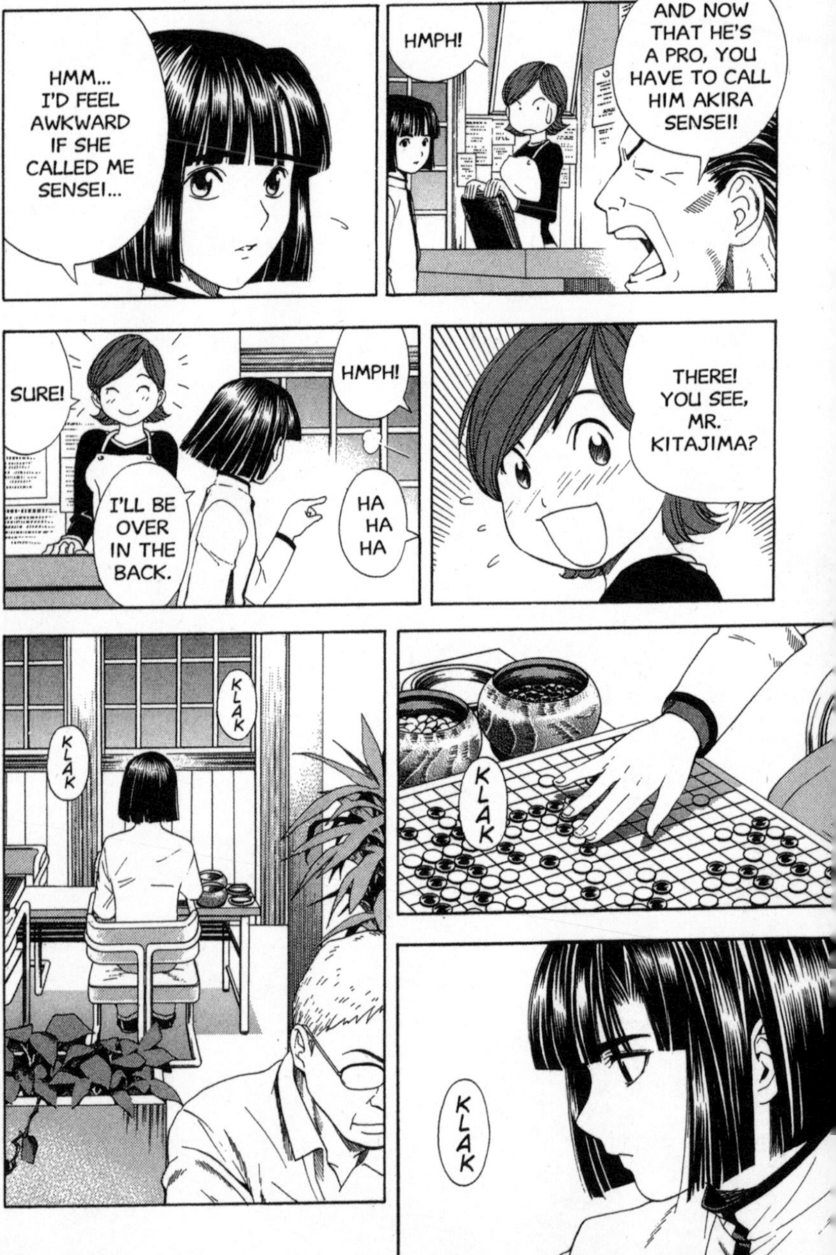
AND NOW THAT HE'S A PRO, YOU HAVE TO CALL HIM AKIRA SENSEI!
HMPH!
HMM... I'D FEEL AWKWARD IF SHE CALLED ME SENSEI...
THERE! YOU SEE, MR. KITAJIMA?
HMPH!
HA HA HA
SURE!
I'LL BE OVER IN THE BACK.
KLAK
KLAK
KLAK
KLAK

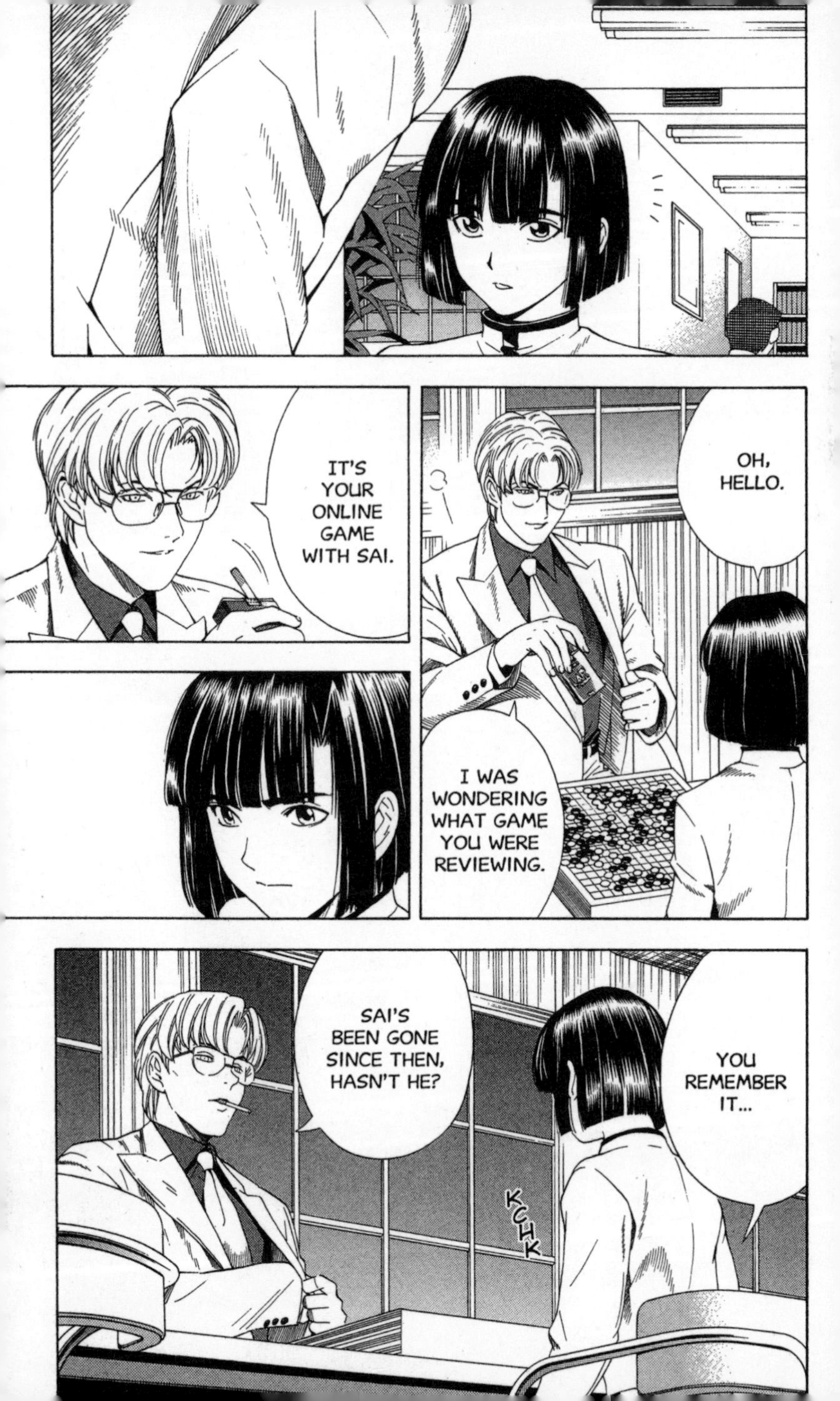
OH, HELLO.
I WAS WONDERING WHAT GAME YOU WERE REVIEWING.
IT'S YOUR ONLINE GAME WITH SAI.
YOU REMEMBER IT...
KCHK
SAI'S BEEN GONE SINCE THEN, HASN'T HE?

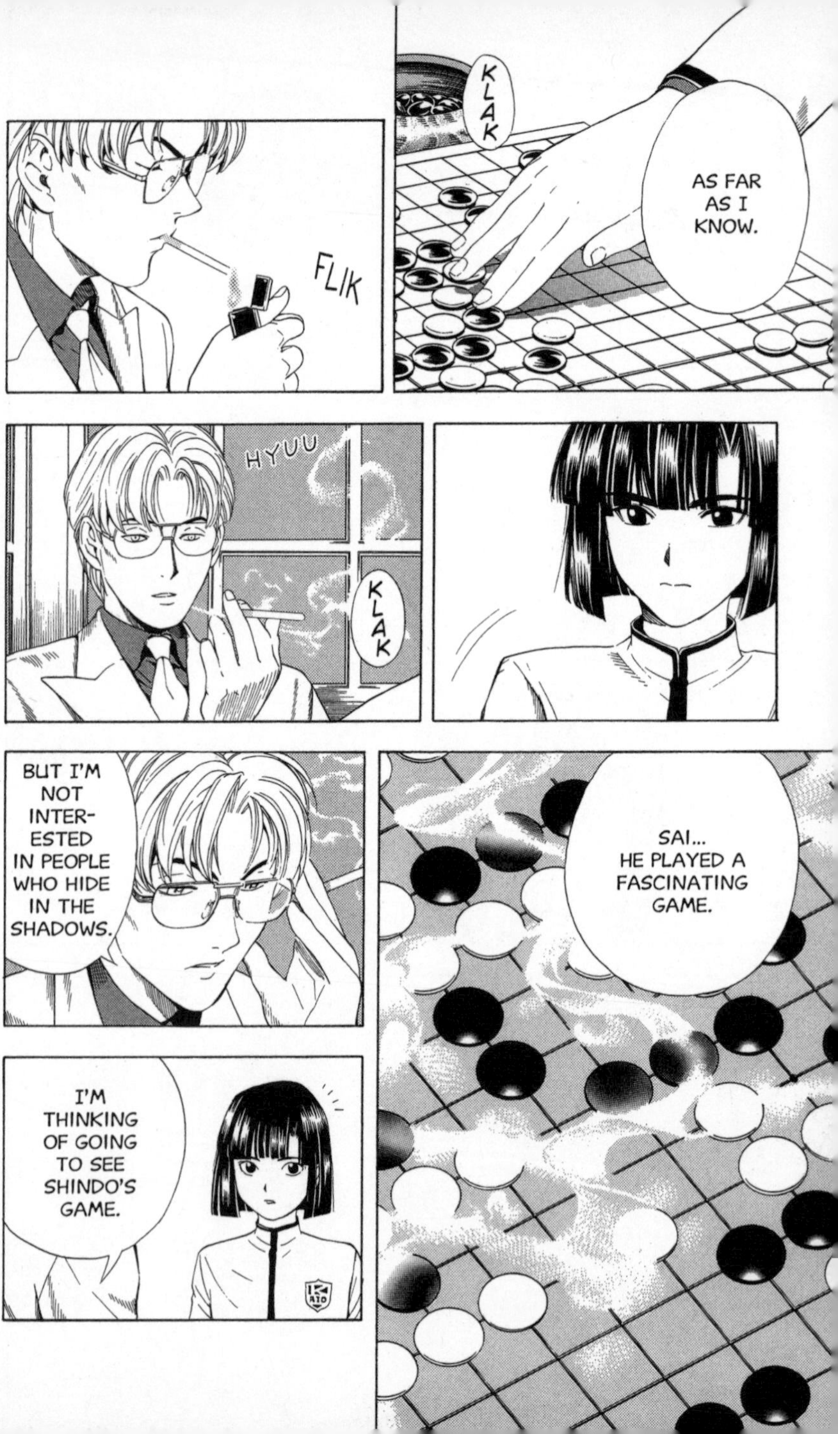
KLAK
AS FAR AS I KNOW.
FLIK
KLAK
HYUU
SAI... HE PLAYED A FASCINATING GAME.
BUT I'M NOT INTER-ESTED IN PEOPLE WHO HIDE IN THE SHADOWS.
I'M THINKING OF GOING TO SEE SHINDO'S GAME.

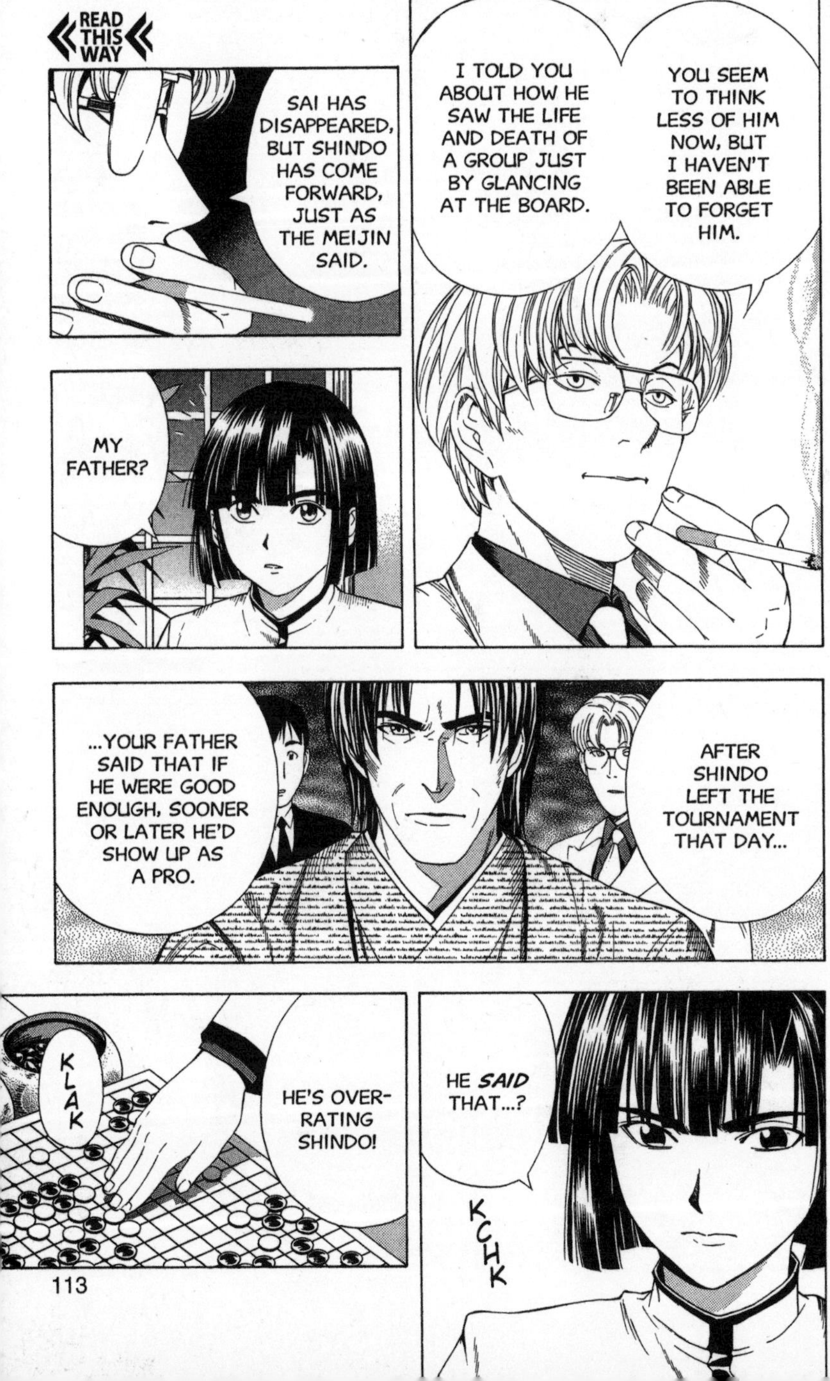
READ THIS WAY
YOU SEEM TO THINK LESS OF HIM NOW, BUT I HAVEN'T BEEN ABLE TO FORGET HIM.
I TOLD YOU ABOUT HOW HE SAW THE LIFE AND DEATH OF A GROUP JUST BY GLANCING AT THE BOARD.
SAI HAS DISAPPEARED, BUT SHINDO HAS COME FORWARD, JUST AS THE MEIJIN SAID.
MY FATHER?
AFTER SHINDO LEFT THE TOURNAMENT THAT DAY...
...YOUR FATHER SAID THAT IF HE WERE GOOD ENOUGH, SOONER OR LATER HE'D SHOW UP AS A PRO.
HE *SAID* THAT...?
KCHK
HE'S OVER-RATING SHINDO!
KLAK

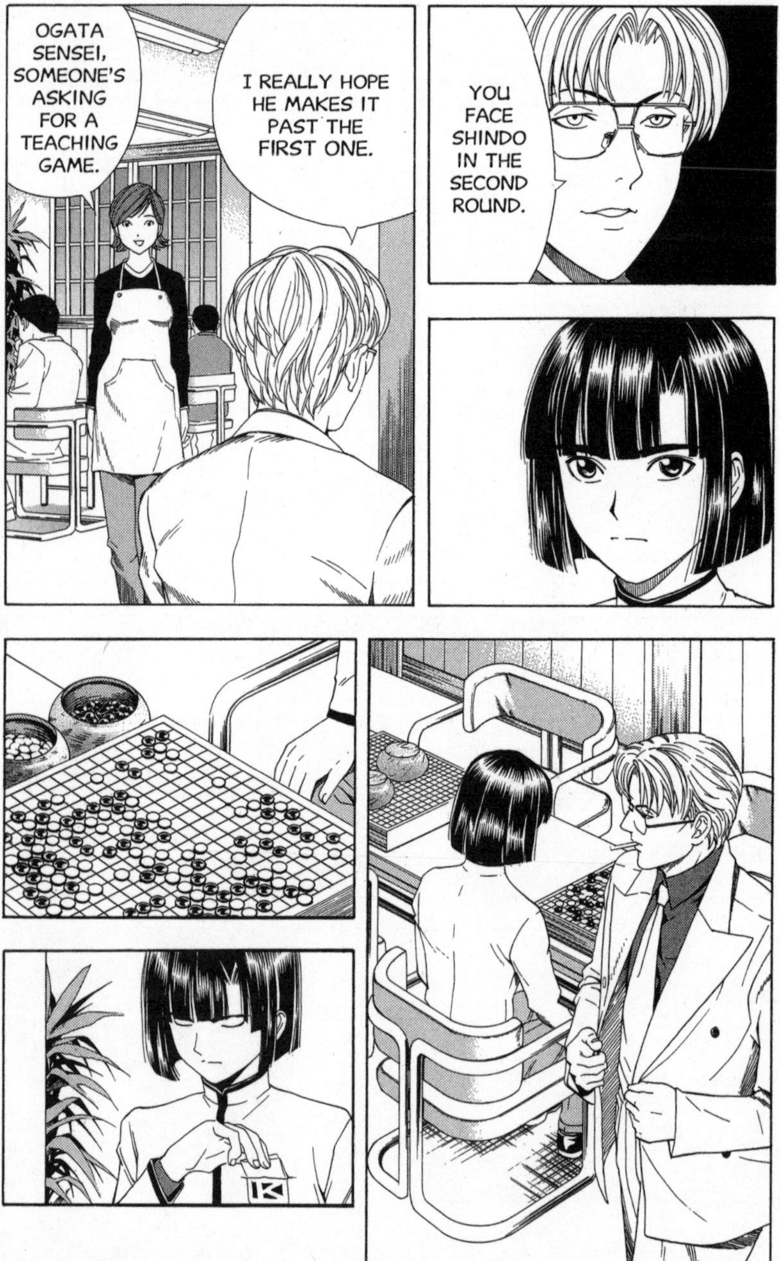
YOU FACE SHINDO IN THE SECOND ROUND.
I REALLY HOPE HE MAKES IT PAST THE FIRST ONE.
OGATA SENSEI, SOMEONE'S ASKING FOR A TEACHING GAME.

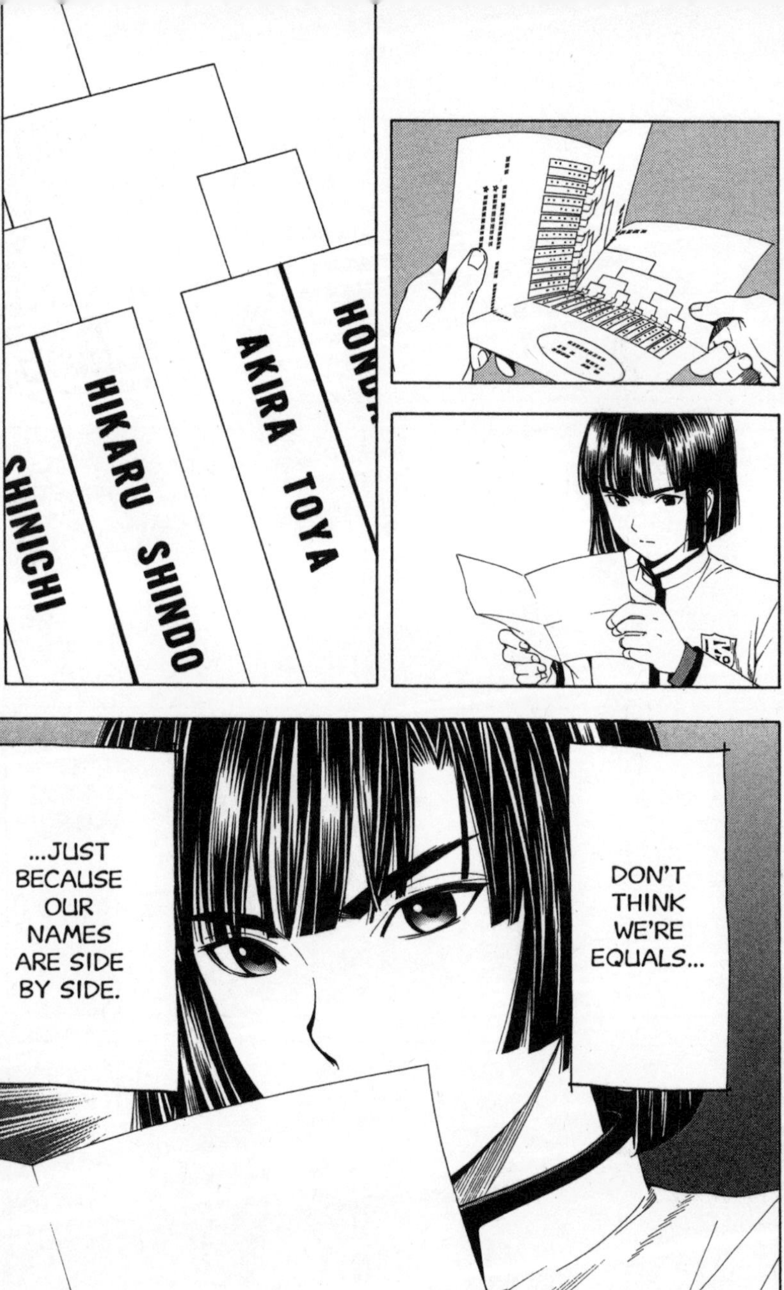
AKIRA TOYA
HIKARU SHINDO
SHINICHI
DON'T THINK WE'RE EQUALS...
...JUST BECAUSE OUR NAMES ARE SIDE BY SIDE.

# HIKARU NO GO STORYBOARDS ⑲

YUMI HOTTA

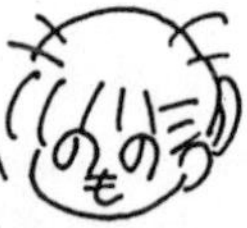

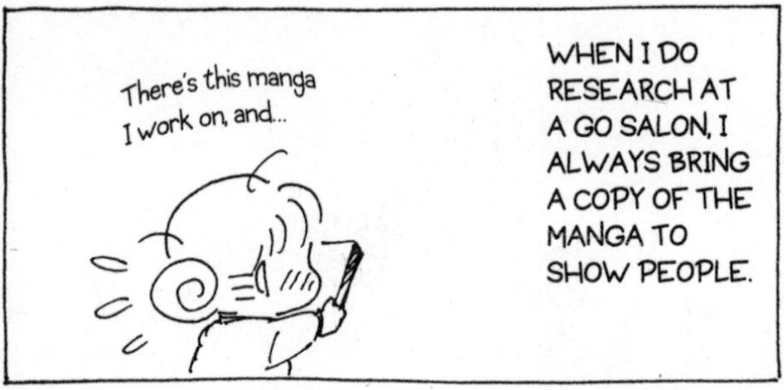
WHEN I DO RESEARCH AT A GO SALON, I ALWAYS BRING A COPY OF THE MANGA TO SHOW PEOPLE.
There's this manga I work on, and...

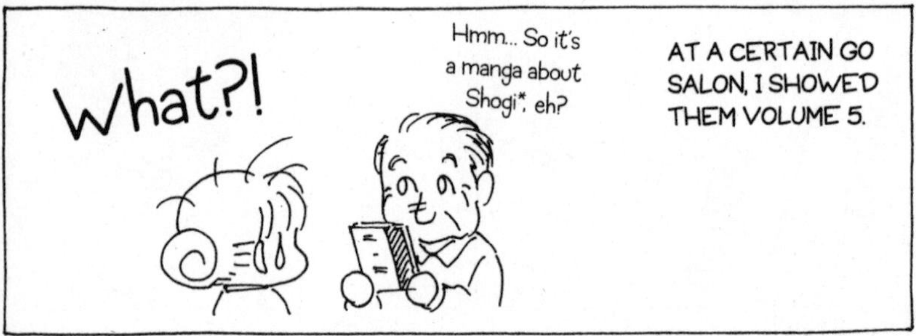
AT A CERTAIN GO SALON, I SHOWED THEM VOLUME 5.
Hmm... So it's a manga about Shogi*, eh?
What?!

*Shogi is a bit like chess.

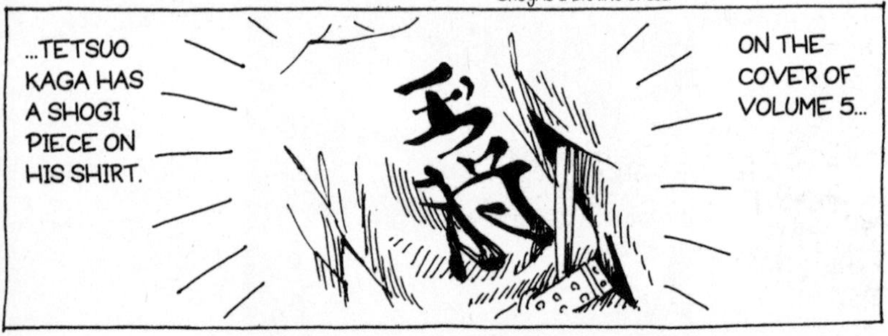
ON THE COVER OF VOLUME 5...
...TETSUO KAGA HAS A SHOGI PIECE ON HIS SHIRT.

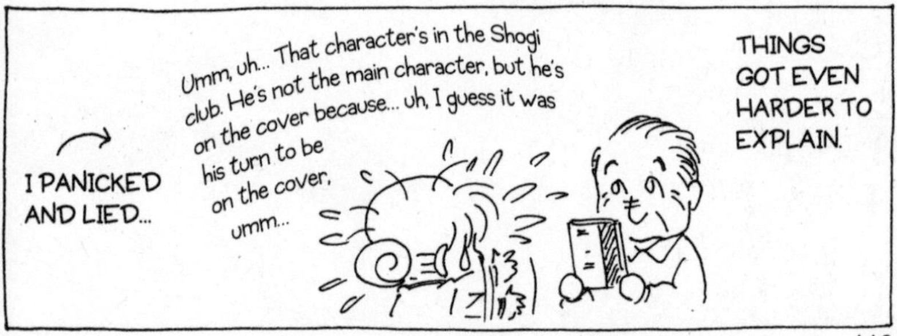
THINGS GOT EVEN HARDER TO EXPLAIN.
Umm, uh... That character's in the Shogi club. He's not the main character, but he's on the cover because... uh, I guess it was his turn to be on the cover, umm...
I PANICKED AND LIED...

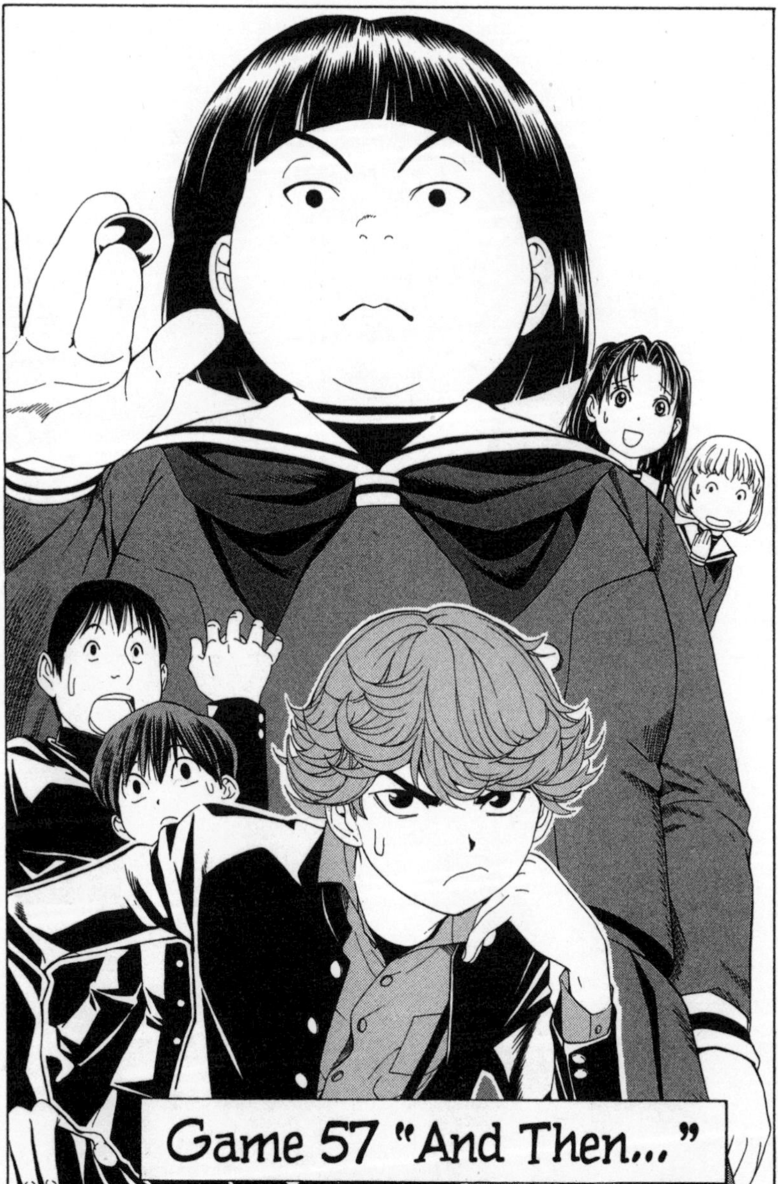
Game 57 "And Then..."

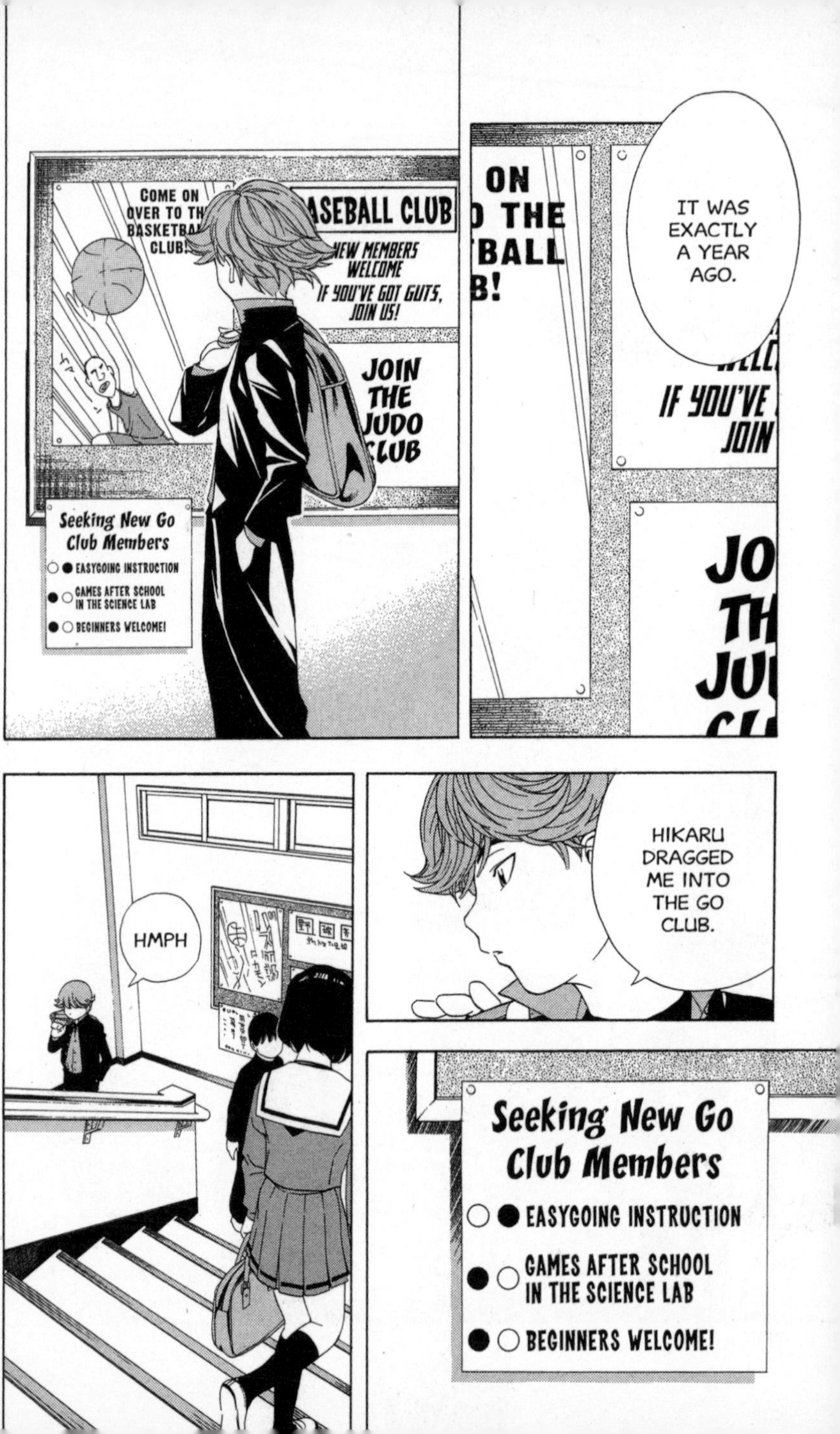
IT WAS EXACTLY A YEAR AGO.
COME ON OVER TO TH BASKETBA CLUB!
ASEBALL CLUB
NEW MEMBERS WELCOME
IF YOU'VE GOT GUTS, JOIN US!
JOIN THE JUDO CLUB
Seeking New Go Club Members
EASYGOING INSTRUCTION
GAMES AFTER SCHOOL IN THE SCIENCE LAB
BEGINNERS WELCOME!
HIKARU DRAGGED ME INTO THE GO CLUB.
Seeking New Go Club Members
EASYGOING INSTRUCTION
GAMES AFTER SCHOOL IN THE SCIENCE LAB
BEGINNERS WELCOME!
HMPH

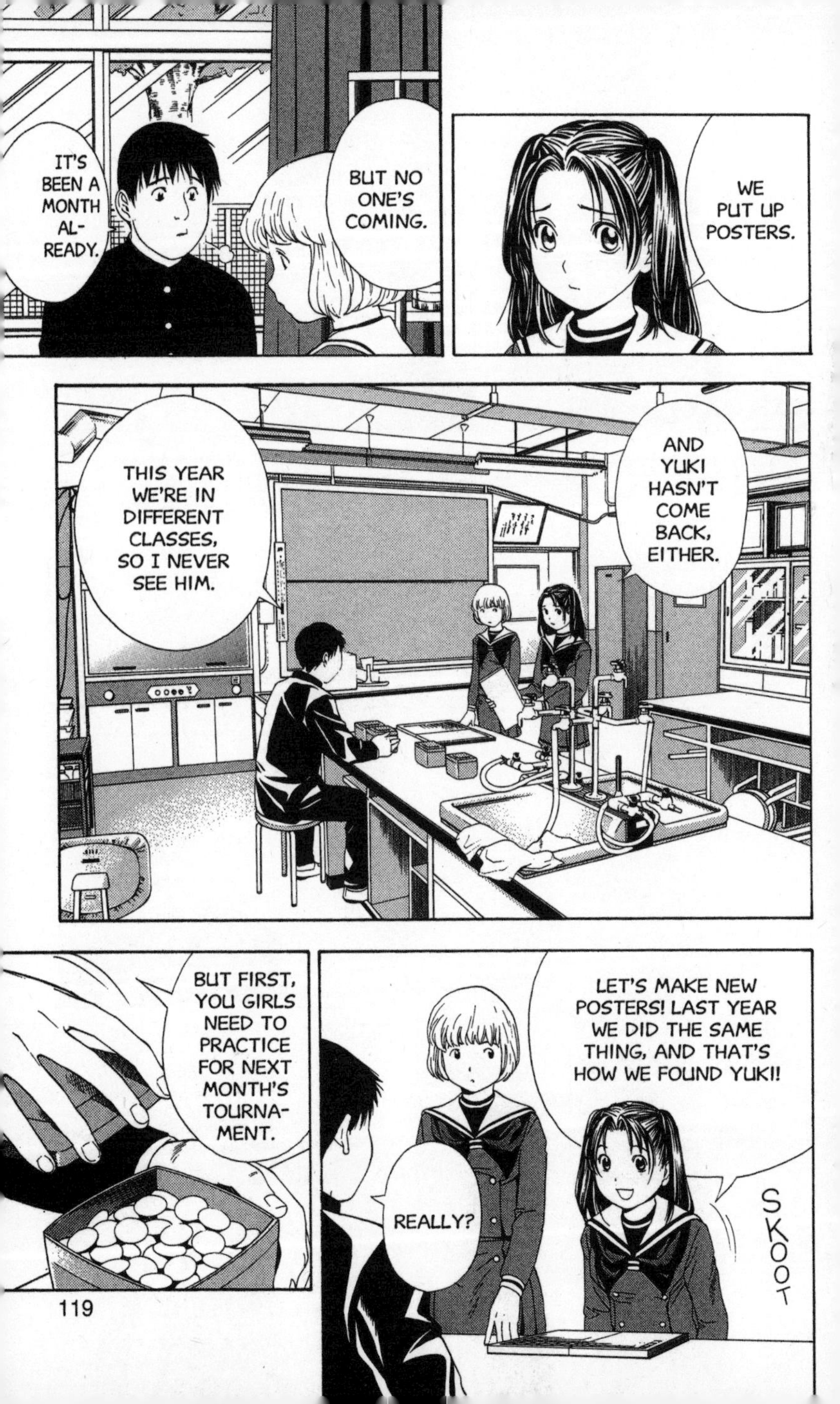
WE PUT UP POSTERS.
BUT NO ONE'S COMING.
IT'S BEEN A MONTH AL-READY.
AND YUKI HASN'T COME BACK, EITHER.
THIS YEAR WE'RE IN DIFFERENT CLASSES, SO I NEVER SEE HIM.
LET'S MAKE NEW POSTERS! LAST YEAR WE DID THE SAME THING, AND THAT'S HOW WE FOUND YUKI!
SKOOT
REALLY?
BUT FIRST, YOU GIRLS NEED TO PRACTICE FOR NEXT MONTH'S TOURNA-MENT.

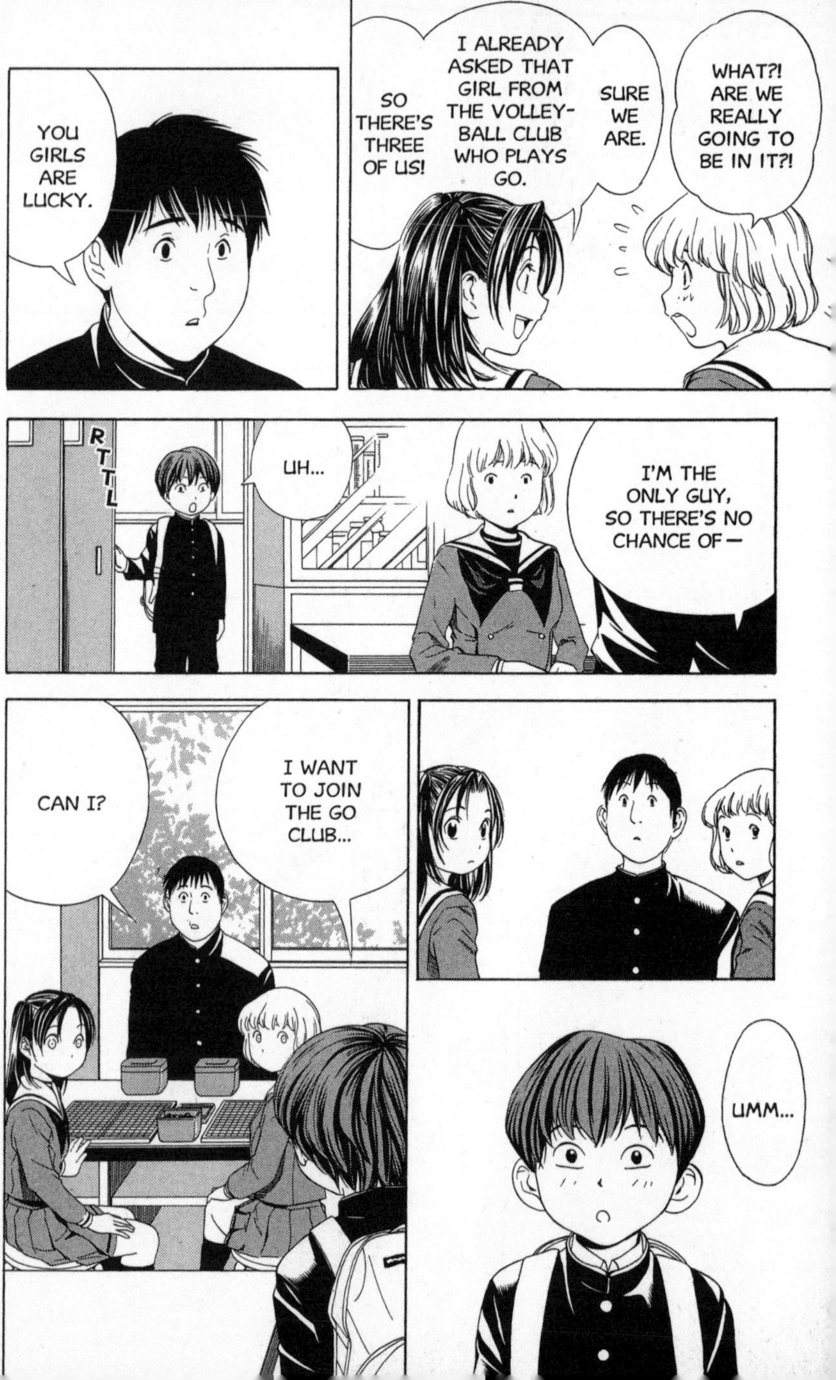
WHAT?! ARE WE REALLY GOING TO BE IN IT?!
SURE WE ARE.
I ALREADY ASKED THAT GIRL FROM THE VOLLEY-BALL CLUB WHO PLAYS GO.
SO THERE'S THREE OF US!
YOU GIRLS ARE LUCKY.
I'M THE ONLY GUY, SO THERE'S NO CHANCE OF—
RTTL
UH...
UMM...
I WANT TO JOIN THE GO CLUB...
CAN I?

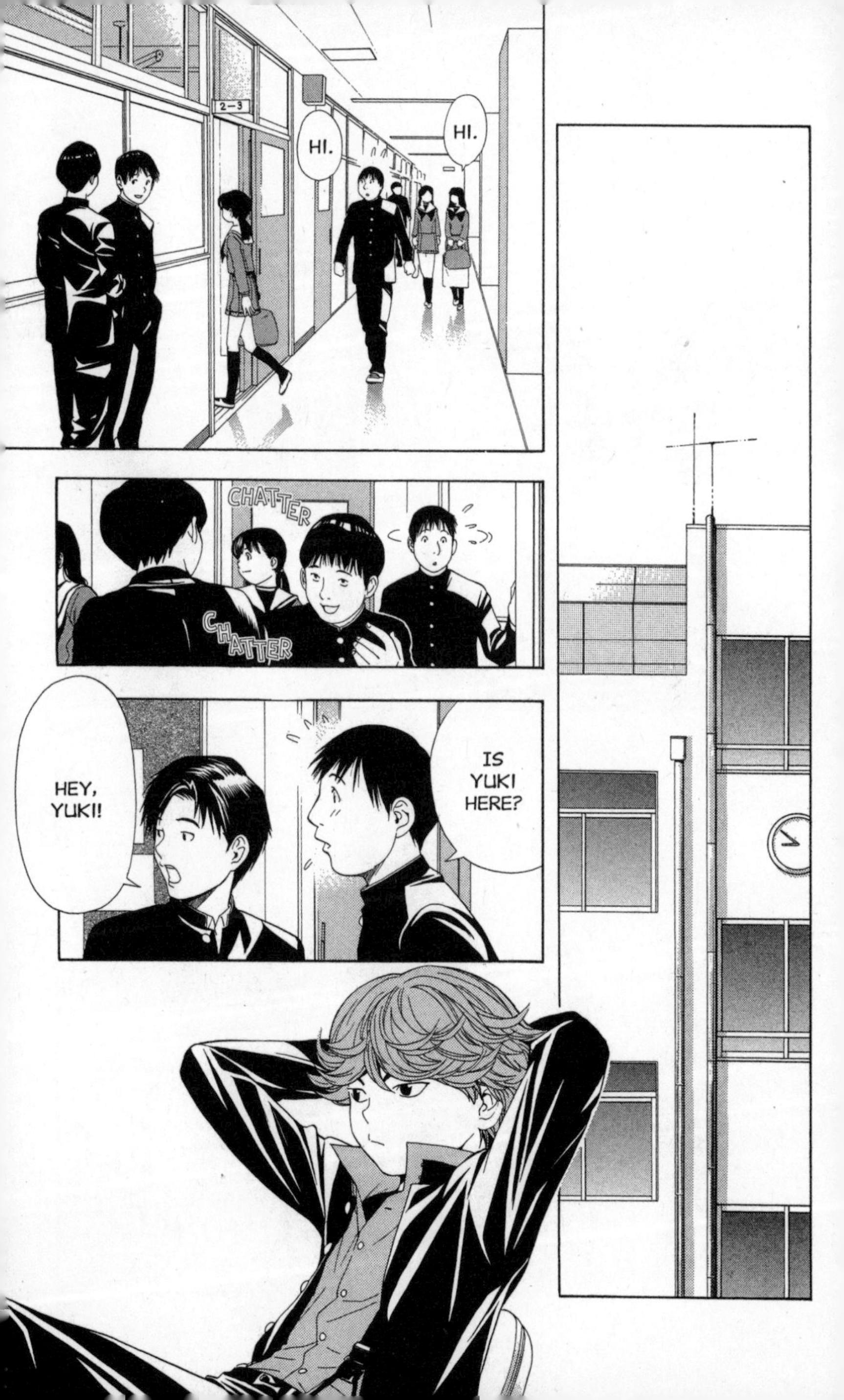
HI.
HI.
CHATTER
CHATTER
IS YUKI HERE?
HEY, YUKI!

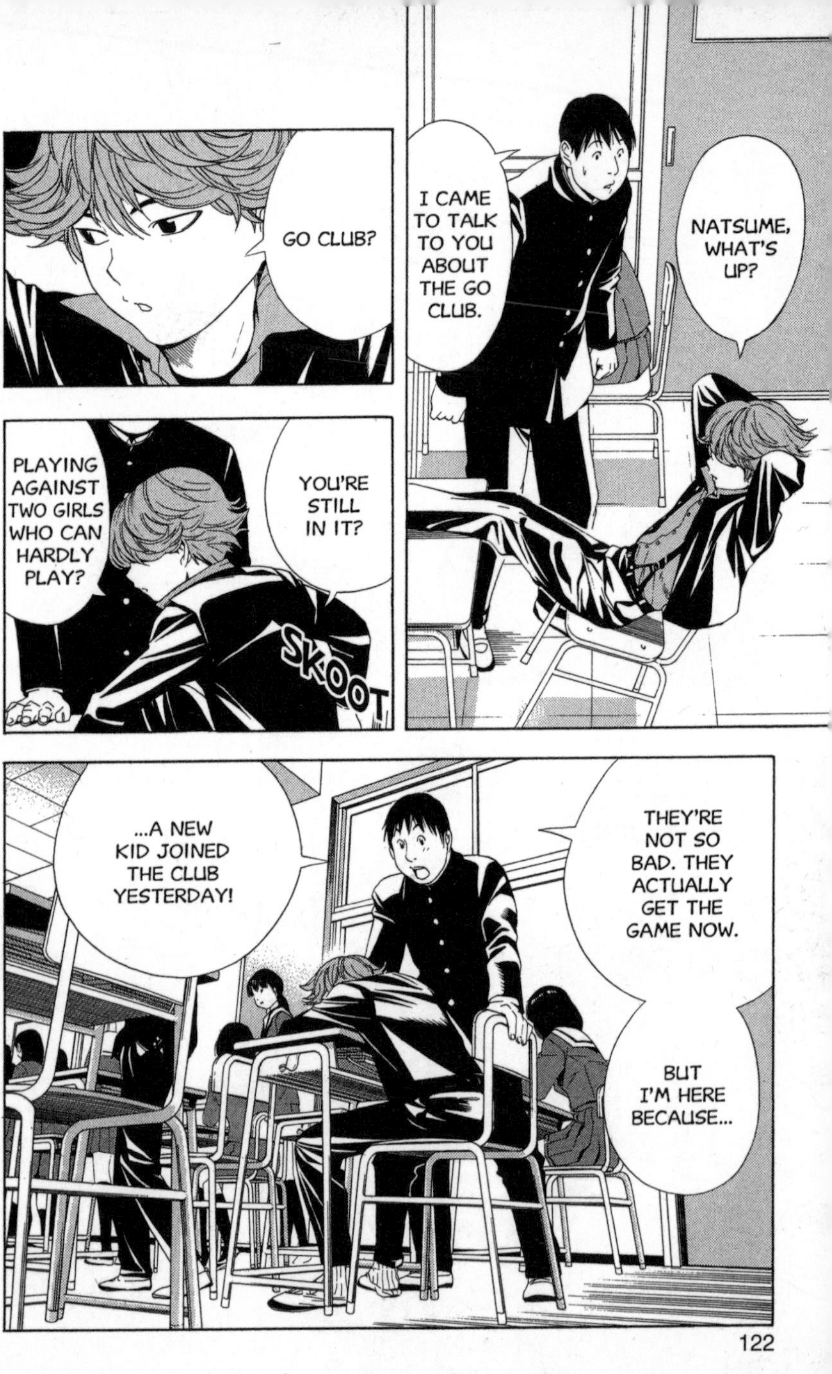
NATSUME, WHAT'S UP?
I CAME TO TALK TO YOU ABOUT THE GO CLUB.
GO CLUB?
YOU'RE STILL IN IT?
PLAYING AGAINST TWO GIRLS WHO CAN HARDLY PLAY?
SKOOT
THEY'RE NOT SO BAD. THEY ACTUALLY GET THE GAME NOW.
BUT I'M HERE BECAUSE...
...A NEW KID JOINED THE CLUB YESTERDAY!

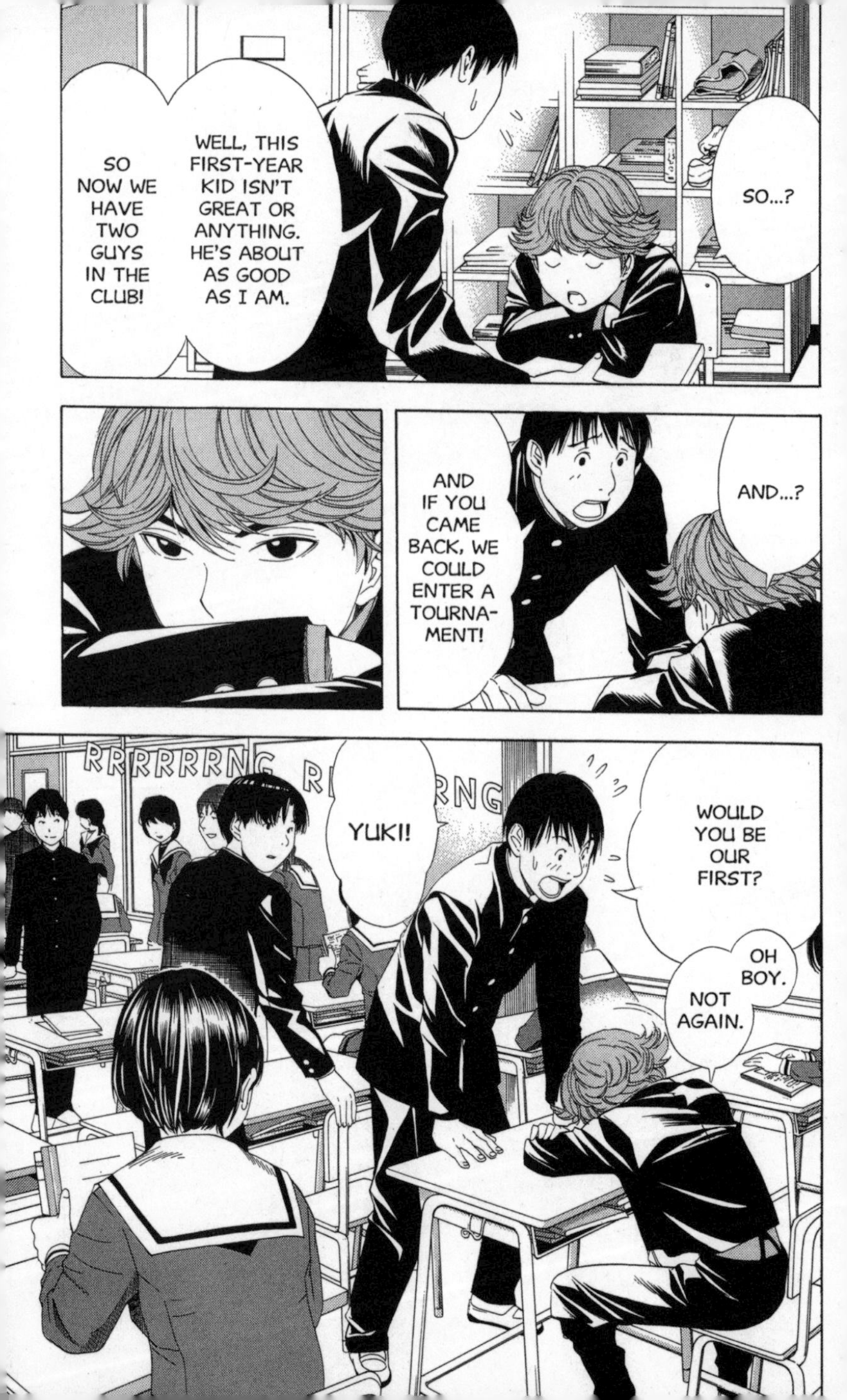
SO...?
WELL, THIS FIRST-YEAR KID ISN'T GREAT OR ANYTHING. HE'S ABOUT AS GOOD AS I AM.
SO NOW WE HAVE TWO GUYS IN THE CLUB!
AND...?
AND IF YOU CAME BACK, WE COULD ENTER A TOURNA-MENT!
WOULD YOU BE OUR FIRST?
YUKI!
RRRRRRNG
RI
RNG
OH BOY. NOT AGAIN.

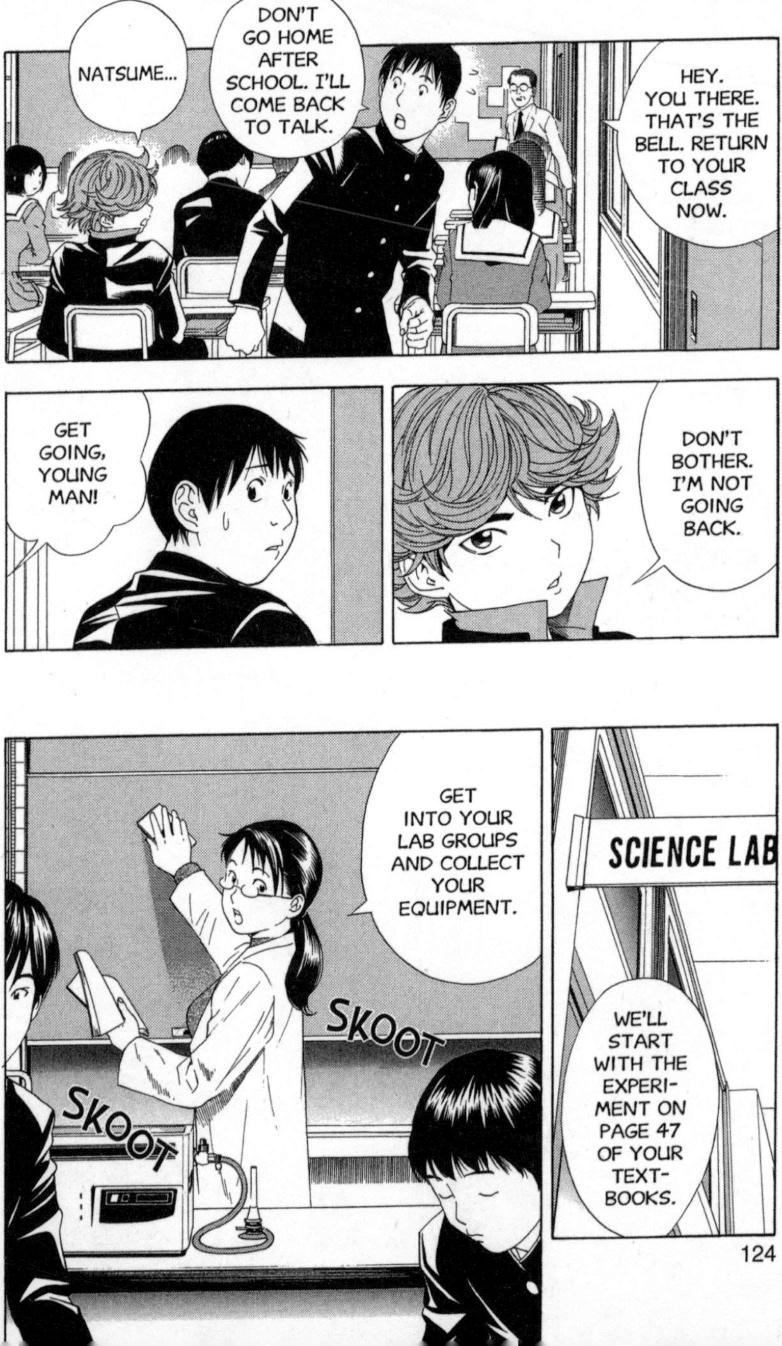
HEY. YOU THERE. THAT'S THE BELL. RETURN TO YOUR CLASS NOW.
DON'T GO HOME AFTER SCHOOL. I'LL COME BACK TO TALK.
NATSUME...
DON'T BOTHER. I'M NOT GOING BACK.
GET GOING, YOUNG MAN!
SCIENCE LAB
WE'LL START WITH THE EXPERIMENT ON PAGE 47 OF YOUR TEXTBOOKS.
GET INTO YOUR LAB GROUPS AND COLLECT YOUR EQUIPMENT.
SKOOT
SKOOT

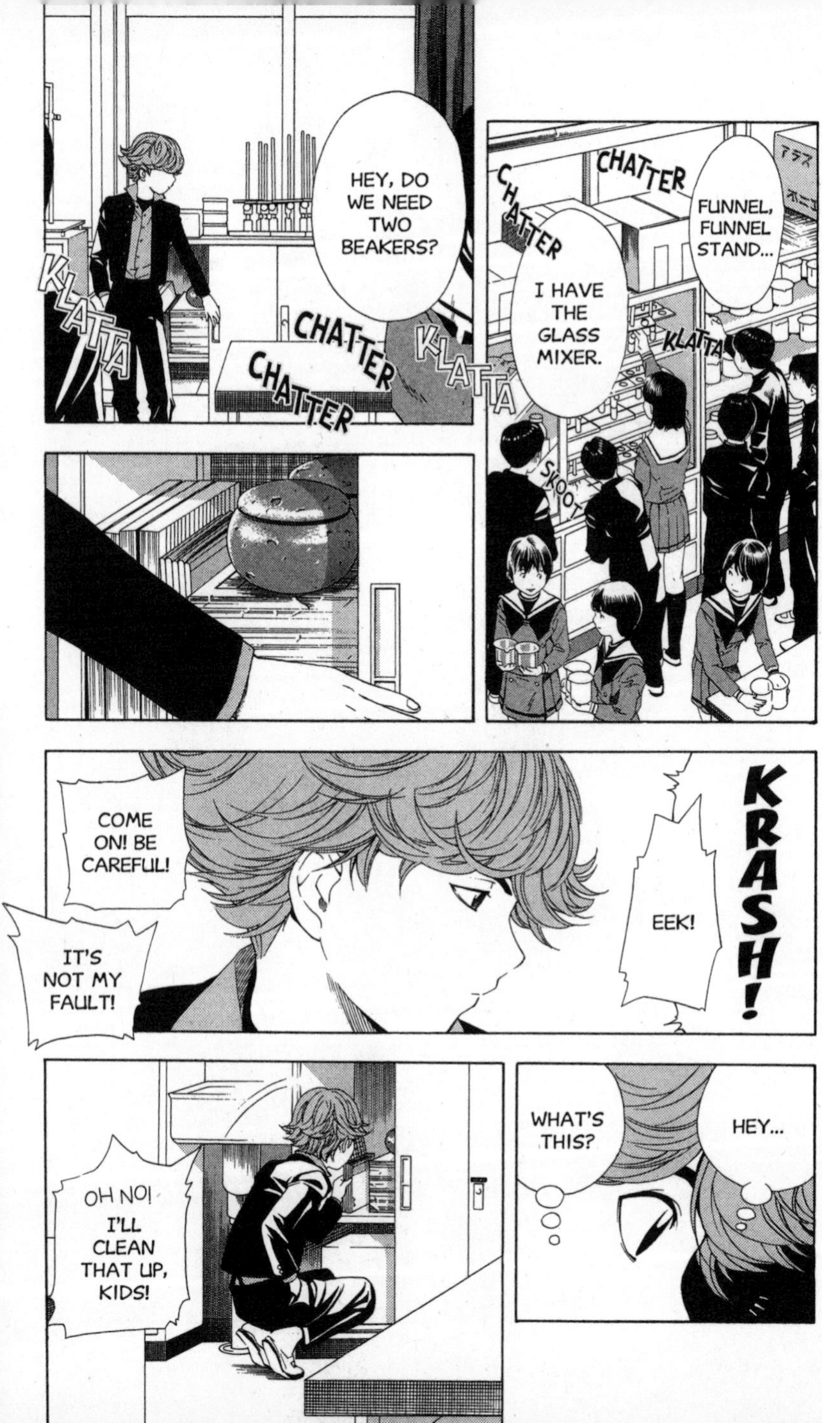
FUNNEL, FUNNEL STAND...
CHATTER
CHATTER
I HAVE THE GLASS MIXER.
KLATTA
SKOOT
HEY, DO WE NEED TWO BEAKERS?
KLATTA
CHATTER
CHATTER
KLATTA
KRASH!
EEK!
COME ON! BE CAREFUL!
IT'S NOT MY FAULT!
HEY...
WHAT'S THIS?
OH NO! I'LL CLEAN THAT UP, KIDS!

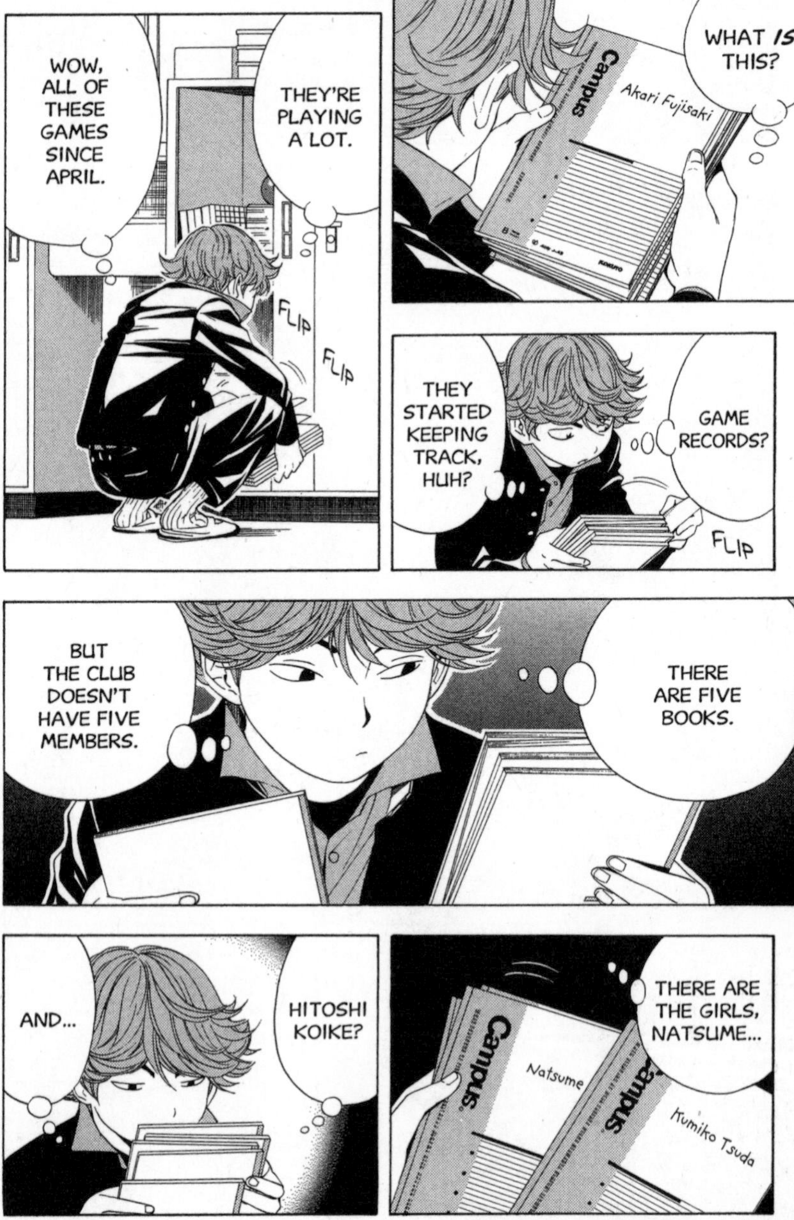
WHAT *IS* THIS?
Campus
Akari Fujisaki
GAME RECORDS?
THEY STARTED KEEPING TRACK, HUH?
FLIP
THEY'RE PLAYING A LOT.
WOW, ALL OF THESE GAMES SINCE APRIL.
FLIP
FLIP
THERE ARE FIVE BOOKS.
BUT THE CLUB DOESN'T HAVE FIVE MEMBERS.
THERE ARE THE GIRLS, NATSUME...
Campus
Natsume
Campus
Kumiko Tsuda
HITOSHI KOIKE?
AND...

READ THIS WAY

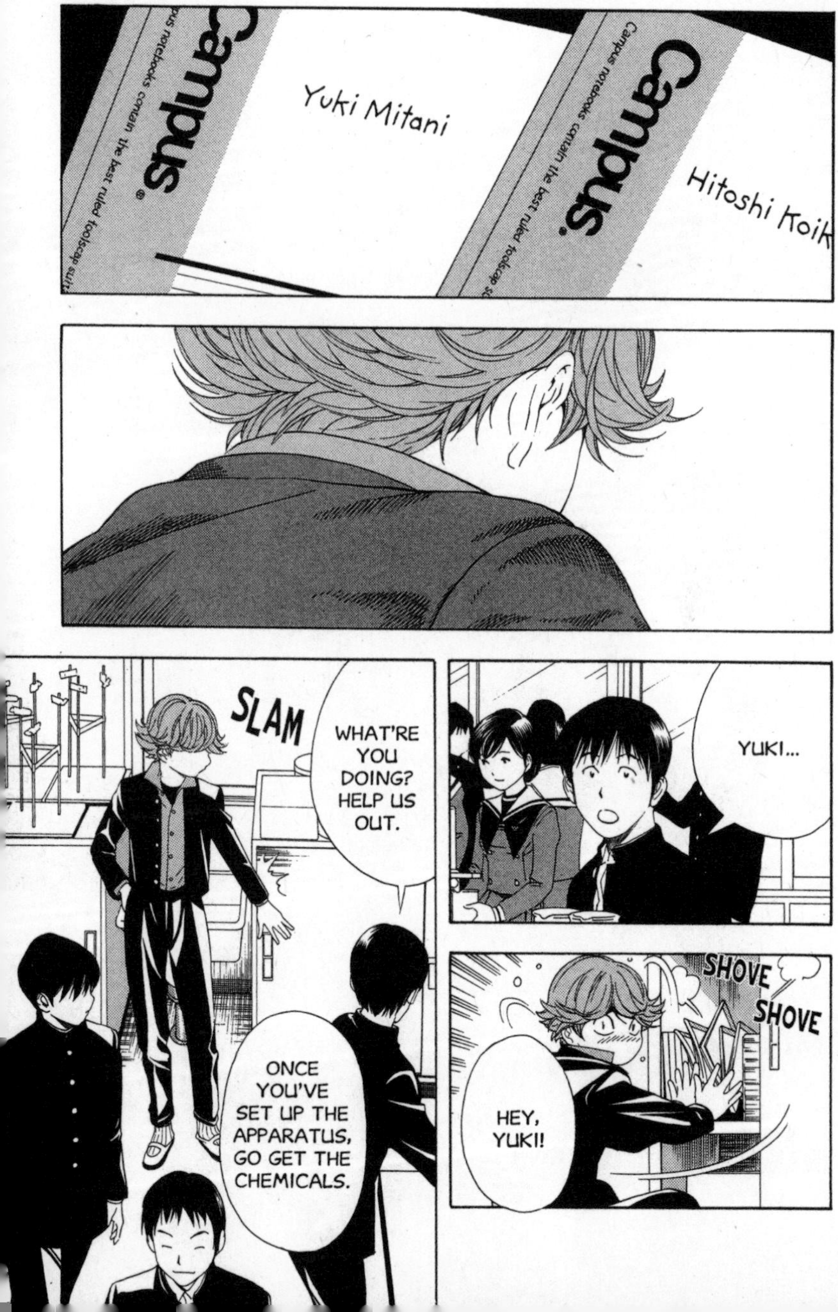
Campus
Yuki Mitani
Campus
Hitoshi Koik
YUKI...
SHOVE
SHOVE
HEY, YUKI!
SLAM
WHAT'RE YOU DOING? HELP US OUT.
ONCE YOU'VE SET UP THE APPARATUS, GO GET THE CHEMICALS.

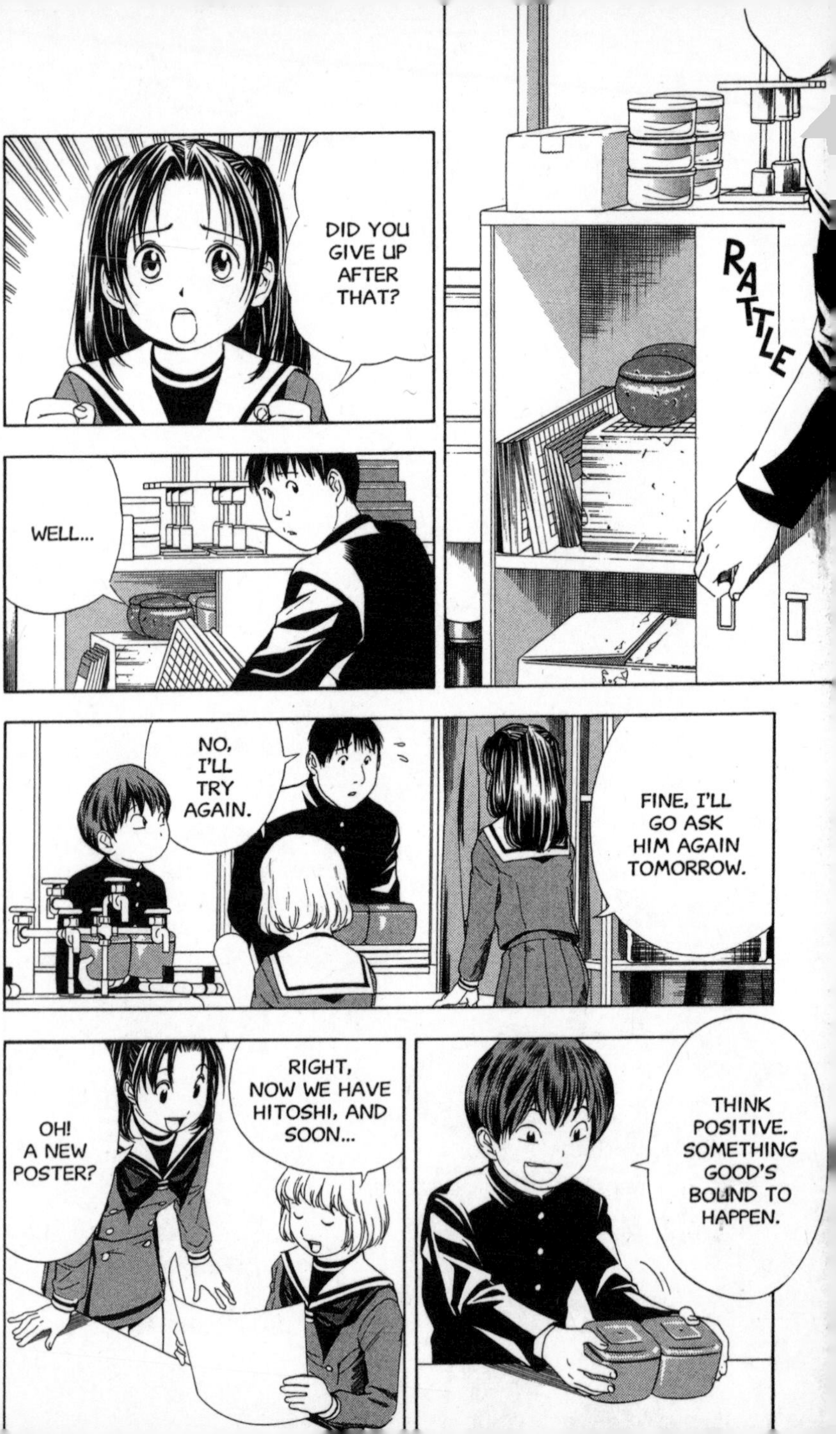
RATTLE
DID YOU GIVE UP AFTER THAT?
WELL...
FINE, I'LL GO ASK HIM AGAIN TOMORROW.
NO, I'LL TRY AGAIN.
THINK POSITIVE. SOMETHING GOOD'S BOUND TO HAPPEN.
RIGHT, NOW WE HAVE HITOSHI, AND SOON...
OH! A NEW POSTER?

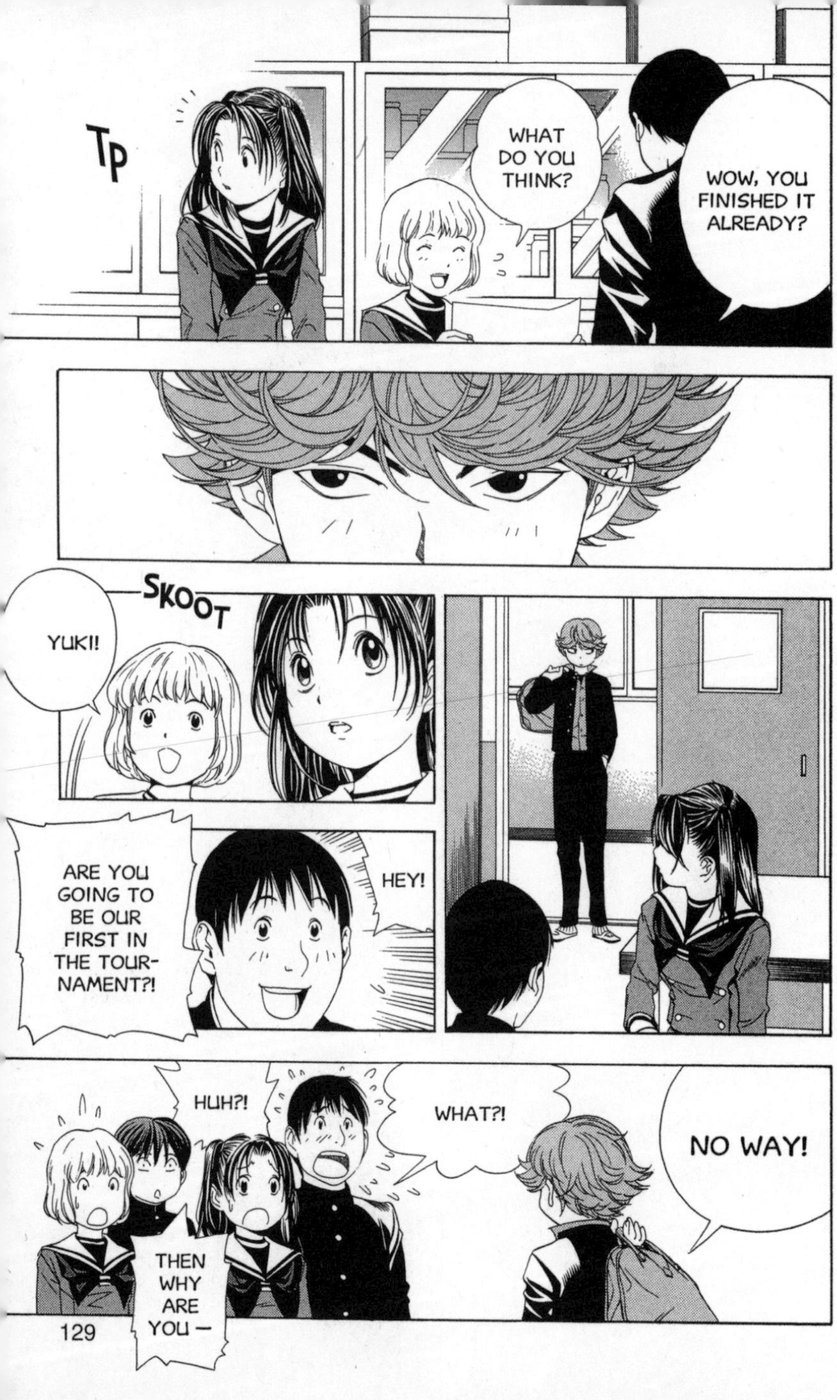
WOW, YOU FINISHED IT ALREADY?
WHAT DO YOU THINK?
TP
SKOOT
YUKI!
HEY!
ARE YOU GOING TO BE OUR FIRST IN THE TOUR-NAMENT?!
NO WAY!
WHAT?!
HUH?!
THEN WHY ARE YOU —

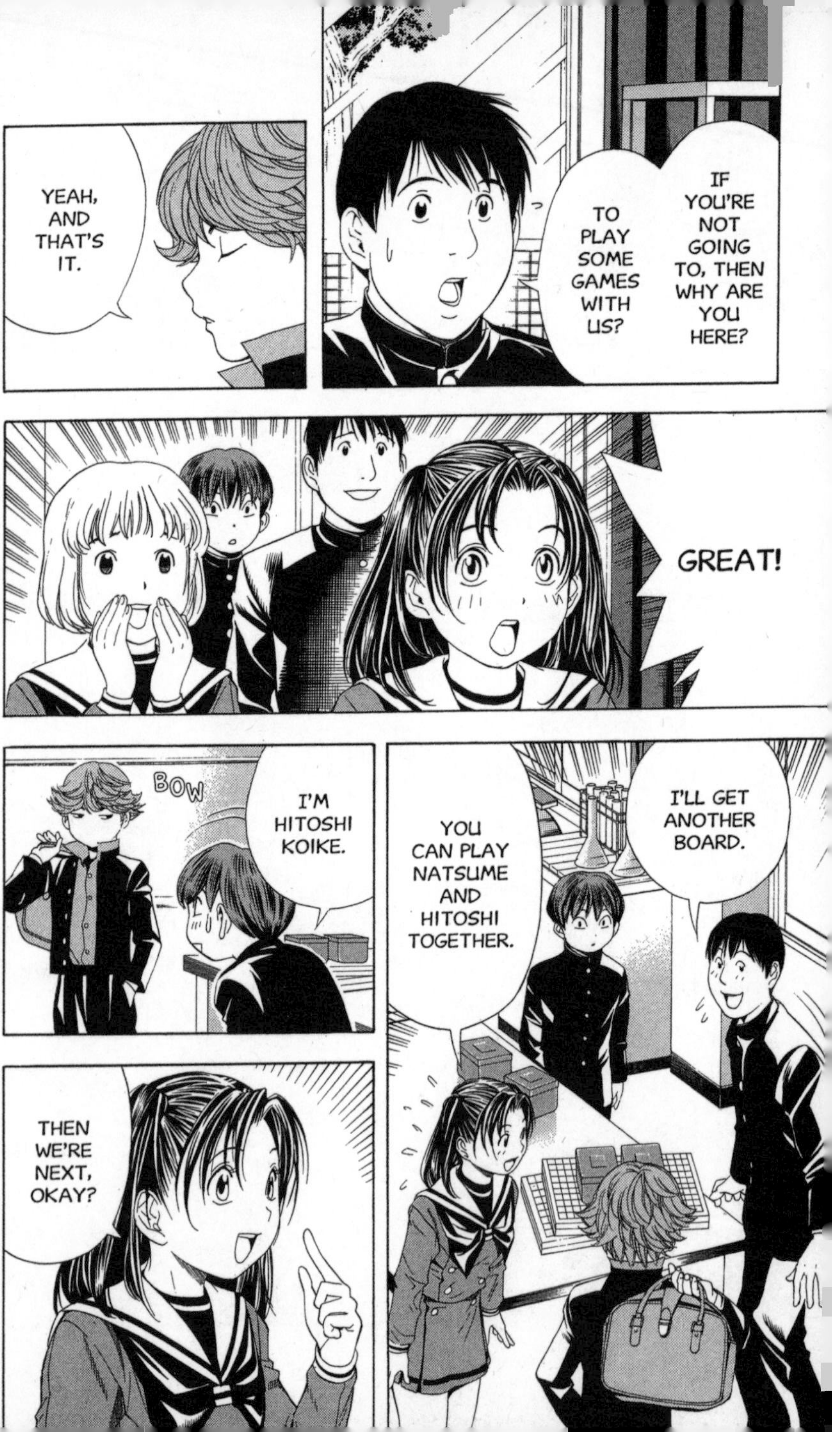
IF YOU'RE NOT GOING TO, THEN WHY ARE YOU HERE?
TO PLAY SOME GAMES WITH US?
YEAH, AND THAT'S IT.
GREAT!
I'LL GET ANOTHER BOARD.
YOU CAN PLAY NATSUME AND HITOSHI TOGETHER.
BOW
I'M HITOSHI KOIKE.
THEN WE'RE NEXT, OKAY?

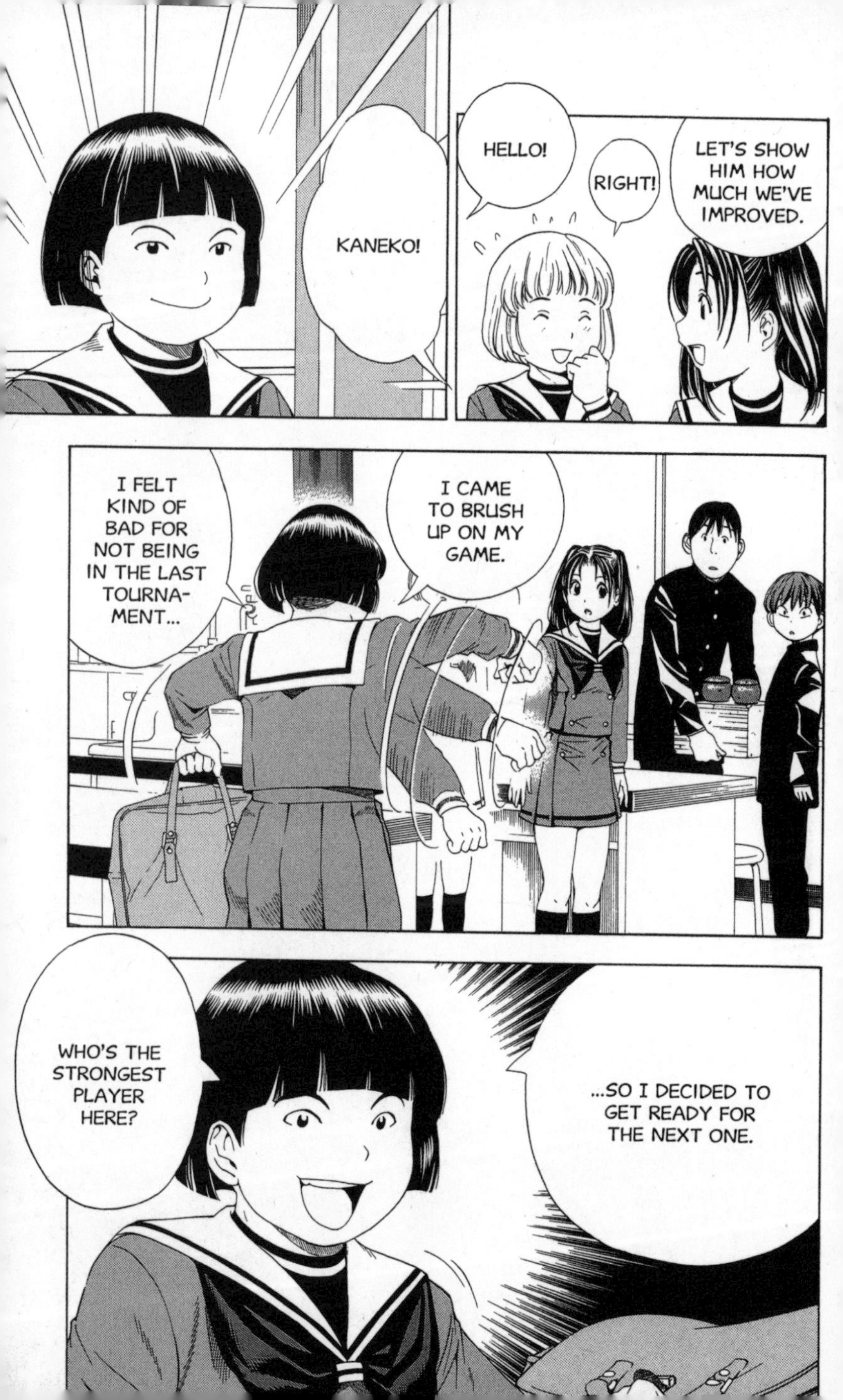
LET'S SHOW HIM HOW MUCH WE'VE IMPROVED.
RIGHT!
HELLO!
KANEKO!
I CAME TO BRUSH UP ON MY GAME.
I FELT KIND OF BAD FOR NOT BEING IN THE LAST TOURNAMENT...
...SO I DECIDED TO GET READY FOR THE NEXT ONE.
WHO'S THE STRONGEST PLAYER HERE?

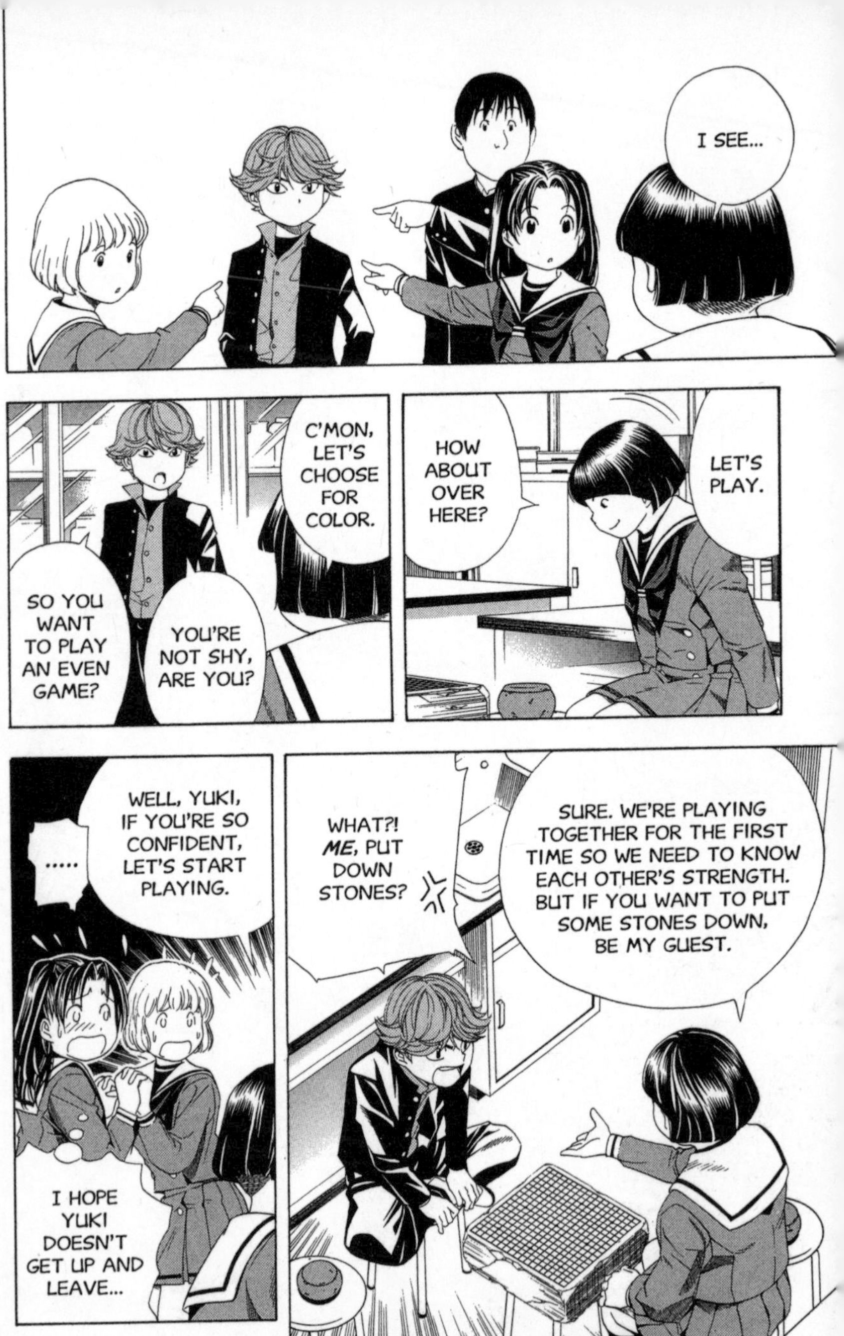
I SEE...
LET'S PLAY.
HOW ABOUT OVER HERE?
C'MON, LET'S CHOOSE FOR COLOR.
YOU'RE NOT SHY, ARE YOU?
SO YOU WANT TO PLAY AN EVEN GAME?
SURE. WE'RE PLAYING TOGETHER FOR THE FIRST TIME SO WE NEED TO KNOW EACH OTHER'S STRENGTH. BUT IF YOU WANT TO PUT SOME STONES DOWN, BE MY GUEST.
WHAT?! *ME*, PUT DOWN STONES?
WELL, YUKI, IF YOU'RE SO CONFIDENT, LET'S START PLAYING.
.....
I HOPE YUKI DOESN'T GET UP AND LEAVE...

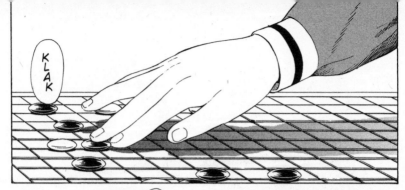

IT'S BEEN SO LONG THAT MY GAME'S OFF.

KLAK

KLAK

I'M NOT PLAYING FOR KEEPS, EITHER.

KLAK

KLAK

KLAK

HEY, KANEKO MANAGED TO CONNECT HER STONES...

KLAK

KLAK

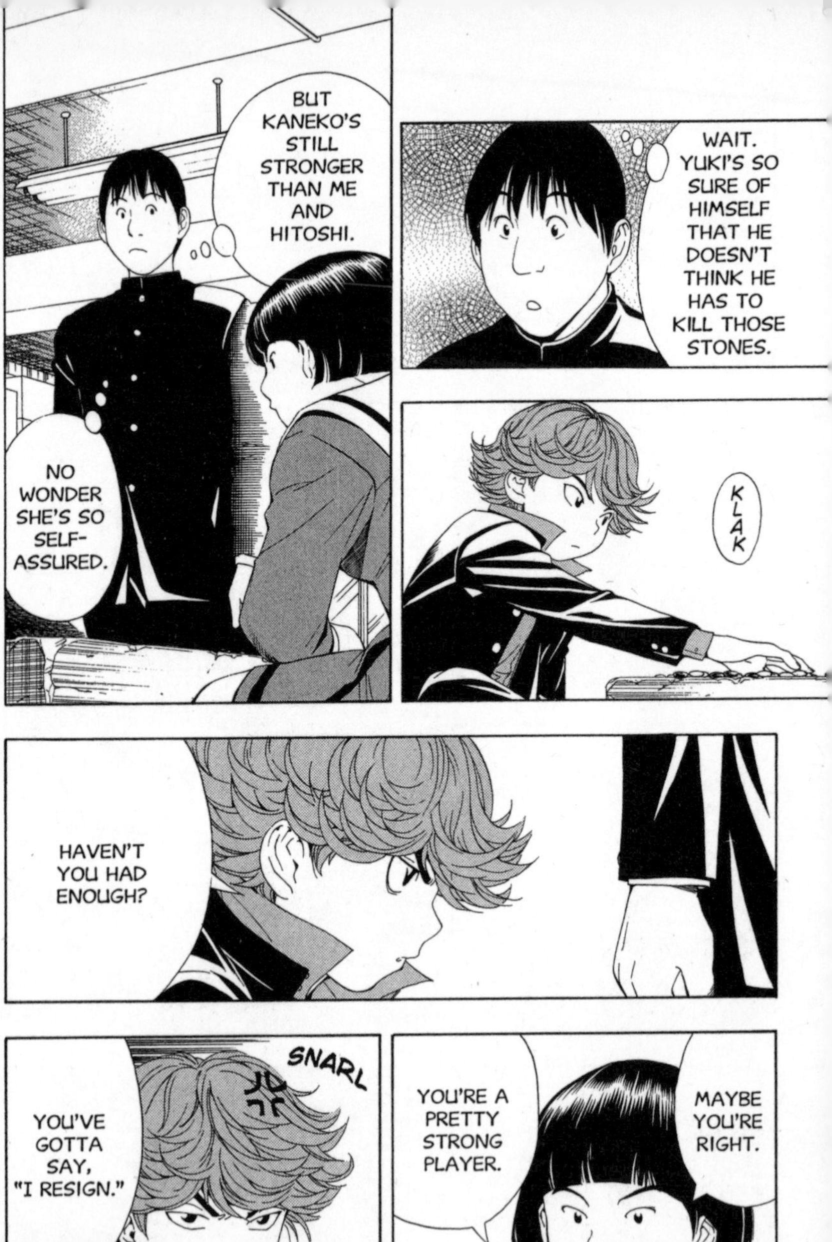

WAIT. YUKI'S SO SURE OF HIMSELF THAT HE DOESN'T THINK HE HAS TO KILL THOSE STONES.
KLAK
BUT KANEKO'S STILL STRONGER THAN ME AND HITOSHI.
NO WONDER SHE'S SO SELF-ASSURED.
HAVEN'T YOU HAD ENOUGH?
MAYBE YOU'RE RIGHT.
YOU'RE A PRETTY STRONG PLAYER.
SNARL
YOU'VE GOTTA SAY, "I RESIGN."

READ THIS WAY

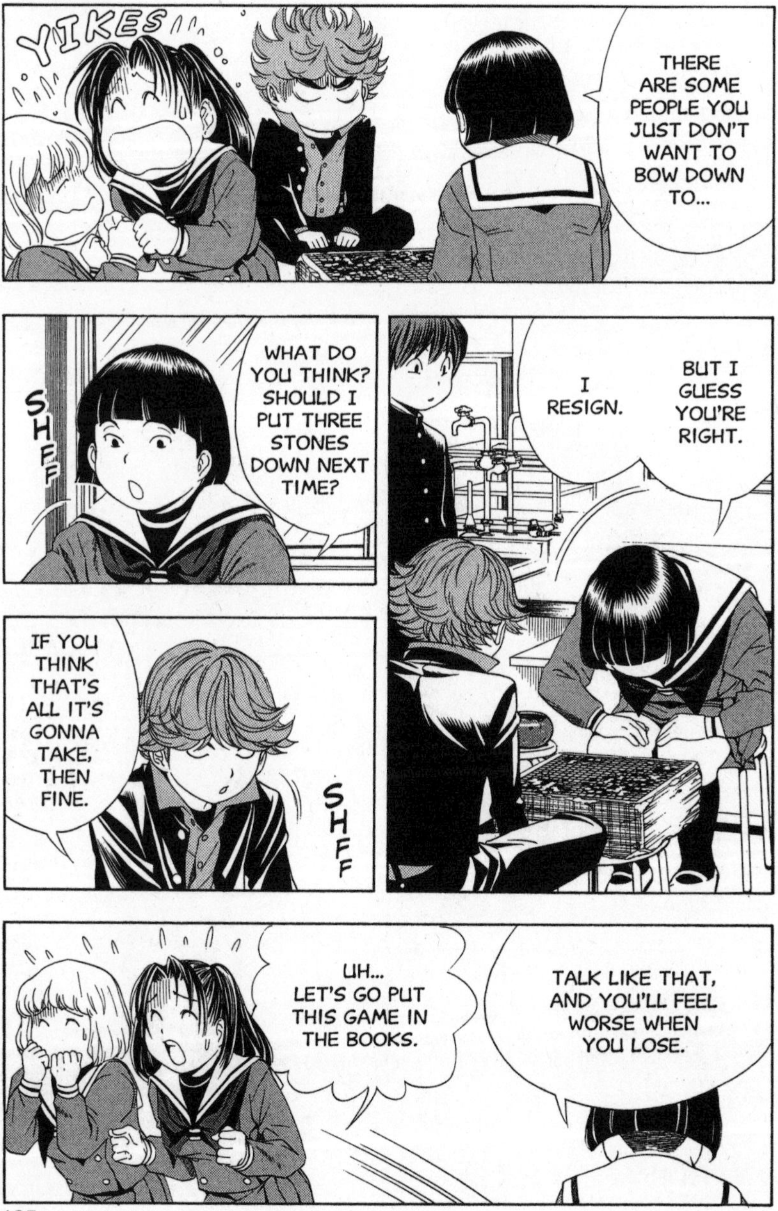
THERE ARE SOME PEOPLE YOU JUST DON'T WANT TO BOW DOWN TO...
YIKES
BUT I GUESS YOU'RE RIGHT.
I RESIGN.
WHAT DO YOU THINK? SHOULD I PUT THREE STONES DOWN NEXT TIME?
SHFF
IF YOU THINK THAT'S ALL IT'S GONNA TAKE, THEN FINE.
SHFF
TALK LIKE THAT, AND YOU'LL FEEL WORSE WHEN YOU LOSE.
UH... LET'S GO PUT THIS GAME IN THE BOOKS.

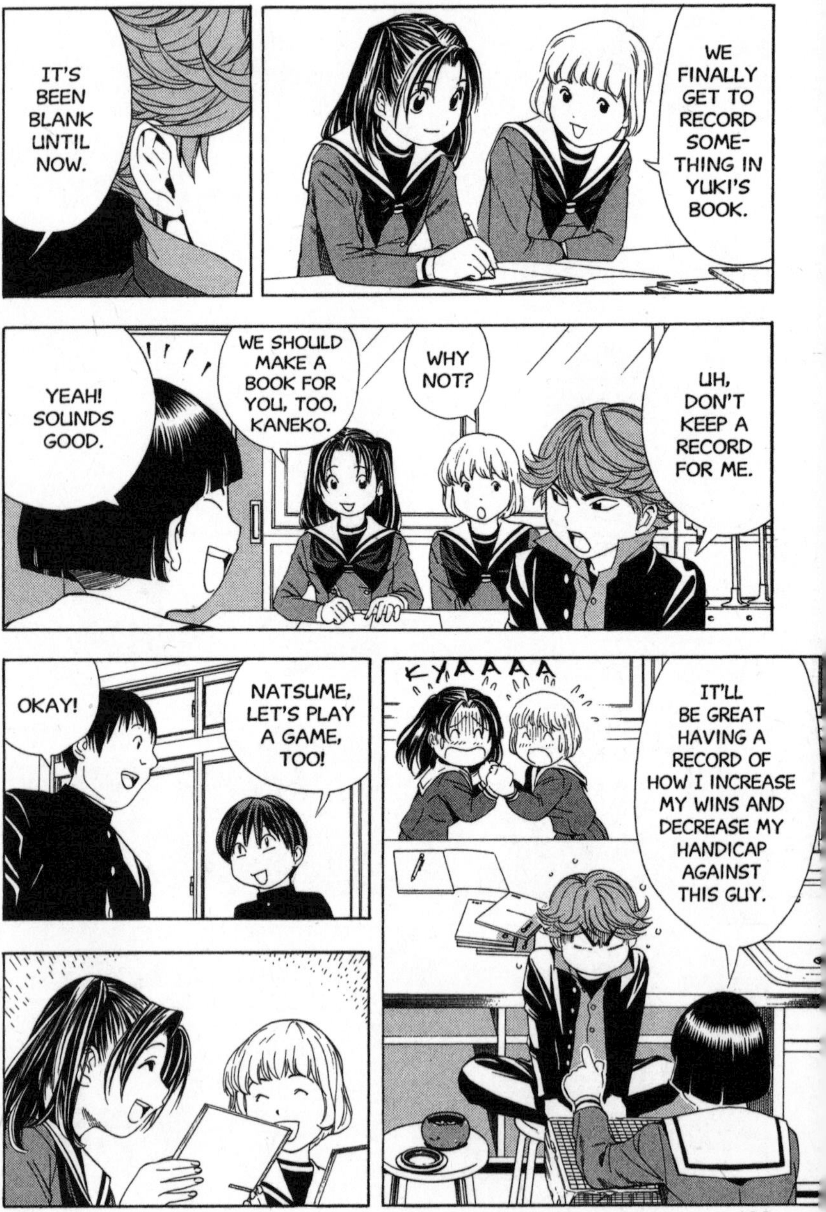
WE FINALLY GET TO RECORD SOME-THING IN YUKI'S BOOK.
IT'S BEEN BLANK UNTIL NOW.
UH, DON'T KEEP A RECORD FOR ME.
WHY NOT?
WE SHOULD MAKE A BOOK FOR YOU, TOO, KANEKO.
YEAH! SOUNDS GOOD.
KYAAAA
IT'LL BE GREAT HAVING A RECORD OF HOW I INCREASE MY WINS AND DECREASE MY HANDICAP AGAINST THIS GUY.
NATSUME, LET'S PLAY A GAME, TOO!
OKAY!

READ THIS WAY

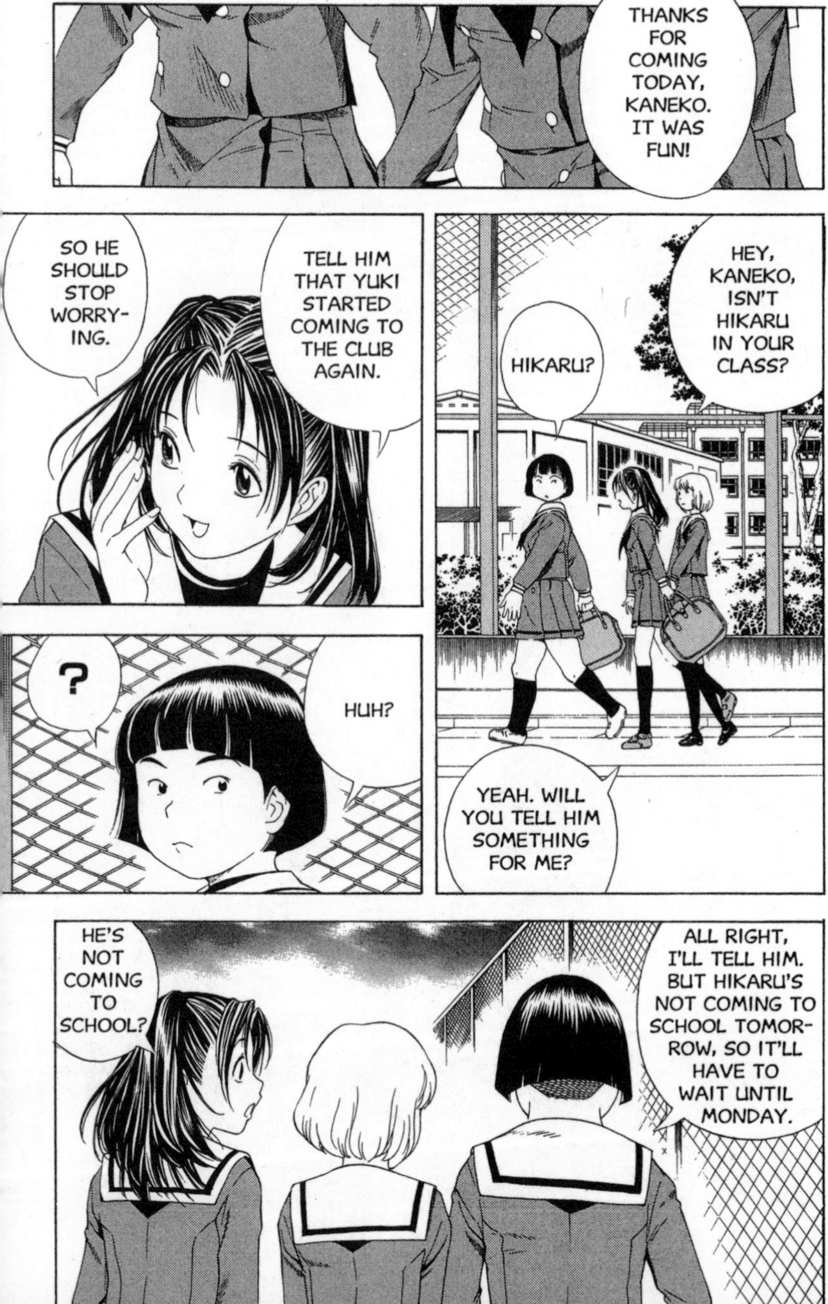
THANKS FOR COMING TODAY, KANEKO. IT WAS FUN!
HEY, KANEKO, ISN'T HIKARU IN YOUR CLASS?
HIKARU?
YEAH. WILL YOU TELL HIM SOMETHING FOR ME?
TELL HIM THAT YUKI STARTED COMING TO THE CLUB AGAIN.
SO HE SHOULD STOP WORRY-ING.
HUH?
?
ALL RIGHT, I'LL TELL HIM. BUT HIKARU'S NOT COMING TO SCHOOL TOMOR-ROW, SO IT'LL HAVE TO WAIT UNTIL MONDAY.
HE'S NOT COMING TO SCHOOL?

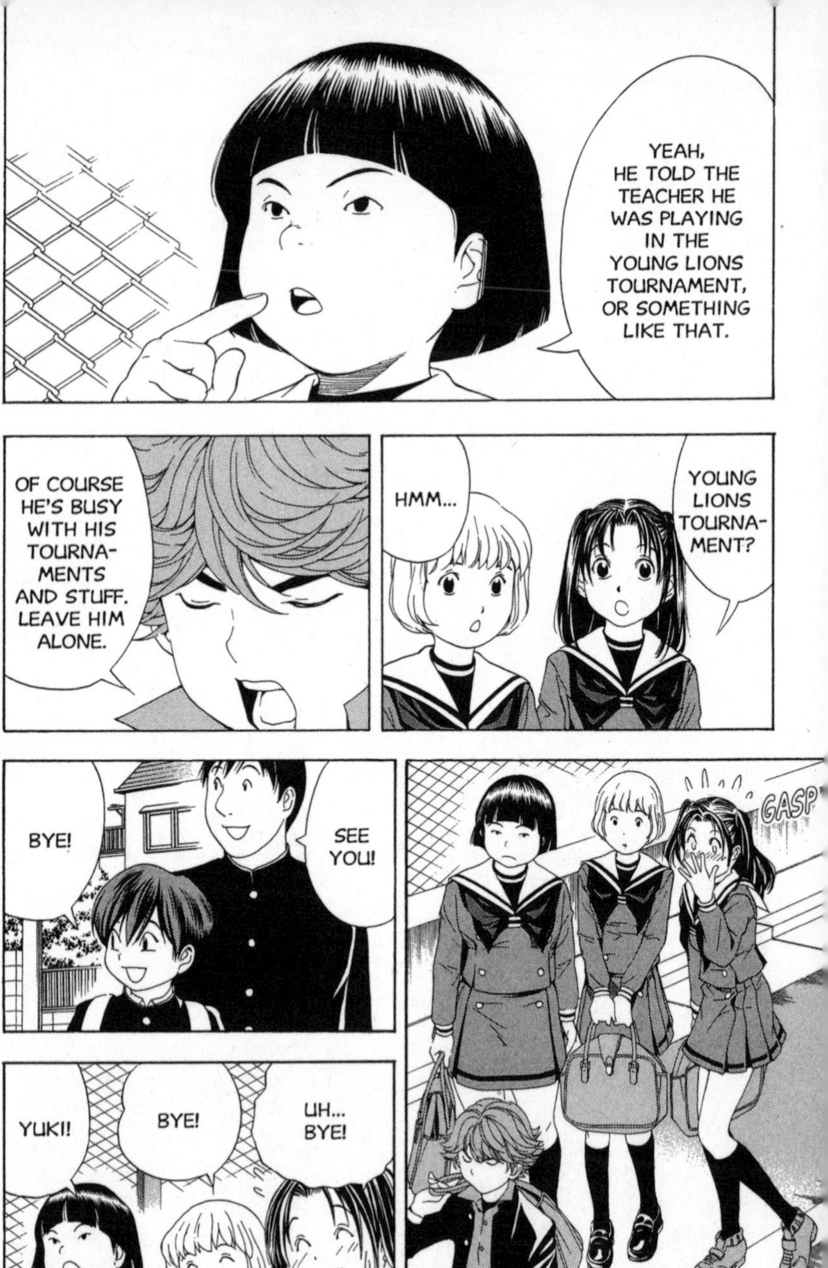
YEAH, HE TOLD THE TEACHER HE WAS PLAYING IN THE YOUNG LIONS TOURNAMENT, OR SOMETHING LIKE THAT.
YOUNG LIONS TOURNA-MENT?
HMM...
OF COURSE HE'S BUSY WITH HIS TOURNA-MENTS AND STUFF. LEAVE HIM ALONE.
GASP
SEE YOU!
BYE!
UH... BYE!
BYE!
YUKI!

READ THIS WAY

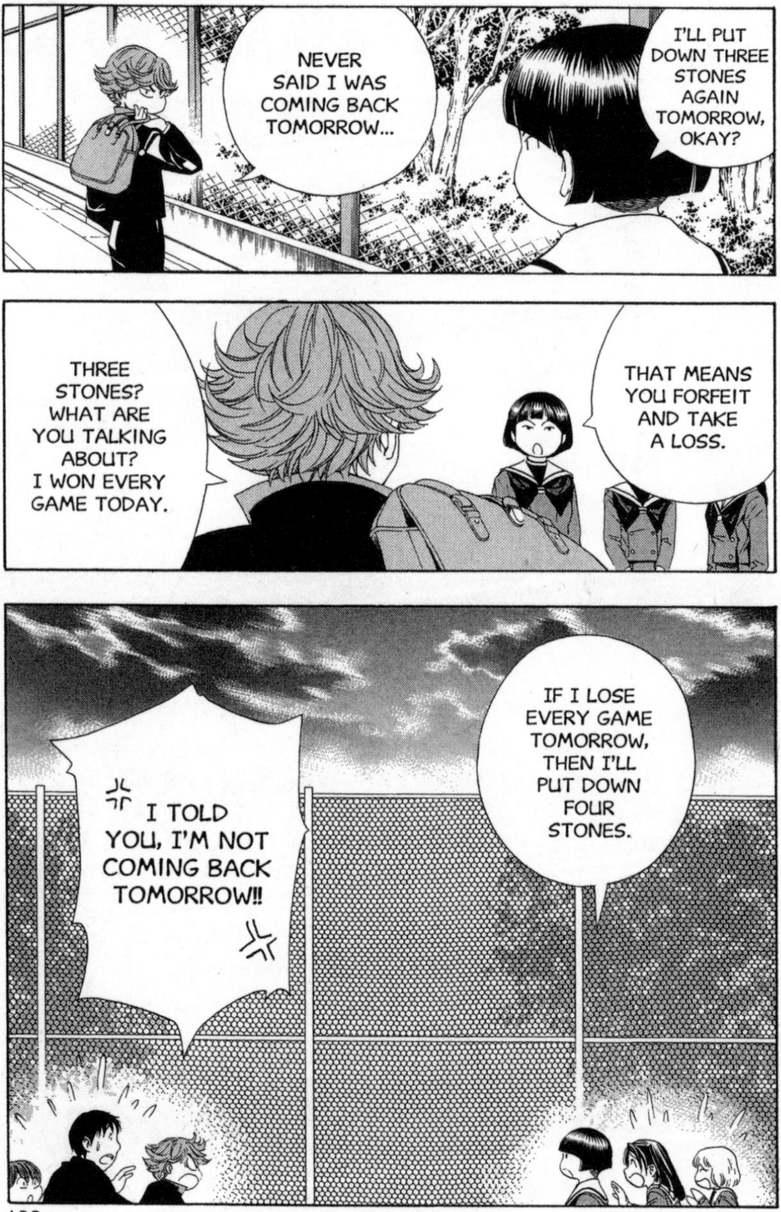

I'LL PUT DOWN THREE STONES AGAIN TOMORROW, OKAY?
NEVER SAID I WAS COMING BACK TOMORROW...
THAT MEANS YOU FORFEIT AND TAKE A LOSS.
THREE STONES? WHAT ARE YOU TALKING ABOUT? I WON EVERY GAME TODAY.
IF I LOSE EVERY GAME TOMORROW, THEN I'LL PUT DOWN FOUR STONES.
I TOLD YOU, I'M NOT COMING BACK TOMORROW!!

# A WORD ABOUT HIKARU NO GO

## FEES FOR TEACHING GAMES

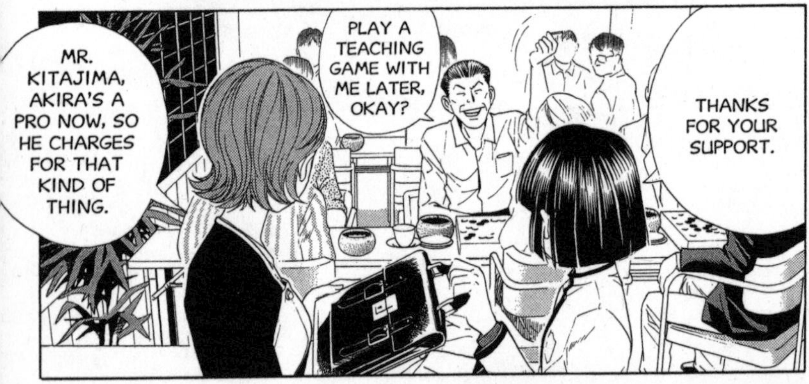
THANKS FOR YOUR SUPPORT.
PLAY A TEACHING GAME WITH ME LATER, OKAY?
MR. KITAJIMA, AKIRA'S A PRO NOW, SO HE CHARGES FOR THAT KIND OF THING.

HOW MUCH DOES IT COST TO PLAY A GAME WITH A PROFESSIONAL PLAYER?

IT DEPENDS ON THE PRO'S DAN LEVEL, AS WELL AS THE LOCATION. IN JAPAN, FEES CAN RANGE FROM 5,000 YEN TO 15,000 YEN.* IF YOU BECOME A MEMBER OF A GO CLUB, YOU'LL PROBABLY PAY A LITTLE LESS. AND IF YOU PAY A SPECIAL FEE, YOU CAN HAVE A PRO COME TO YOUR HOUSE TO TEACH YOU. HIKARU GETS TO PLAY AGAINST SAI EVERY DAY — NOT A BAD DEAL!

*ABOUT US $44-132

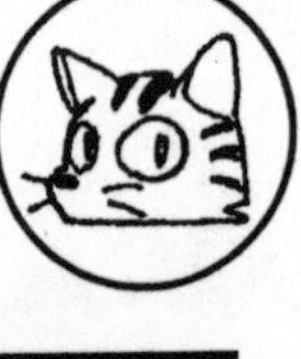

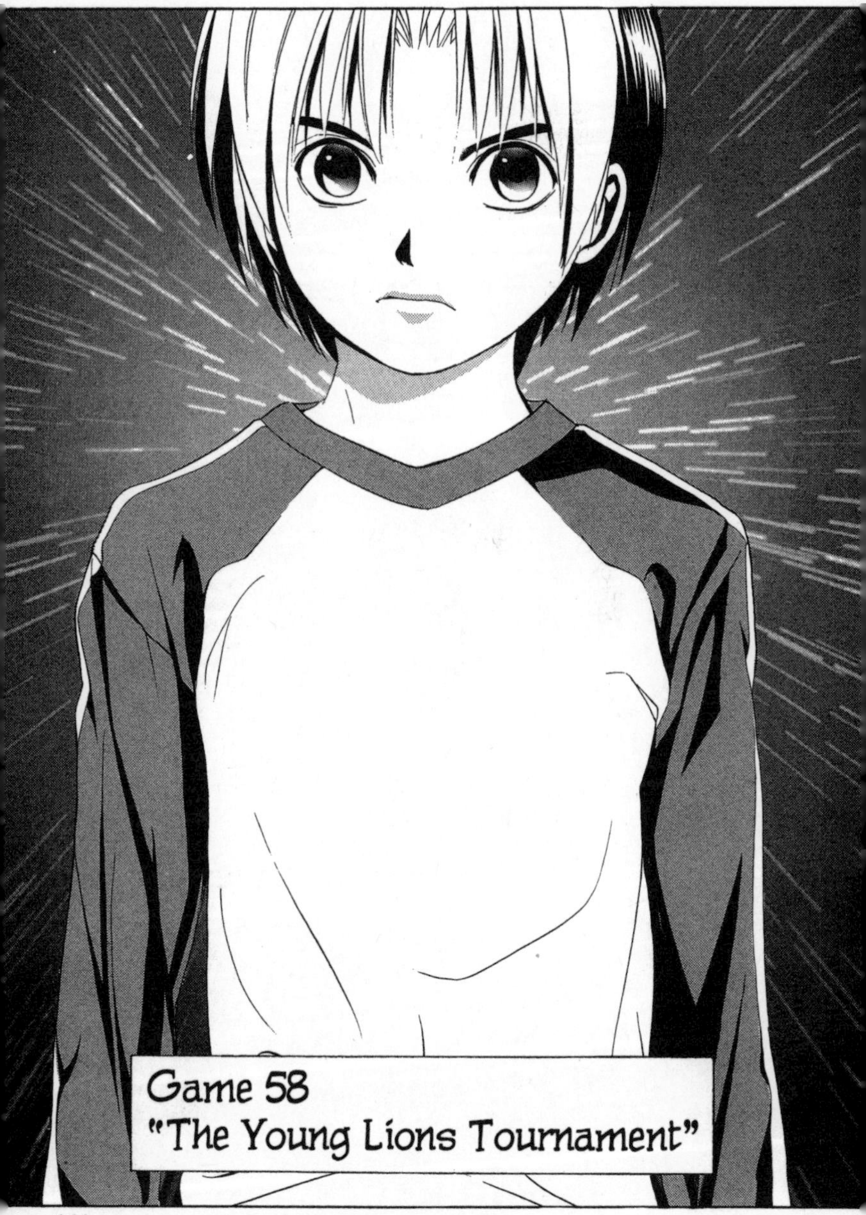
Game 58
"The Young Lions Tournament"

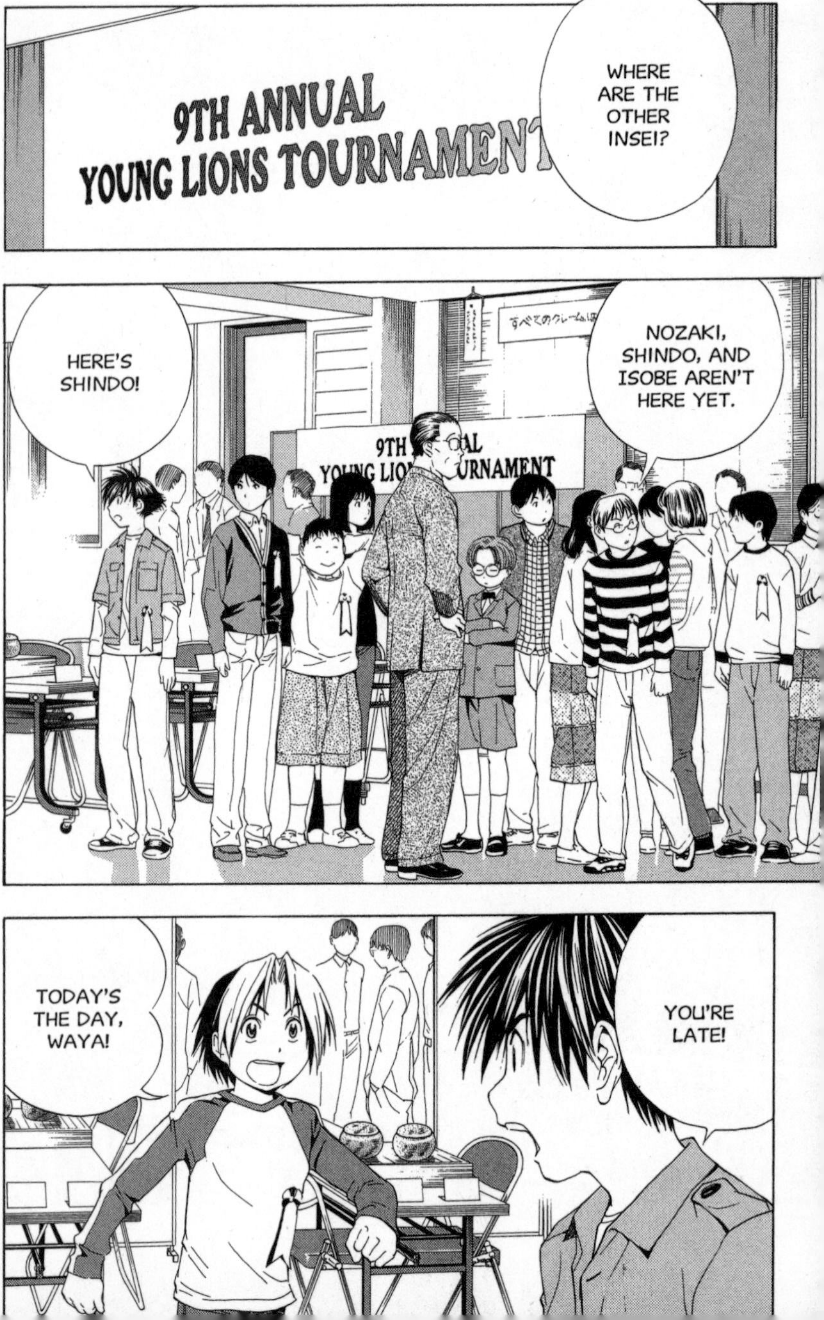
WHERE ARE THE OTHER INSEI?
9TH ANNUAL YOUNG LIONS TOURNAMENT
NOZAKI, SHINDO, AND ISOBE AREN'T HERE YET.
HERE'S SHINDO!
YOU'RE LATE!
TODAY'S THE DAY, WAYA!

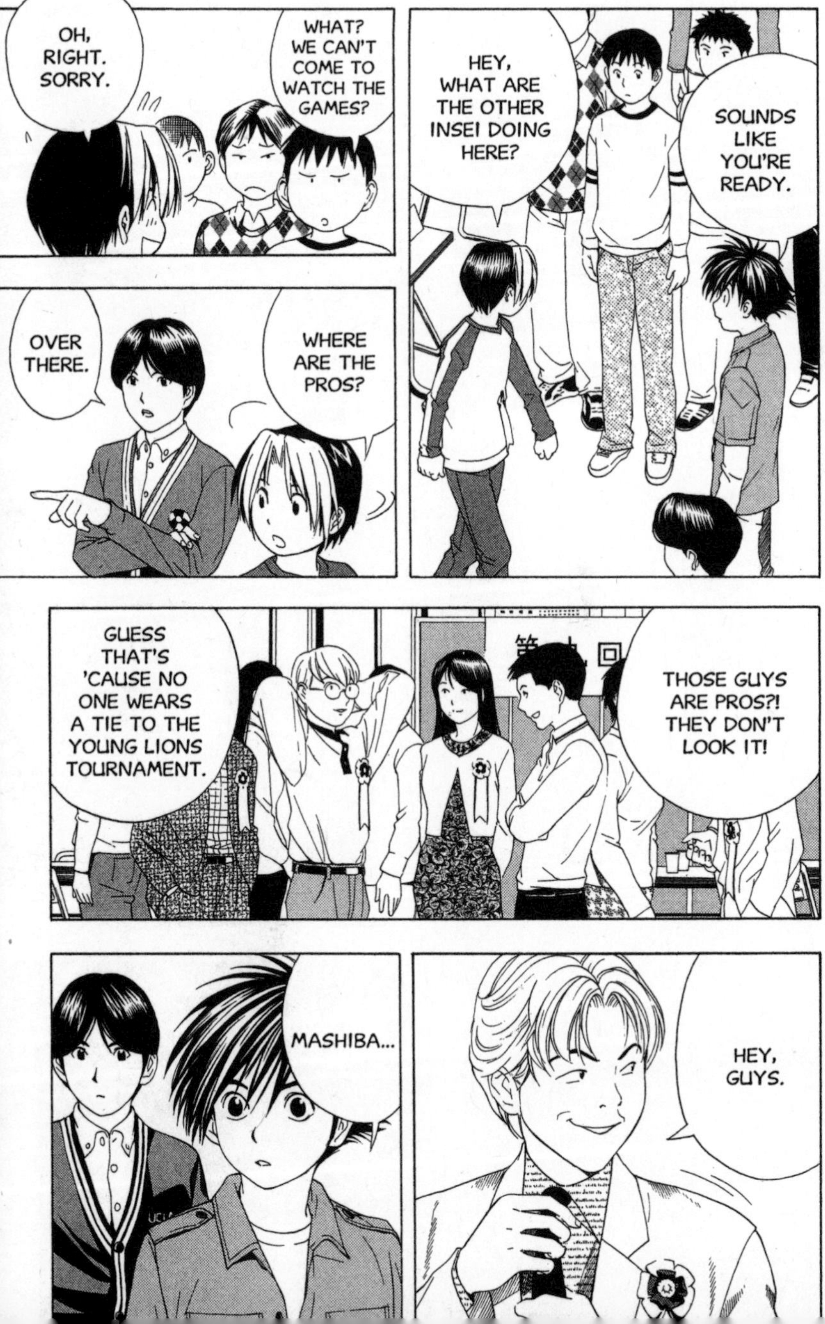
SOUNDS LIKE YOU'RE READY.
HEY, WHAT ARE THE OTHER INSEI DOING HERE?
WHAT? WE CAN'T COME TO WATCH THE GAMES?
OH, RIGHT. SORRY.
WHERE ARE THE PROS?
OVER THERE.
THOSE GUYS ARE PROS?! THEY DON'T LOOK IT!
GUESS THAT'S 'CAUSE NO ONE WEARS A TIE TO THE YOUNG LIONS TOURNAMENT.
HEY, GUYS.
MASHIBA...

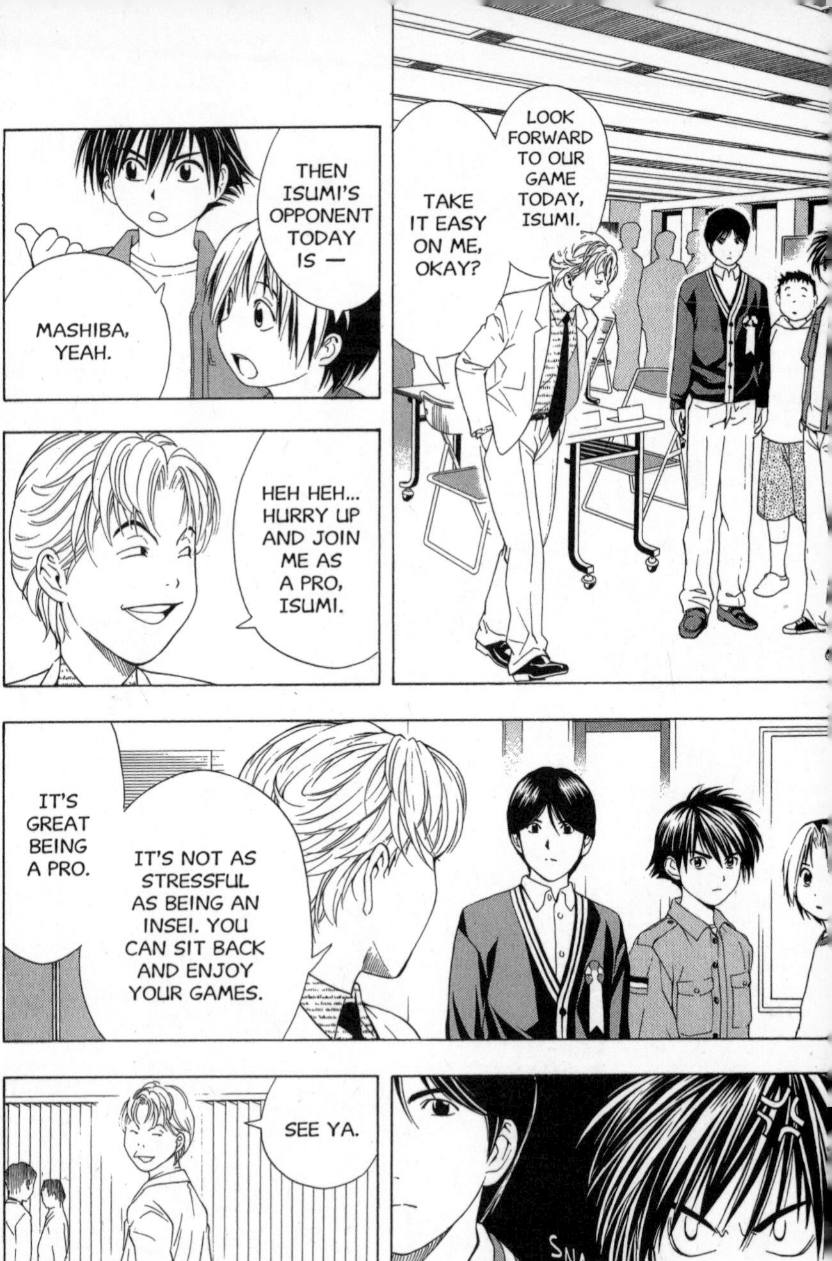
LOOK FORWARD TO OUR GAME TODAY, ISUMI.
TAKE IT EASY ON ME, OKAY?
THEN ISUMI'S OPPONENT TODAY IS —
MASHIBA, YEAH.
HEH HEH... HURRY UP AND JOIN ME AS A PRO, ISUMI.
IT'S GREAT BEING A PRO.
IT'S NOT AS STRESSFUL AS BEING AN INSEI. YOU CAN SIT BACK AND ENJOY YOUR GAMES.
SNAP
SEE YA.

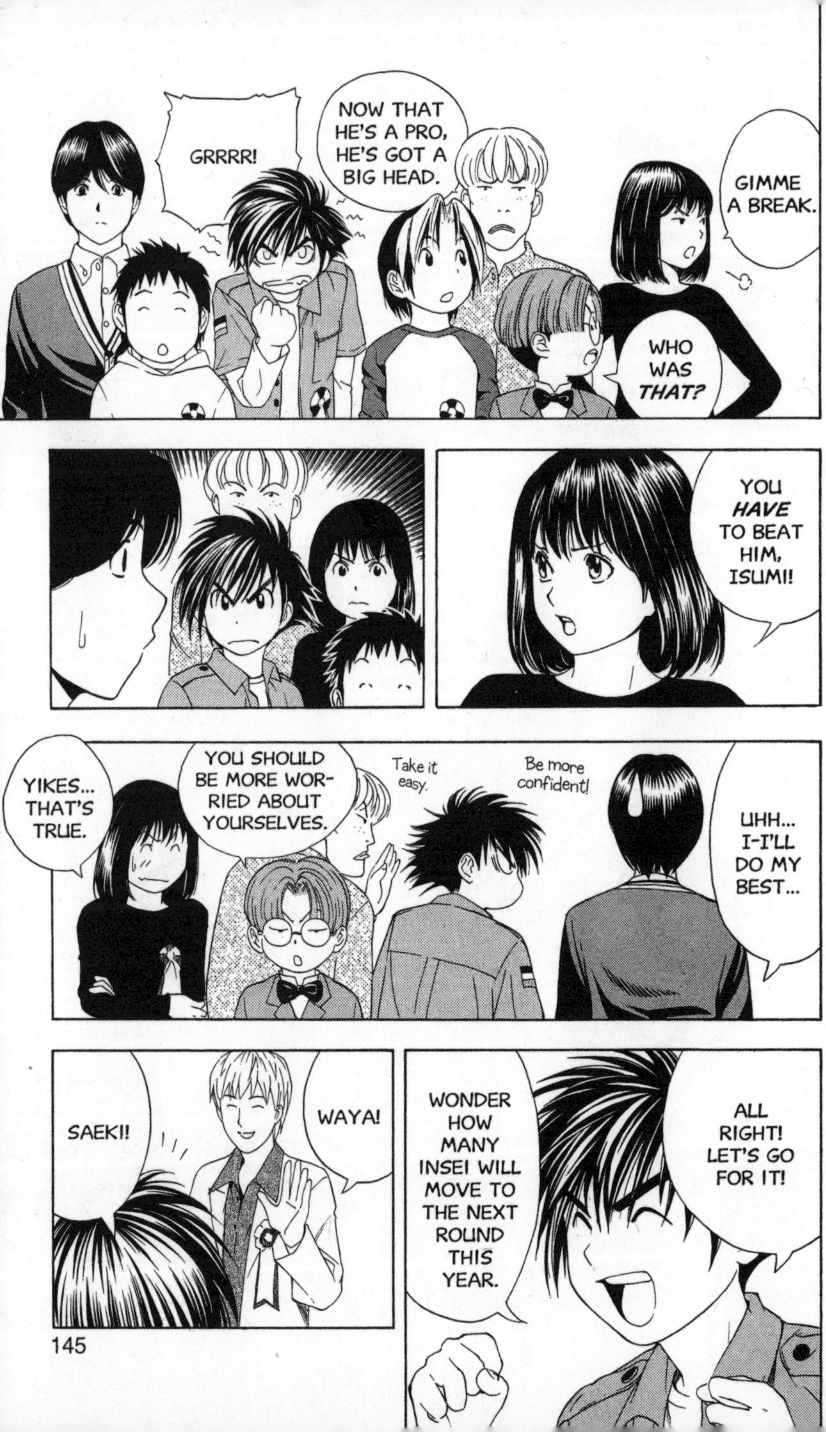

GIMME A BREAK.
NOW THAT HE'S A PRO, HE'S GOT A BIG HEAD.
GRRRR!
WHO WAS *THAT?*
YOU *HAVE* TO BEAT HIM, ISUMI!
UHH... I-I'LL DO MY BEST...
Be more confident!
Take it easy.
YOU SHOULD BE MORE WOR-RIED ABOUT YOURSELVES.
YIKES... THAT'S TRUE.
ALL RIGHT! LET'S GO FOR IT!
WONDER HOW MANY INSEI WILL MOVE TO THE NEXT ROUND THIS YEAR.
WAYA!
SAEKI!

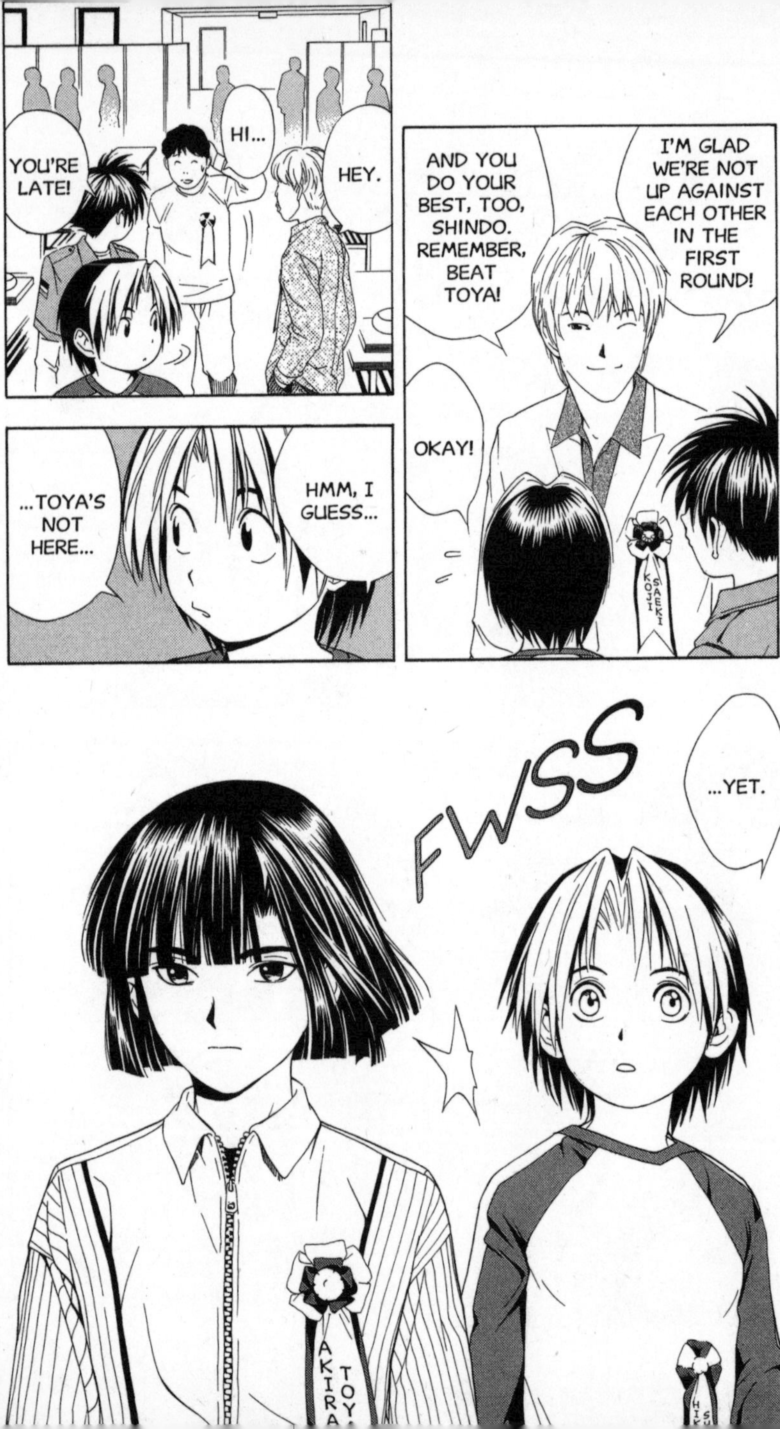
I'M GLAD WE'RE NOT UP AGAINST EACH OTHER IN THE FIRST ROUND!
AND YOU DO YOUR BEST, TOO, SHINDO. REMEMBER, BEAT TOYA!
OKAY!
KOJI SAEKI
HEY.
HI...
YOU'RE LATE!
HMM, I GUESS...
...TOYA'S NOT HERE...
...YET.
FWSS

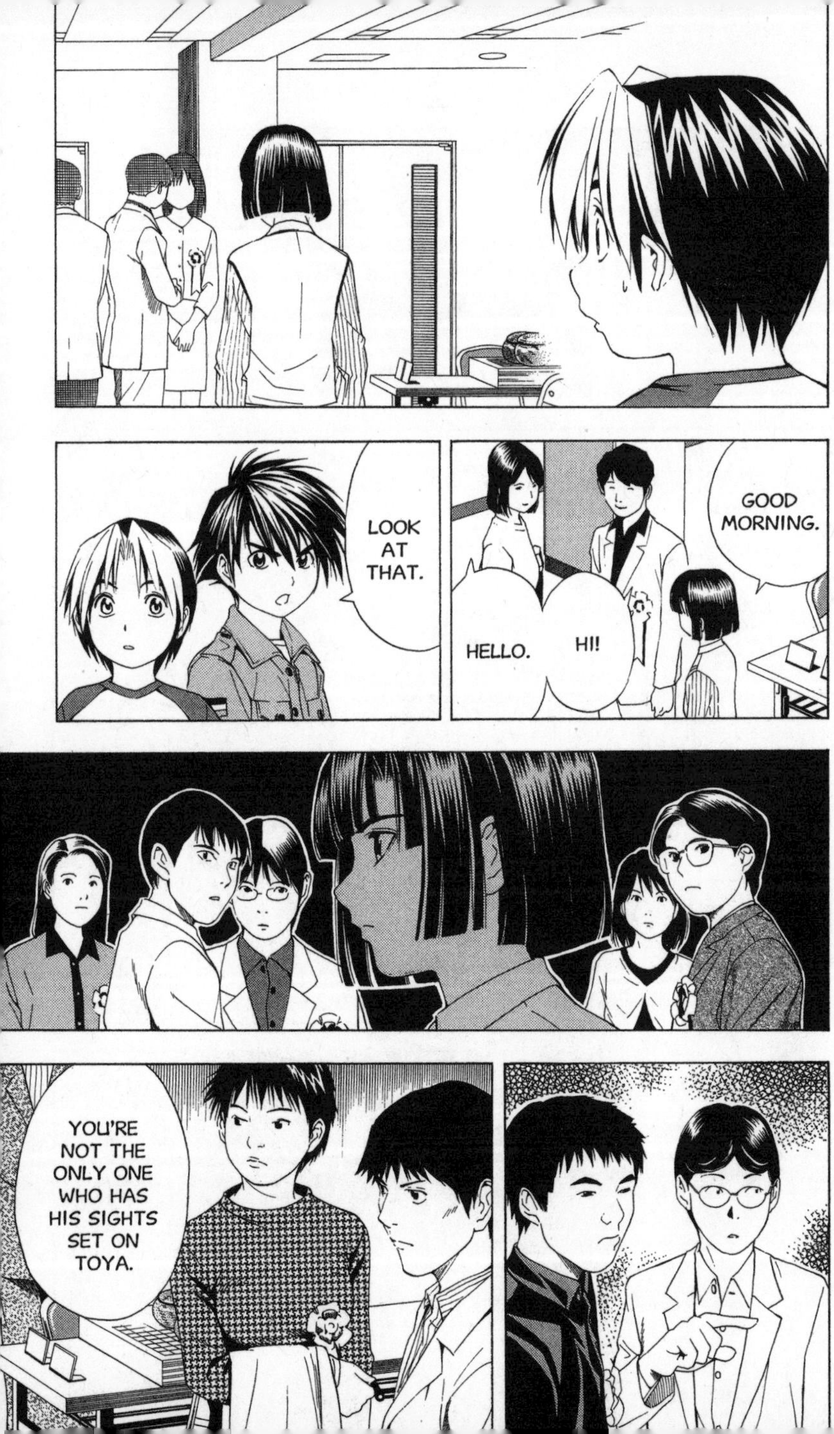
GOOD MORNING.
HI!
HELLO.
LOOK AT THAT.
YOU'RE NOT THE ONLY ONE WHO HAS HIS SIGHTS SET ON TOYA.

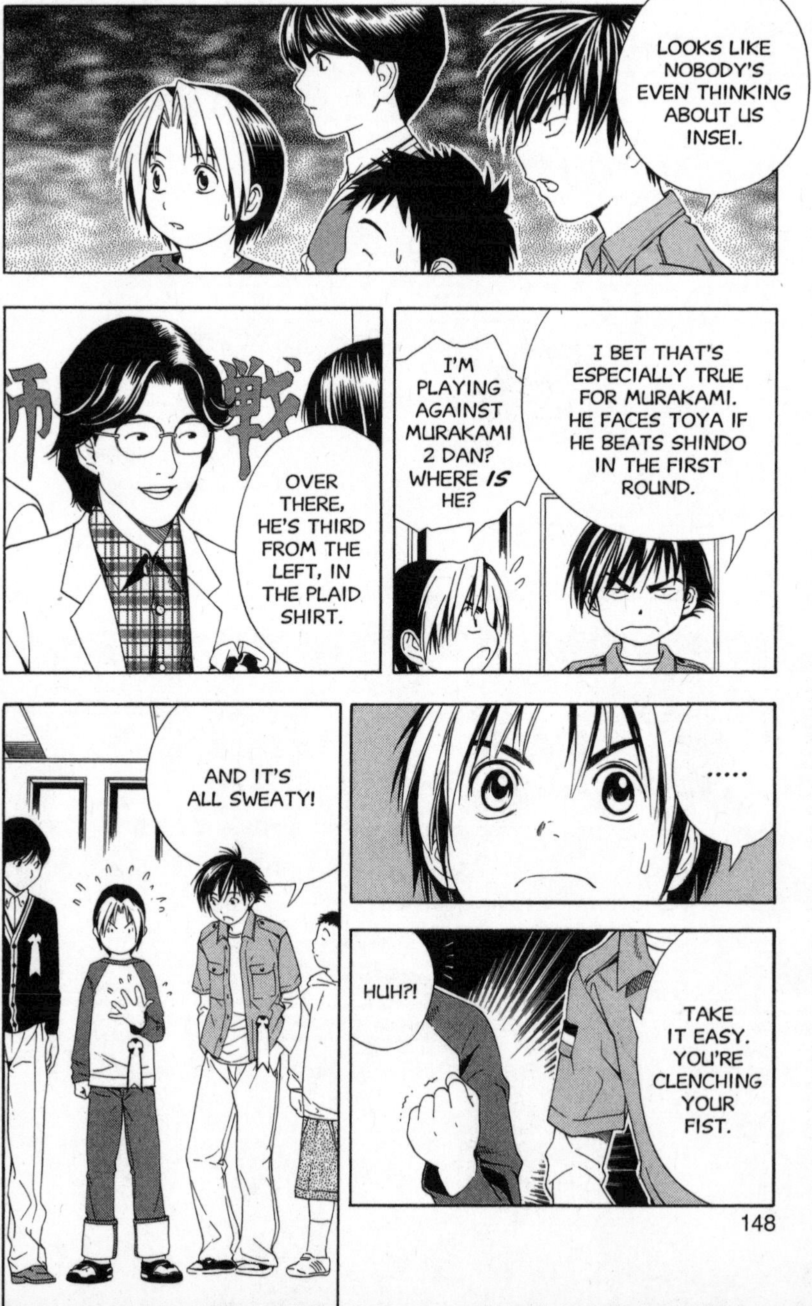
LOOKS LIKE NOBODY'S EVEN THINKING ABOUT US INSEI.
I BET THAT'S ESPECIALLY TRUE FOR MURAKAMI. HE FACES TOYA IF HE BEATS SHINDO IN THE FIRST ROUND.
I'M PLAYING AGAINST MURAKAMI 2 DAN? WHERE *IS* HE?
OVER THERE, HE'S THIRD FROM THE LEFT, IN THE PLAID SHIRT.
.....
TAKE IT EASY. YOU'RE CLENCHING YOUR FIST.
HUH?!
AND IT'S ALL SWEATY!

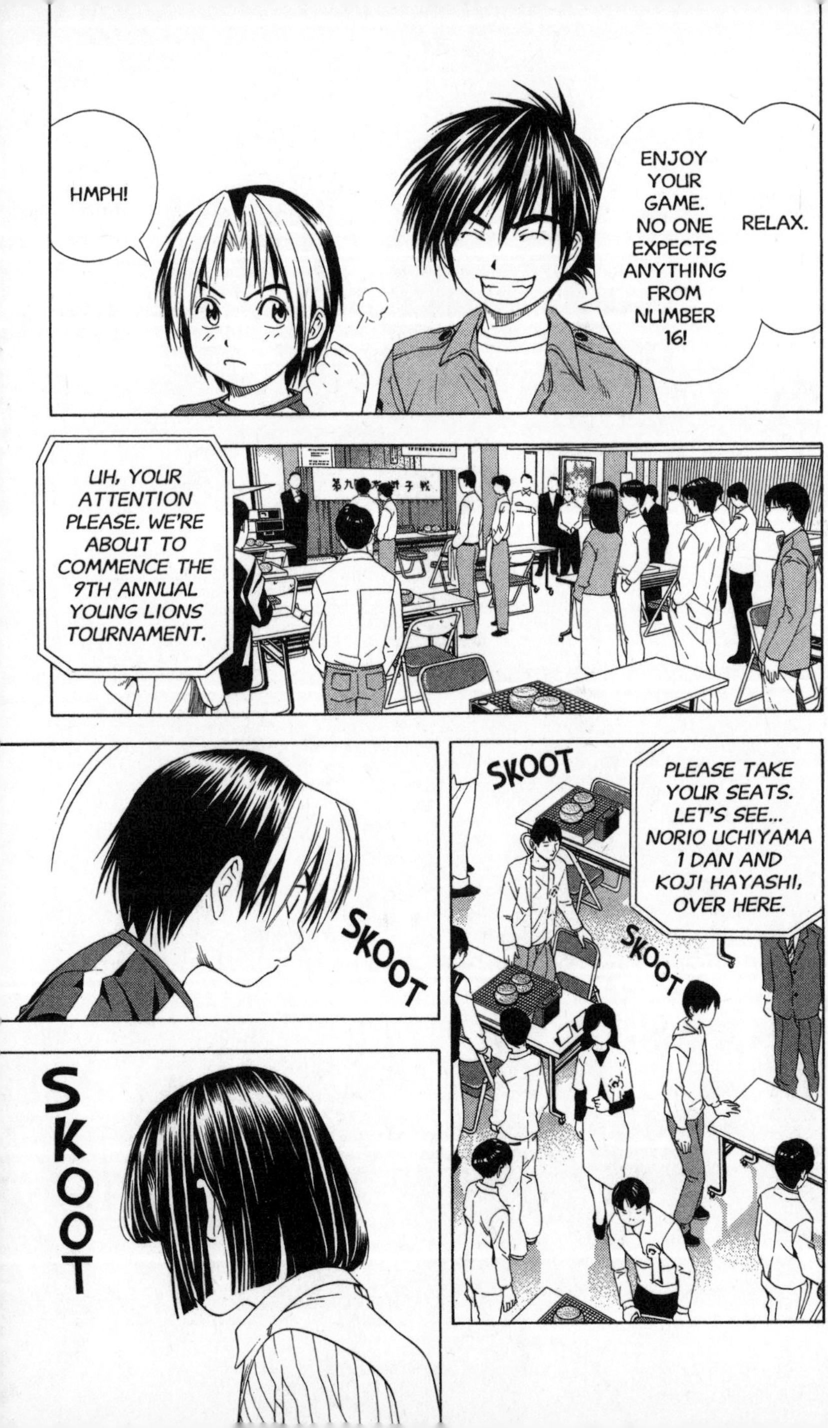
RELAX.
ENJOY YOUR GAME. NO ONE EXPECTS ANYTHING FROM NUMBER 16!
HMPH!
UH, YOUR ATTENTION PLEASE. WE'RE ABOUT TO COMMENCE THE 9TH ANNUAL YOUNG LIONS TOURNAMENT.
PLEASE TAKE YOUR SEATS. LET'S SEE... NORIO UCHIYAMA 1 DAN AND KOJI HAYASHI, OVER HERE.
SKOOT
SKOOT
SKOOT
SKOOT

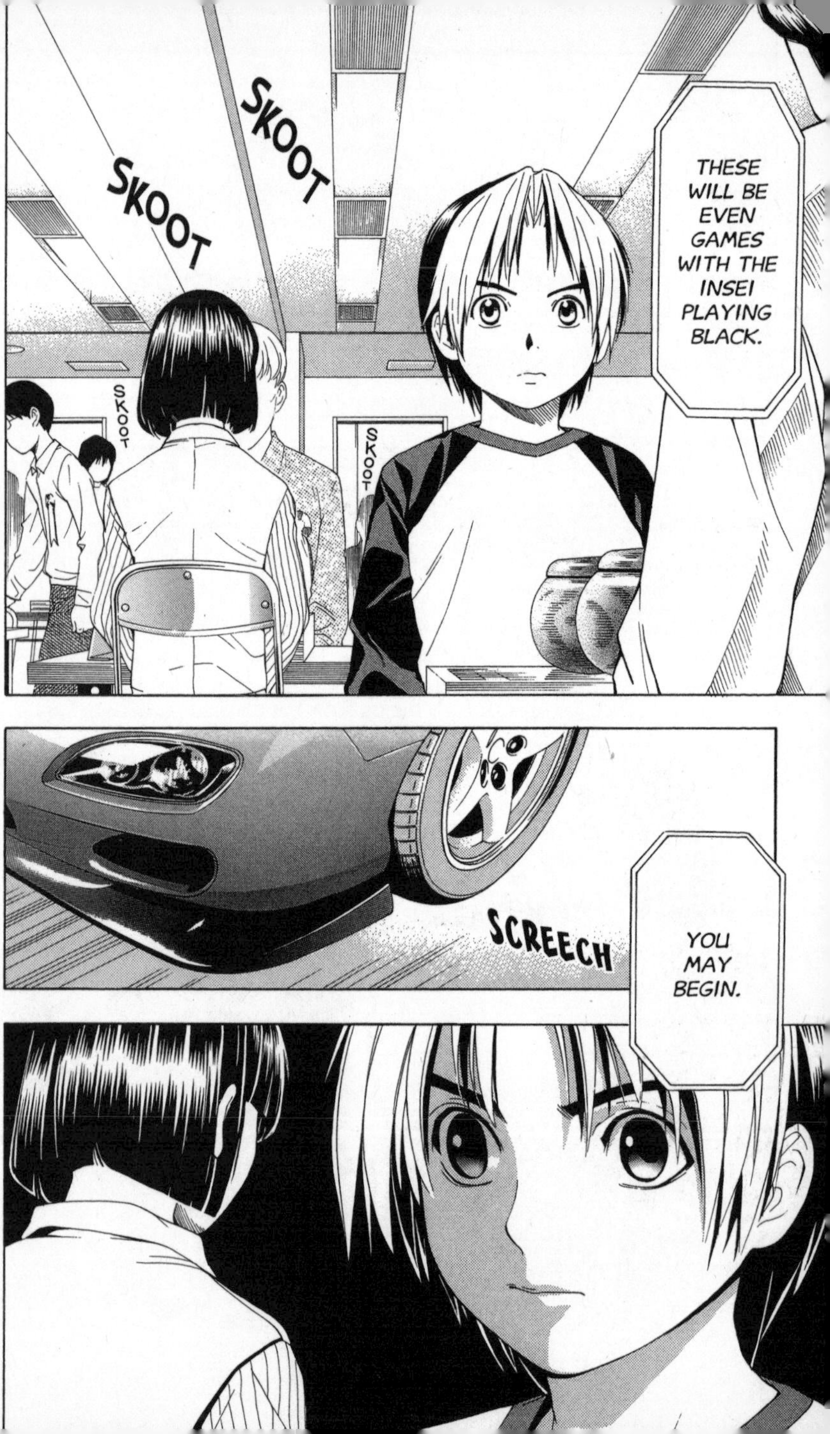
THESE WILL BE EVEN GAMES WITH THE INSEI PLAYING BLACK.
SKOOT
SKOOT
SKOOT
SKOOT
YOU MAY BEGIN.
SCREECH

READ THIS WAY

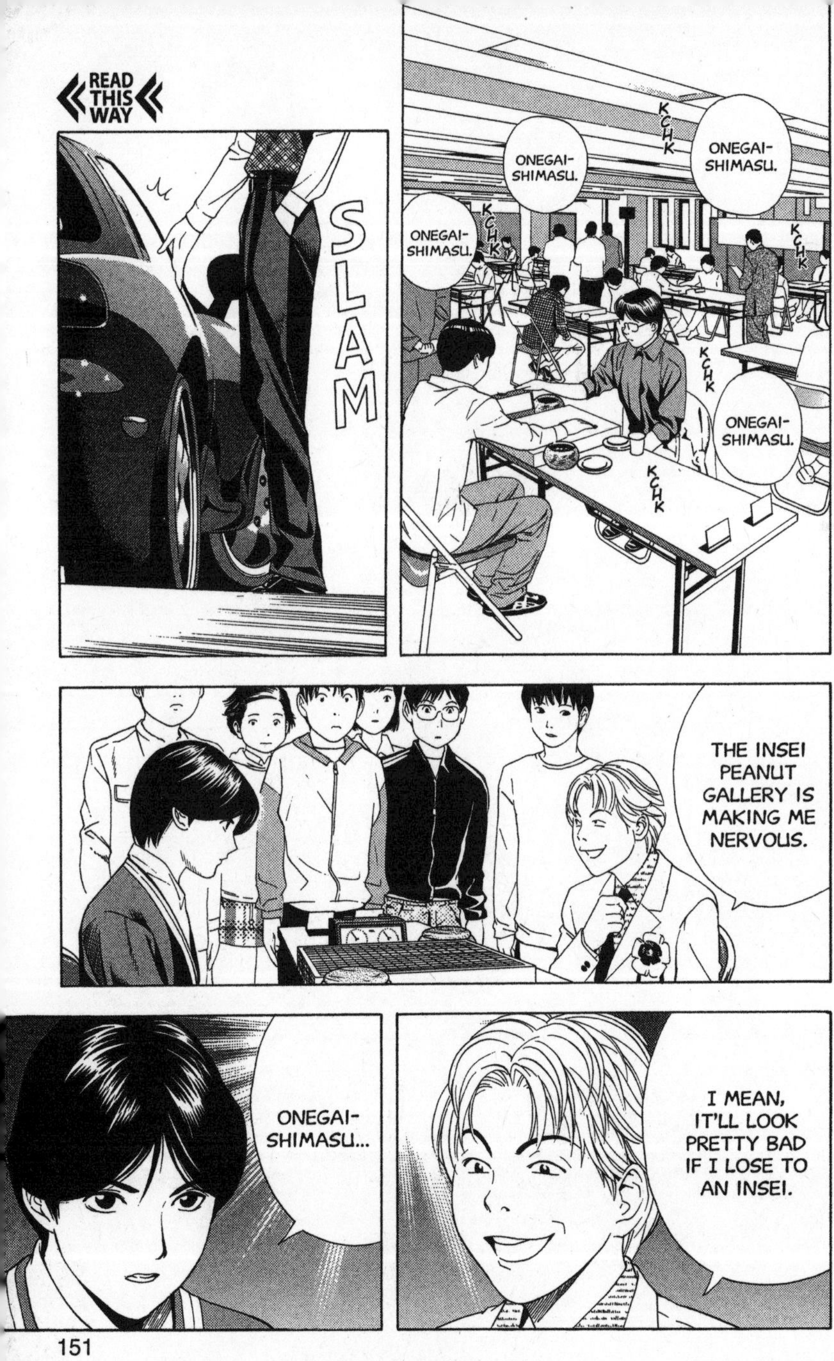
ONEGAI-SHIMASU.
KCHK
ONEGAI-SHIMASU.
KCHK
KCHK
ONEGAI-SHIMASU.
KCHK
ONEGAI-SHIMASU.
KCHK
SLAM
THE INSEI PEANUT GALLERY IS MAKING ME NERVOUS.
I MEAN, IT'LL LOOK PRETTY BAD IF I LOSE TO AN INSEI.
ONEGAI-SHIMASU...

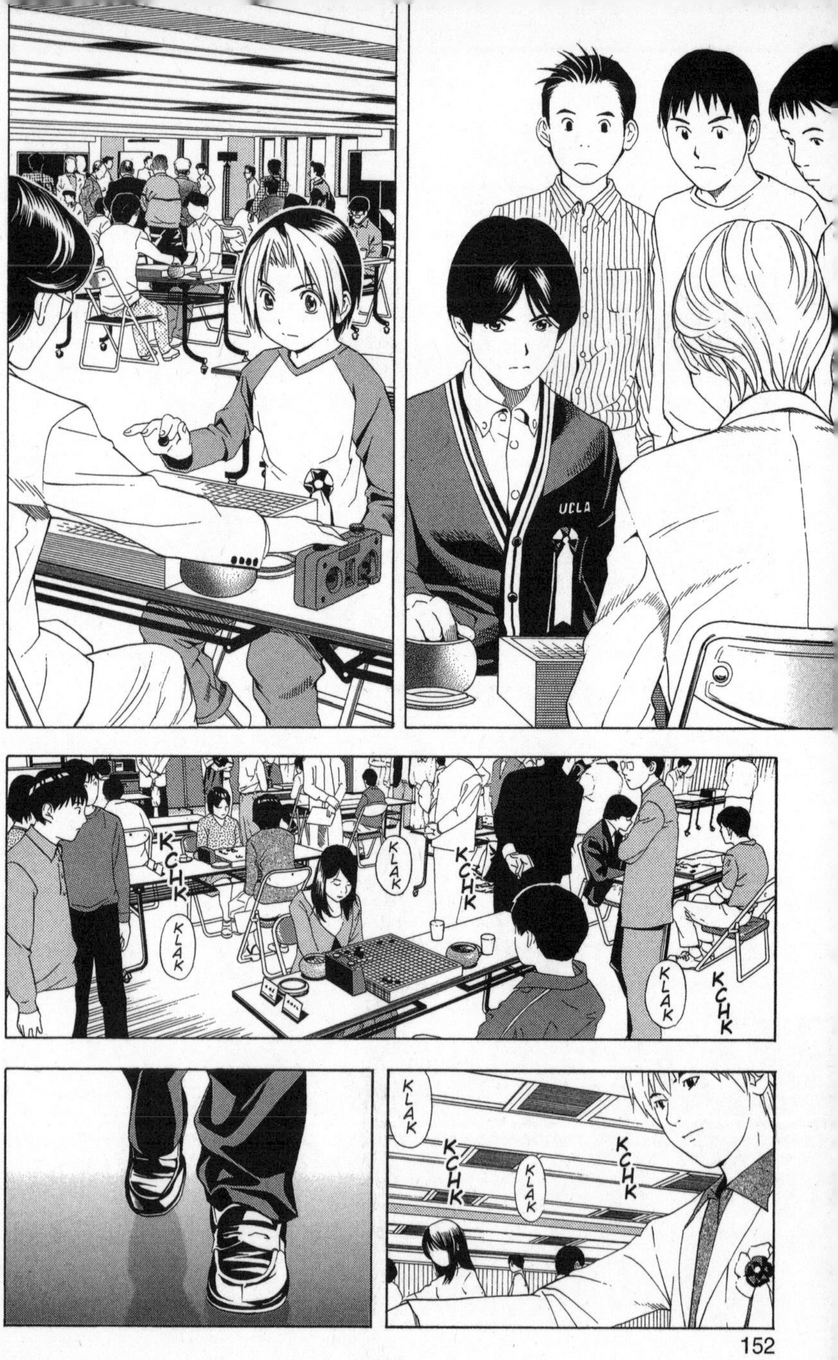
UCLA
KCHK
KLAK
KCHK
KLAK
KCHK
KLAK
KCHK
KLAK
KCHK
KLAK

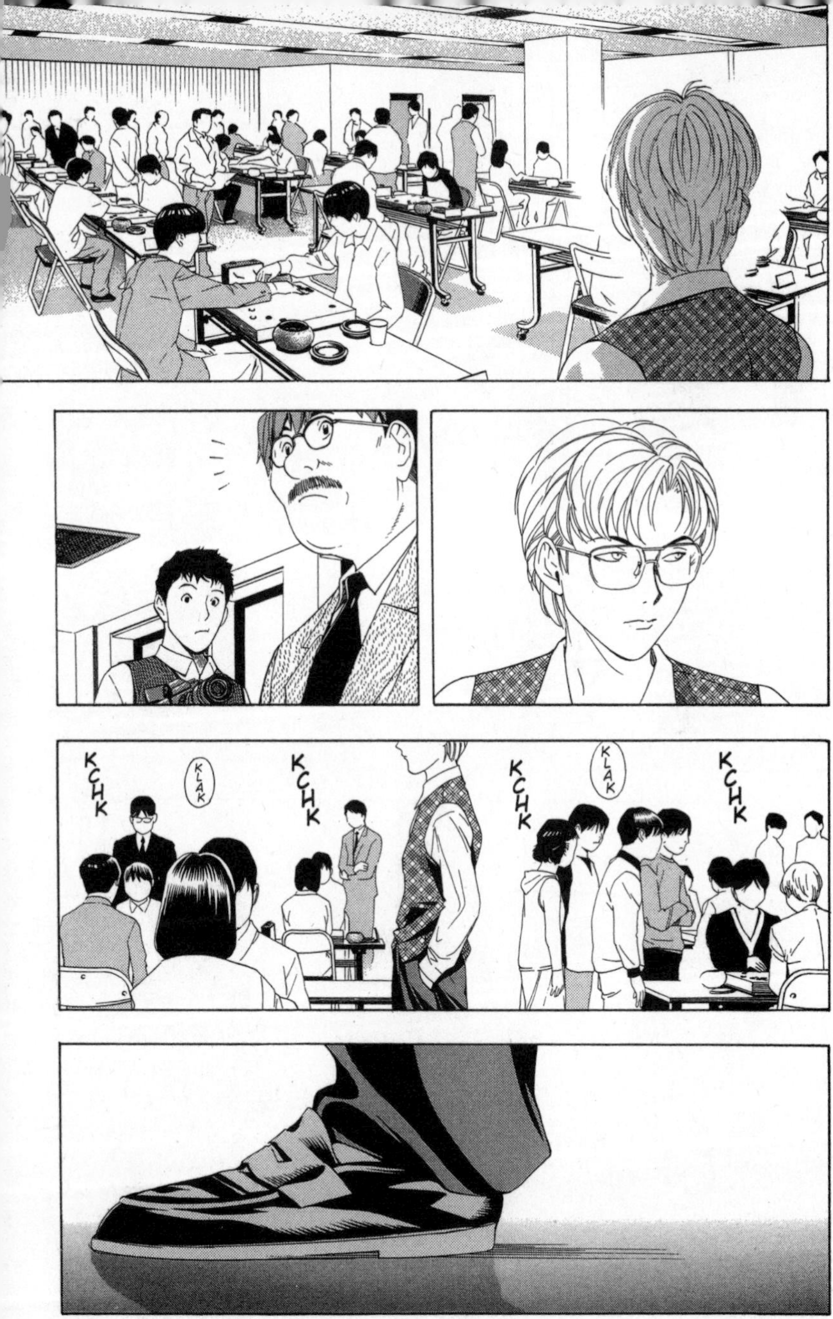
KCHK
KLAK
KCHK
KCHK
KLAK
KCHK

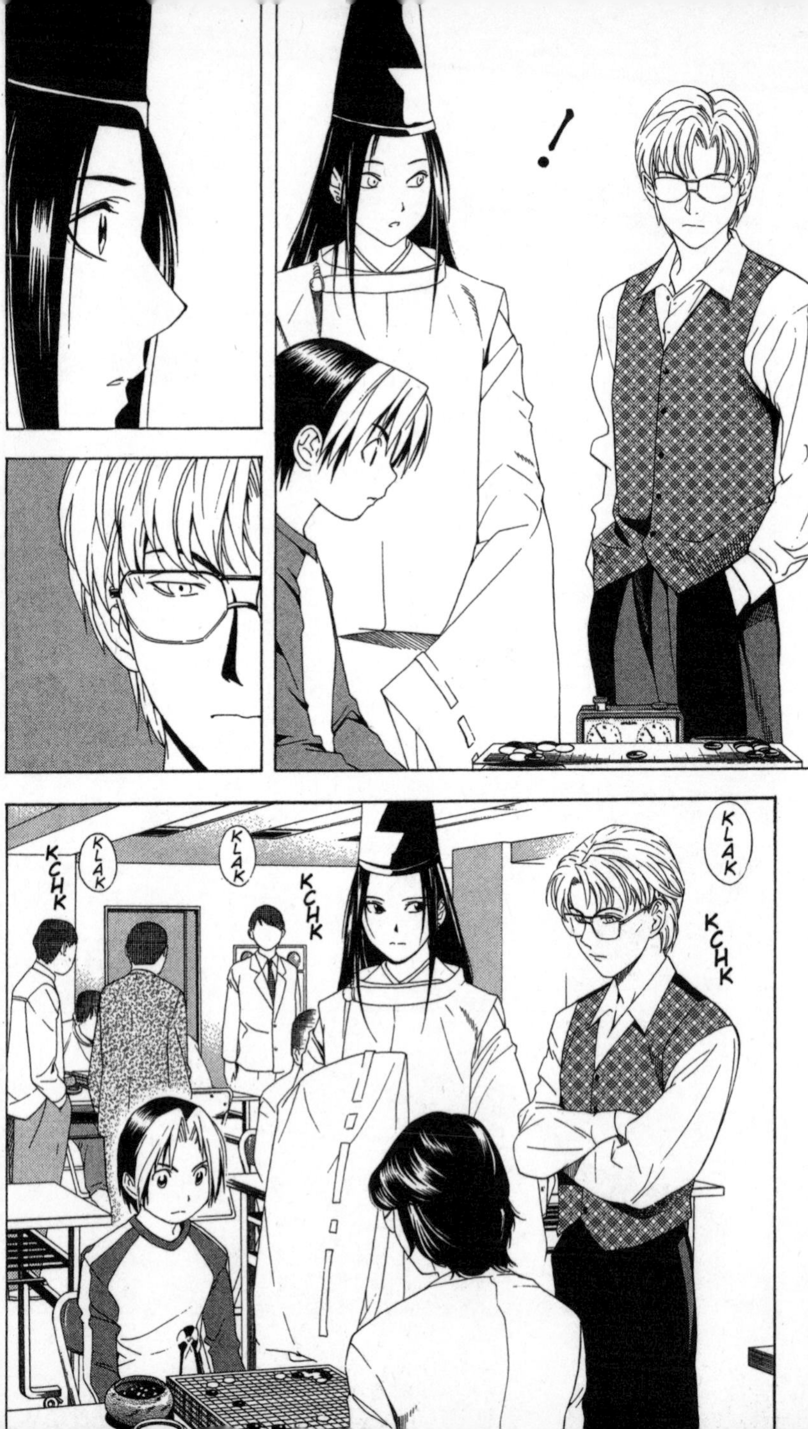
!
KLAK
KCHK
KCHK
KLAK
KLAK
KCHK

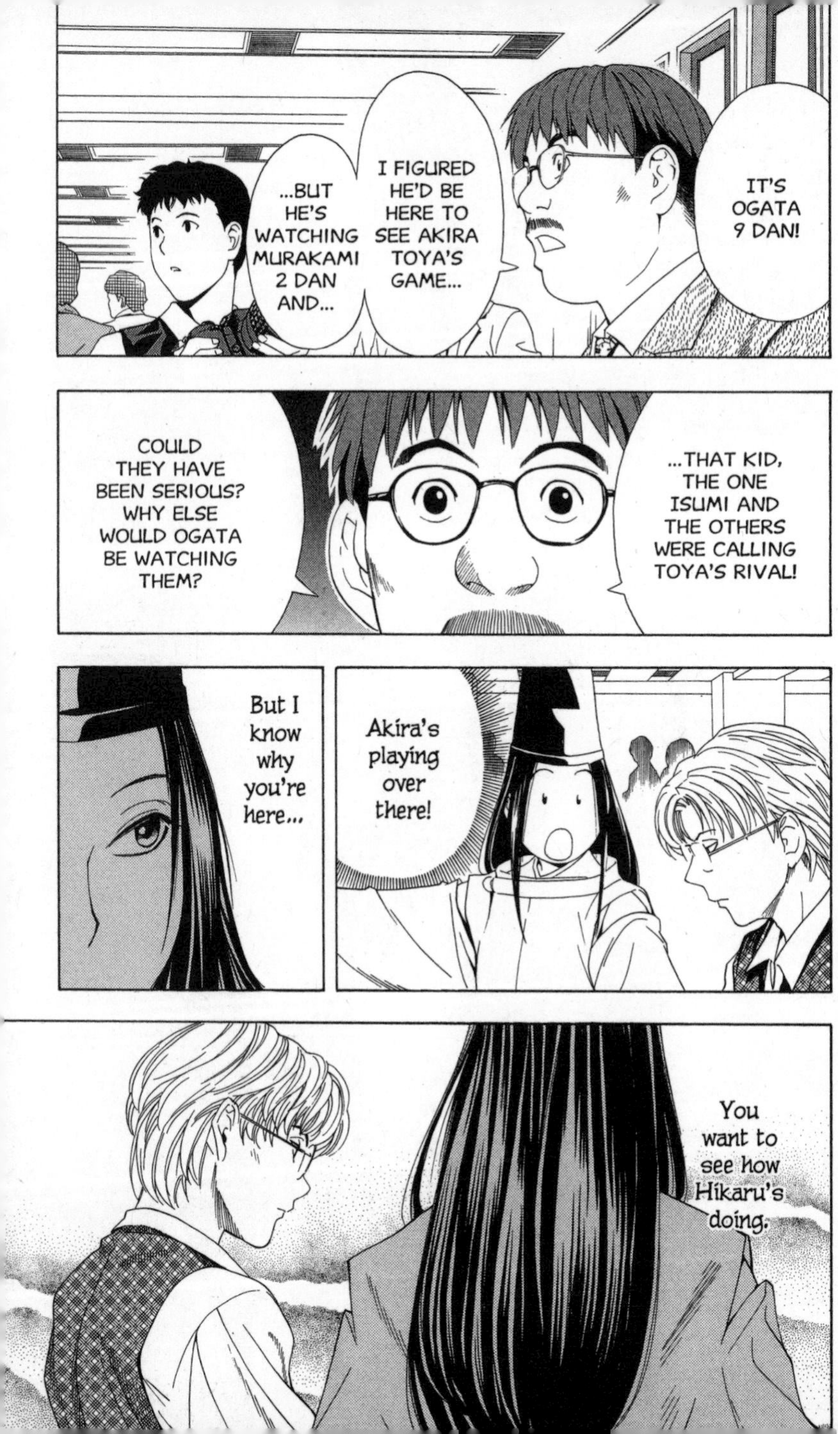
IT'S OGATA 9 DAN!
I FIGURED HE'D BE HERE TO SEE AKIRA TOYA'S GAME...
...BUT HE'S WATCHING MURAKAMI 2 DAN AND...
...THAT KID, THE ONE ISUMI AND THE OTHERS WERE CALLING TOYA'S RIVAL!
COULD THEY HAVE BEEN SERIOUS? WHY ELSE WOULD OGATA BE WATCHING THEM?
Akira's playing over there!
But I know why you're here...
You want to see how Hikaru's doing.

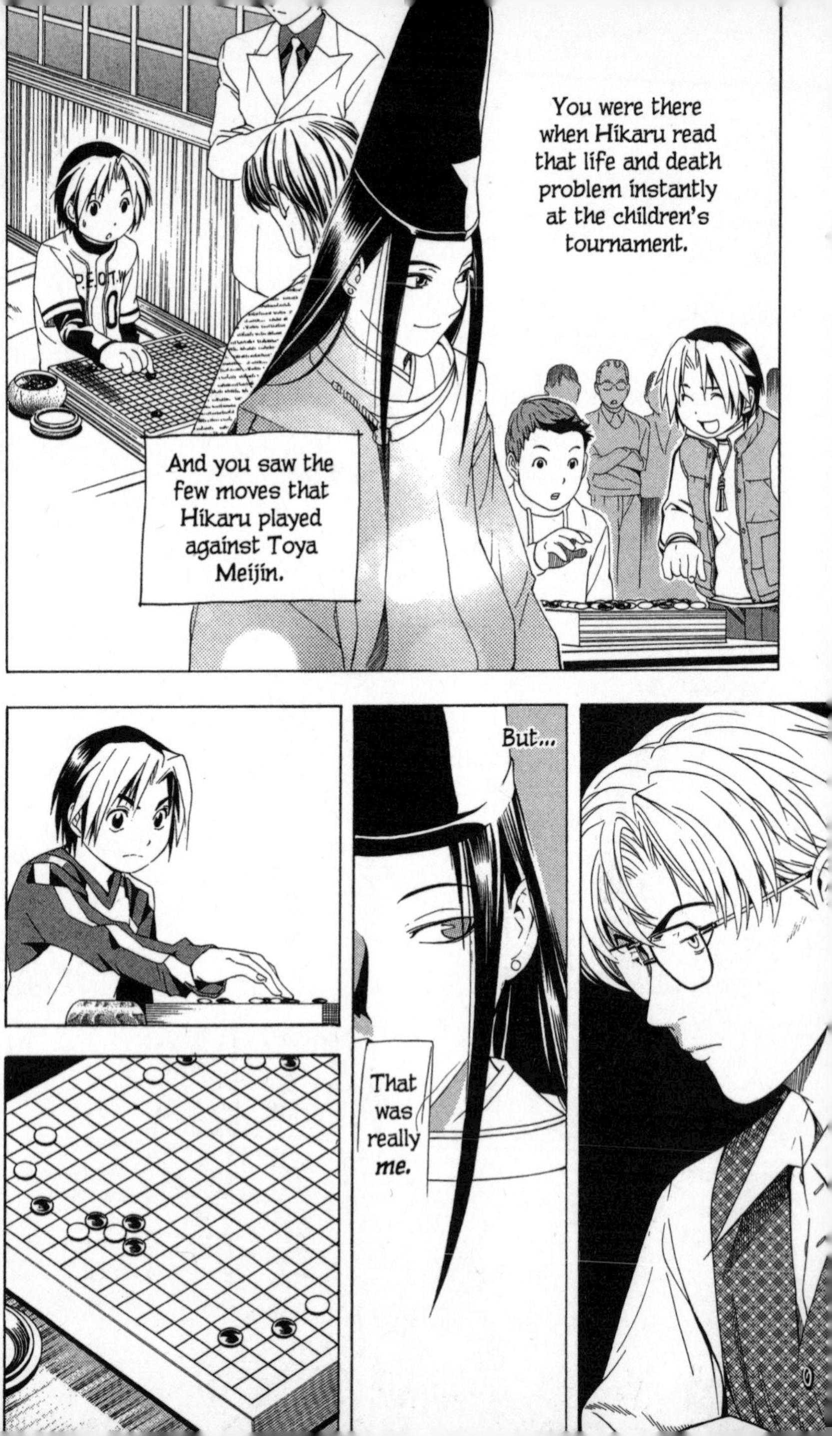
You were there when Hikaru read that life and death problem instantly at the children's tournament.
And you saw the few moves that Hikaru played against Toya Meijin.
But...
That was really *me*.

Now, every day I play only against Hikaru.

And that's fun, too, in its own way.

You are a go player.

If the chance should arise, I would enjoy playing a game with you, too.

In the past, I've played so many games with so many different players.

The memories come flooding back to me.

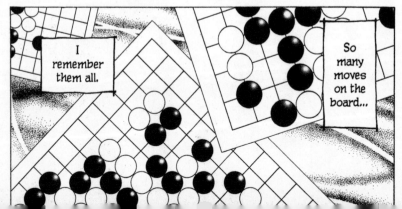

So many moves on the board...

I remember them all.

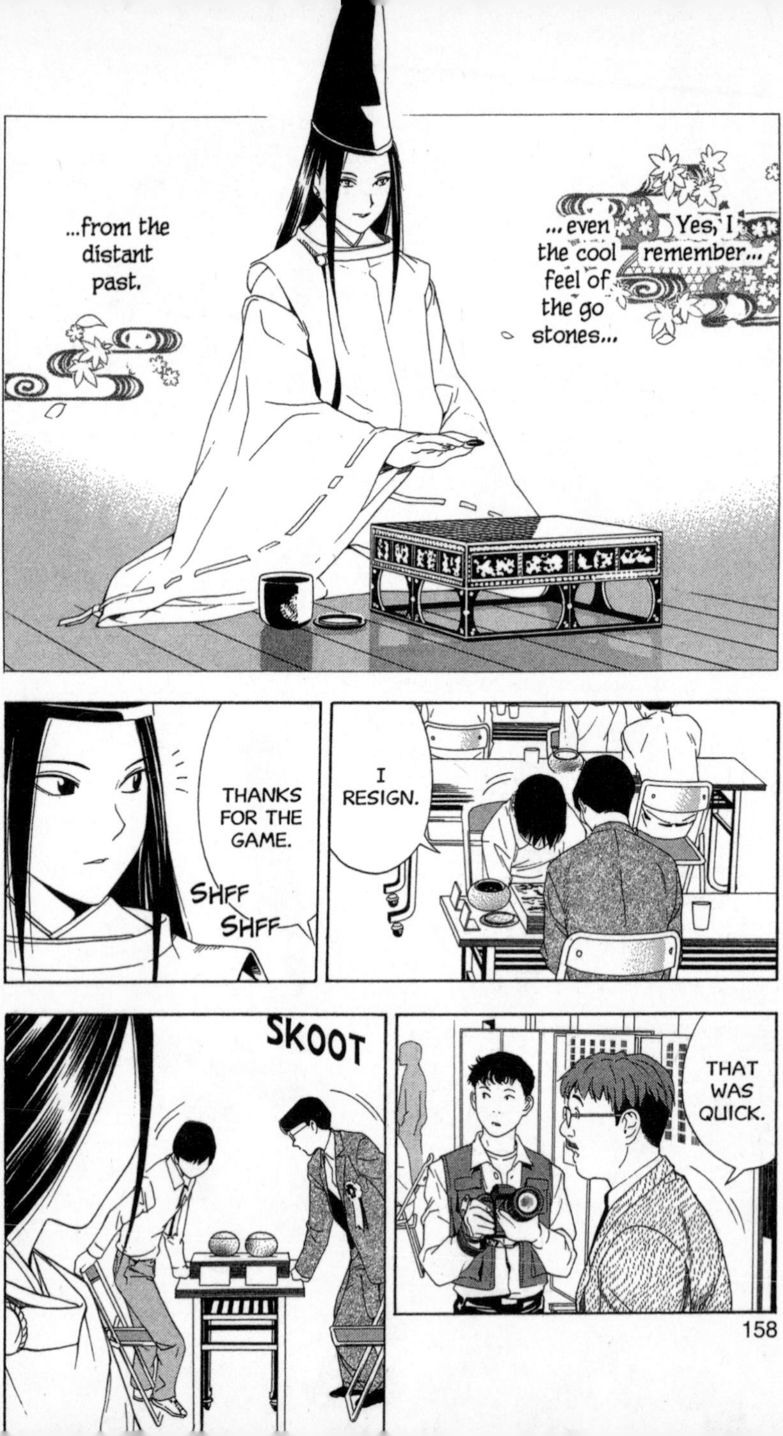
Yes, I remember...
...even the cool feel of the go stones...
...from the distant past.
I RESIGN.
THANKS FOR THE GAME.
SHFF SHFF
THAT WAS QUICK.
SKOOT

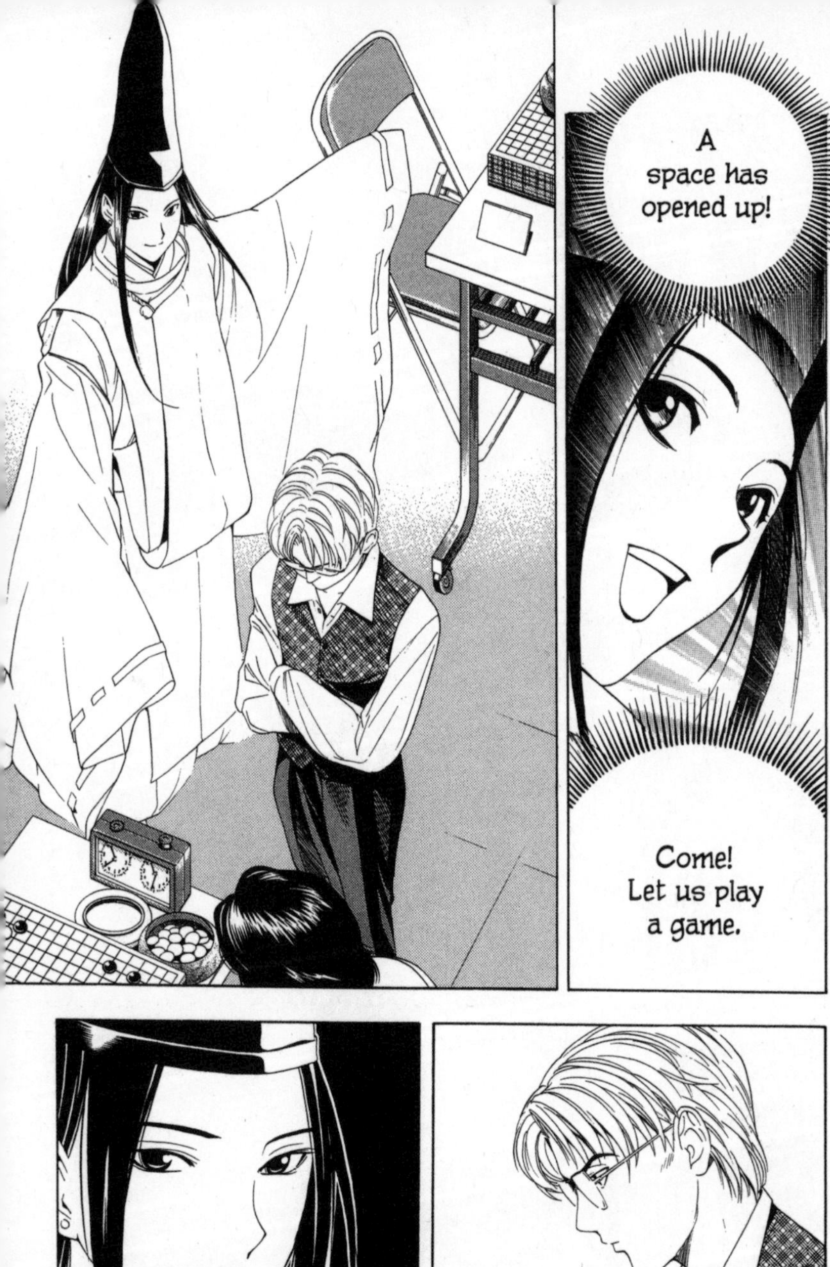
A space has opened up!
Come! Let us play a game.

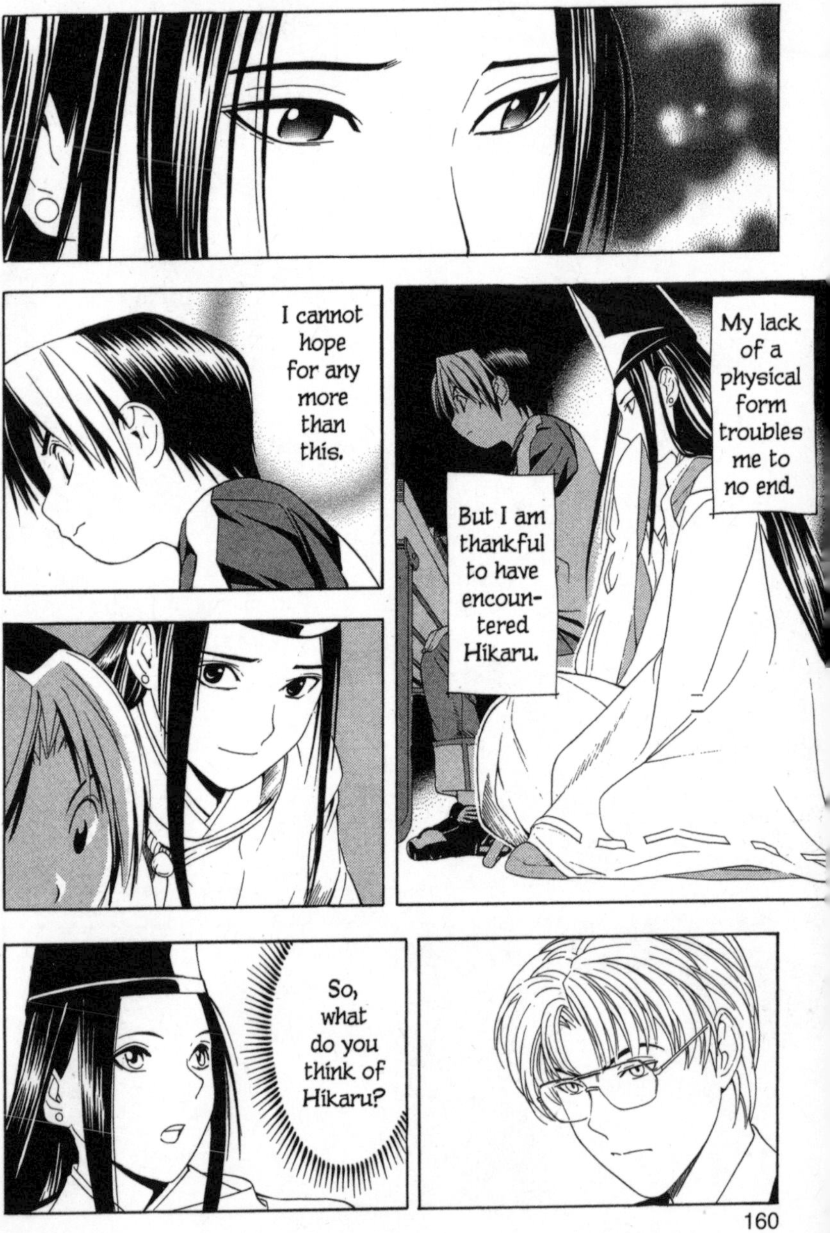
My lack of a physical form troubles me to no end.
But I am thankful to have encountered Hikaru.
I cannot hope for any more than this.
So, what do you think of Hikaru?

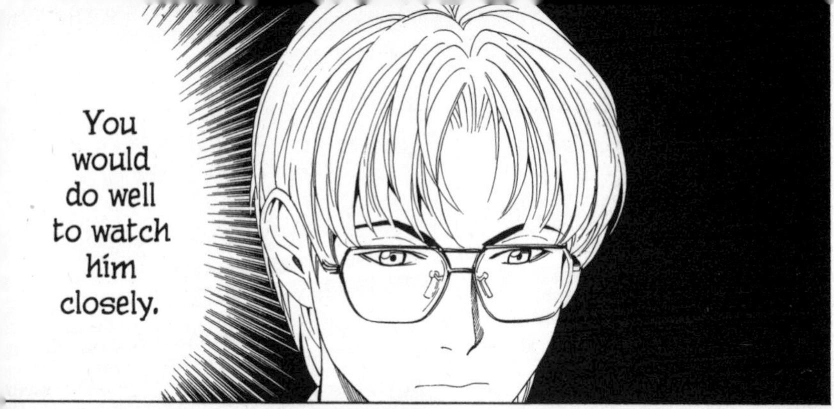
You would do well to watch him closely.
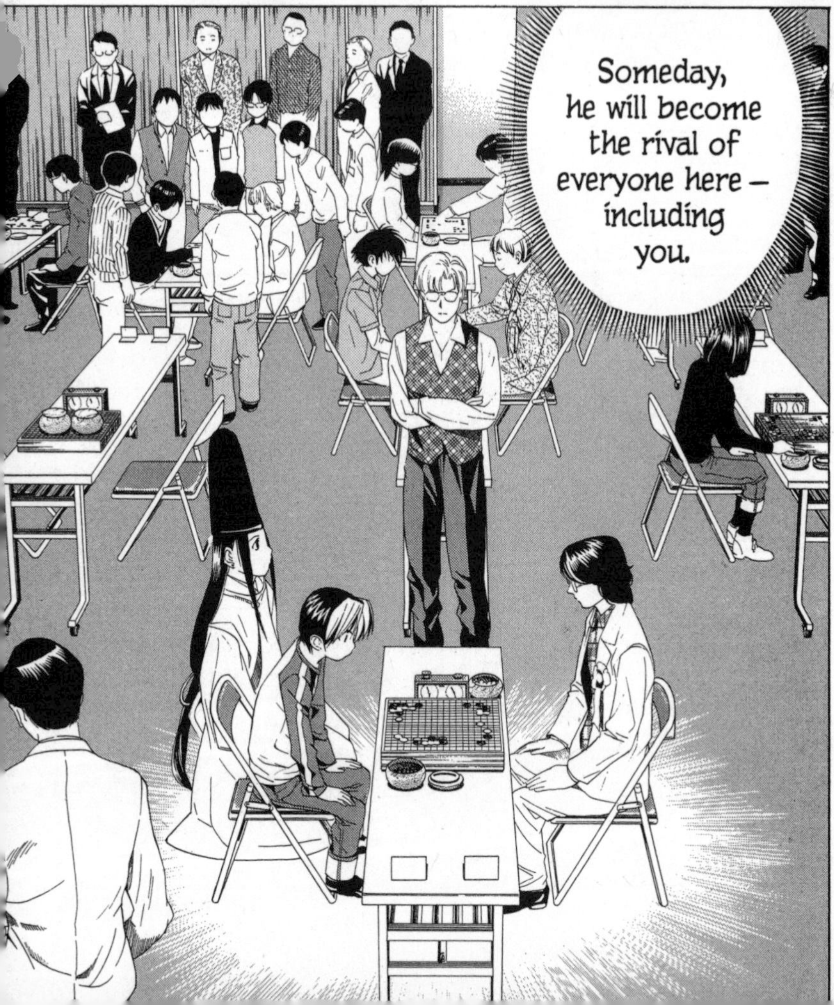
Someday, he will become the rival of everyone here – including you.

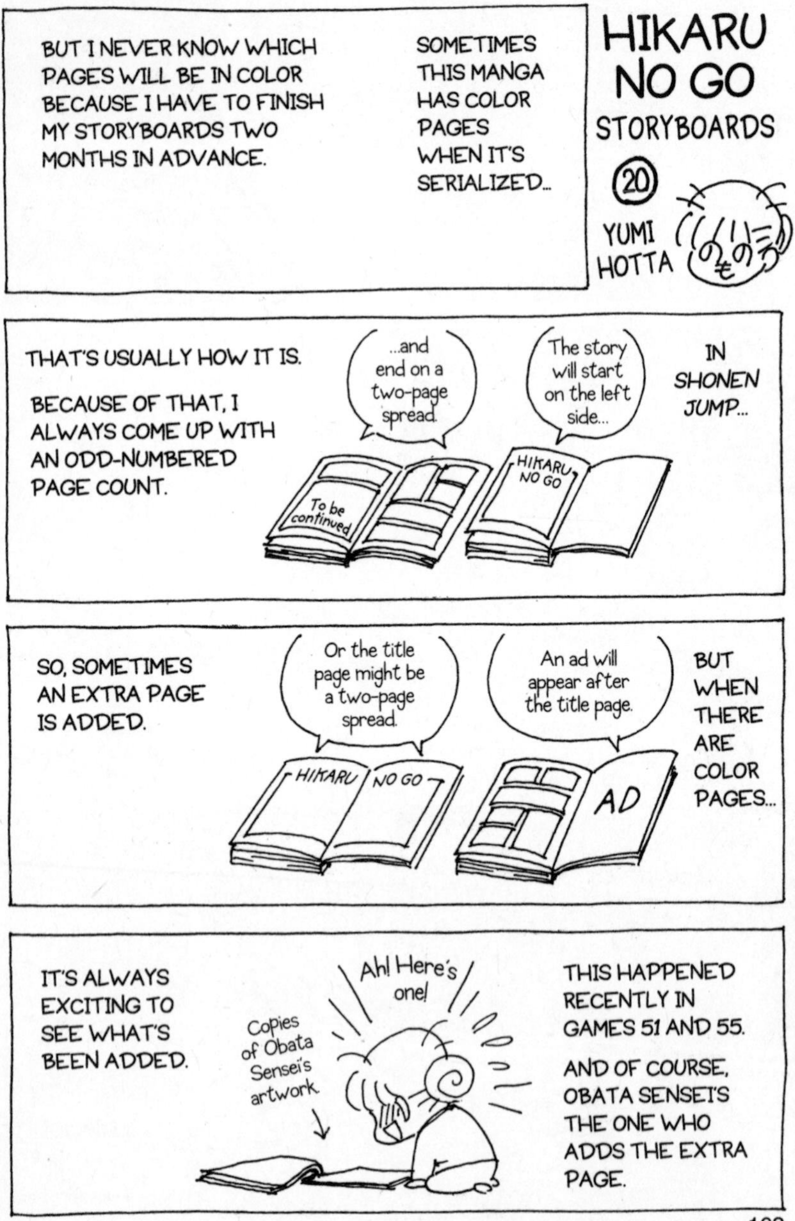
HIKARU NO GO
STORYBOARDS
20
YUMI HOTTA
SOMETIMES THIS MANGA HAS COLOR PAGES WHEN IT'S SERIALIZED...
BUT I NEVER KNOW WHICH PAGES WILL BE IN COLOR BECAUSE I HAVE TO FINISH MY STORYBOARDS TWO MONTHS IN ADVANCE.
IN SHONEN JUMP...
The story will start on the left side...
HIKARU NO GO
...and end on a two-page spread.
To be continued
THAT'S USUALLY HOW IT IS.
BECAUSE OF THAT, I ALWAYS COME UP WITH AN ODD-NUMBERED PAGE COUNT.
BUT WHEN THERE ARE COLOR PAGES...
An ad will appear after the title page.
AD
Or the title page might be a two-page spread.
HIKARU
NO GO
SO, SOMETIMES AN EXTRA PAGE IS ADDED.
THIS HAPPENED RECENTLY IN GAMES 51 AND 55.
AND OF COURSE, OBATA SENSEI'S THE ONE WHO ADDS THE EXTRA PAGE.
Ah! Here's one!
Copies of Obata Sensei's artwork
IT'S ALWAYS EXCITING TO SEE WHAT'S BEEN ADDED.

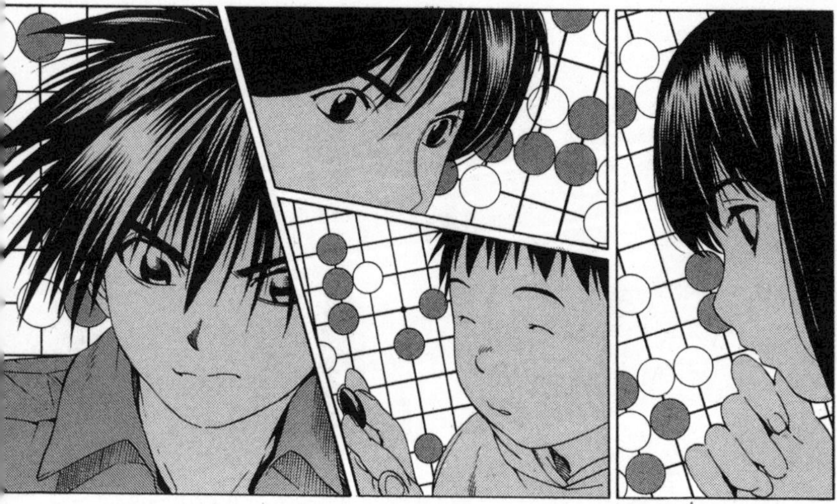

# Game 59 "Toya Looks Back"

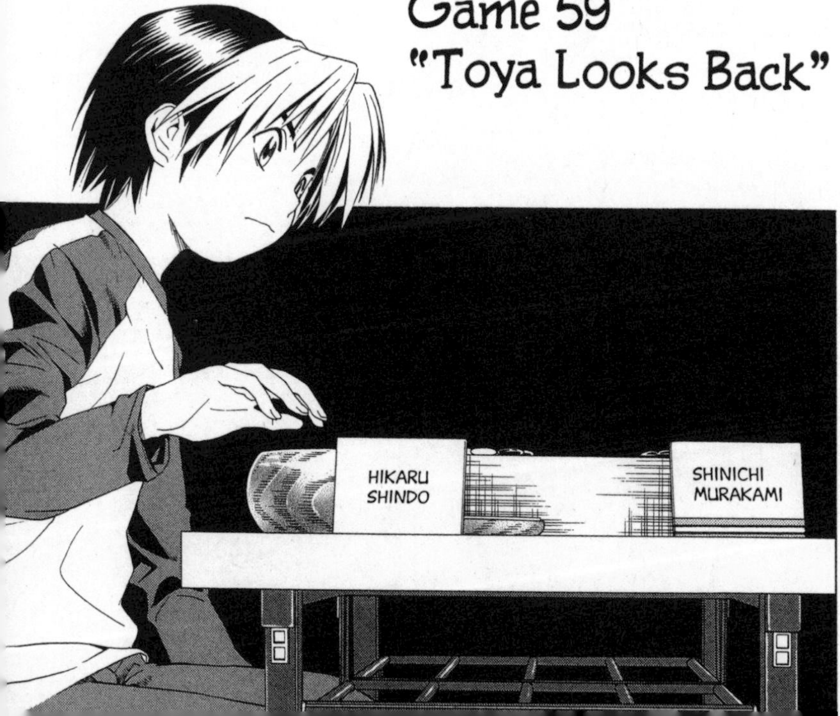
SHINICHI MURAKAMI
HIKARU SHINDO

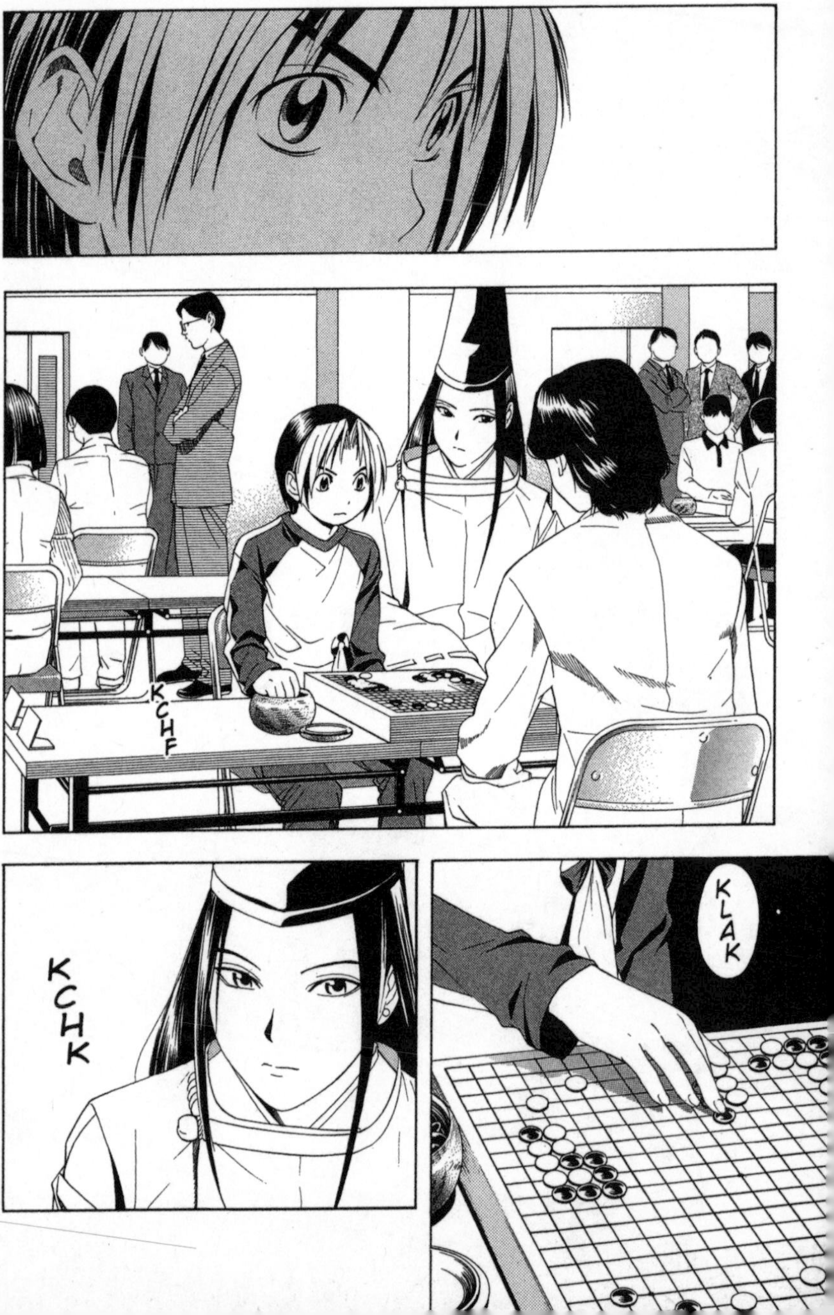
KCHF
KLAK
KCHK

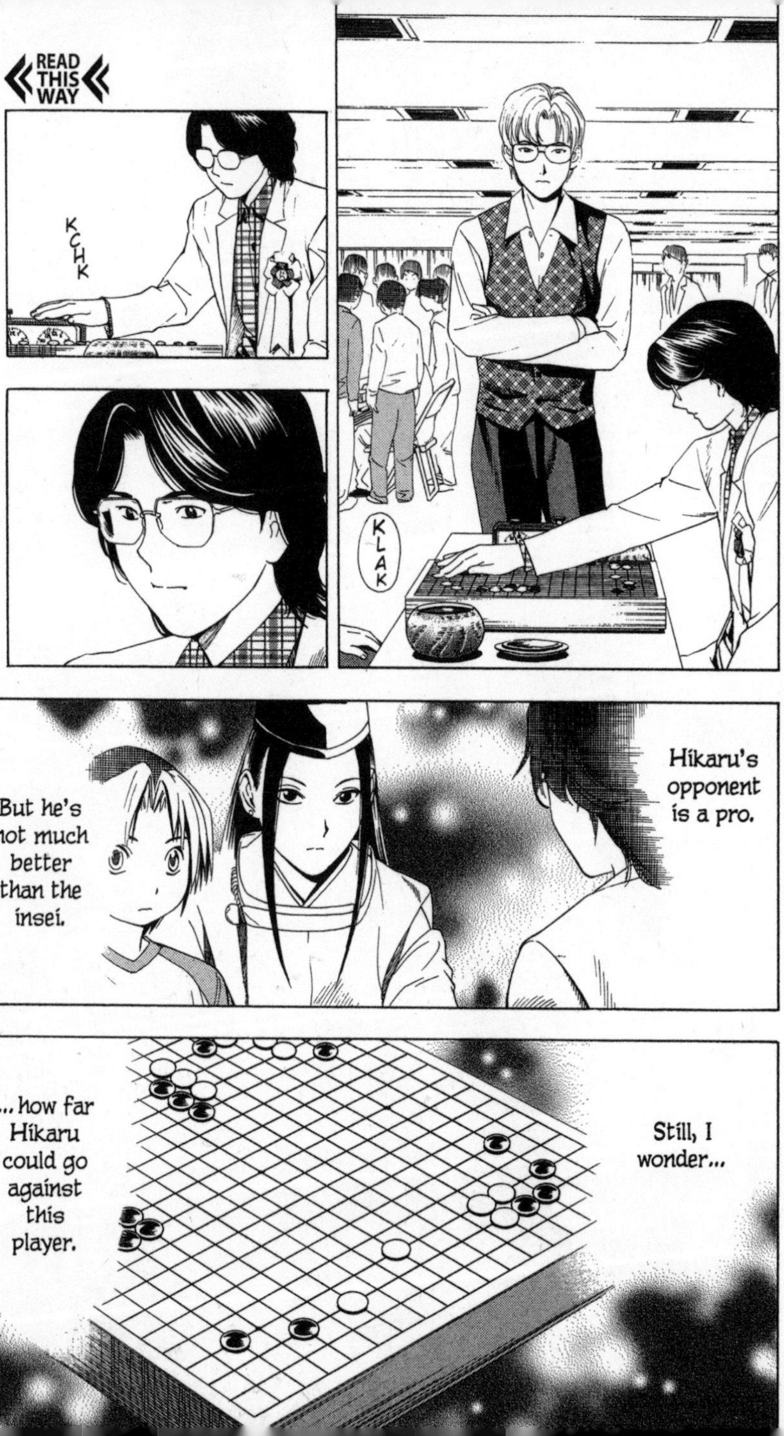
READ THIS WAY
KLAK
KCHK
Hikaru's opponent is a pro.
But he's not much better than the insei.
Still, I wonder...
...how far Hikaru could go against this player.

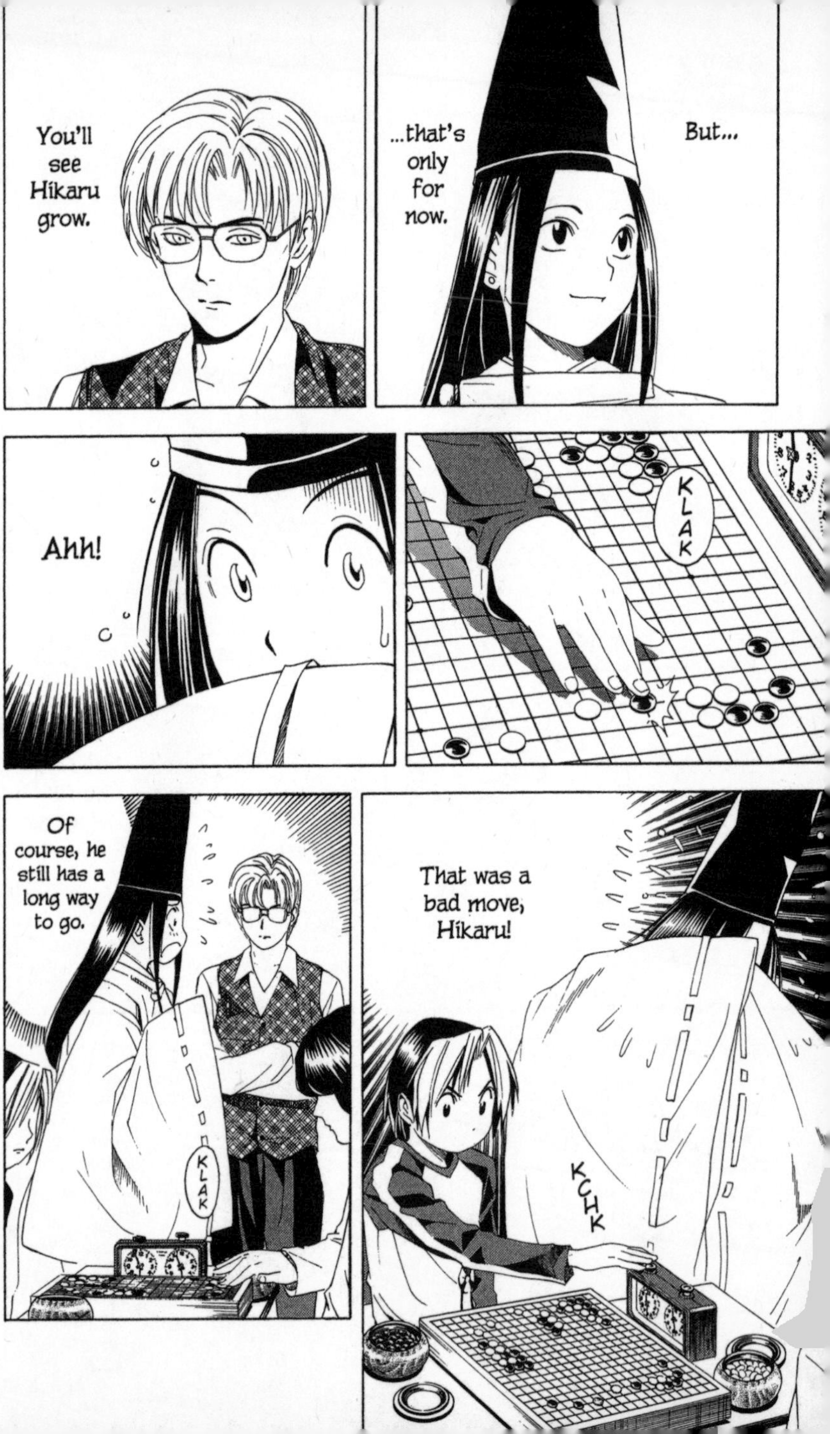

But...
...that's only for now.
You'll see Hikaru grow.
KLAK
Ahh!
That was a bad move, Hikaru!
KCHK
Of course, he still has a long way to go.
KLAK

READ THIS WAY

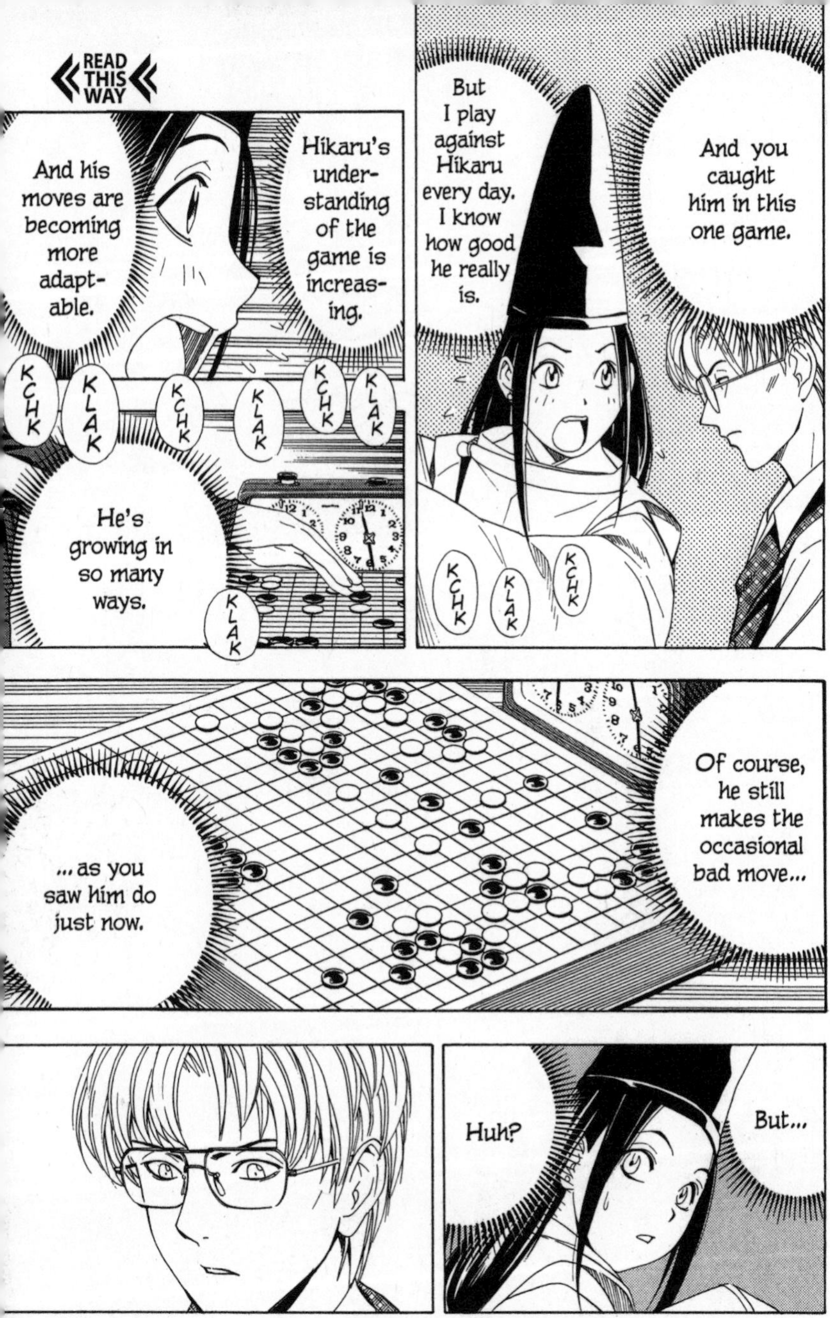
And you caught him in this one game.
But I play against Hikaru every day. I know how good he really is.
KCHK
KLAK
KCHK
Hikaru's under-standing of the game is increas-ing.
And his moves are becoming more adapt-able.
KLAK
KCHK
KLAK
KCHK
KLAK
KCHK
He's growing in so many ways.
KLAK
Of course, he still makes the occasional bad move...
...as you saw him do just now.
But...
Huh?

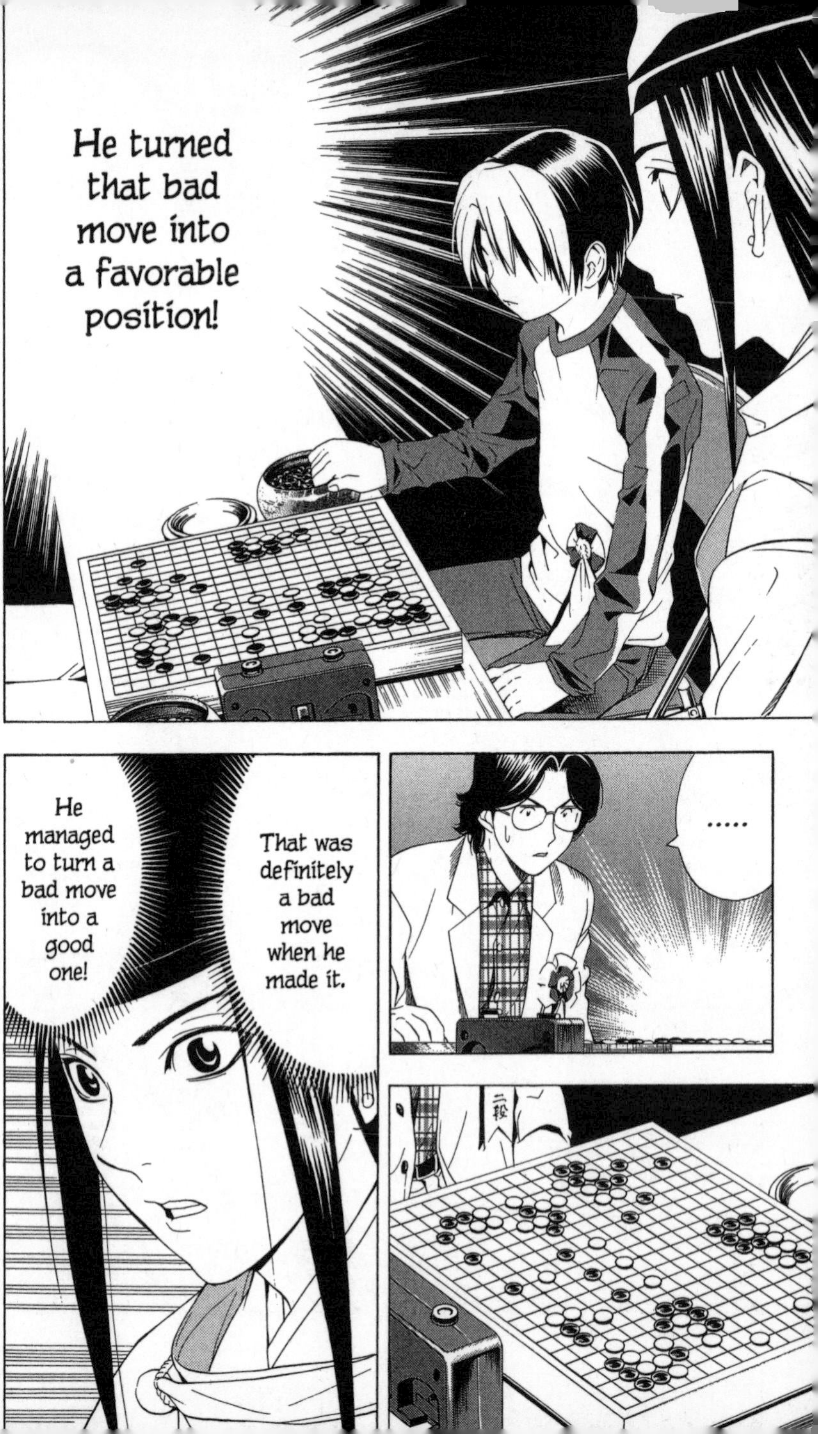
He turned that bad move into a favorable position!
.....
That was definitely a bad move when he made it.
He managed to turn a bad move into a good one!
二段

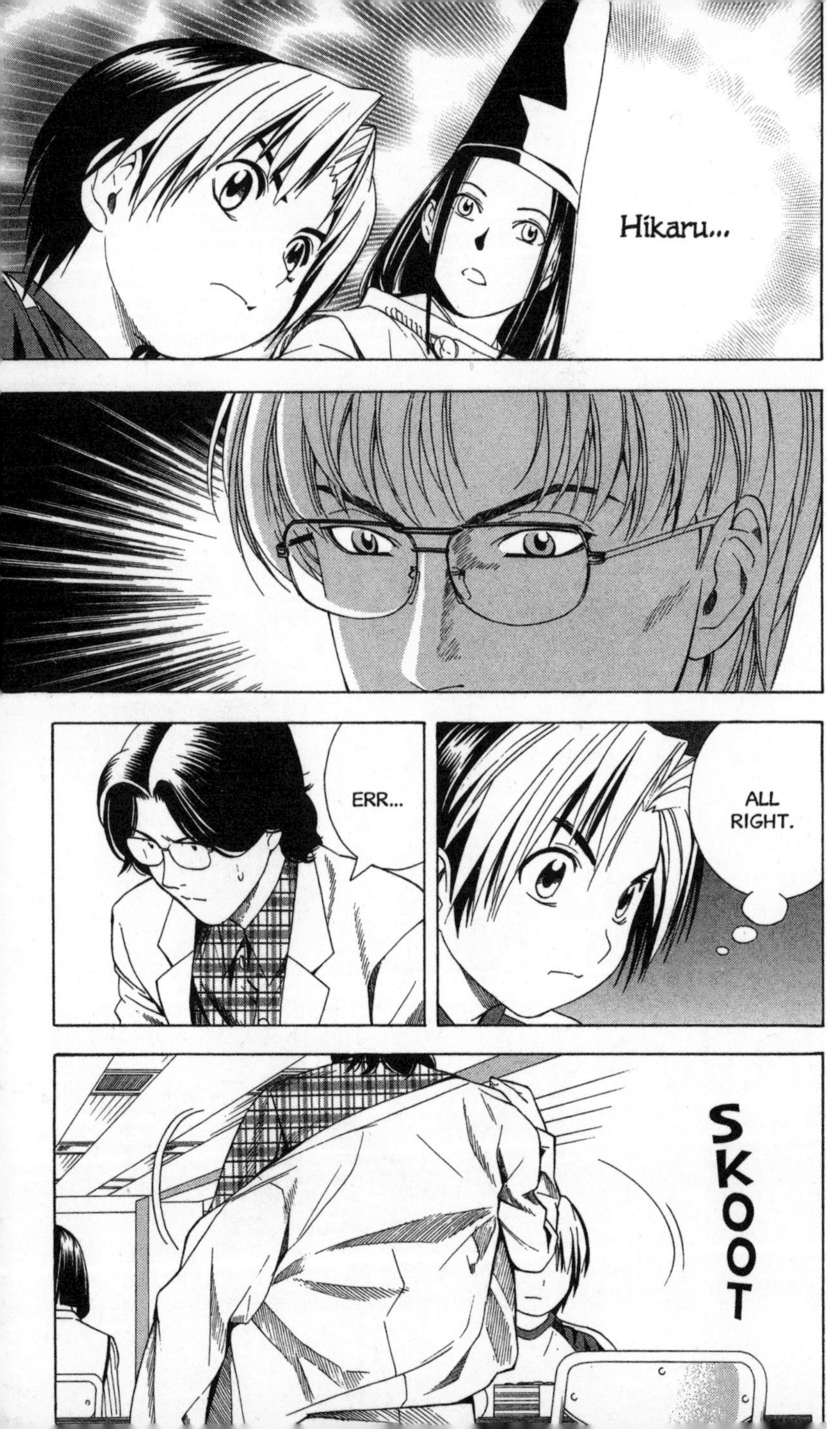
Hikaru...
ALL RIGHT.
ERR...
SKOOT

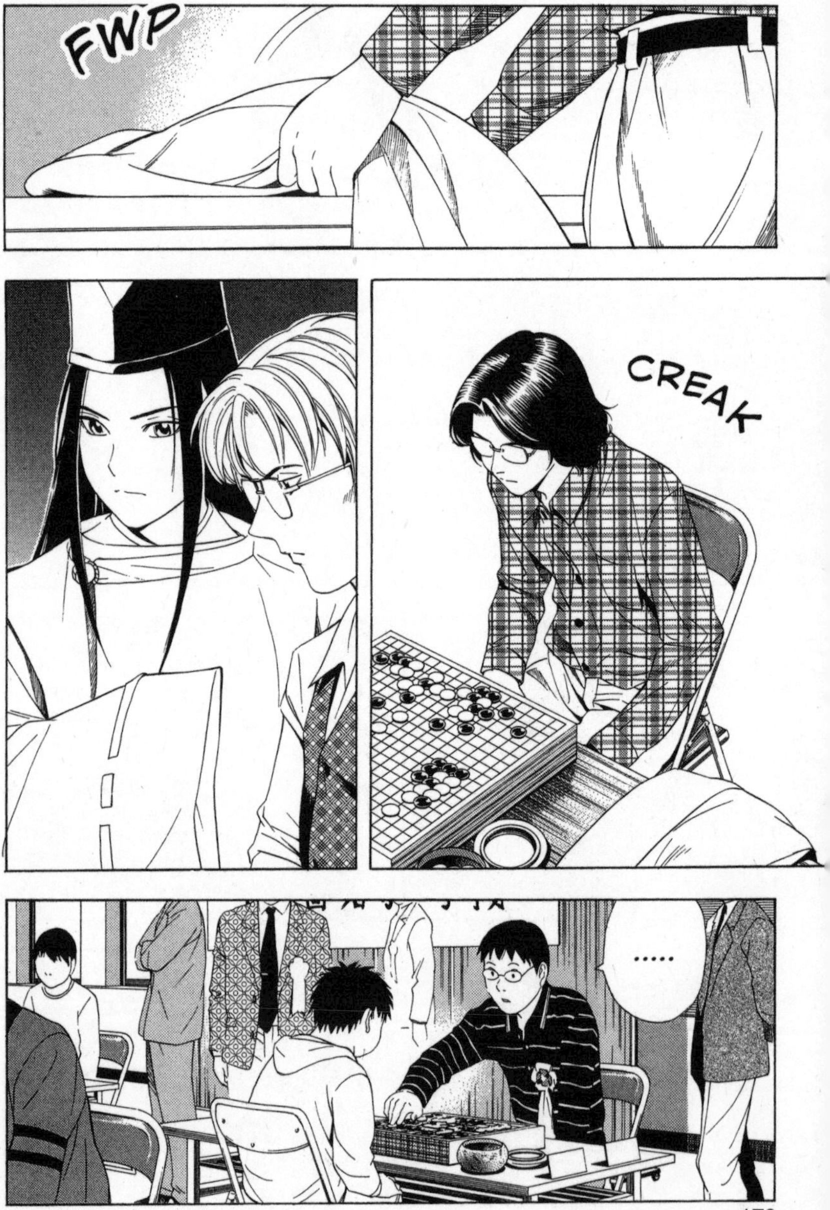
FWP
CREAK
.....

READ THIS WAY

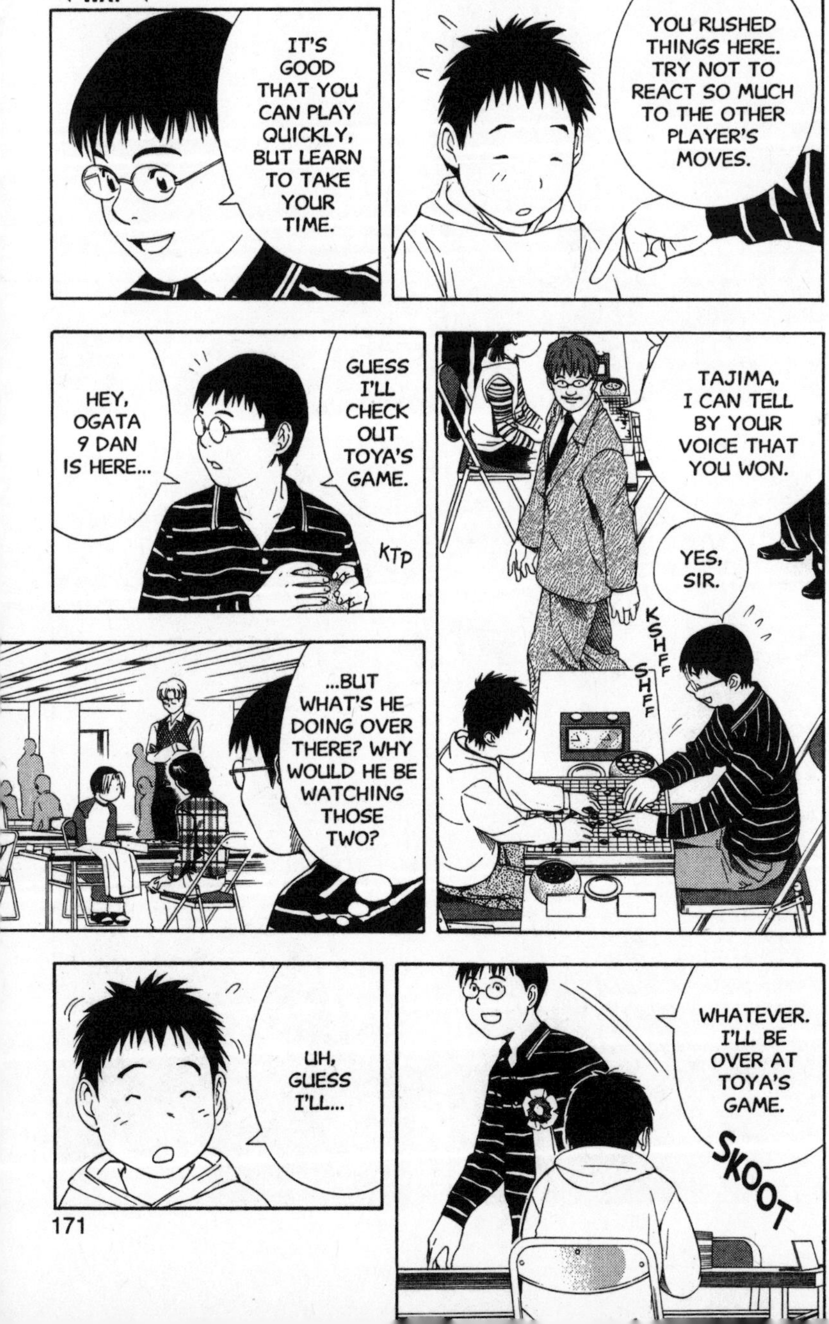
YOU RUSHED THINGS HERE. TRY NOT TO REACT SO MUCH TO THE OTHER PLAYER'S MOVES.
IT'S GOOD THAT YOU CAN PLAY QUICKLY, BUT LEARN TO TAKE YOUR TIME.
TAJIMA, I CAN TELL BY YOUR VOICE THAT YOU WON.
YES, SIR.
KSHFF
SHFF
GUESS I'LL CHECK OUT TOYA'S GAME.
KTP
HEY, OGATA 9 DAN IS HERE...
...BUT WHAT'S HE DOING OVER THERE? WHY WOULD HE BE WATCHING THOSE TWO?
WHATEVER. I'LL BE OVER AT TOYA'S GAME.
SKOOT
UH, GUESS I'LL...

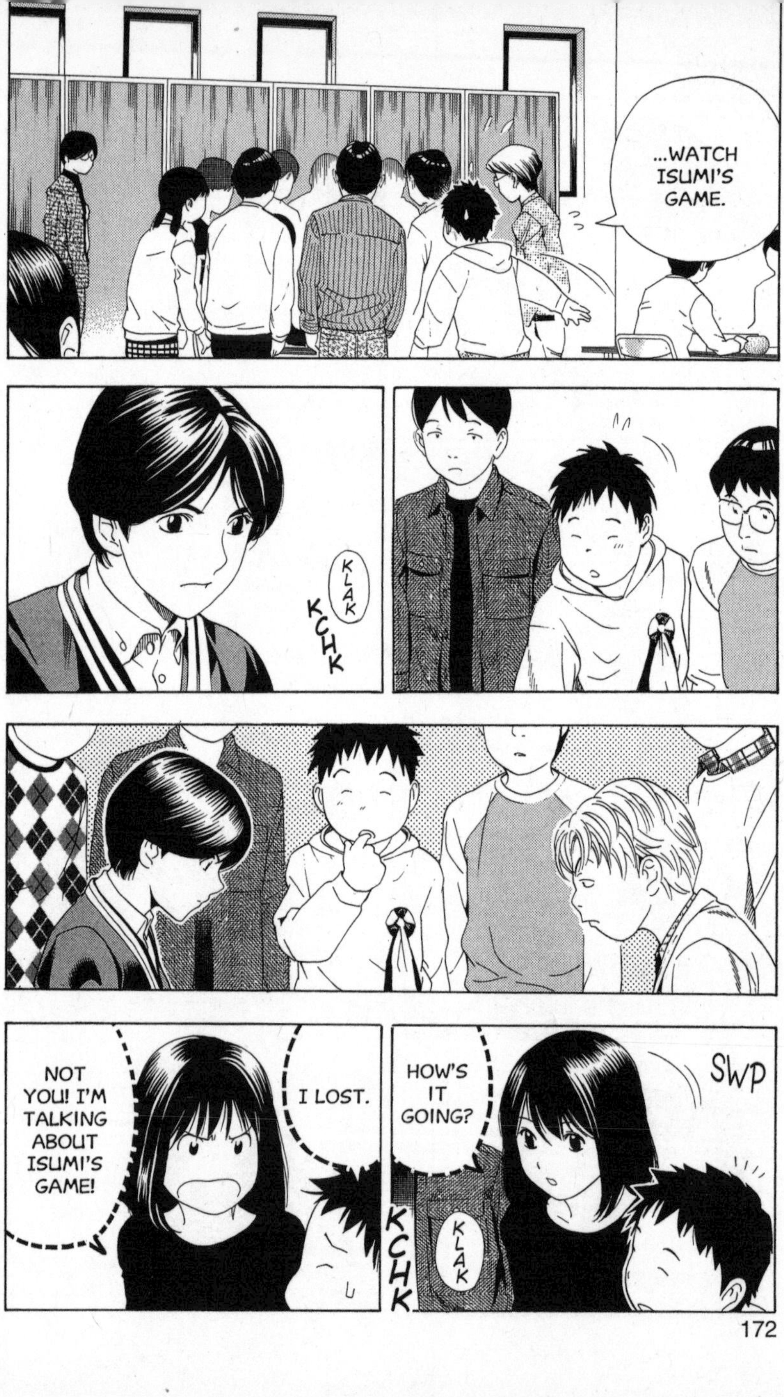
...WATCH ISUMI'S GAME.
KLAK
KCHK
SWP
HOW'S IT GOING?
KLAK
KCHK
I LOST.
NOT YOU! I'M TALKING ABOUT ISUMI'S GAME!

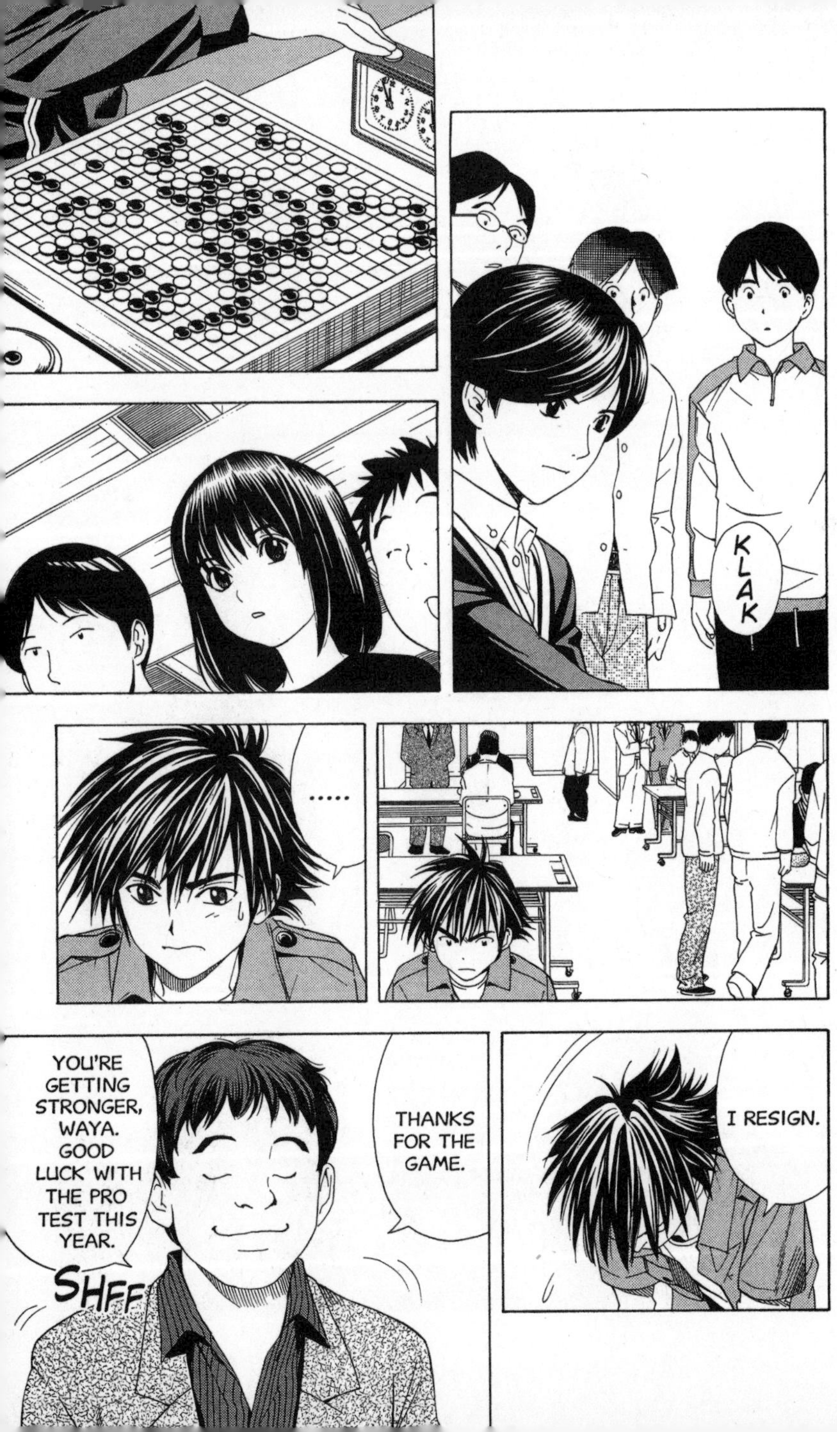
KLAK
.....
I RESIGN.
THANKS FOR THE GAME.
YOU'RE GETTING STRONGER, WAYA. GOOD LUCK WITH THE PRO TEST THIS YEAR.
SHFF

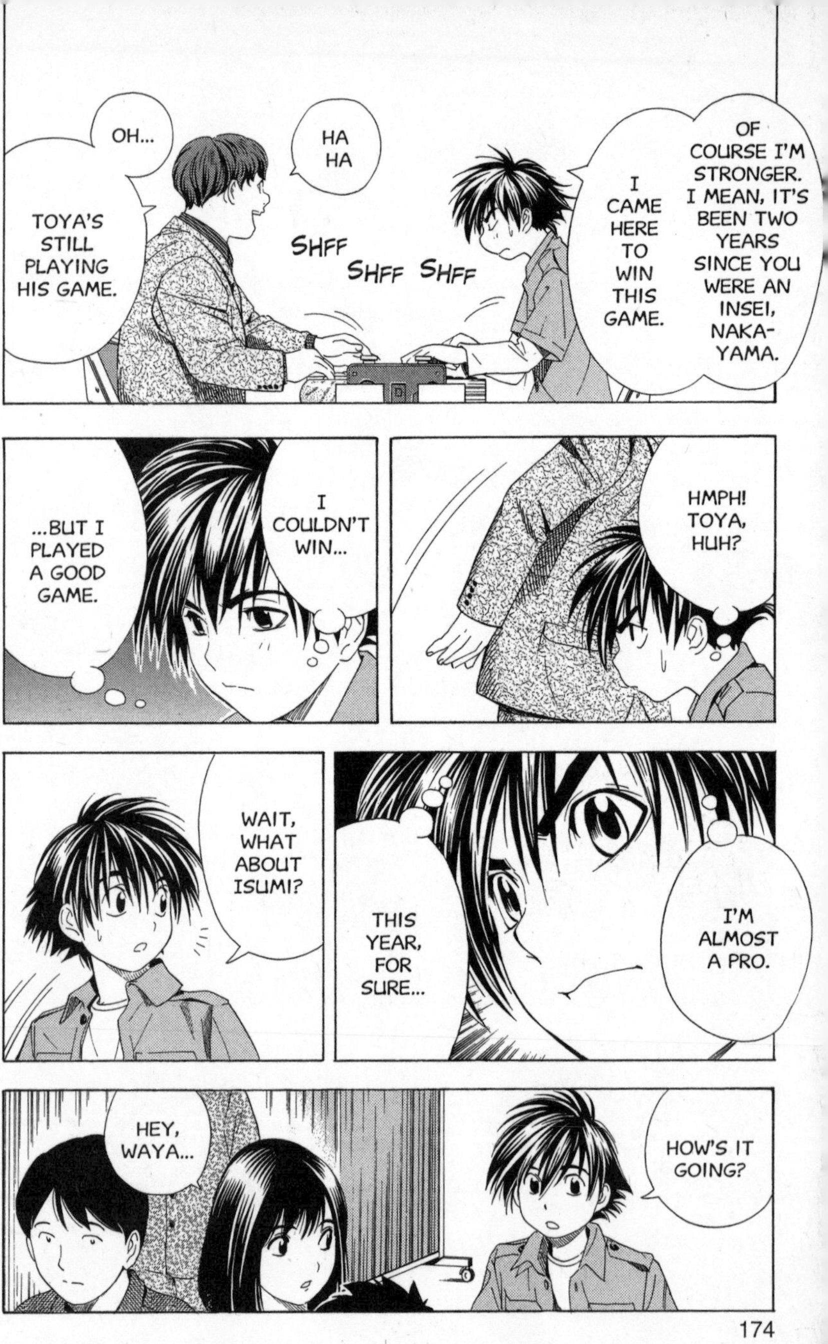
OF COURSE I'M STRONGER. I MEAN, IT'S BEEN TWO YEARS SINCE YOU WERE AN INSEI, NAKAYAMA.
I CAME HERE TO WIN THIS GAME.
SHFF SHFF SHFF
HA HA
OH...
TOYA'S STILL PLAYING HIS GAME.
HMPH! TOYA, HUH?
I COULDN'T WIN...
...BUT I PLAYED A GOOD GAME.
I'M ALMOST A PRO.
THIS YEAR, FOR SURE...
WAIT, WHAT ABOUT ISUMI?
HOW'S IT GOING?
HEY, WAYA...

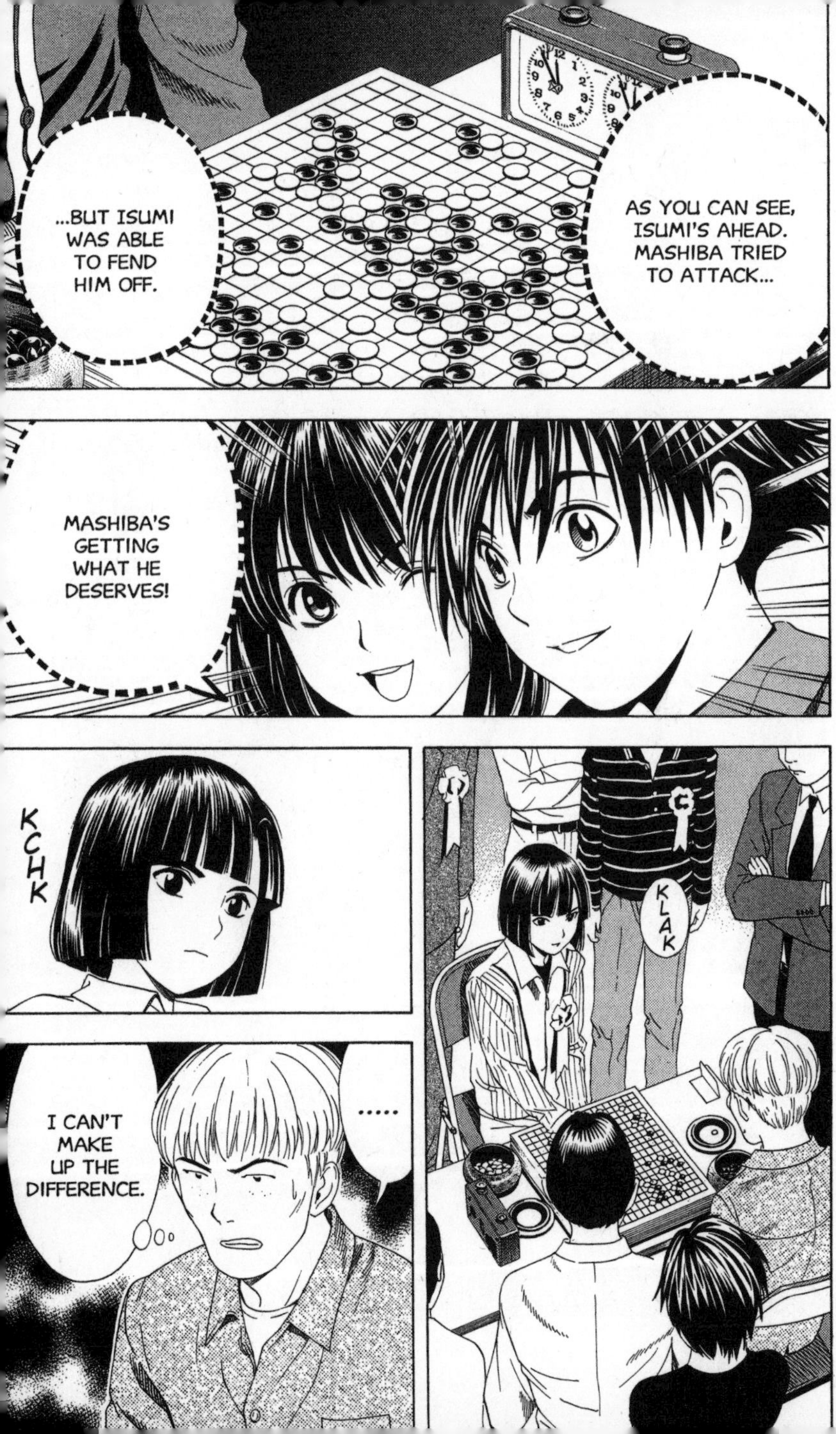
AS YOU CAN SEE, ISUMI'S AHEAD. MASHIBA TRIED TO ATTACK...
...BUT ISUMI WAS ABLE TO FEND HIM OFF.
MASHIBA'S GETTING WHAT HE DESERVES!
KLAK
KCHK
.....
I CAN'T MAKE UP THE DIFFERENCE.

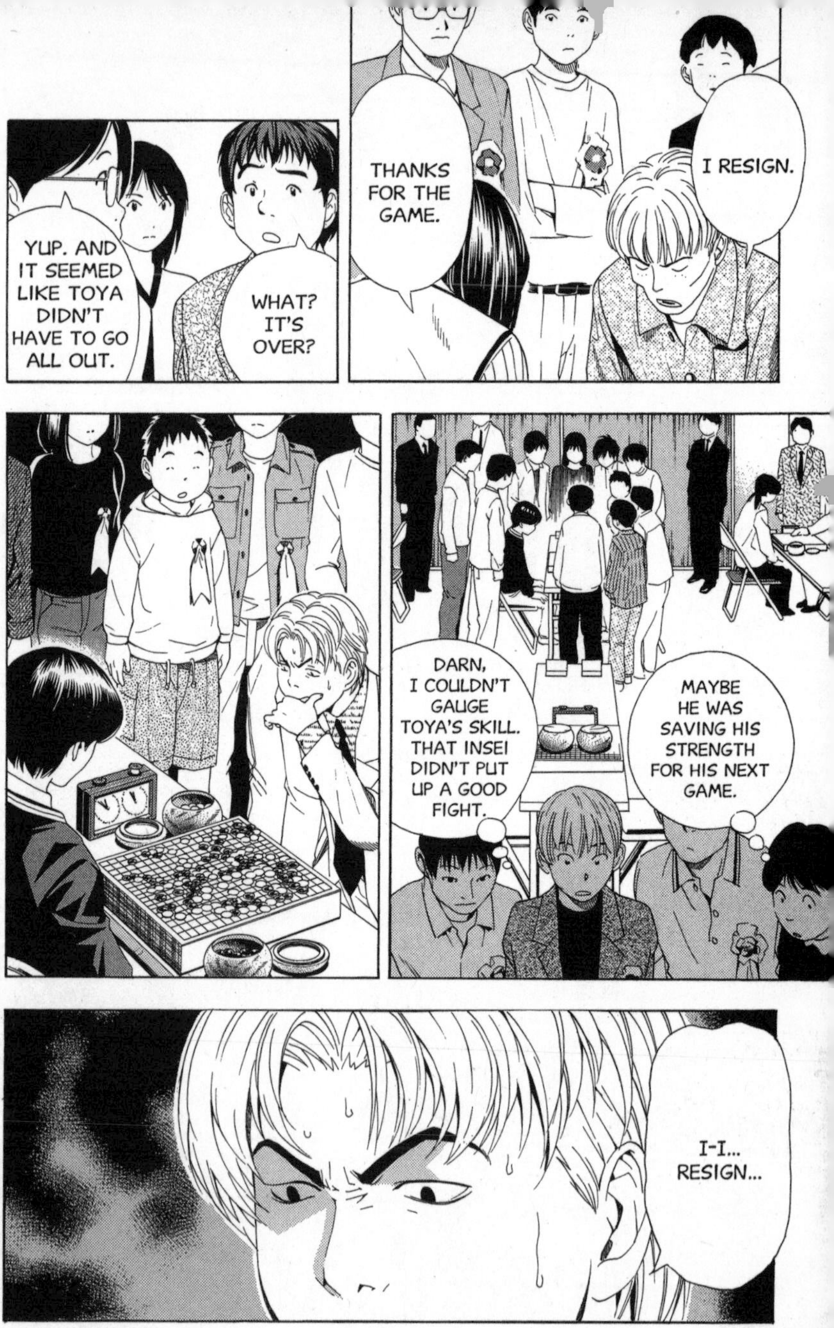
I RESIGN.
THANKS FOR THE GAME.
WHAT? IT'S OVER?
YUP. AND IT SEEMED LIKE TOYA DIDN'T HAVE TO GO ALL OUT.
MAYBE HE WAS SAVING HIS STRENGTH FOR HIS NEXT GAME.
DARN, I COULDN'T GAUGE TOYA'S SKILL. THAT INSEI DIDN'T PUT UP A GOOD FIGHT.
I-I... RESIGN...

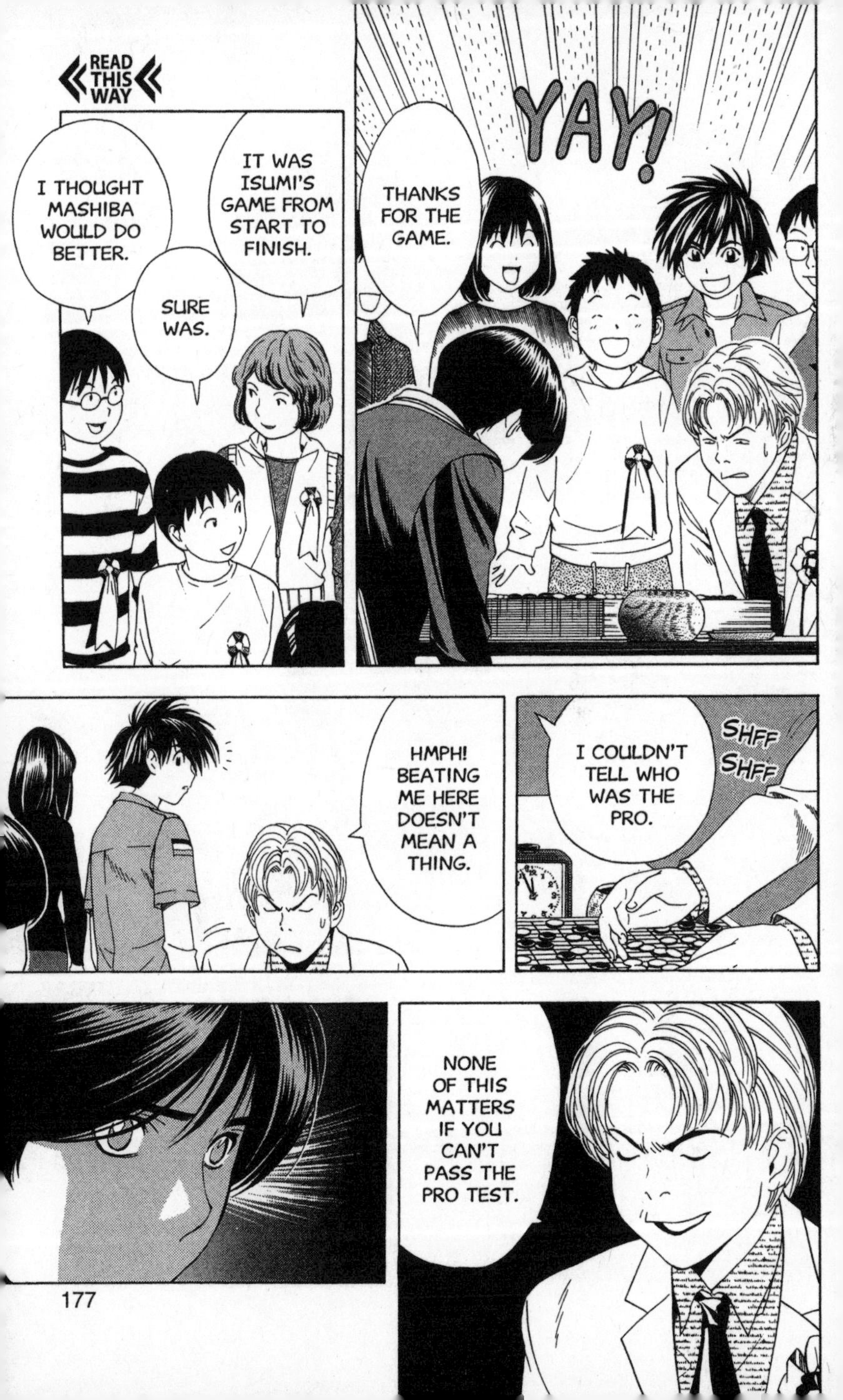
READ THIS WAY
YAY!
THANKS FOR THE GAME.
IT WAS ISUMI'S GAME FROM START TO FINISH.
I THOUGHT MASHIBA WOULD DO BETTER.
SURE WAS.
SHFF SHFF
I COULDN'T TELL WHO WAS THE PRO.
HMPH! BEATING ME HERE DOESN'T MEAN A THING.
NONE OF THIS MATTERS IF YOU CAN'T PASS THE PRO TEST.

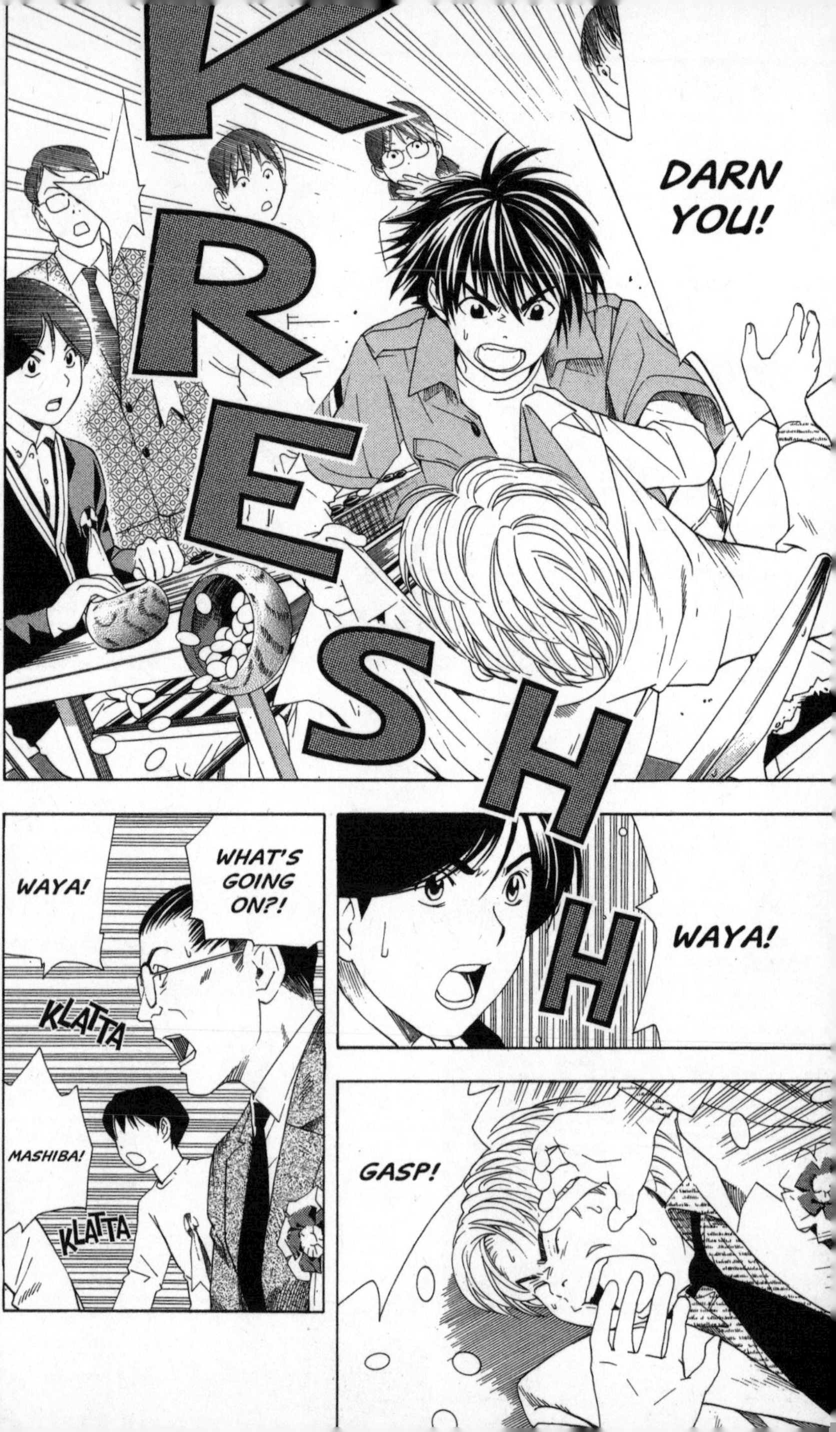
KRESHH
DARN YOU!
WAYA!
GASP!
WHAT'S GOING ON?!
WAYA!
KLATTA
MASHIBA!
KLATTA

READ THIS WAY

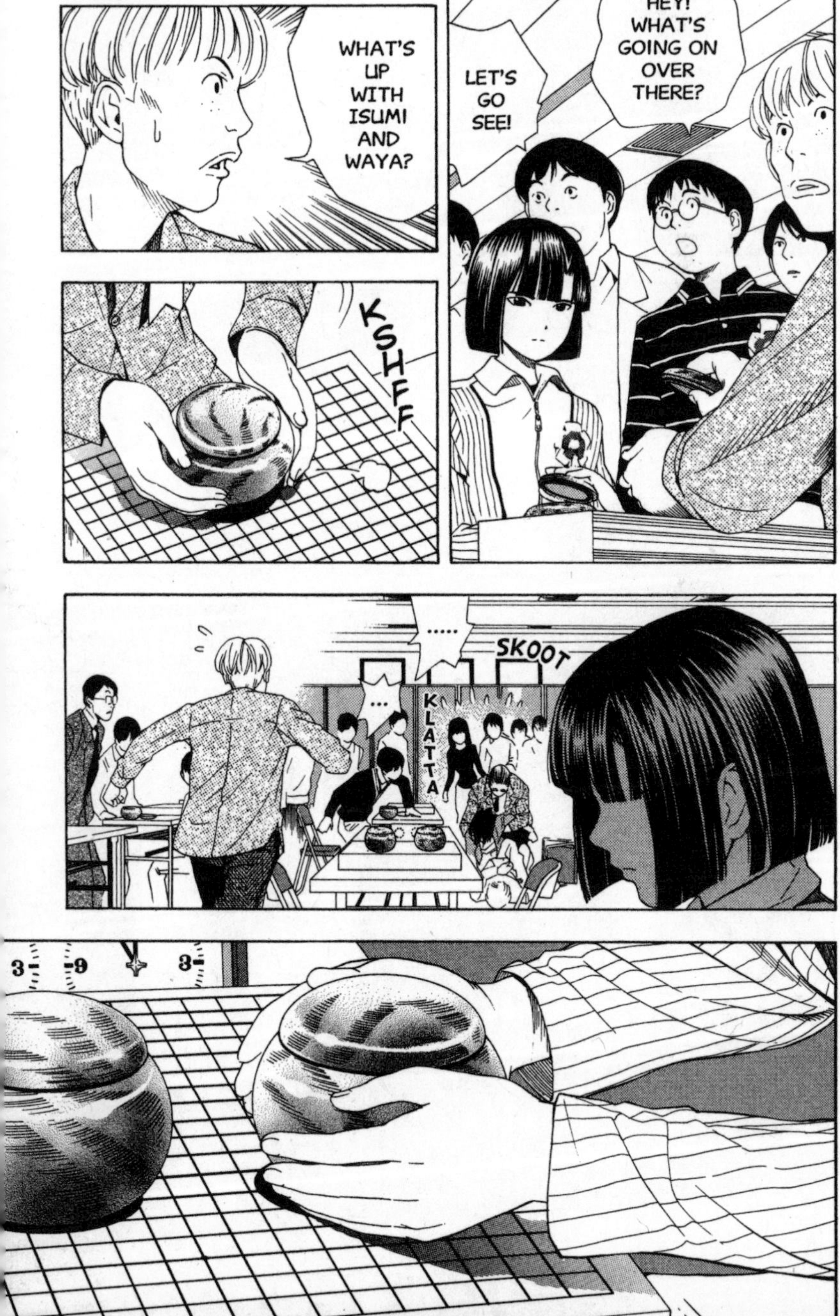
HEY! WHAT'S GOING ON OVER THERE?
LET'S GO SEE!
WHAT'S UP WITH ISUMI AND WAYA?
KSHFF
.....
SKOOT
...
KLATTA

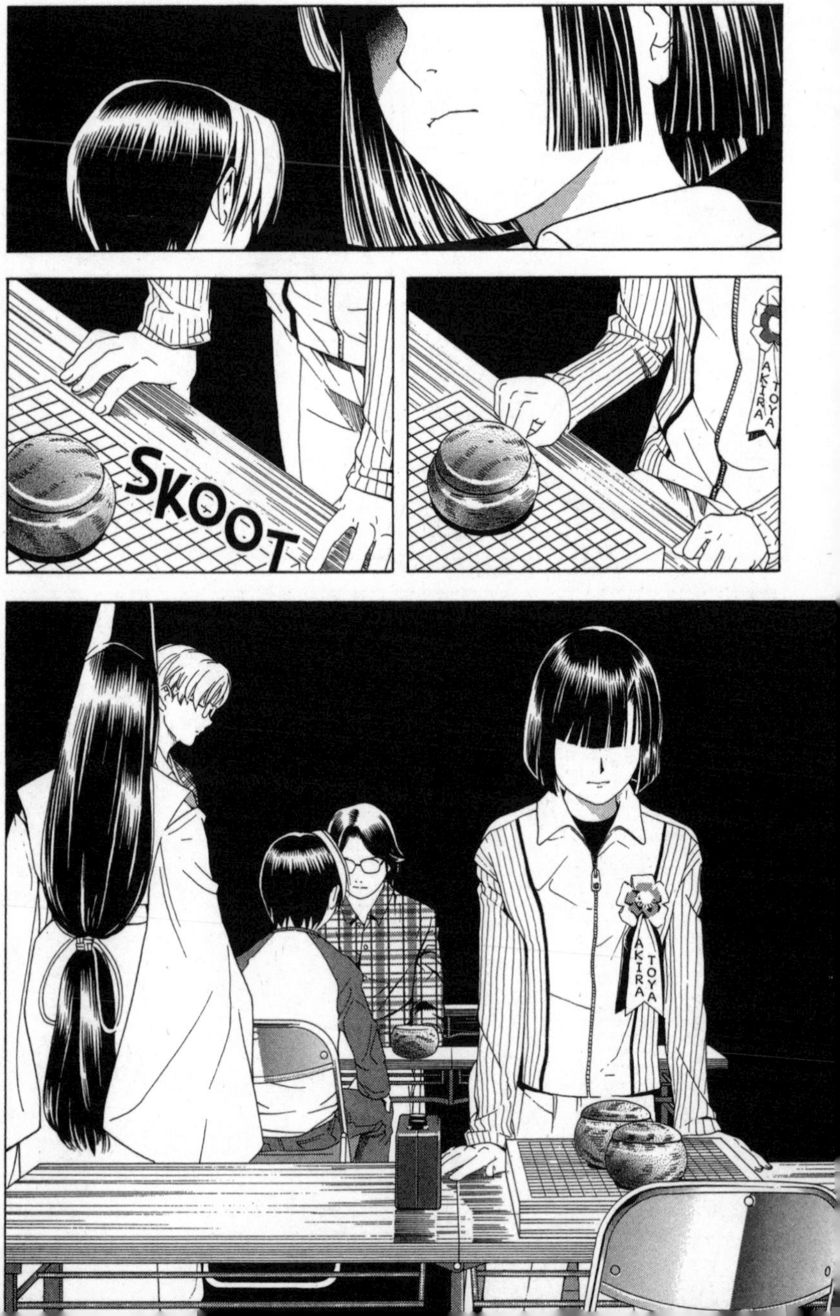
AKIRA TOYA
SKOOT
AKIRA TOYA

READ THIS WAY

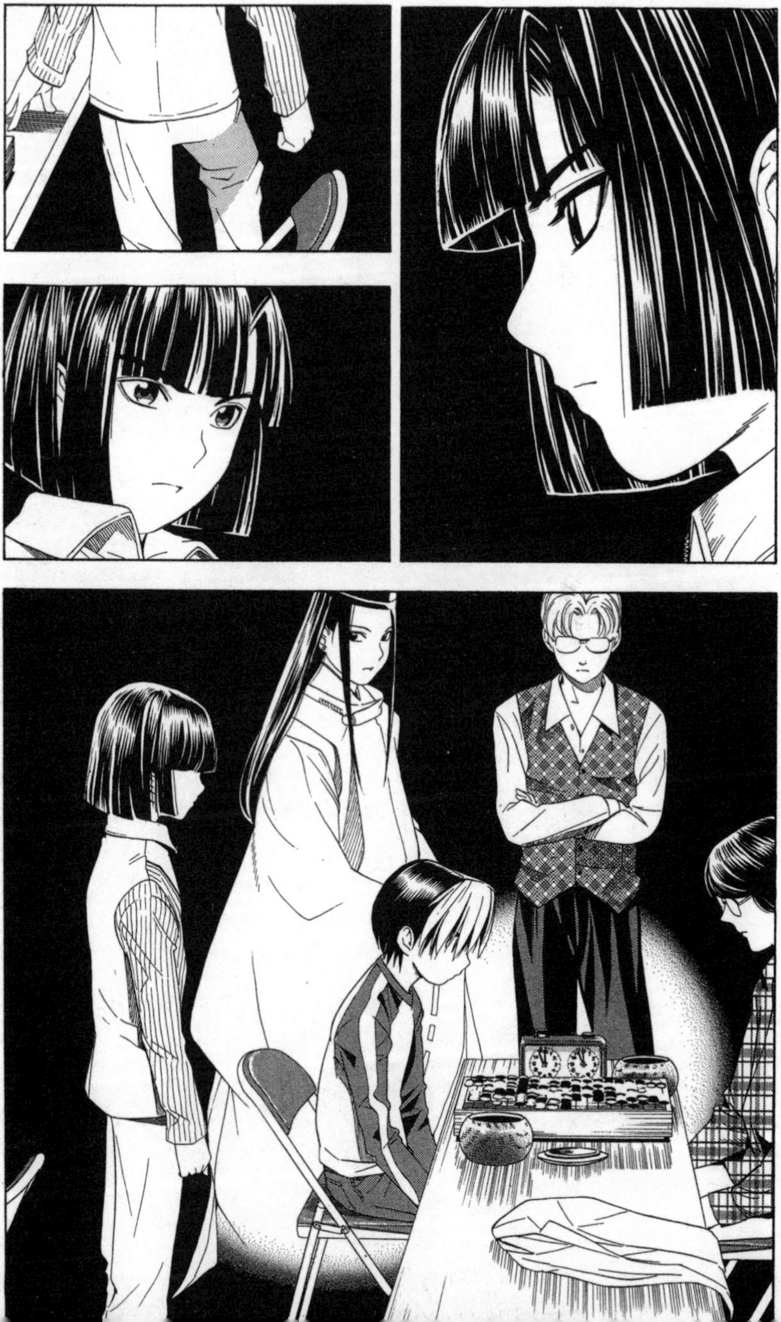

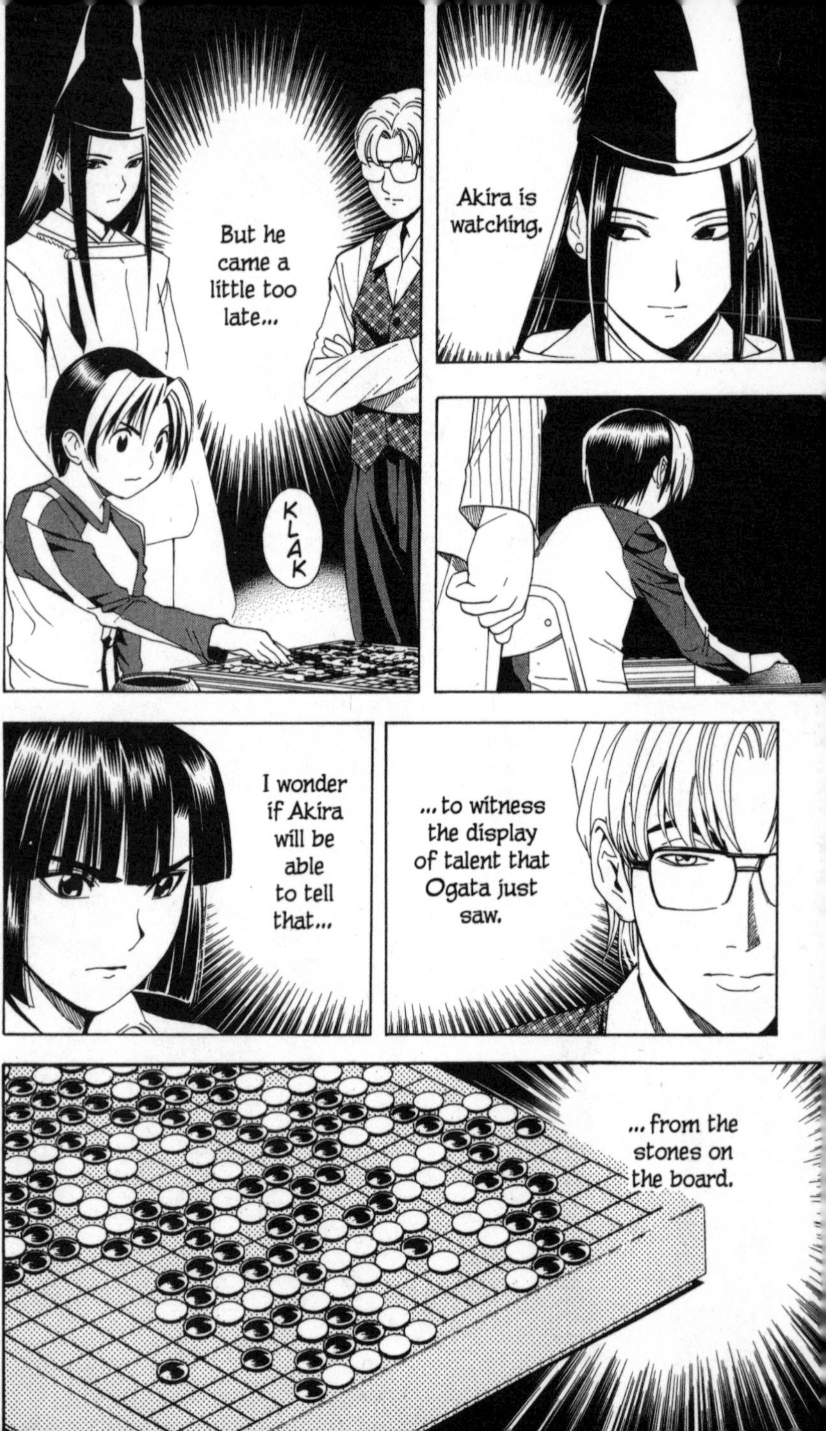
Akira is watching.
But he came a little too late...
KLAK
...to witness the display of talent that Ogata just saw.
I wonder if Akira will be able to tell that...
...from the stones on the board.

READ THIS WAY

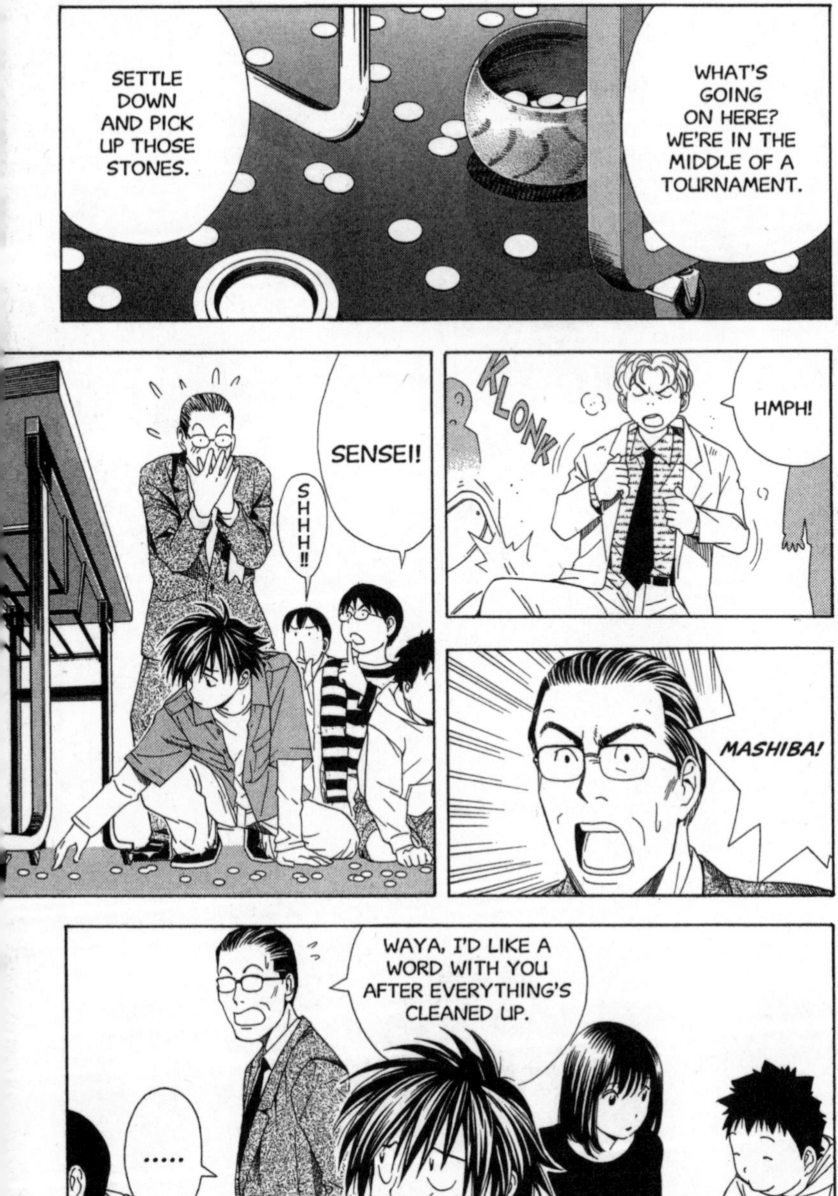
WHAT'S GOING ON HERE? WE'RE IN THE MIDDLE OF A TOURNAMENT.
SETTLE DOWN AND PICK UP THOSE STONES.
HMPH!
KLONK
MASHIBA!
SENSEI!
SHHH!!
WAYA, I'D LIKE A WORD WITH YOU AFTER EVERYTHING'S CLEANED UP.
......

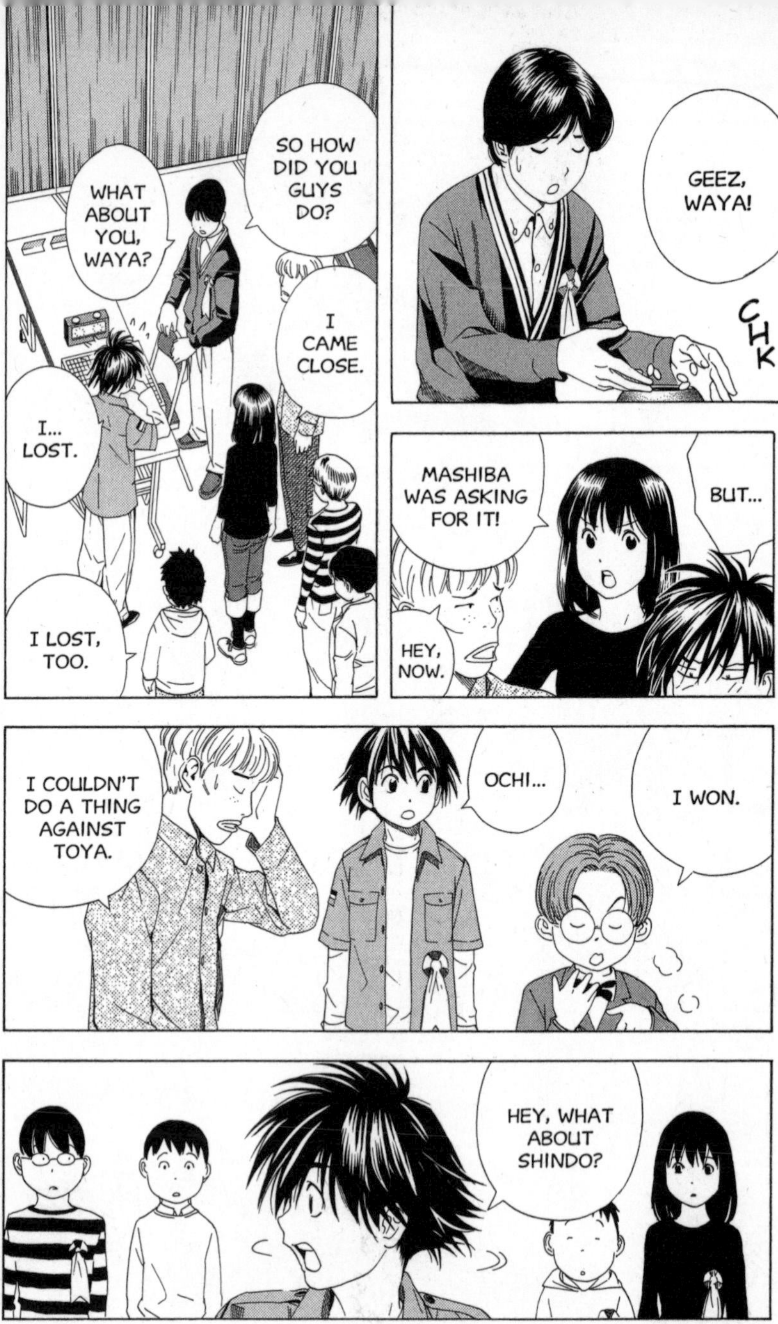
GEEZ, WAYA!
CHK
BUT...
MASHIBA WAS ASKING FOR IT!
HEY, NOW.
SO HOW DID YOU GUYS DO?
WHAT ABOUT YOU, WAYA?
I CAME CLOSE.
I... LOST.
I LOST, TOO.
I WON.
OCHI...
I COULDN'T DO A THING AGAINST TOYA.
HEY, WHAT ABOUT SHINDO?

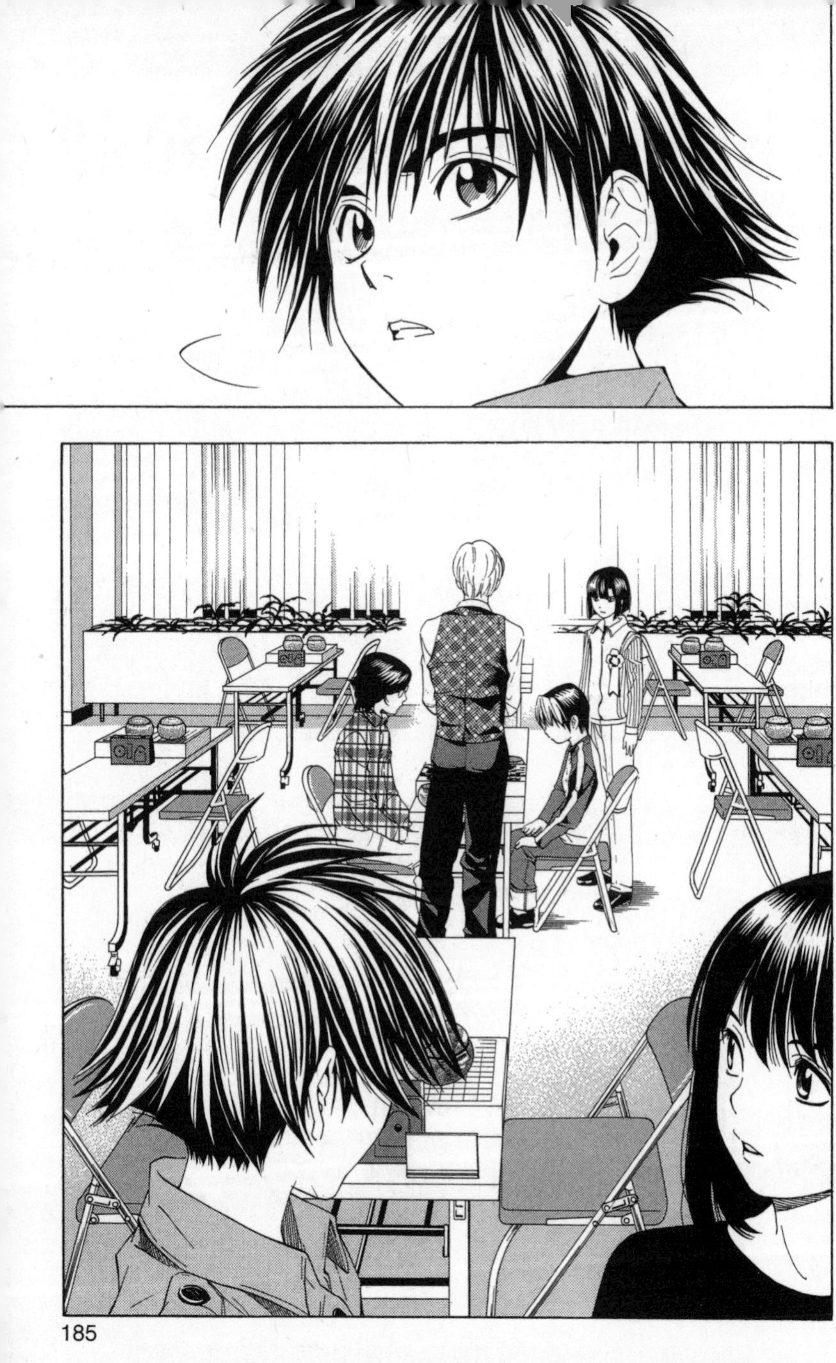

# A WORD ABOUT HIKARU NO GO

## THE YOUNG LIONS TOURNAMENT

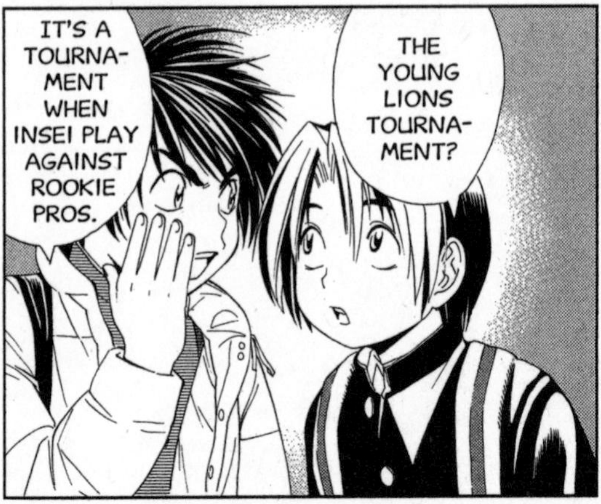
THE YOUNG LIONS TOURNAMENT?
IT'S A TOURNAMENT WHEN INSEI PLAY AGAINST ROOKIE PROS.

THE YOUNG LIONS TOURNAMENT IS BASED ON THE HOSU SEN (YOUNG PHOENIX TOURNAMENT). THE GENERAL PUBLIC CAN WATCH THIS TOURNAMENT FOR FREE. THE FIRST AND SECOND ROUNDS TAKE PLACE EVERY YEAR IN THE MIDDLE OF MAY. THE THIRD AND FOURTH ROUNDS AND THE FINALS HAPPEN IN JUNE. GO INSEI!

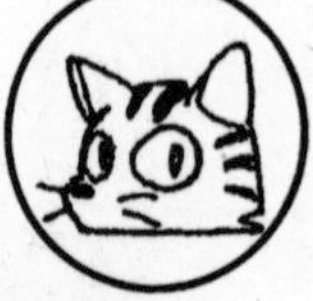

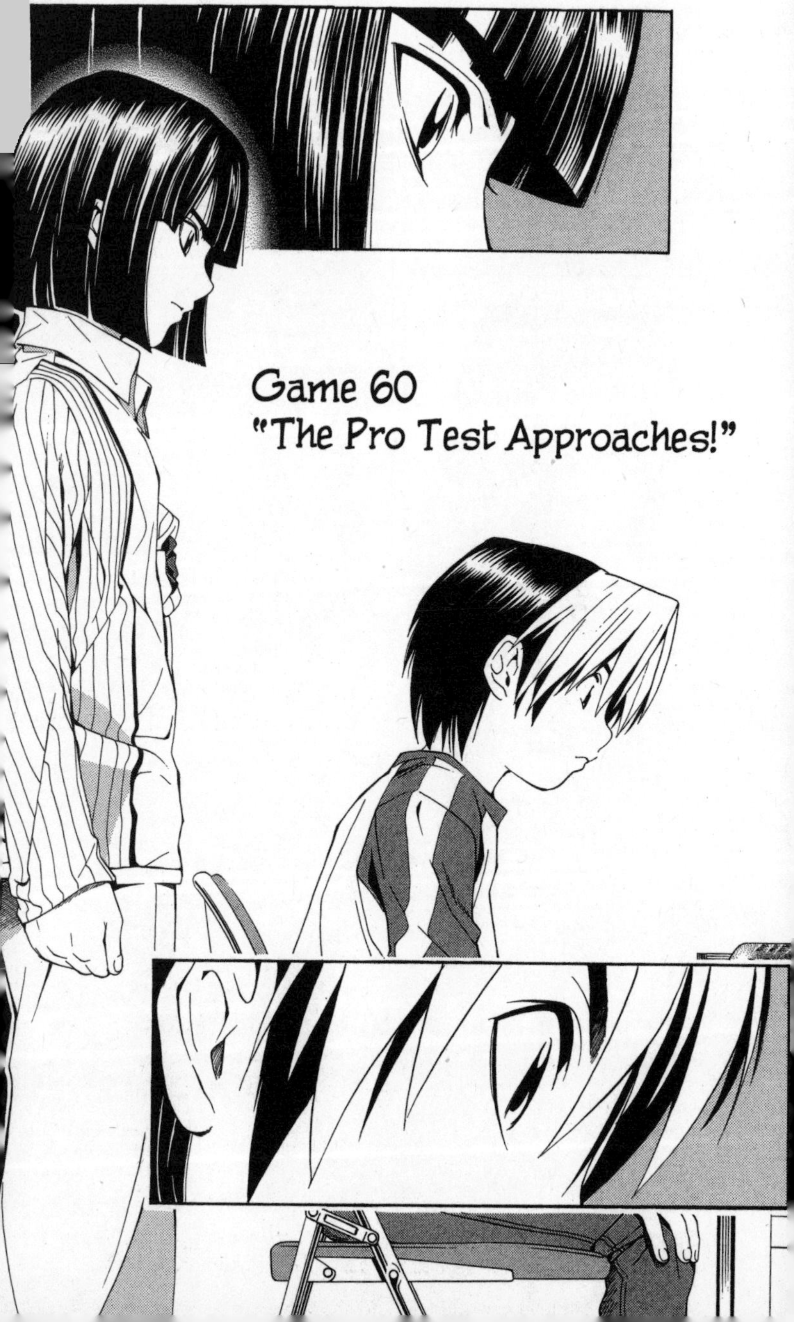
Game 60
"The Pro Test Approaches!"

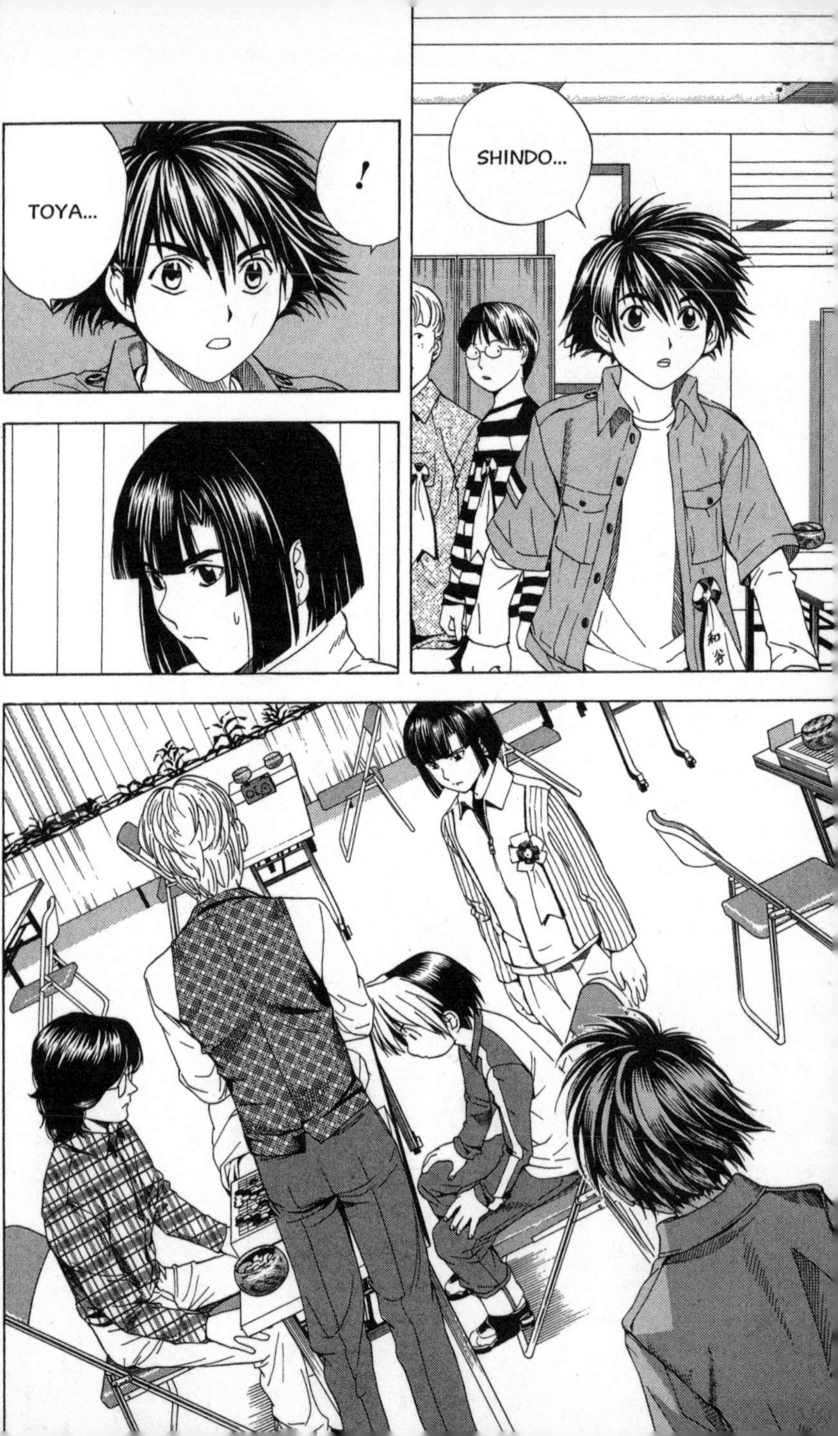
SHINDO...
!
TOYA...

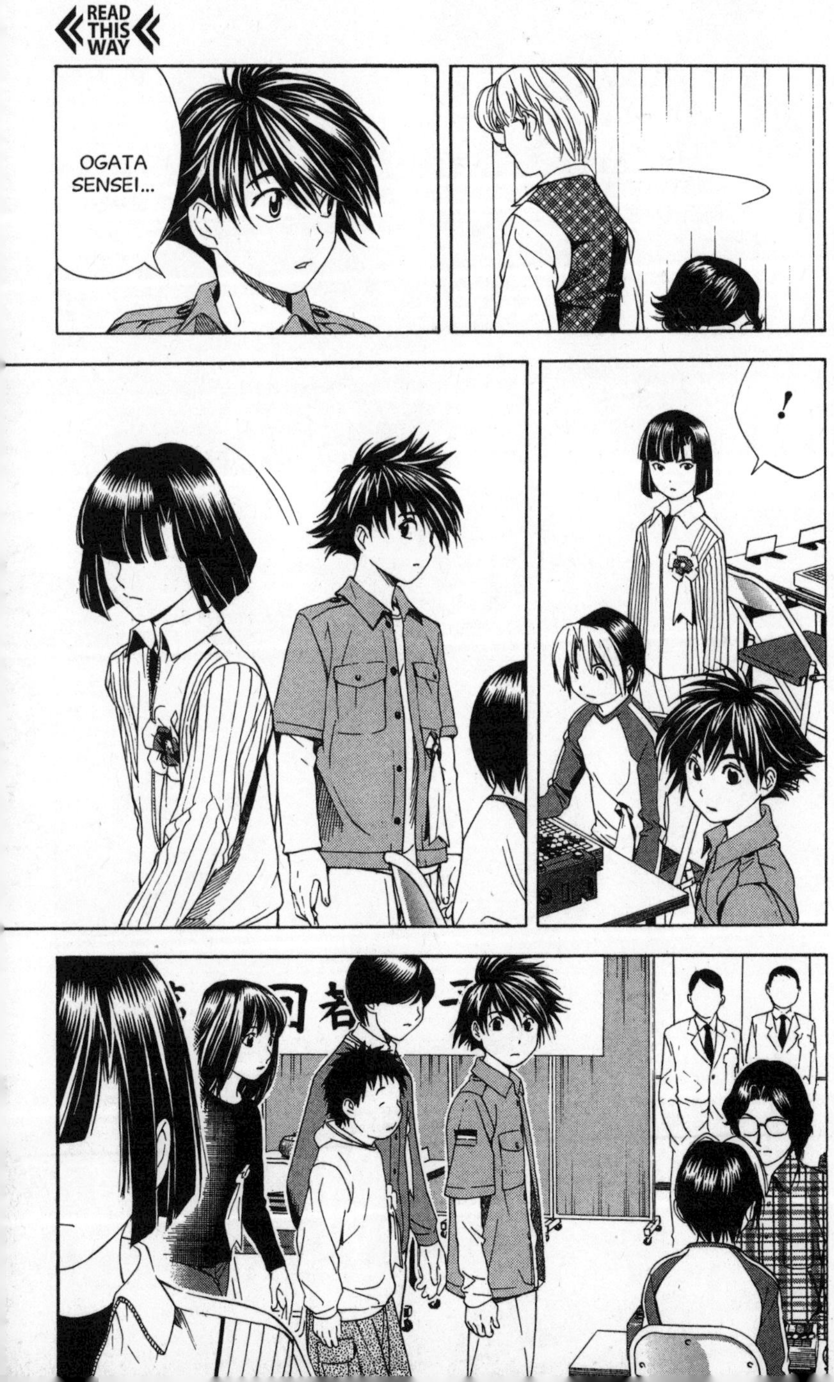
READ THIS WAY
OGATA SENSEI...
!

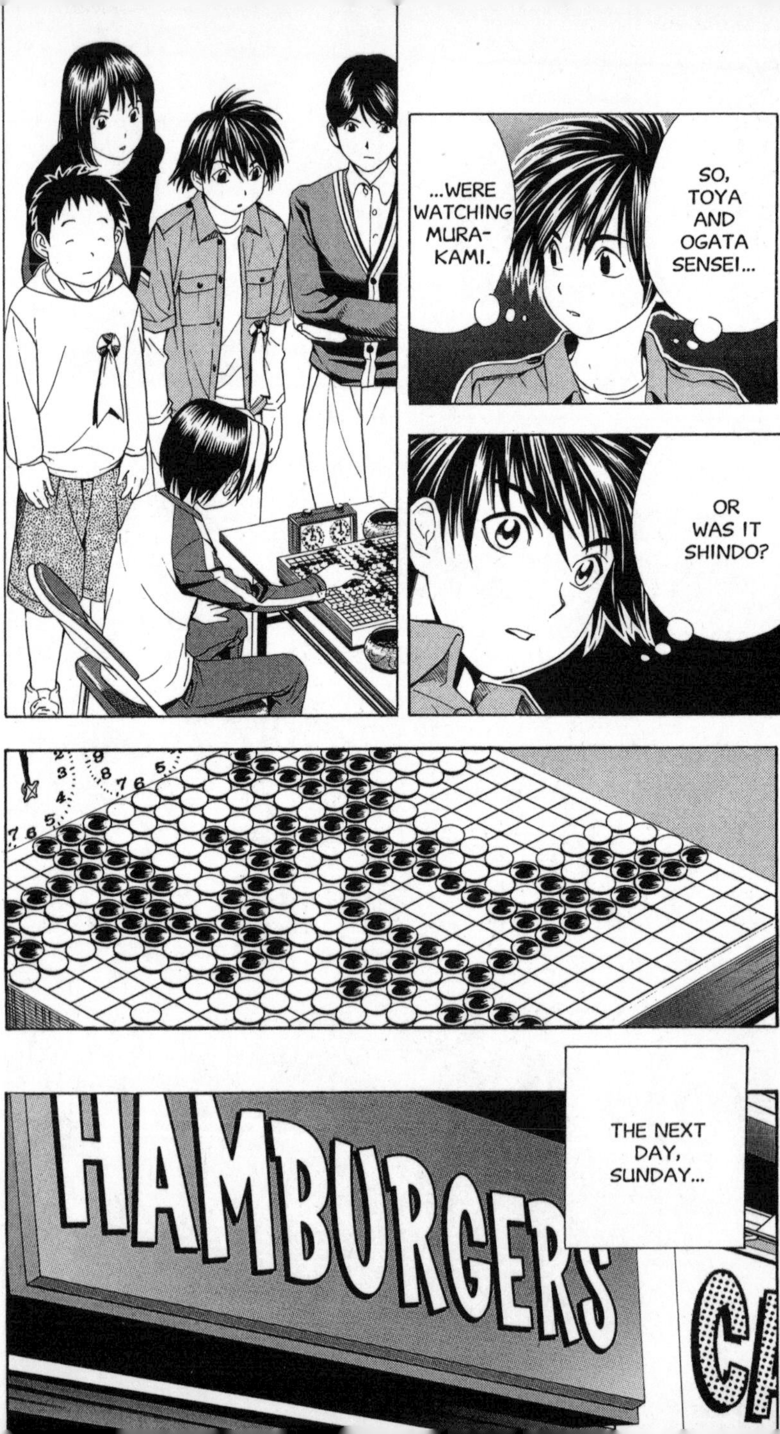
SO, TOYA AND OGATA SENSEI...
...WERE WATCHING MURA-KAMI.
OR WAS IT SHINDO?
THE NEXT DAY, SUNDAY...
HAMBURGERS

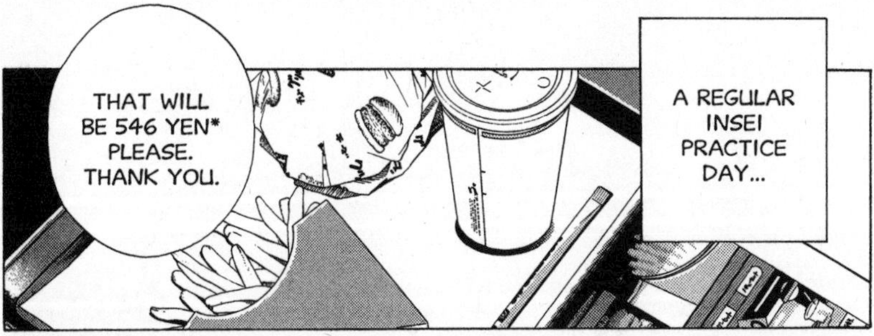
A REGULAR INSEI PRACTICE DAY...
THAT WILL BE 546 YEN* PLEASE. THANK YOU.

*About US $5

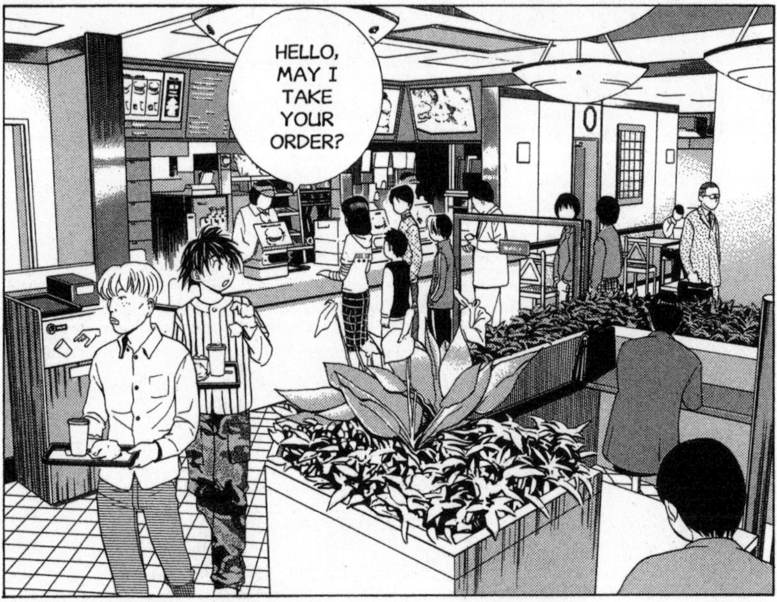
HELLO, MAY I TAKE YOUR ORDER?

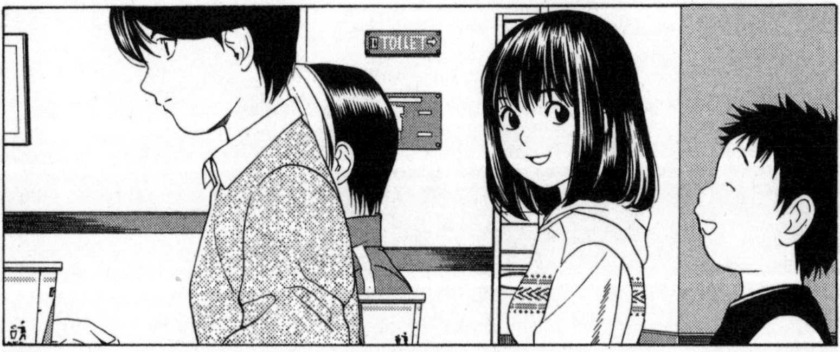
TOILET

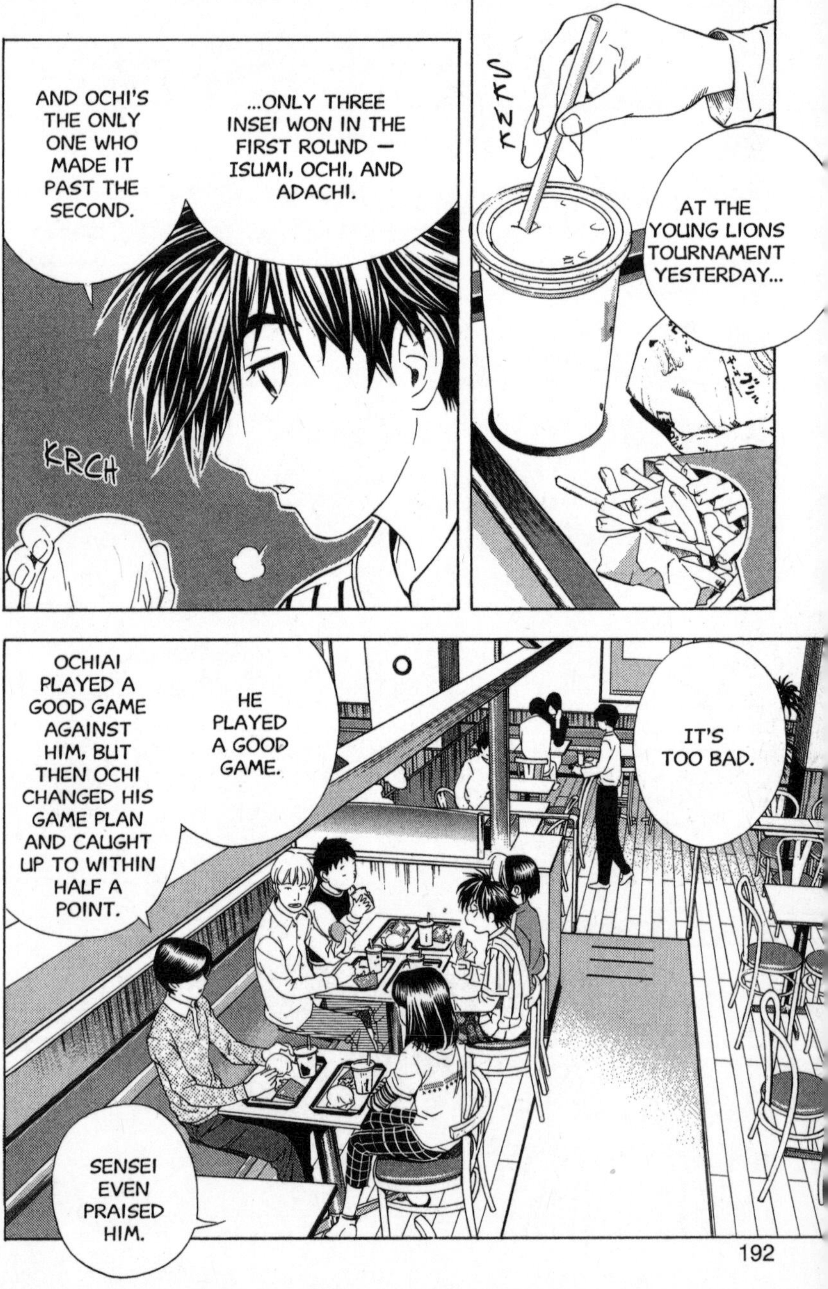
SKWK
AT THE YOUNG LIONS TOURNAMENT YESTERDAY...
...ONLY THREE INSEI WON IN THE FIRST ROUND — ISUMI, OCHI, AND ADACHI.
AND OCHI'S THE ONLY ONE WHO MADE IT PAST THE SECOND.
KRCH
IT'S TOO BAD.
HE PLAYED A GOOD GAME.
OCHIAI PLAYED A GOOD GAME AGAINST HIM, BUT THEN OCHI CHANGED HIS GAME PLAN AND CAUGHT UP TO WITHIN HALF A POINT.
SENSEI EVEN PRAISED HIM.

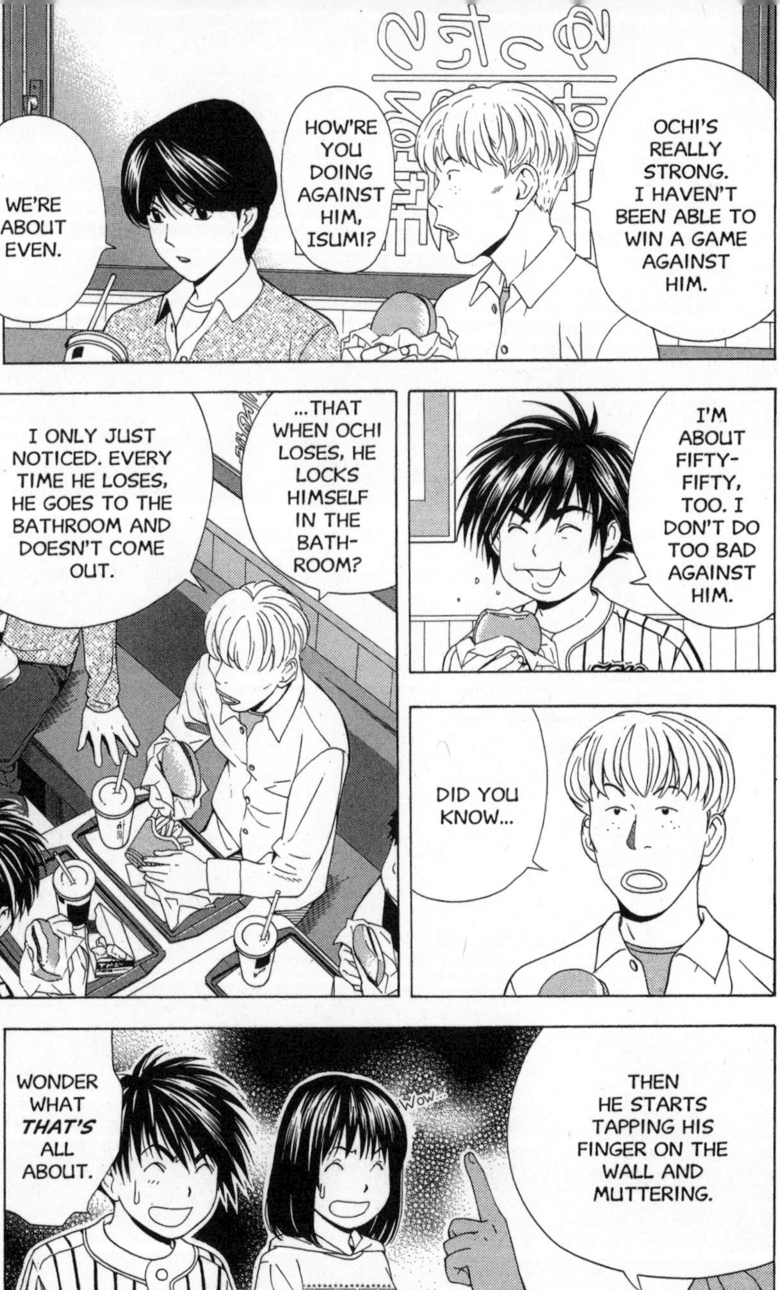
OCHI'S REALLY STRONG. I HAVEN'T BEEN ABLE TO WIN A GAME AGAINST HIM.
HOW'RE YOU DOING AGAINST HIM, ISUMI?
WE'RE ABOUT EVEN.
I'M ABOUT FIFTY-FIFTY, TOO. I DON'T DO TOO BAD AGAINST HIM.
DID YOU KNOW...
...THAT WHEN OCHI LOSES, HE LOCKS HIMSELF IN THE BATH-ROOM?
I ONLY JUST NOTICED. EVERY TIME HE LOSES, HE GOES TO THE BATHROOM AND DOESN'T COME OUT.
THEN HE STARTS TAPPING HIS FINGER ON THE WALL AND MUTTERING.
WOW...
WONDER WHAT *THAT'S* ALL ABOUT.

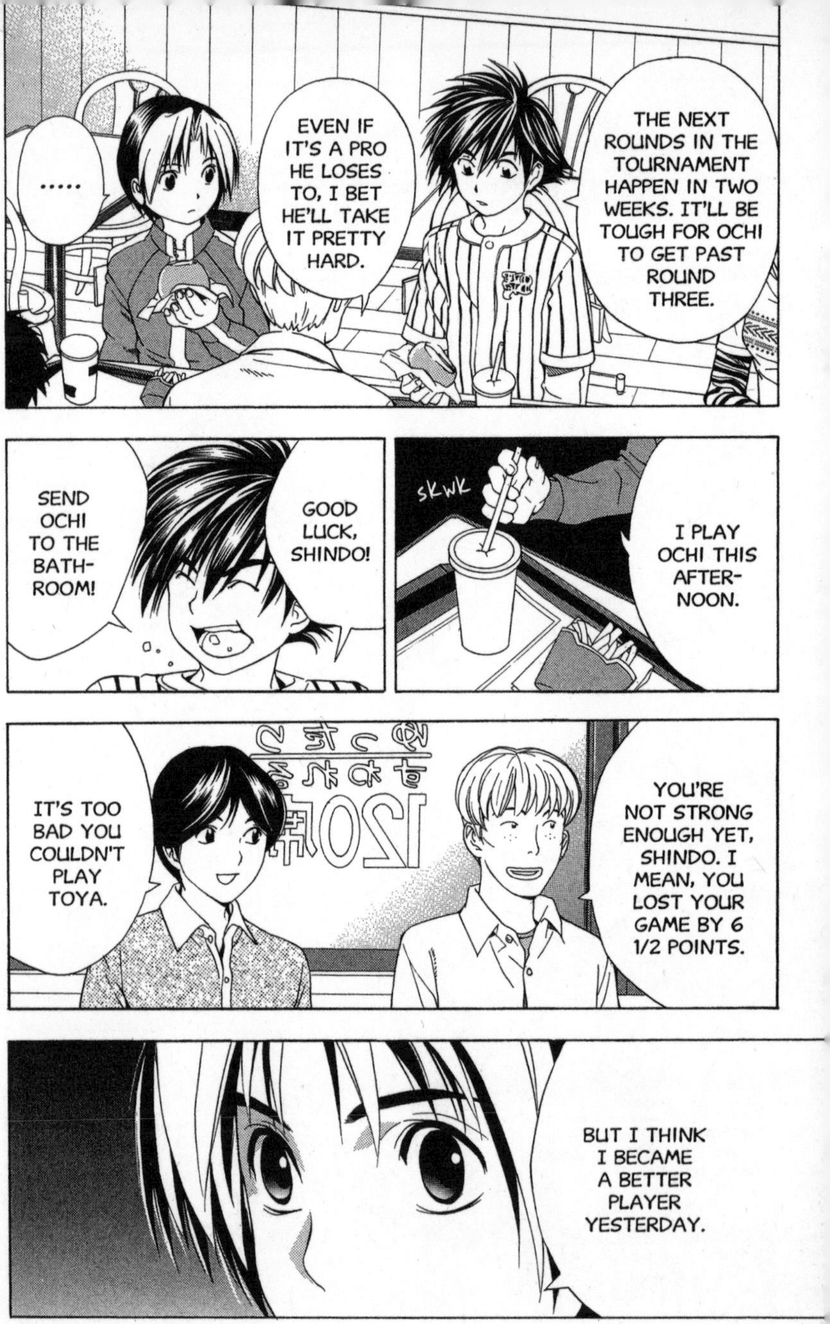
THE NEXT ROUNDS IN THE TOURNAMENT HAPPEN IN TWO WEEKS. IT'LL BE TOUGH FOR OCHI TO GET PAST ROUND THREE.
EVEN IF IT'S A PRO HE LOSES TO, I BET HE'LL TAKE IT PRETTY HARD.
.....
I PLAY OCHI THIS AFTERNOON.
SKWK
GOOD LUCK, SHINDO!
SEND OCHI TO THE BATH-ROOM!
YOU'RE NOT STRONG ENOUGH YET, SHINDO. I MEAN, YOU LOST YOUR GAME BY 6 1/2 POINTS.
IT'S TOO BAD YOU COULDN'T PLAY TOYA.
BUT I THINK I BECAME A BETTER PLAYER YESTERDAY.

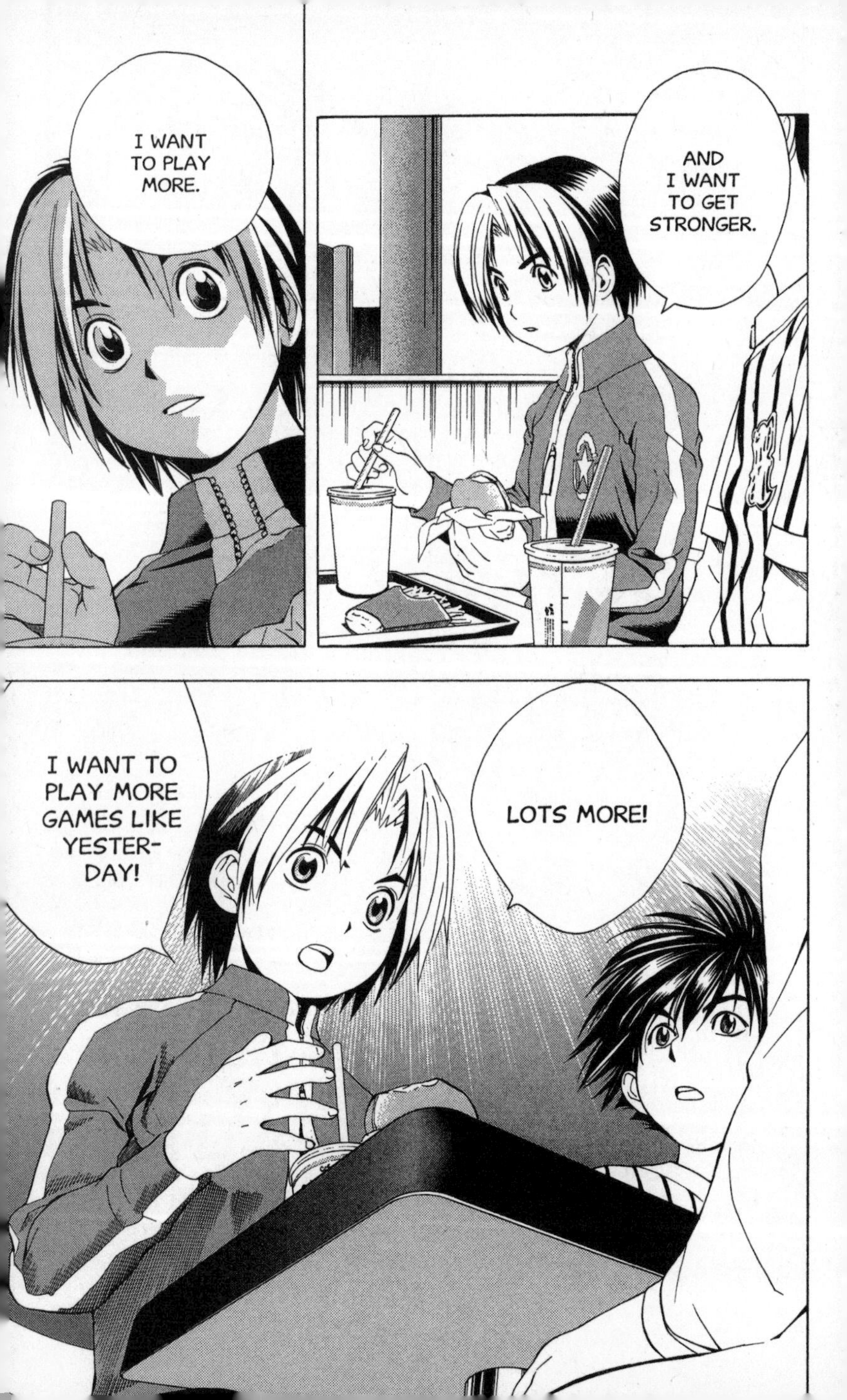
AND I WANT TO GET STRONGER.
I WANT TO PLAY MORE.
LOTS MORE!
I WANT TO PLAY MORE GAMES LIKE YESTER-DAY!

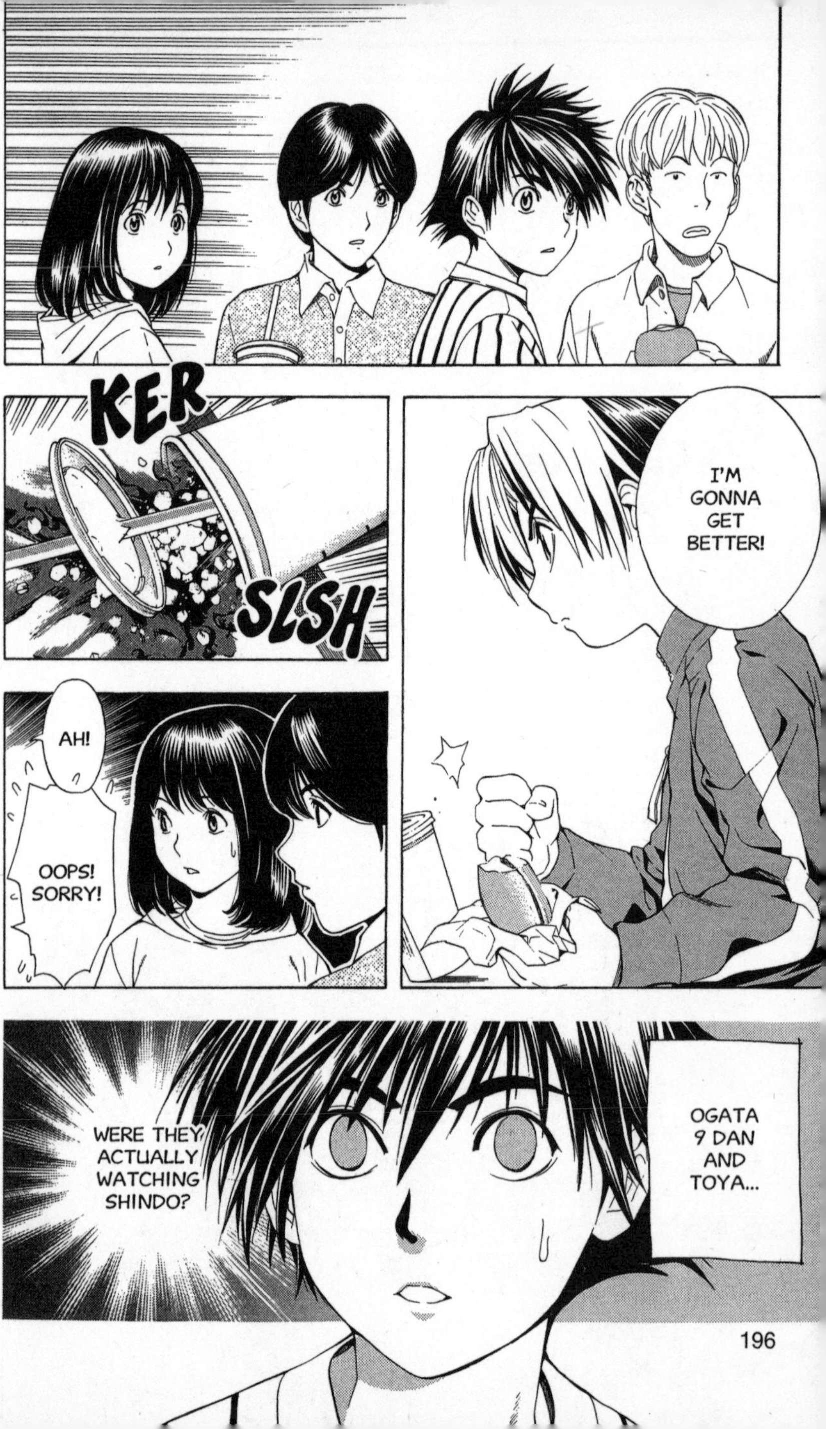
I'M GONNA GET BETTER!
KER
SLSH
AH!
OOPS! SORRY!
OGATA 9 DAN AND TOYA...
WERE THEY ACTUALLY WATCHING SHINDO?

READ THIS WAY

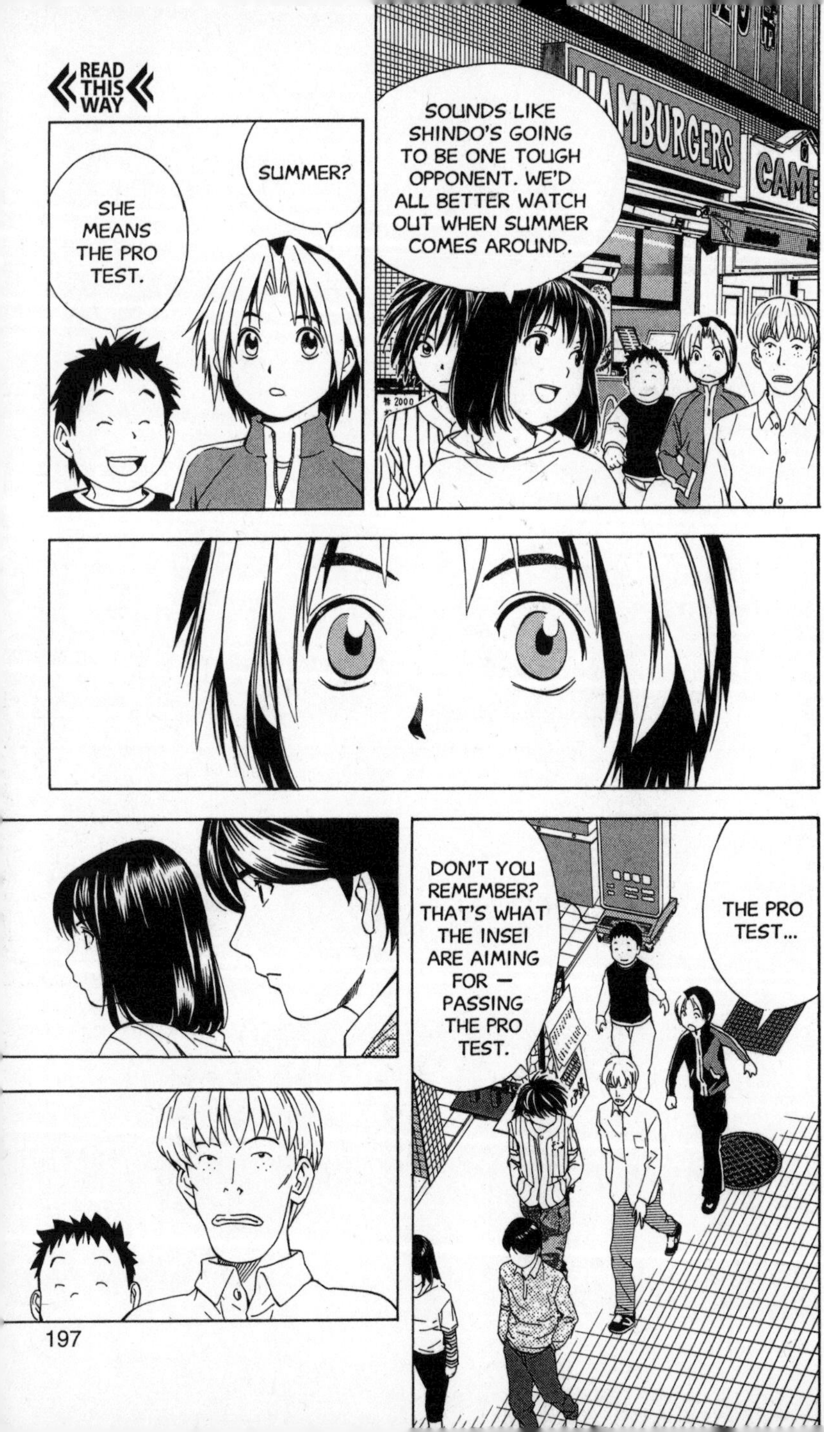
SOUNDS LIKE SHINDO'S GOING TO BE ONE TOUGH OPPONENT. WE'D ALL BETTER WATCH OUT WHEN SUMMER COMES AROUND.
HAMBURGERS
SUMMER?
SHE MEANS THE PRO TEST.
THE PRO TEST...
DON'T YOU REMEMBER? THAT'S WHAT THE INSEI ARE AIMING FOR — PASSING THE PRO TEST.

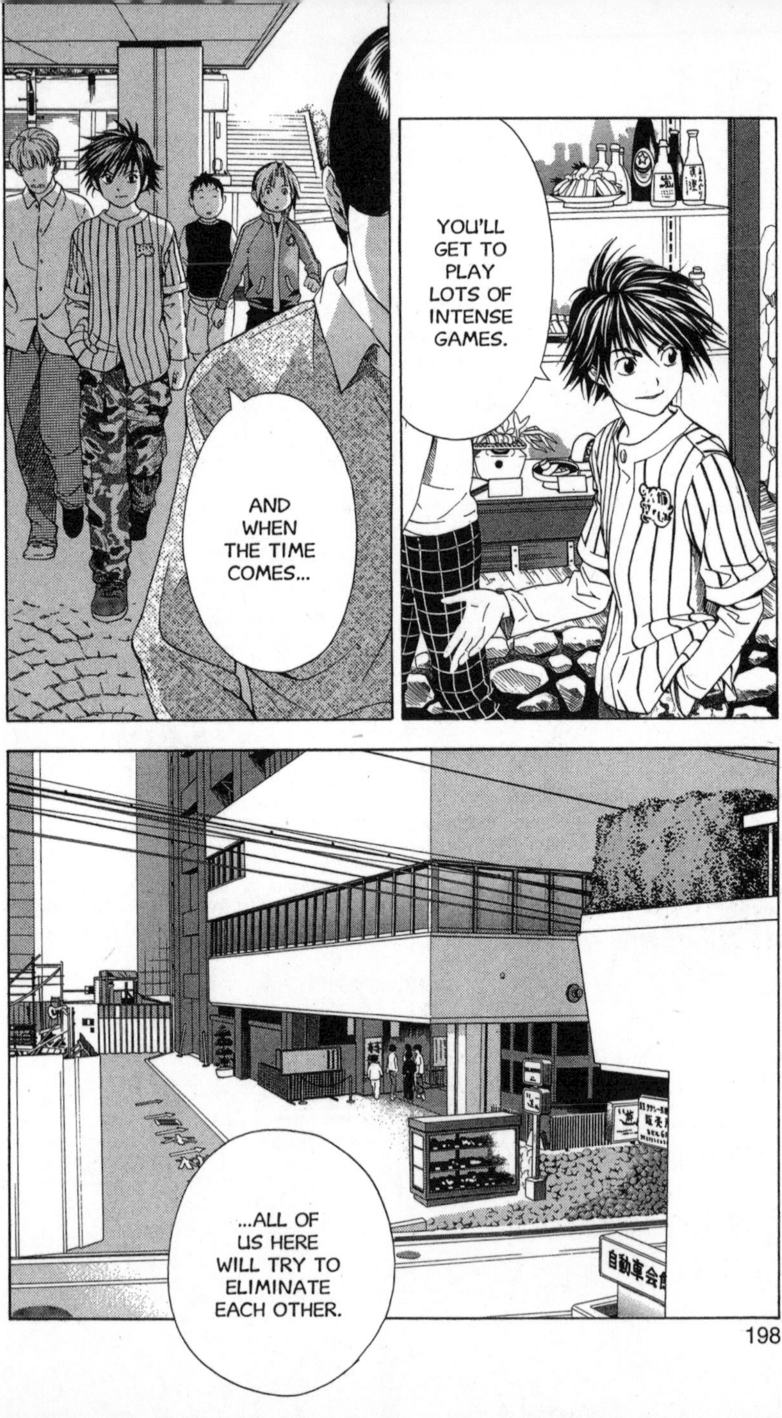
YOU'LL GET TO PLAY LOTS OF INTENSE GAMES.
AND WHEN THE TIME COMES...
自動車会館
...ALL OF US HERE WILL TRY TO ELIMINATE EACH OTHER.

READ THIS WAY

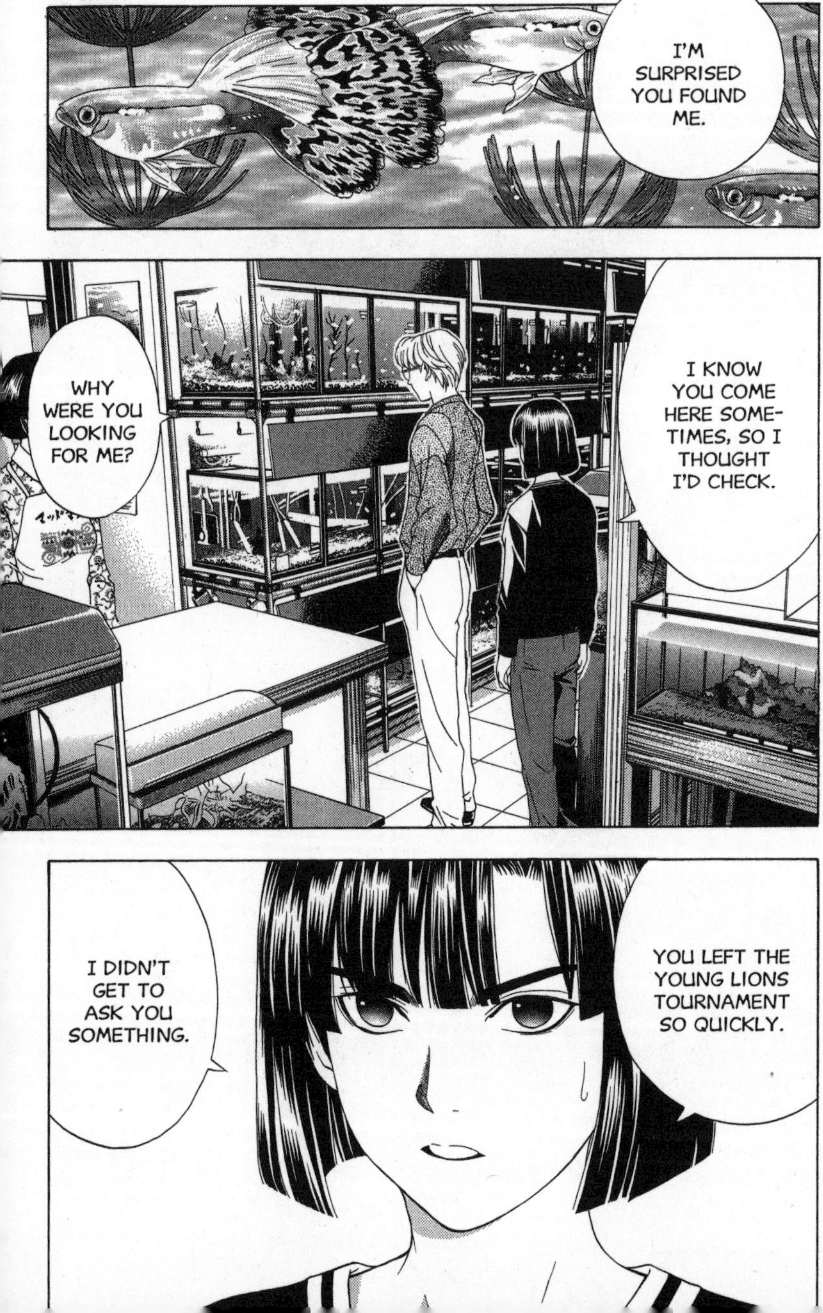
I'M SURPRISED YOU FOUND ME.
I KNOW YOU COME HERE SOME-TIMES, SO I THOUGHT I'D CHECK.
WHY WERE YOU LOOKING FOR ME?
YOU LEFT THE YOUNG LIONS TOURNAMENT SO QUICKLY.
I DIDN'T GET TO ASK YOU SOMETHING.

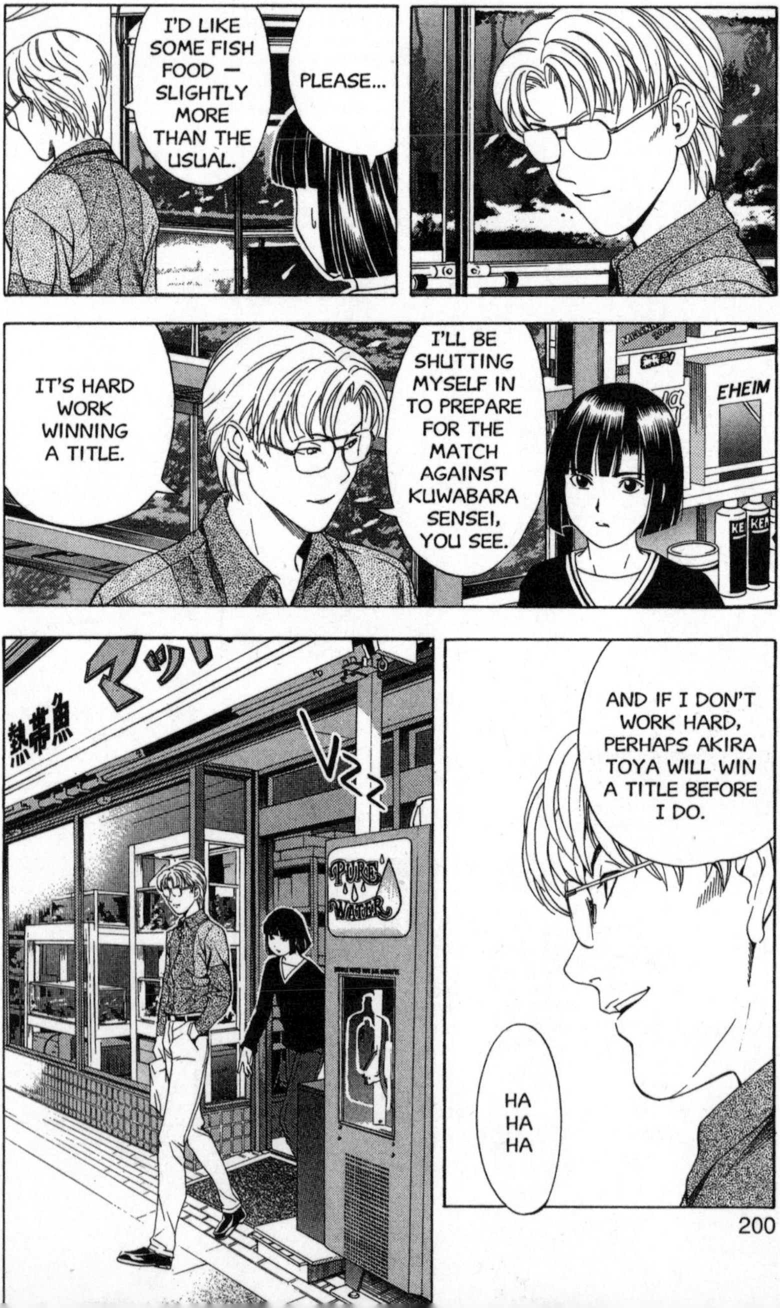
I'D LIKE SOME FISH FOOD — SLIGHTLY MORE THAN THE USUAL.
PLEASE...
I'LL BE SHUTTING MYSELF IN TO PREPARE FOR THE MATCH AGAINST KUWABARA SENSEI, YOU SEE.
IT'S HARD WORK WINNING A TITLE.
EHEIM
AND IF I DON'T WORK HARD, PERHAPS AKIRA TOYA WILL WIN A TITLE BEFORE I DO.
HA HA HA
熱帯魚
VZZ
PURE WATER

READ THIS WAY

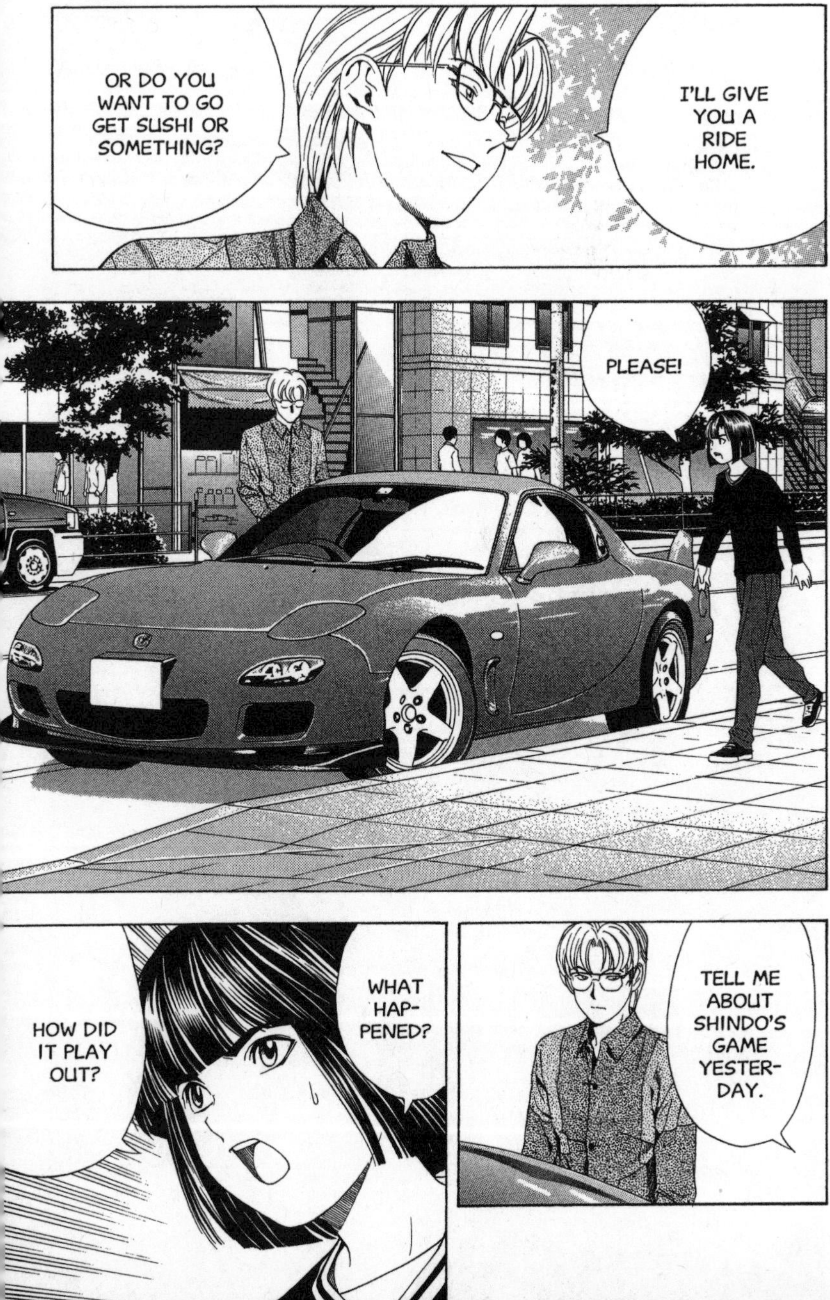
I'LL GIVE YOU A RIDE HOME.
OR DO YOU WANT TO GO GET SUSHI OR SOMETHING?
PLEASE!
TELL ME ABOUT SHINDO'S GAME YESTER-DAY.
WHAT HAP-PENED?
HOW DID IT PLAY OUT?

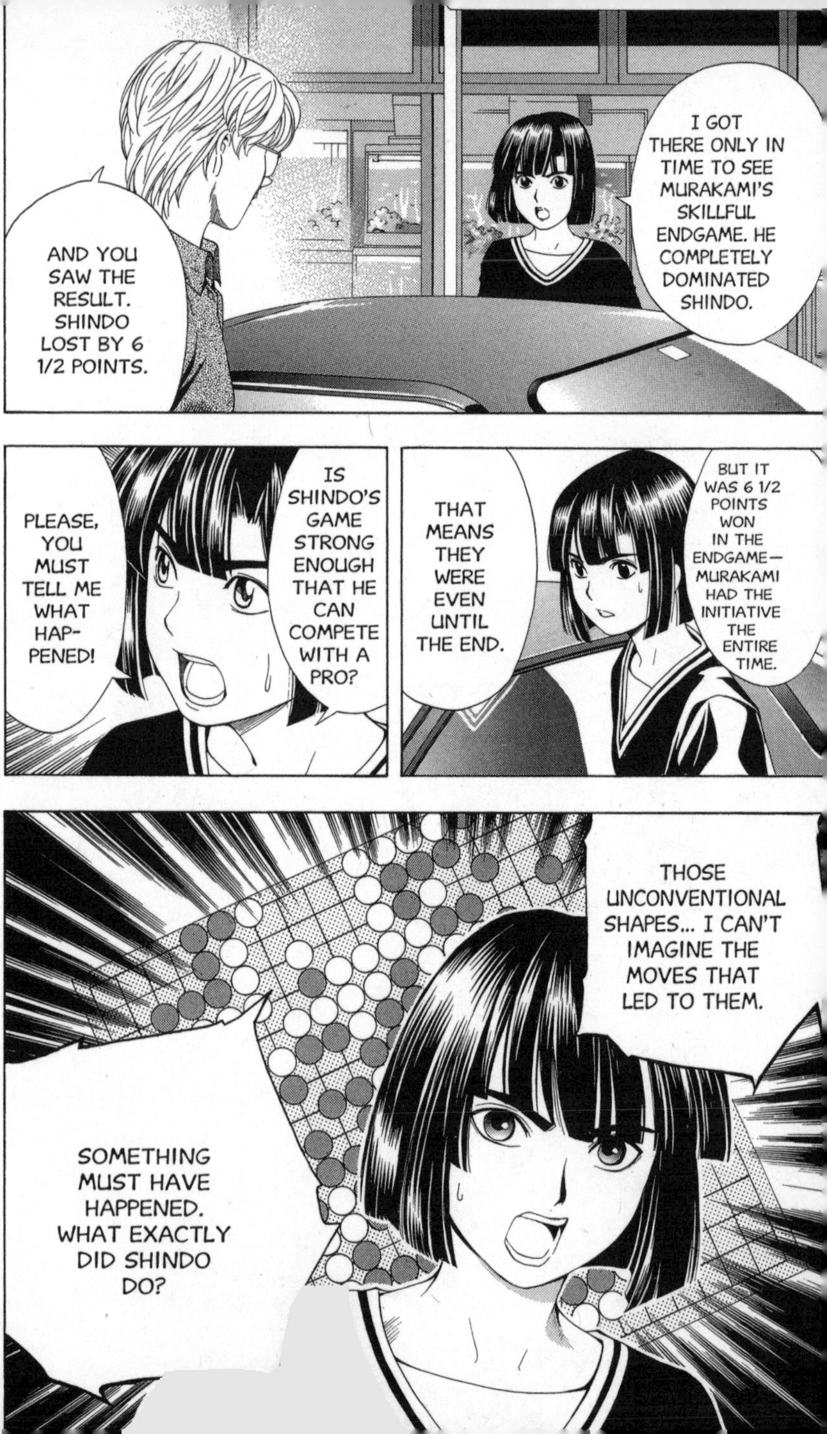
I GOT THERE ONLY IN TIME TO SEE MURAKAMI'S SKILLFUL ENDGAME. HE COMPLETELY DOMINATED SHINDO.
AND YOU SAW THE RESULT. SHINDO LOST BY 6 1/2 POINTS.
BUT IT WAS 6 1/2 POINTS WON IN THE ENDGAME— MURAKAMI HAD THE INITIATIVE THE ENTIRE TIME.
THAT MEANS THEY WERE EVEN UNTIL THE END.
IS SHINDO'S GAME STRONG ENOUGH THAT HE CAN COMPETE WITH A PRO?
PLEASE, YOU MUST TELL ME WHAT HAP-PENED!
THOSE UNCONVENTIONAL SHAPES... I CAN'T IMAGINE THE MOVES THAT LED TO THEM.
SOMETHING MUST HAVE HAPPENED. WHAT EXACTLY DID SHINDO DO?

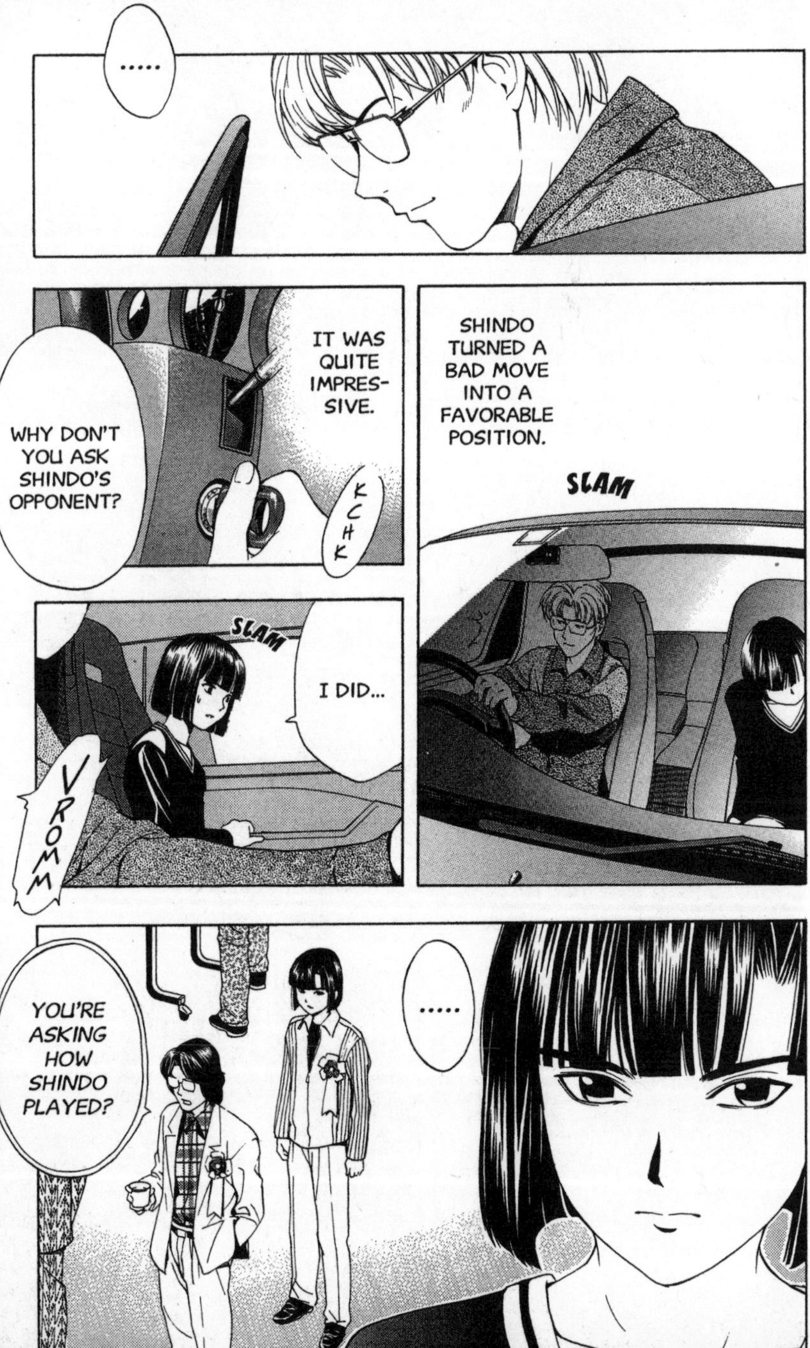
......
SHINDO TURNED A BAD MOVE INTO A FAVORABLE POSITION.
SLAM
IT WAS QUITE IMPRES-SIVE.
KCHK
WHY DON'T YOU ASK SHINDO'S OPPONENT?
SLAM
I DID...
VROMM
......
YOU'RE ASKING HOW SHINDO PLAYED?

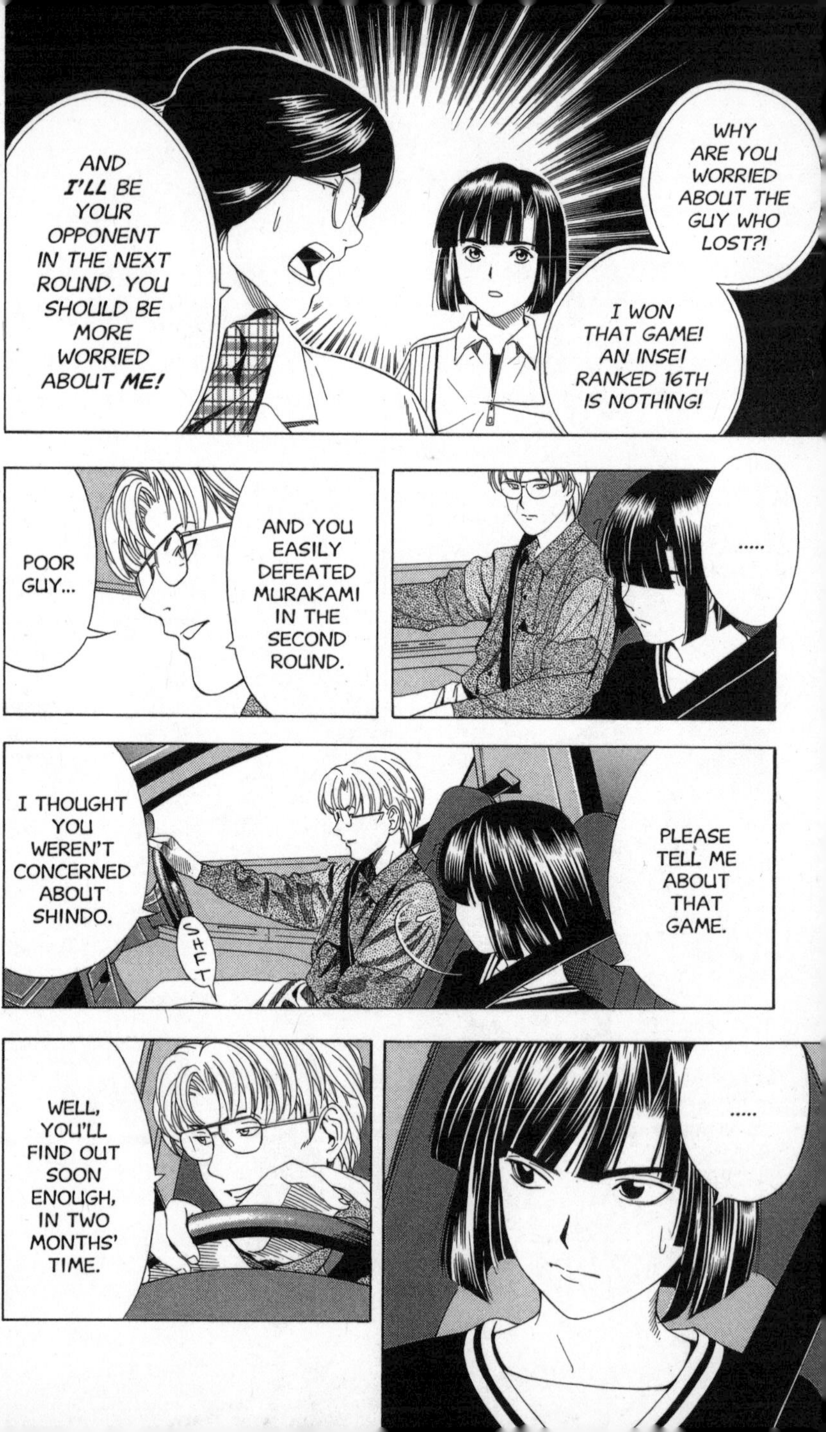
WHY ARE YOU WORRIED ABOUT THE GUY WHO LOST?!
I WON THAT GAME! AN INSEI RANKED 16TH IS NOTHING!
AND I'LL BE YOUR OPPONENT IN THE NEXT ROUND. YOU SHOULD BE MORE WORRIED ABOUT ME!
.....
AND YOU EASILY DEFEATED MURAKAMI IN THE SECOND ROUND.
POOR GUY...
PLEASE TELL ME ABOUT THAT GAME.
SHFT
I THOUGHT YOU WEREN'T CONCERNED ABOUT SHINDO.
.....
WELL, YOU'LL FIND OUT SOON ENOUGH, IN TWO MONTHS' TIME.

READ THIS WAY

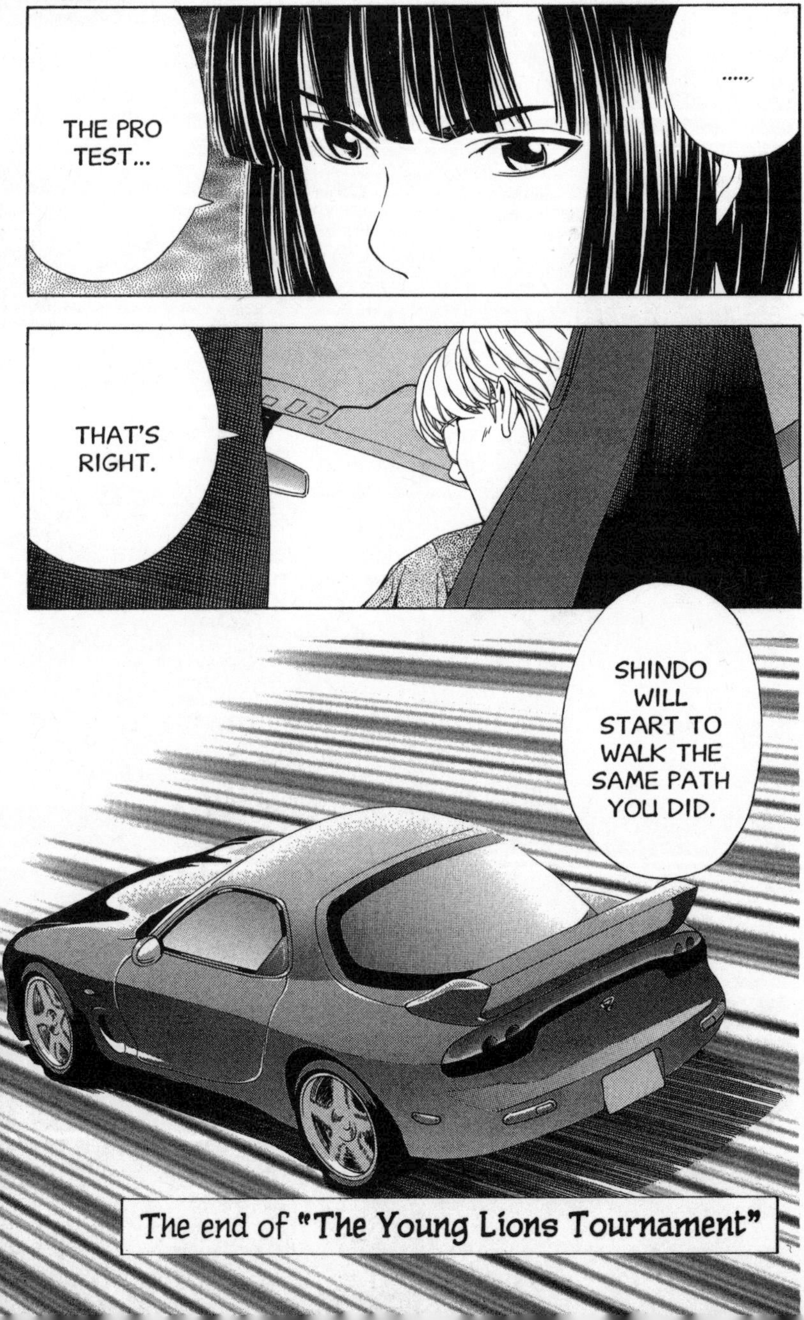
.....
THE PRO TEST...
THAT'S RIGHT.
SHINDO WILL START TO WALK THE SAME PATH YOU DID.
The end of "The Young Lions Tournament"

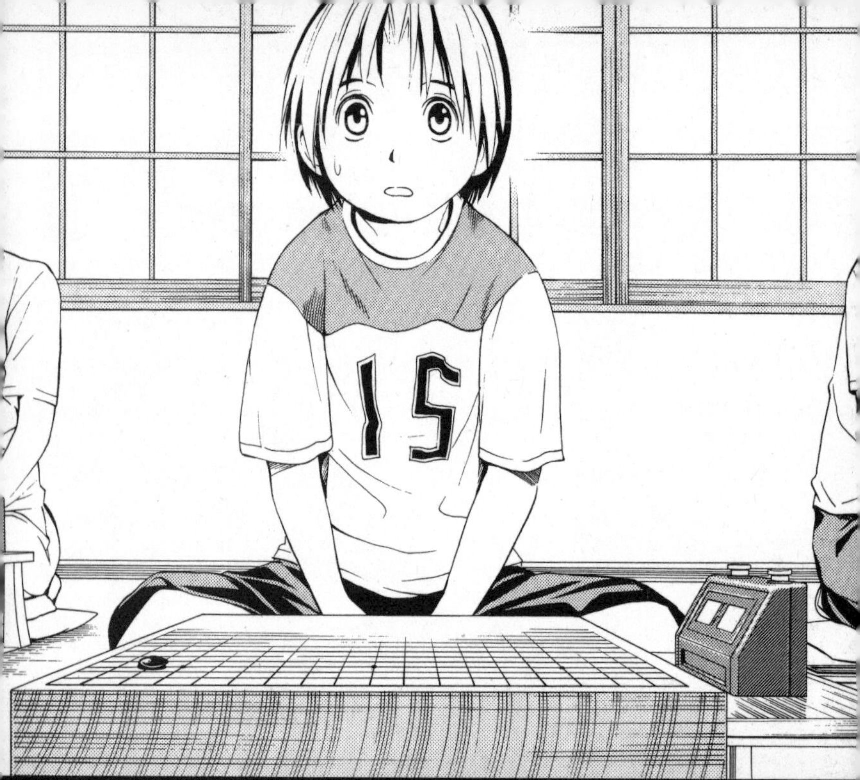

The preliminary rounds of the Pro Test begin, and the insei students find themselves competing not just with each other but with applicants from outside the school. Hikaru's first opponent, Mr. Tsubaki, is nothing like the players Hikaru has faced so far. The man is loud and rude, and everything he does sets Hikaru's teeth on edge!

## AVAILABLE NOW

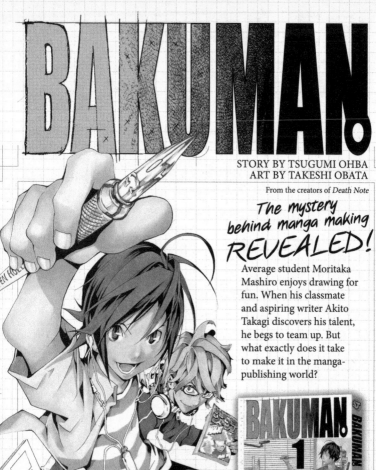

# BAKUMAN。

STORY BY TSUGUMI OHBA
ART BY TAKESHI OBATA

From the creators of *Death Note*

## The mystery behind manga making REVEALED!

Average student Moritaka Mashiro enjoys drawing for fun. When his classmate and aspiring writer Akito Takagi discovers his talent, he begs to team up. But what exactly does it take to make it in the manga-publishing world?

Bakuman。 Vol. 1
ISBN: 978-1-4215-3513-5
$9.99 US / $12.99 CAN.*

# The mystery behind *manga-making* revealed

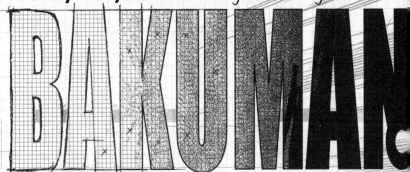

**BAKUMAN**

*Story by* **TSUGUMI OHBA** ✎ *Art by* **TAKESHI OBATA**

**From the creators of Death Note**

**BAKUMAN COMPLETE BOX SET**
Volumes 1–20

Comes with a *two-sided poster* and the *Otter No. 11* mini-comic!

Average student Moritaka Mashiro enjoys drawing for fun. When his classmate and aspiring writer Akito Takagi discovers his talent, he begs Moritaka to team up with him as a manga-creating duo. But what exactly does it take to make it in the manga-publishing world?

## This *bestselling series* is now available in a COMPLETE BOX SET!

**A 20% SAVINGS OVER BUYING THE INDIVIDUAL VOLUMES!**

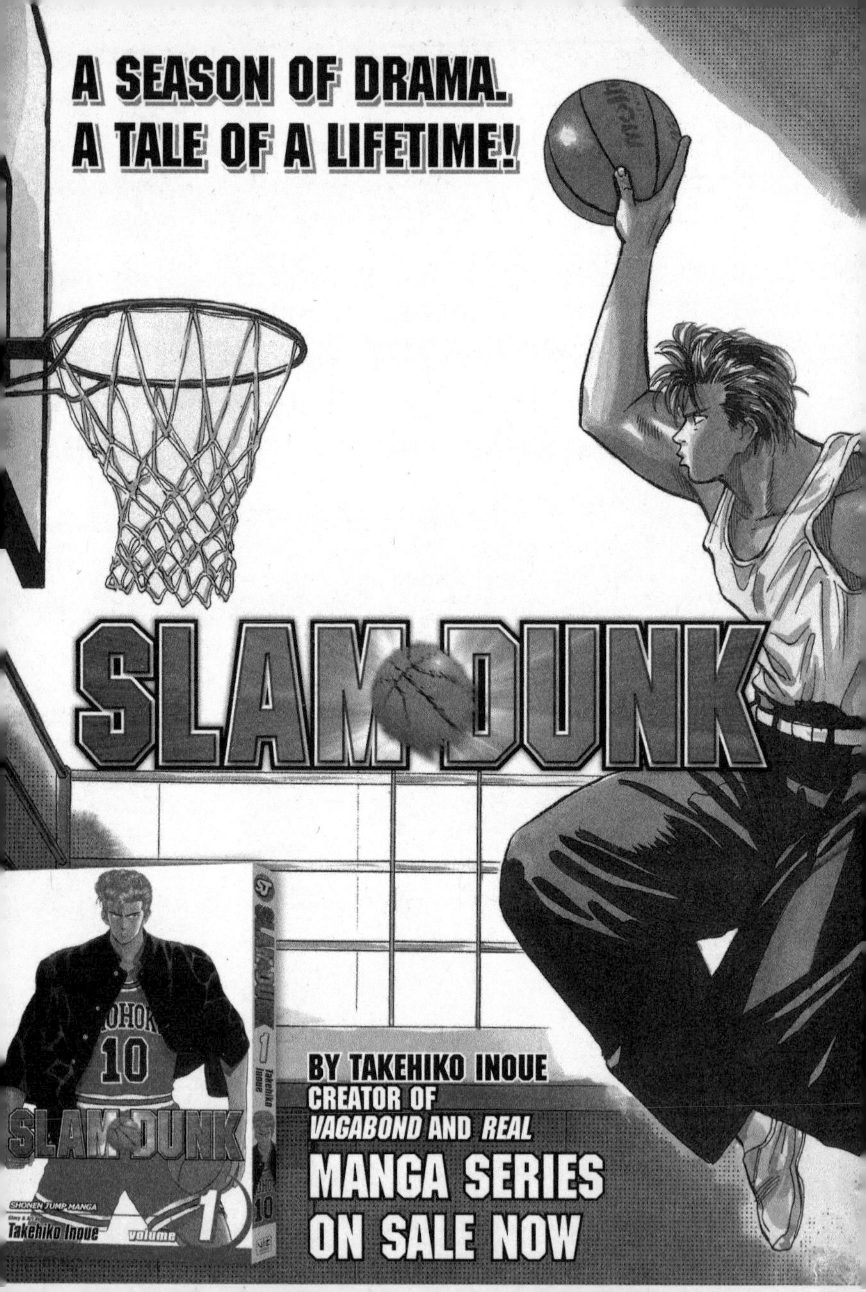
A SEASON OF DRAMA.
A TALE OF A LIFETIME!
SLAM DUNK
SLAM DUNK
SHONEN JUMP MANGA
Takehiko Inoue
volume 1
BY TAKEHIKO INOUE
CREATOR OF
VAGABOND AND REAL
MANGA SERIES
ON SALE NOW

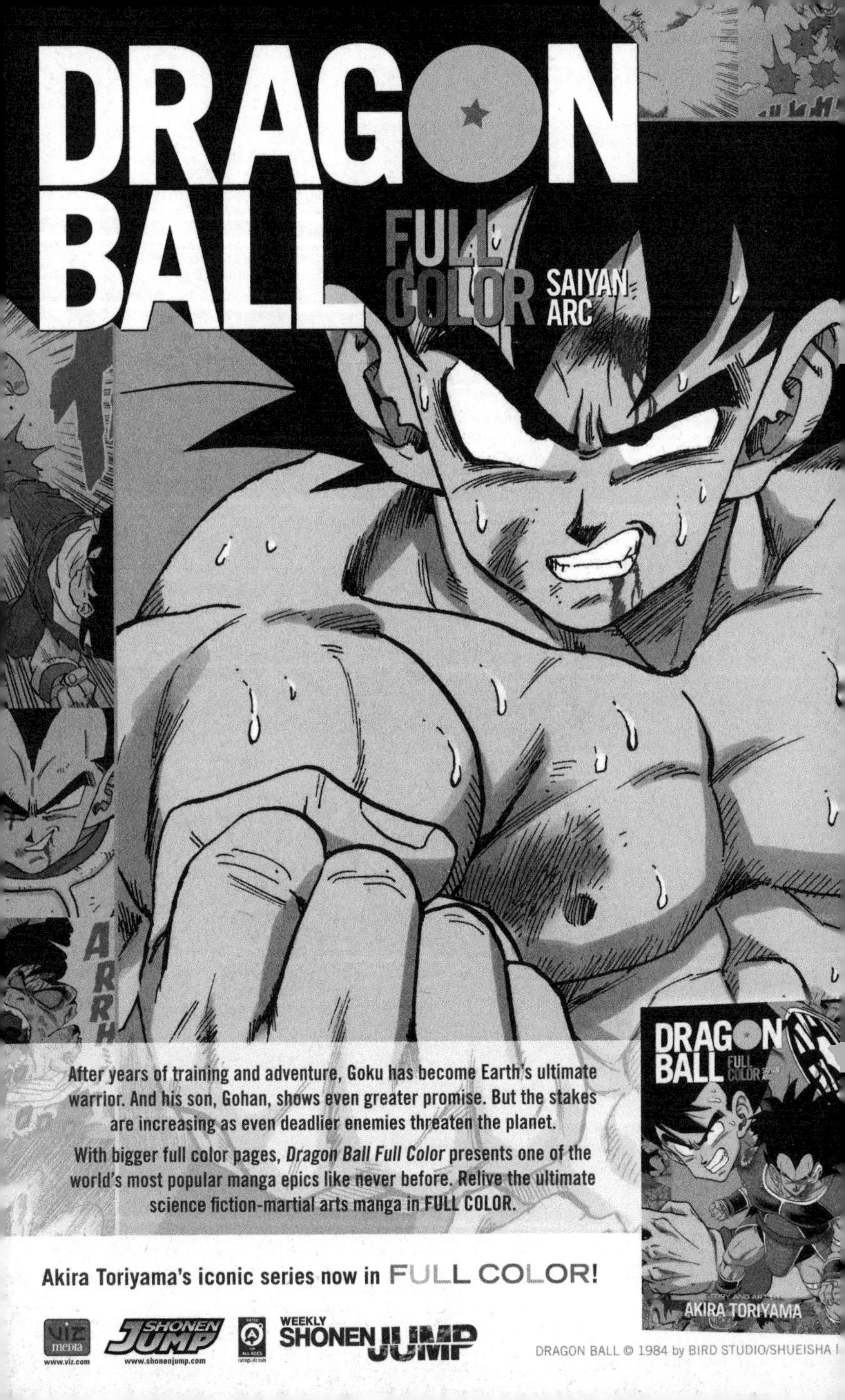

# DRAGON BALL
# BALL FULL COLOR SAIYAN ARC

After years of training and adventure, Goku has become Earth's ultimate warrior. And his son, Gohan, shows even greater promise. But the stakes are increasing as even deadlier enemies threaten the planet.

With bigger full color pages, *Dragon Ball Full Color* presents one of the world's most popular manga epics like never before. Relive the ultimate science fiction-martial arts manga in FULL COLOR.

**Akira Toriyama's iconic series now in FULL COLOR!**

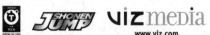

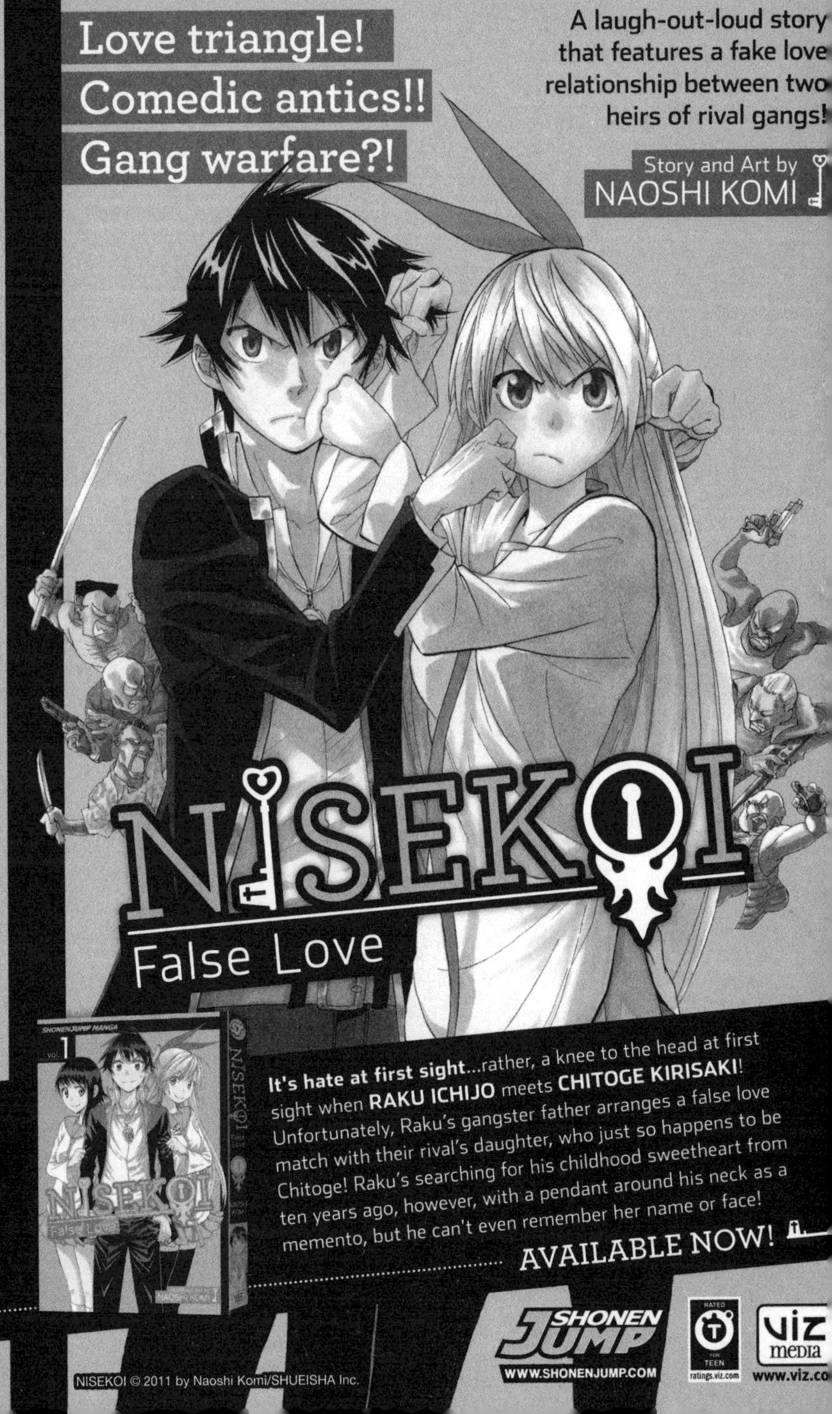
Love triangle!
Comedic antics!!
Gang warfare?!
A laugh-out-loud story that features a fake love relationship between two heirs of rival gangs!
Story and Art by
NAOSHI KOMI
NISEKOI
False Love
SHONENJUMP MANGA
vol. 1
NISEKOI
False Love
NAOSHI KOMI
It's hate at first sight...rather, a knee to the head at first sight when RAKU ICHIJO meets CHITOGE KIRISAKI! Unfortunately, Raku's gangster father arranges a false love match with their rival's daughter, who just so happens to be Chitoge! Raku's searching for his childhood sweetheart from ten years ago, however, with a pendant around his neck as a memento, but he can't even remember her name or face!
AVAILABLE NOW!
SHONEN JUMP
WWW.SHONENJUMP.COM
RATED T FOR TEEN
ratings.viz.com
VIZ media
www.viz.co
NISEKOI © 2011 by Naoshi Komi/SHUEISHA Inc.

IN A SAVAGE WORLD RULED BY THE PURSUIT OF THE MOST DELICIOUS FOODS, IT'S EITHER EAT OR BE EATEN!

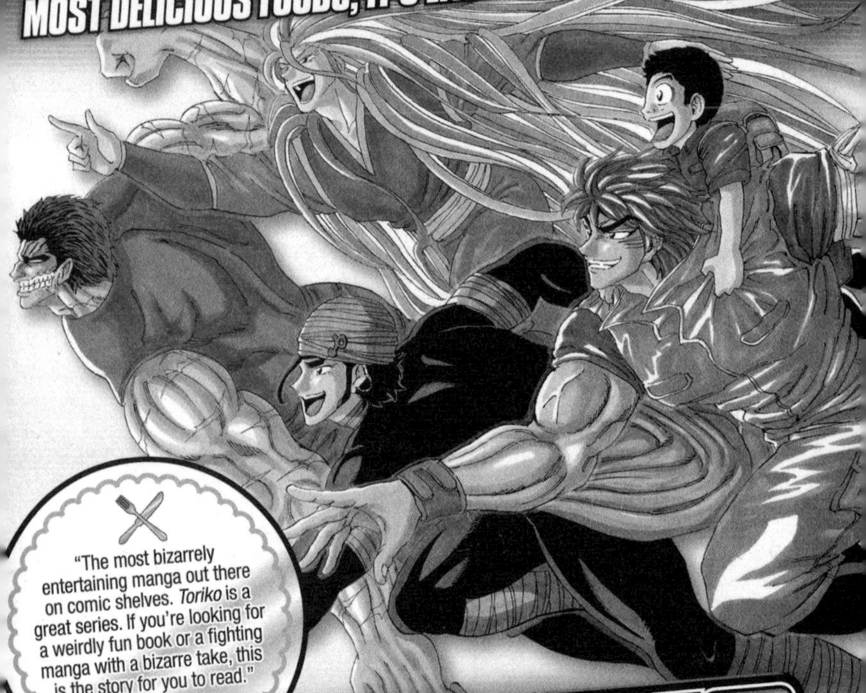

"The most bizarrely entertaining manga out there on comic shelves. *Toriko* is a great series. If you're looking for a weirdly fun book or a fighting manga with a bizarre take, this is the story for you to read."
—ComicAttack.com

# TORIKO

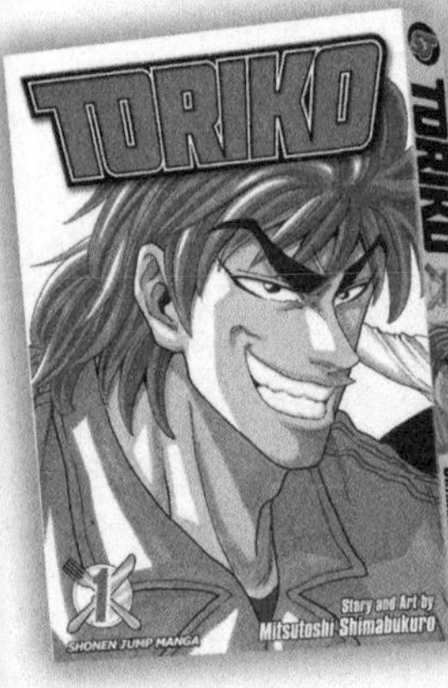
TORIKO
TORIKO
Mitsutoshi Shimabukuro
1
SHONEN JUMP MANGA
Story and Art by
Mitsutoshi Shimabukuro

**Story and Art by Mitsutoshi Shimabukuro**

In an era where the world's gone crazy for increasingly bizarre gourmet foods, only Gourmet Hunter Toriko can hunt down the ferocious ingredients that supply the world's best restaurants. Join Toriko as he tracks and defeats the tastiest and most dangerous animals with his bare hands.

RATED T FOR TEEN ratings.viz.com

SHONEN JUMP
www.shonenjump.com

VIZ media
www.viz.com

# You're Rea

...ion!!

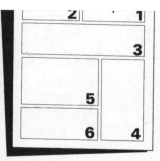

Guess what? You're
...t the wrong end of the

...It's true! In keeping with the
original Japanese format, **Hikaru no Go** is
meant to be read from right to left,
starting in the upper-right corner.

Unlike English, which is read from
left to right, Japanese is read from right to
left, meaning that action, sound effects
and word-balloon order are completely
reversed... something which can make
readers unfamiliar with Japanese feel
pretty backwards themselves. For this
reason, manga or Japanese comics published in the U.S. in English have
sometimes been published "flopped"—that is, printed in exact reverse
order, as though seen from the other side of a mirror.

By flopping pages, U.S. publishers can avoid confusing readers, but the
compromise is not without its downside. For one thing, a character in a
flopped manga series who once wore in the original Japanese version a
T-shirt emblazoned with "M A Y" (as in "the merry month of") now wears
one which reads "Y A M"! Additionally, many manga creators in Japan are
themselves unhappy with the process, as some feel the mirror-imaging of
their art skews their original intentions.

We are proud to bring you Yumi Hotta and Takeshi
Obata's **Hikaru no Go** in the original unflopped
format. For now, though, turn to the other side
of the book and let the adventure begin...!

—Editor

◀ • • • • • • • • • • • • • • • • • •